Resurrection and moral order

Resurrection and moral order

An outline for evangelical ethics

Oliver O'Donovan, M.A., D.Phil.

*Regius Professor of Moral and Pastoral Theology
in the University of Oxford and Canon of Christ Church*

Second Edition

APOLLOS
Leicester, England

William B. Eerdmans Publishing Company
Grand Rapids, Michigan

APOLLOS (an imprint of Inter-Varsity Press)
38 De Montfort Street, Leicester LE1 7GP, England

Wm. B. Eerdmans Publishing Company
255 Jefferson S.E., Grand Rapids, MI 49503

First published 1986
Second edition 1994

Reprinted 1996

British Library Cataloguing in Publication Data
A catalogue record for this book is available from the British Library.

UK ISBN 0–85111–433–4

Eerdmans ISBN (USA) 0-8028-0692-9

Set in Linotron Sabon
Phototypeset in Great Britain by Intype, London
Printed in the United States of America

Contents

Preface

It will be apparent from the first sentences of this book in what sense its approach to ethics is 'evangelical'. No doubt there will be those who do not penetrate so far. But there may also be those who do, but who still find themselves puzzled at the way in which the author has conceived his task; and to them these few words of explanation are addressed.

Some years ago I was attempting to teach a course in that area that is variously designated as 'general' Christian ethics, 'fundamental' Christian ethics, Christian 'metaethics' or 'foundations' of Christian ethics – my own preference is for the name 'Christian moral concepts' – when there came upon me, partly through the blank faces of my students and partly through self-generated doubts, a deep frustration with the current options for approaching it.

I was, I suppose, discovering without knowing it the force of what has come to be called in some circles 'anti-foundationalism'. I had grown up on an approach which treated this area simply as a form of apologetics. There seem to be, we used to say, this, that and the other difficulties with the idea of a Christian ethics; but the difficulties turn out on examination to be less conclusive than they first appeared; Christian ethics may, therefore, proceed on its way unimpeached.

With such an apologetic strategy, undertaken and sustained on its own terms, I have no quarrel; and towards its most skilful practitioners I feel nothing but gratitude. My unease arose from the substitution of this exercise for a study of Christian moral concepts. I found my students in Toronto justifiably disconcerted to see their professor parrying unheard-of attacks upon supposedly well-understood positions which no-one had expounded to them. And as I reflected, I came to realize that Christian moral concepts never *were* expounded in the tradition that I knew; for the apologetic strategy had, on the whole, found it convenient to work on the assumption of a simple divine-command theory, which had been the object of sceptical attack.

There was a further point that dawned on me then, though I should have understood it earlier. My teacher Paul Ramsey once wrote: 'Christian theological ethics is metaethics, and the Christian community in all ages is a standing metaethical community of discourse.' It required only a little reflection to turn this proposition around, and to conclude that the exploration of Christian moral concepts must always, in the first place, be the work of theology. This book grows out of my belated recognition of the fact. It is an assertion of the 'moral theology' which ought to be present in any 'Christian ethic'.

This background may serve as a commentary upon the manner, plan and procedure of what follows. So far as the manner is concerned, the style is didactic rather than dialectical. The plan is dictated by the desire to provide an *outline* of theological ethics, the shape determined by systematic rather than apologetic factors. In order to assist the reader's sense of the shape of the exposition, I have followed certain well-known exemplars in putting discursive material in smaller type. As for procedure: I have entered into discussion with greater thinkers than myself, contemporary and of the past, only in order to mark the critical points of convergence and divergence which define the shape of Christian moral thought as I see it.

Nobody will imagine that I have done these thinkers justice on their own terms, and I hope nobody will imagine that I think I have. (Among my contemporaries, for example, I would wish to have given a fuller account of the contributions made by the more recent work of Stanley Hauerwas and John Finnis.) I have tried to be fairly thorough in tracing Christian moral concepts back to their roots in biblical exegesis. The discerning reader will be able to judge how much I have been grateful to learn, and how much unwilling to learn, from contemporary traditions of biblical study; and I have not felt it necessary or desirable to explain my every move in such a way as to cover my flank against the possibility of challenge from that quarter.

The debts I ought to acknowledge are too many and too varied. However, it is a matter of hard fact that the book would appear without bibliography or index were it not for the generous labours of two kind friends, the Rev. Tom Breidenthal and Mr Stephen Spencer. And it would not have appeared at all apart from the patient encouragement over several years of the editorial staff at IVP, who have been everything that a theological publisher should be and more.

OLIVER O'DONOVAN

Prologue to the second edition

To re-read one's own book is a curious experience of divine judgment and divine grace. Judgment, because its faults are so obviously one's own; grace, because its merits strike one unexpectedly, as though the author had been someone else. For me the experience has been made more gracious by reading Jean-Yves Lacoste's limpid French translation (*Résurrection et Expérience Morale*, Paris: Presses Universitaires de France, 1992), to which I confidently refer those who find my native English too involved. The task of adding a prologue to the second edition has caused me some hesitation. To rewrite or defend what one has written looks like quibbling with the divine verdict. Can one improve upon the gift of God or argue down his criticism? There is something to be said, it would seem, for saying nothing. Yet there is one thing which may help the reader now approaching *Resurrection and Moral Order* for the first time; and that is to locate the positions taken in the book in relation to some current alternatives. It was a reasonable complaint that I did too little of this in the first place, preferring to set the argument against the wider backdrop of the Western philosophical and theological tradition and scriptural exegesis. I do not apologize for that priority, which was intended to say something rather pointed to contemporary practitioners. But if I can make good the lack, I shall be glad, especially since a decade of considerable activity in Christian ethics has now passed since the discussions in these pages reached their final shape.

The principal orientations of the book are sketched out in the first part. Purposeful action is determined by what is true about the world into which we act; this can be called the 'realist' principle. That truth is constituted by what God has done for his world and for humankind in Jesus Christ; this is the 'evangelical' principle. The act of God which liberates our action is focused on the resurrection of Jesus from the dead, which restored and fulfilled the intelligible order of creation; this we can call the 'Easter' principle. Each of these contentions has been challenged, or in some way qualified, in the recent literature of Christian ethics. They offer us, then, a grid on which to register some of the most important alternatives to the account of Christian ethics which this book advocates.

Prologue to the second edition

The realist principle

In chapter 2 I pitted Christian realism against the alternative of a radical voluntarism, current in both philosophical and popular moral culture of our times. But can a Christian thinker qualify the direct correspondence which I have urged between action and reality without surrendering to the arbitrariness of this voluntarism? That question is posed by the work of my Oxford colleague John Finnis, advocating a traditional style of Roman Catholic morality in practice and a rather original concept of it in theory. There are few writing today in this field who can elicit, and reward, such intense intellectual attention as he does.

To his *Natural Law and Natural Rights*, noted in the Bibliography, add *Fundamentals of Ethics* (Oxford and Georgetown University Presses, 1983) and *Moral Absolutes: tradition, revision and truth* (Catholic University of America Press, 1991). The position I address here is advocated especially in *Fundamentals of Ethics*, but has been maintained with consistency elsewhere.

A central contention of Finnis' writing is the independence of practical from theoretical reason. The goods of human action are grasped pre-reflectively and immediately by practical reason; they are not derived from any account of human nature or the world. In support of this contention Finnis at first appealed to the 'is–ought' dichotomy characteristic of the empiricist tradition of twentieth-century philosophy; but he has since become more guarded about aligning himself with that school of thought. While continuing to insist on a distinction between 'descriptions' and 'evaluations', he will not speak of 'fact' and 'value', 'for no clear sense can be given to "factual" other than objective and true' (*Fundamentals of Ethics*, p. 66). Clearly he is no voluntarist. The distinction he wishes to make (with Aristotle and Thomas) is not between reason and will but between kinds of reasoning. He does not deny right practical judgments a coherence with reality. But that coherence cannot itself be known by practical reason, so that it cannot form right practical judgments. In this way the realist principle, while not denied, is rendered practically ineffective. Our knowledge of the truth about the world will not provide a content for our rational decisions about how to live and act.

Here, possibly, may be a 'Christian' ethics, but not, I think, a theological ethics. The moral arguments of the New Testament epistles often pivot on the word 'therefore', which links the evangelical proclamation with moral inferences. It is not clear to me that Finnis can follow them. His own account of 'a specifically Christian and evangelical morality' – and I am grateful for his permission to quote a private letter – is 'not because there are specifically Christian first principles to supplant the first principles of natural law, but because the Christian sees the world and its potentialities more accurately, the revelation completed in Christ having disclosed what it has . . . and having confirmed and clarified what it has'. This 'more accurate' perception, not convertible into distinct first principles, allows the believer to make moral judgments in a context of enhanced intelligibility. It is clear to his or her reflective reason why morality (as such) makes good sense. But there is no evangelical content to the moral reasoning. The difference between Finnis and myself, then, seems to amount to this: while I believe that a distinct behaviour is demanded by the resurrection of Jesus, he believes that the same behaviour is demanded which was demanded anyway, but that the demand is clearer and more cogently perceived.

It is forbidden by good logic, Finnis believes, to pretend to derive a practical judgment from an account of human nature or the world. But this prohibition operates only in the one direction. Deliveries of practical reason may become a matter of reflection, and so contribute to a theoretical view of reality. 'There is', he tells us, 'a legitimate theoretical investigation and description of human nature, and it cannot be a satisfactory description unless it incorporates results which cannot be obtained except by the practical pursuit that Aristotle called ethics' (*Fundamentals of Ethics*, p. 21). So from our practical grasp of the good of friendship we may reach the general theory that human beings are social animals. But it will not work the other way, that the truth of human sociality convinces us that friendship is a good. We should not be misled by Finnis' use of the term 'theoretical' – which is simply the traditional opposite to 'practical'. What he is attacking is not simply an intellectualist *psychology* of moral judgment. With the strictly psychological question of whether inclinations precede rationalizations or are themselves formed by rational prejudgments he is not concerned. What he denies (and what I maintain) is that the sociality of human nature affords a *reason* for us to pursue our friendships; and what we both affirm is that our friendships afford an *evidence* of the sociality of human nature.

If we were mere observers of our own behaviour, we could know about ourselves, on the same terms that we know it about others, that we formed friendships *in fact*, and so were social animals. *This* strictly descriptive knowledge might be irrelevant to our deliberations. If that, after all, is the way I am, what difference can I make to it by taking thought? But Finnis knows that theoretical knowledge of our sociality is not like that. It incorporates 'results obtained by ethics', *i.e.*, the grasp of friendship as a good which is the work of practical reason, not merely the observation of our own or other people's behaviour. It includes, then, a knowledge of that good which practical reason grasps. (Finnis' books, nothing if not exercises of theoretical reason, claim unambiguously to know what the goods of practical reason are.) *That* knowledge cannot be irrelevant to our deliberation about how to live, for it challenges false deliveries of practical reason, such as the notion that the only or chief good is sensual pleasure. But if theoretical reason can correct practical misjudgments – if it can even, by approving false-hoods, corrupt practical judgment – then the supposed logical bar seems to have lost its force entirely.

The evangelical principle

If Finnis loses purchase on an evangelical morality, that is only an unintended consequence of his relegation of the reality principle. The opposite is the case with the German theologian, Martin Honecker, for whom the realist principle as such presents no prob-lems. But not all reality is evangelical reality; and quite specifically the reality to which ethics responds is not. It is the backdrop *against which* redemption can appear in dialectical contrast. This is expressed in traditional Lutheran terms by the description of morality as law: 'The Law is an experience of reality grasped theologically.' Yet, Lutheran as this conceptuality is, what emerges is a view that can be paralleled in other traditions. The ethical is a sphere of social values with its own autonomy in relation to faith, a 'secular' sphere in the sense that that term used to have in the theology of church and state. Faith in the gospel challenges and disturbs it, provoking its constant change and transformation, but it does not provide an alternative of its own.

In what follows I concentrate on pp. 80–82 of Honecker's *Ein-führung in die theologische Ethik* (Berlin: de Gruyter, 1990), where the systematic conclusions are drawn from a long and useful dis-cussion of the law–gospel theme. I cannot here defend my view that these pages provide the interpretative key to Honecker's ethics as a whole, nor can I venture on the worthwhile task of measuring this Lutheran approach against others that move in parallel to it. But the 'autonomists' of recent Roman Catholic debate suggest some fruitful comparisons, and perhaps particularly Josef Fuchs (see his *Christian Morality: The Word becomes Flesh*; Georgetown University Press and Dublin: Gill & Macmillan, 1987).

Honecker expounds his opening statement about the law in six propositions, of which the first is that 'the human being discovers the claim of Law historically'. This is explained as a denial that there is *one* law, a 'timeless, supernatural and otherworldly procla-mation of God's will'. There have been many 'laws', each arising in the context of a particular historical moment: for Paul the Jewish torah, for Luther the late-medieval piety of works, for Barth the ideology of a compelling national identity. Each moment 'is expressed' (the third proposition continues) 'in the historical mediation of values and norms. The norms of each age rest upon a particular historical point of view. Only the moral orientation as such is anthropologically conditioned.'

In his eagerness to deny the 'timeless' and 'otherworldly' character of law, Honecker seems to have forgotten to deny the *placeless* character of any age's moral affirmations. Like other historical relativists he is not on his guard against the cultural absolutism which holds that for each age there is [one set] of prevailing moral principles. This is to overlook the most perennially obvious feature of morality in every age: its judgments are always contested. Morality takes no form in history at all if it does not take the form of deep disagreements, showing up the fissured nature of any civilization's hold on reality. This omission explains, perhaps, the two most perplexing words in Honecker's presentation, the words which connect the first proposition to the second. The second proposition is 'that philosophical, general and theological ethics are not to be differentiated on the basis of a particular concept of revelation'; and the perplexing connectives are '*Daraus folgt*', 'It follows . . .'. Of course, it does not follow. The fact that each age has its own characteristic moral concepts and priorities *cannot* imply that different types of ethic are not differentiated by different ideas of revelation. The inference would follow only if there were, in fact, uncontested and homogeneous moral convictions in every age, common to those who believed in Christian revelation and to those who believed in some other revelation or no revelation at all. But since in every age arguments sufficiently rational (in terms of that age) have been deployed in support of contradictory positions, we might as well conclude precisely the opposite: *either* a revelation of some sort must resolve the conflicts *or* there can be no intelligibility about morality at all.

But Honecker has set up this ideal of a homogeneous morality only in order to set the disturbance in relief when it arrives, and to claim for the gospel the exclusive privilege of causing trouble. 'The ambiguity and ambivalence of all human experience of reality', he tells us in his fourth proposition, 'is brought to light only through the Gospel'; and adds in his fifth, 'the Gospel puts a question against the ultimacy of the experience of reality encountered in Law'. It is the role of gospel to shake our confidence in prevailing moral conceptions, to expose the 'misuse' of moral behaviour for self-affirmation and self-justification; and as such it is '*kein Quietiv*', but a motive for practical engagement. Practical, certainly, but, if we are meant to take the initial claims about reality-perception with full seriousness, decidedly antisocial. To shake a society's (homogeneous!) perceptions of reality is not to render any service unless one can contribute to formulating better ones. Without a social programme of its own, the life of the gospel is a pure expression of discontent.

Perhaps it is to guard against the destructiveness of this line of thought that Honecker completes his series of propositions: 'the reality-dialectic of Law and Gospel corresponds to worldly reality'. It is not, that is, a form of the real–ideal dialectic. The world contains this dynamism within it, whereby the oppression born of prevalent reality-perception is overcome by the promise of God's nearness. We ought to take seriously this wish to build the gospel into the dialectic of world history as a force that perpetually liberates. Still, it liberates only as a *negating* force. It offers no hope for the fulfilment of practical and moral reason in *constructive* action. As we read the editorial or foreign pages of our newspapers we find it comforting to know that God will shake those complacent bastards up. But when we turn from newspaper to business, what has the gospel to say to us? Only that we, too, will be shaken up. We live 'not under' but 'with' the law, hopeful radicals while we read the papers, resigned and unself-deceiving conformists when we are at our desks.

Honecker concludes that 'precisely a self-consciously rational, realistic, intelligently-argued ethic is the result of a reflective and self-consciously theological starting-point'. Yet we know that it is not the rationality or reality of the gospel that has shaped this ethic, for the gospel has no public rationality except in dialectical opposition. It has, to borrow John Milbank's telling phrase, no 'social space'. The only social space there is is the one which the gospel has to call in question. We should not overlook the alarming suggestion that this space might in the 1930s have been legitimately occupied by Nazi ideology. Honecker, of course, is no Nazi sympathizer; but he has left himself no way of preferring one social and moral order to another. Nazi ideology, human rights, Jewish torah, early Christian anti-Semitism, medieval works-piety, Renaissance capitalism, all have simply *been there* in their time, and all in turn have been shaken and dismissed. The gospel always bowls, never goes in to bat.

In my discussion of historicism I failed to identify the kind of historical relativism which Honecker represents, in which history is deployed as a sceptical rather than an ideological force. There is no necessary progress here, merely a series of shifting images insusceptible to final judgment. In response to this I would now formulate some rather stronger statements than will be found in this book about history as the stage on which God has disclosed the fulfilment of our practical endeavours. Our life, given back to us in Jesus' resurrection from the dead, has been granted its place at the right hand of the throne of God. History since Christ bears the mark of that in Christian civilization. True, this must not lead us back to a doctrine of necessary progress. The orders which inherit the imprint of Christ's ascension may be the worst corrupted, and the struggle for the gospel's social space must be renewed in every generation in different forms. Yet it will not do to classify all social orders indiscriminately as 'law', or, as in other secularist traditions, 'natural law'. This is to refuse the gospel's call to discern the signs of the times – a refusal that historicism can make by asserting that while all ages are different, no age is more different than any other.

The Easter principle

When I wrote *Resurrection and Moral Order* I was concerned to overcome the confrontation between advocates of 'creation ethics' and of 'kingdom ethics', and I claimed that, in the resurrection of Christ, where creation is restored and fulfilment promised, ethics had a foundation which embraced the partial truths of both these points of view. This claim did not convince everybody. The connexion that I made between resurrection and created order allowed some commentators, and by no means unfriendly ones, to conclude that I was using resurrection simply as a way back to creation ethics. 'What I think O'Donovan seeks is an account of natural law which is not governed by the eschatological witness of Christ's resurrection,' Stanley Hauerwas wrote. 'We cannot write about Resurrection and Moral Order because any order that we know as Christians is resurrection.'

I am inclined to allow something here for the distorting effect of Hauerwas' own self-definition. This has two aspects to it. One, familiar to all Hauerwas' readers by now, is an ecclesiological one. In the next sentence he writes: 'we know nothing about what we mean by creation separate from the new order we find *through the concrete practices of baptism and eucharist correlative as they are to* Christ's resurrection'. That is a sentence which, apart from the words I have italicized, I might have written myself. We walk together in agreement about the non-self-evidence of creation order. But where I turn to the Christ-event and to the apostolic witness, he turns first to the practices of the church. That suggests a rather traditional Protestant–Catholic parting of the ways. The other aspect, increasingly in evidence in his more recent writing, is a tendency to privilege the crucifixion over the other moments of the Christ-event, in keeping with an emphasis on martyrdom and death as the normative expression of Christian witness. This suggests a different parting of the ways, with Hauerwas, focusing on Good Friday, following the Western tradition, and myself, on Easter Sunday, the Eastern. In the light of that I am disturbed by a trace of crucimonism in the suggestion that *any* order that we know as Christians 'is resurrection'. Are there not surrogates which Christians may accept in substitution for the true world order established in the resurrection? And may not one of them be an order in which ascetic practice and martyrdom come to be valued in themselves, apart from confidence in divine vindication? I fear that Hauerwas may not be averse to a Bultmann-like volatilization of the resurrection. He would not be the first to find it an embarrassment to a programme of pious readiness to embrace death. Is Easter anything more than an assurance that Good Friday was quite good enough all on its own?

I would be unjust to the characteristic generosity of Hauerwas if I did not mention that this quotation arises from a friendly appreciation of some remarks I made elsewhere on the place of compassion in medicine ('Killing Compassion', to be published in his forthcoming *Dispatches from the Front*). The author's ecclesiological priorities are everywhere in evidence in his recent works, but note especially *The Priestly Kingdom* (Notre Dame, 1983). The martyrdom theme emerges sharply in the opening essay of *After Christendom?* (Nashville: Abingdon, 1991), and note also 'Creation, Contingency and Non-Violence' in *Dispatches from the Front*.

Still, Hauerwas' self-definition apart, I did not say enough about how resurrection ought to relate to other christological moments (advent, cross, ascension). This failure was forced upon my notice by what seems to me the most important publishing event of the eighties, the appearance fifty years after its composition of Karl Barth's *Ethics* of 1931 (ed. D. Braun, tr. G. Bromiley, New York: Seabury and Edinburgh: T. & T. Clark, 1981). In it Barth adopts the governing principle that Christian ethics must conform to the shape of salvation-history, and so has a threefold pattern corresponding to creation, reconciliation and redemption (*i.e.*, eschatology): an ethics of life, an ethics of law, and an ethics of promise. James McClendon, writing about the time of the Barth publication, came up with a similar suggestion: ethics covers 'the sphere of the organic', 'the sphere of the communal' and 'the sphere of the anastatic' – which means we are 'part of the natural order', 'part of a social world' and 'part of an eschatological realm' (*Ethics*, Nashville: Abingdon, 1986).

Clearly, this approach promises a fuller account of theological ethics than any monothematic programme based on creation, kingdom or even resurrection. There are, however, some instructive difficulties to be met with as the details of the scheme begin to be worked out. The way the specific subject areas of ethics are distributed across the three headings can look quite arbitrary. For example, both Barth and McClendon discuss political life in their second sections, but neither of them chooses that place to discuss warfare. McClendon, who is a pacifist, deals with the matter in his third section under the heading 'A Future for Peace?' Barth, who was not, put the discussion of war in his first section under 'The Command of Life'. There are further signs of strain in Barth: he found himself almost without specific content for his third section on the ethics of redemption (which contains, however, some wonderful observations on conscience and on humour). And he could not decide where the concept 'neighbour' belonged: in *Ethics* it appears in the second section with the other social concepts; but this committed Barth to the implication that coexistence with the fellow human was a result of God's reconciling work alone, making creation altogether a Rousseauian affair, so that in the *Dogmatics* we find it moved back to the creation section.

The conclusion we should draw is that the organization of ethics into creation, reconciliation and eschaton cannot provide a self-evident principle for arranging the *specific* subject areas that ethics interests itself in. It was a mistake to think that everything that needed to be said about human society could be included under the doctrine of reconciliation. Each area has to be given, as it were, a salvation-history of its own. Marriage is a gift of creation; it is taken into the reconciling fellowship of Christ; it is confronted with the challenge of the eschatological kingdom. Telling the truth is a task entrusted to Adam as he names the animals; it is a responsibility of redeemed humankind which has been told the truth about itself in Jesus; and the full disclosure of the truth is the content of God's future judgment. Work is a gift of creation; it is ennobled into mutual service in the fellowship of Christ; it gives place to the final sabbath rest. And so on.

There is a second difficulty, which has to do with the triad creation–reconciliation–redemption itself. There is a formal beauty about triads, and it is pleasing to be able to speak of salvation-history triadically, in terms of its beginning, middle and end. But it can only be convention, and such conventions have to be held up to the test of Christ's own work. We must speak about creation, because in Jesus' resurrection God has given back the created world. We must speak about final redemption, because Jesus sits at God's right hand, and the Spirit is given us as a guarantee. And we can be confident in speaking of reconciliation because of the work of Christ upon the cross. But that is not enough to prove the triad adequate. The gospels do not tell only of the death, resurrection and exaltation of Christ, but of his appearing and his ministry on earth. We need an advent moment (including in that term the incarnation, the appearing and the ministry of Jesus in fulfilment of the hopes of Israel); otherwise our gospel will be preposterously truncated. Here Barth's scheme betrays him into silence.

Granting this axiom, that Christian thought will be concerned with *all* the moments of the Christ-event and *all* the moments will shape the lives of Christians, what can be said for the *particular* significance of the resurrection? The Christian life takes its beginning in the act of faith, an act which renders all other acts comparatively indifferent; this corresponds to the advent moment. The Christian life involves obedient suffering in the pattern of Christ's own suffering. It confers the power of prayer and prophecy under the authority of Christ's eternal throne. All these are included when we speak of our 'conformity' to Christ. Yet when we think quite specifically about Christian *action* we have to single out the resurrection moment which vindicates the creation into which our actions can be ventured with intelligibility. In action the integrity of the world order is supposed, and that integrity is answered for by the empty tomb, where God has stood by the life he made and has not allowed it to be brought to nothing.

If ethics abstracts the resurrection moment in order to speak of liberated action, that is not to deny that that moment really does belong to this context. Faced with the Lutheran or Roman Catholic who wants to found an ethics on justification by faith, or on the 'fundamental option'; faced with Hauerwas and others who see the cross as the matrix of our Christian life; faced with idealists who point to an ever-beckoning horizon which forms the limit of our hopes and imaginations, I cannot deny them their legitimacy as theological approaches to describing the Christian life. I can only warn them that their moment, like mine, will fail to yield conformity to Christ if it is absolutized over against the others. But I can add that while a *theologian* may properly begin from any of these points, a *theological moralist* has a special reason to begin with the moment in which liberated action is assured. Much so-called 'Christian ethics' never addresses human action at all; some even make a boast of not doing so. I have no reason to think it a more noble thing to reflect on human action than on – say – belief or martyrdom; but there is, after all, an intellectual propriety to be observed, and it is fitting for each question to be addressed in its proper turn and in its proper way.

A church principle?

Let us return to the most important things that Hauerwas has been saying: that the church is a community of moral formation, where moral practices and concepts are communicated by precept, example and (most importantly) sacrament. Can the evangelical realism of *Resurrection and Moral Order* find a point of contact with this high-church moral programme? There are points of disagreement that arise over what I see as a tendency to describe the church–world frontier in exclusively confrontational terms, disagreements which require negotiating on the territory of Christian political thought and not here. But the broader thesis is one to which I believe I can be hospitable.

The section of this book which cost me most labour, which strikes me still as most imperfect, and yet as most worth having attempted, is the second part (chs. 5–8) in which I turn from the objective to the subjective ground of Christian morality by way of the doctrine of the Holy Spirit. Here I think I have marked out a terrain within which some of Hauerwas' claims could find themselves at home. My reservations about them are largely with their apparent lack of context: the theological space within which the church must be located has not been marked out with sufficient clarity. My criticism of his early writing on character (pp. 211–218) could be transferred to his ecclesiology: the moral community is given an epistemological priority, self-posited and self-justified. But its necessity can, and must, be demonstrated on the basis of what God has done for us in Christ. It is a part of the subjective chapter of ethics which must *follow* (and *must* follow) from the objective chapter. This most Catholic of Protestant ethicists might have heard less of the complaint that he was trying to bounce us into a sectarian community had he paid more attention to this point.

He might also have gained internal cogency had he unified this space, as I have tried to do, in terms of a doctrine of freedom and authority. Hauerwas is frequently found pointing to the importance of authority; but when a general account of it is called for, which would imply some rendering of the authority of the state, he shies away from the task. I can understand that my own example might not look too encouraging from his point of view. He might wonder why I put the authority of the church at the end, and the authority of conscience (albeit in a deconstructive mode – I had not then read Barth's *Ethics*!) near the beginning. He might wonder why the authority of the state was treated so comparatively early. To which I can only say in my excuse that I admitted that the order was not satisfactory. I can imagine, though not execute, an exposition in which the authority of the church would come first after the authority of Christ. All other authorities and freedoms would then be seen to follow from it. That would certainly be a better way of handling things.

Perhaps, however, that is not enough to meet the high-church interest. Roman Catholic readers have found my chapter on the authority of the church (ch. 8) distinctly Protestant in orientation – which maybe should surprise neither them nor me, except that I had hoped to make some kind of ecumenical opening with it, and was disappointed to discover that I had not done so! (But how many Protestant theologians will give any space to the moral authority of the church, unless it be to attack the idea?) The starting-point of the discussion is, in truth, a characteristically Protestant one: the sharp distinction between didactic and political authority. This distinction, promoted first by the canon-lawyers, was much used in the fourteenth century by theologians defending the Franciscan cause, and from there became a central plank in early Reformation Erastianism. Didactic authority, the authority of the Word, was associated exclusively with the church; political authority, the authority of the sword, with civil government. It followed that all administrative questions of church government became subject to the state. My response was to make a corrective move within this Franciscan framework and to ascribe to the church *both* authority to instruct *and* authority to command, thus allowing it authority over its own moral discipline. Of course, such a corrective move was nothing new. Calvin was the most influential of the Reformers to make it; and it has been made constantly since, especially in my own Anglican communion, never entirely comfortable with its Erastian beginnings.

That having been said in my defence, I had better admit that I find that discussion very unsatisfying. The trouble arose from an over-ambitious attempt to juggle simultaneously with two different distinctions, the distinction between counsel and precept and the distinction between didactic and political authority. Using the former to illustrate the latter, I made the church's didactic authority less genuinely *authoritative* than it ought to be. Consequently, when confronted with the practice of excommunication, I started babbling about a 'mixed form' (p. 174), instead of seeing it as a proper expression of the authority of the Word. I could have learned something from Calvin's better way of making the corrective move, not by ascribing two different kinds of authority to the church but by extending the church's evangelical authority to structures of ministry and discipline. This in turn would mean correcting the way the original Franciscan distinction was framed. My own suggested formula for understanding political authority, as might, right and tradition (pp. 128f. – I now prefer to say 'power' rather than 'might'), points in a direction I might have followed further. Instead of contrasting a purely positive authority of might with a purely truth-based authority of word, we should contrast a structure which combines the authority of truth with those of tradition *and power* with one which mediates the authority of truth through the authority of tradition alone. A fuller account of church authority as involving the authority of tradition would not only explain such a practice as excommunication, but would show how and why church authority may sometimes be corrected by the authority of the prophet speaking directly out of God's Word.

But I have not succumbed to the temptation to rewrite, or to draft new work within the covers of the old. Perhaps I shall have said just enough to persuade some readers that the second part of the book may be as worth engaging with as the first and the third. I believe that there is some potential in the ideas I explored there, and most of my attention since has been devoted to them. They may provide a stimulus for further conversation. That there are those who have conversed with me through the means of this book, and who yet will do so, is a constant cause of gratitude to me, even though I cannot be aware of most of what has been thought and said in reply. Our conversation with each other by this means

may be the occasion, if God wills, for that higher and more important conversation to supervene in which we all must listen together
and be addressed.

1

The gospel and Christian ethics

The foundations of Christian ethics must be evangelical foundations; or, to put it more simply, Christian ethics must arise from the gospel of Jesus Christ. Otherwise it could not be *Christian* ethics.

It is, of course, quite possible – for it has often happened and often does happen – that Christian believers may have ethical convictions which do not arise from their faith in Jesus. There can be ethical Christians without there being Christian ethics. It is possible, too, that such believers may actually produce theological arguments for separating their faith from their ethical convictions. Certain forms of belief in natural law or in the opposition of law and gospel make a virtue of denying that 'Christian ethics' in the strict sense can exist. Such theories may allow that Christian faith has a bearing on ethics indirectly, in that Christian spirituality promotes a heightened concern for the moral dimension of life and a strengthened ability to cope with it. But the substance of ethical questions, they hold, is not open to special illumination from the gospel; the believer is in no more favoured a position than the unbeliever when it comes to discerning the difference between good and evil. But we must observe what follows from separating faith and morality in this fashion: we become either moralists or antinomians. By 'moralism' we mean the holding of moral convictions unevangelically, so that they are no longer part of the Christian good news, and can, therefore, have the effect only of qualifying it, whether as *praeparatio evangelica*, as a 'ministry of condemnation' (as Saint Paul said of the Mosaic law, 2 Cor. 3:9), or as a rule which is supposed to govern an area of life which Chri t has not touched or transformed. By 'antinomianism' we mean the holding of the Christian faith in a way that expresses disregard, or insufficient regard, for moral questions. Once it is decided that morality is not part of the good news that Christians welcome and proclaim, believers will have to choose between being thoroughly evangelical and ignoring it, and respecting it at the cost of being only half evangelical. A belief in Christian ethics is a belief that certain ethical and moral judgments belong to the gospel itself; a belief, in other words, that the church can be committed to ethics without moderating the tone of its voice as a bearer of glad tidings.

Already in Saint Paul's letters to Galatia and Rome the twin temptations of antinomianism and moralism are identified as dangers. What Paul observed, however, is that they are simply two sides of one and the same temptation, which he called 'the flesh'. This highly suggestive association of law and licence, anticipating certain modern psychological observations, sprang from the perception that all alternatives to evangelical ethics, which Paul presents as life in the Holy Spirit, have something fundamental in common. Every way of life not lived by the Spirit of God is lived by 'the flesh', by man taking responsibility for himself whether in libertarian or legalistic ways, without the good news that God has taken responsibility for him. Consequently we cannot admit the suggestion that Christian ethics should pick its way between the two poles of law and licence in search of middle ground. Such an approach could end up by being only what it was from the start, an oscillation between two sub-Christian forms of life. A consistent Christianity must take a different path altogether, the path of an integrally evangelical ethics which rejoices the heart and gives light to the eyes because it springs from God's gift to mankind in Jesus Christ.

We first meet the term 'flesh' (*sarx*) in Galatians in respect of the merely human, which of itself has no power to effect its own justification (2:16), though its life may be the natural context for life lived 'by faith in the Son of God' (2:20). But the flesh becomes dangerous when it is conceived as an alternative source of strength to the Spirit (3:3). In the Christian life there must always be maintained a paradoxical tension between the weakness of the flesh and the strength of the gospel which is heard and lived through it (4:13–14). The tendency of the natural to degenerate into the rebellious is illustrated by the story of Ishmael and Isaac: the one who was born 'naturally' (*kata sarka*) and who becomes hostile to the one born of divine promise (4:23), who represents an alternative source of strength, the Spirit (4:29). Up to this point the rivalry is conceived entirely in terms of moral power, of the pretensions of the flesh to justify man through 'works of the law'. But inevitably an autonomous human power seeks fulfilment in its own self-expression, and so we find the flesh taking occasion not only of law but of freedom to assert itself against the Spirit (5:13). The mutual antipathy of Spirit and flesh (5:17) unites both flesh as 'desire' (*epithymia*) and flesh as 'law' (*nomos*) (5:16,18). Saint Paul will reject at least one reading of Aristotle's doctrine that 'sin is multiple'. The unity of the principle of life by the Spirit evokes a kind of shadow-unity among the different modes of rebellion. Whether it appears as law or as licence, the ultimate fact about life according to flesh is that it is a refusal of life in the Spirit. In the last resort legalism is not characterized by its delight in the law, but simply by its taking the merely and exclusively human, the flesh, as the object of its 'boasting', rather than the divine work of the cross of Christ (6:13–14).

Resurrection and creation

Yet it is too imprecise to say merely that Christian ethics 'springs from' God's gift in Jesus Christ. What is the logic of this 'springing'? What is it about God's gift that carries the promise of ethical illumination with it? We shall argue for the theological proposition that Christian ethics depends upon the resurrection of Jesus Christ from the dead.

We call it a 'theological proposition' since it cannot be substantiated directly by quoting from the text of the New Testament. Certainly we might mention Colossians 3:1: 'If then you have been raised with Christ, seek the things that are above, where Christ is, seated at the right hand of God.' But then somebody would reply by quoting 2:20: 'If with Christ you died to the elemental spirits of the universe. . . .' And do we not receive the impression, as we read Colossians 3 and the corresponding passage in Ephesians 4, that it is the ascension as much as the resurrection of Christ that is central to the apostle's thought? Looking elsewhere we can find other 'ifs' that reinforce our commitment to the moral life, for instance in Philippians 2:1. In the ethical instruction of the New Testament there is great freedom in reaching for aspects of the Christian kerygma that will afford us a motive for Christian obedience. The advent of Christ, his death, resurrection and ascension, his sending of the Spirit and his expected return to judge, all these can and do incite believers to ethical seriousness. Even the simple example of Christ can incite us to imitate him (Phil. 2:5, notwithstanding the strenuous efforts of exegetes, theologians and translators to expunge the idea from this verse). We are not attempting to deny the richness of the New Testament's ethical appeal; but it is the task of theology to uncover the hidden relation of things that gives the appeal force. We are driven to concentrate on the resurrection as our starting-point because it tells us of God's vindication of his creation, and so of our created life. Just so does 1 Peter, the most consistently theological New Testment treatise on ethics, begin by proclaiming the reality of the new life upon which the very possibility of ethics depends: 'By his great mercy we have been born anew to a living hope through the resurrection of Jesus Christ from the dead' (1:3).

The meaning of the resurrection, as Saint Paul presents it, is that it is God's final and decisive word on the life of his creature, Adam. It is, in the first place, God's reversal of Adam's choice of sin and death: 'As in Adam all die, so also in Christ shall all be made alive'

(1 Cor. 15:22). In the second place, and precisely because it is a reversal of Adam's decision to die, the resurrection of Christ is a new affirmation of God's first decision that Adam should live, an affirmation that goes beyond and transforms the initial gift of life: 'The first man Adam became a living being; the last Adam became a life-giving spirit' (15:45). The work of the Creator who made Adam, who brought into being an order of things in which humanity has a place, is affirmed once and for all by this conclusion. It might have been possible, we could say, before Christ rose from the dead, for someone to wonder whether creation was a lost cause. If the creature consistently acted to uncreate itself, and with itself to uncreate the rest of creation, did this not mean that God's handiwork was flawed beyond hope of repair? It might have been possible before Christ rose from the dead to answer in good faith, Yes. Before God raised Jesus from the dead, the hope that we call 'gnostic', the hope for redemption *from* creation rather than for the redemption *of* creation, might have appeared to be the only possible hope. 'But in fact Christ has been raised from the dead . . .' (15:20). That fact rules out those other possibilities, for in the second Adam the first is rescued. The deviance of his will, its fateful leaning towards death, has not been allowed to uncreate what God created.

In making the resurrection our starting-point we do not intend to isolate it from the other saving events which the Gospel narrative proclaims, least of all from the death of Christ which preceded it and from the ascension which followed it, both of them bound up with the resurrection in a knot of mutual intelligibility. If, still instructed by Saint Paul, we follow the first strand of thought back from Easter Sunday to Good Friday, we shall find God's reversal of Adam's choice already visible in Christ's representative death, where 'in the likeness of sinful flesh and for sin, [God] condemned sin in the flesh' (Rom. 8:3). There was pronounced God's No to life in the flesh, which was the condition of his Yes to life in the Spirit. The ethics of the gospel, too, has its aspect of condemnation, which judges and puts to death all that stands in the way of human life. And if we follow the second strand of thought forward from Easter to Ascension Day, we shall see the transformation of human life made explicit, though not visible, in Christ's passing beyond the terms and possibilities of existence in history. The ethics of the gospel has also its world-transcending aspect, in which we are to 'seek the things that are above, where Christ is, seated at the right hand of God' (Col. 3:1). Yet these aspects, of abnegation and transcendence in personal ethics, of criticism and revolution in social ethics, are prevented from becoming negative and destructive by the fact that they are interpreted from the centre, the confirmation of the world-order which God has made. Man's life on earth is important to God; he has given it its order; it matters that it should conform to the order he has given it. Once we have grasped that, we can understand too how this order requires of us both a denial of all that threatens to become disordered and a progress towards a life which goes beyond this order without negating it. But when the gospel is preached without a resurrection (as it was preached by the romantic idealists more or less throughout the nineteenth century), then, of course, the cross and the ascension, collapsed together without their centre, become symbols for a gnostic other-worldliness.

The resurrection carries with it the promise that 'all shall be made alive' (1 Cor. 15:22). The raising of Christ is representative, not in the way that a symbol is representative, expressing a reality which has an independent and prior standing, but in the way that a national leader is representative when he brings about for the whole of his people whatever it is, war or peace, that he effects on their behalf. And so this central proclamation directs us back also to the message of the incarnation, by which we learn how, through a unique presence of God to his creation, the whole created order is taken up into the fate of this particular representative man at this particular moment of history, on whose one fate turns the redemption of all. And it directs us forward to the end of history when that particular and representative fate is universalized in the resurrection of mankind from the dead. 'Each in his own order: Christ the first fruits, then at his coming those who belong to Christ' (15:23). The sign that God has stood by his created order implies that this order, with mankind in its proper place within it, is to be totally restored at the last.

This invites a comment upon a debate which has occupied too much attention, the debate between the so-called 'ethics of the kingdom' and the 'ethics of creation'. This way of posing the alternatives is not acceptable, for the very act of God which ushers in his kingdom is the resurrection of Christ from the dead, the reaffirmation of creation. A kingdom ethics which was set up in opposition to creation could not possibly be interested in the same eschatological kingdom as that which the New Testament proclaims. At its root there would have to be a hidden dualism which interpreted the progress of history to its completion not as a fulfilment, but as a denial of its beginnings. A creation ethics, on the other hand, which was set up in opposition to the kingdom, could not possibly be evangelical ethics, since it would fail to take note of the good news that God had acted to bring all that he had made to its fulfilment. In the resurrection of Christ creation is restored and the kingdom of God dawns. Ethics which starts from this point may sometimes emphasize the newness, sometimes the primitiveness of the order that is there affirmed. But it will not be tempted to overthrow or deny either in the name of the other.

15

The natural ethic

Since creation, and human nature with it, are reaffirmed in the resurrection, we must firmly reject the idea that Christian ethics is esoteric, opted into by those who so choose, irrelevant to those who do not choose.

It is easy to see how this misconception has gained favour. Western moral thought since the Enlightenment has been predominantly 'voluntarist' in its assumptions. That is to say, it has understood morality as the creation of man's will, by which he imposes order on his life, both individually and socially. Moral reasoning is subservient to the commitment of the will; any ethic, however 'reasonable' it may be in terms of practicality or internal consistency, is originally a posit of the will, a choice to which either individual or society has, in free self-determination, committed itself. Moral disagreements, then, may reveal ultimate clashes of commitment which are incapable of resolution. This account of morality has had a strong appeal for those traditions of Christian thought which, on the one hand, oppose a morality of the law apart from faith, and, on the other, give to faith a mainly irrationalist content. Kierkegaard, perhaps, provides the pattern for modern Christian voluntarism, in which neither faith nor morality can rest upon the foundation of reason but must simply be chosen. (Kierkegaard also *distinguished* very sharply between faith and morality, but that is of less importance for those contemporary Christians who have followed him in assigning to both a voluntarist foundation.) In this modern 'faith-ethic' Christian moral obligation becomes a function of the believer's decision, something that he has opted into. It is esoteric, meaningful only to those who, by a process in which moral awareness has apparently played no part (so much for the summons '*Repent* and believe'!), have placed themselves within the closed circle. Thus all Christian moral duties become analogous to such ecclesiastical house-rules as respect for the clergy or giving to the church, duties which presuppose membership of the church community and lay no claim on those outside it. Even the prohibitions of adultery and murder are, apparently, house-rules of this type; the failure of the non-believer to respect his marriage or his neighbour's life is nothing extraordinary, since, lacking the faith-commitment of a Christian, he does not have any reason to respect his marriage or his neighbour's life!

This view is evidently mistaken, if only because so many unbelievers do respect their marriages and their neighbour's lives, and, more significantly, so many non-Christian cultures require that they should do so. The theological weakness which has led to such a result is a failure to reckon with creation, and so with the reality of a divinely-given order of things in which human nature itself is located. True, man has rejected, despised and flouted this order.

16

Human nature, as Christians believe, is flawed not only in its instances but in its mould, so that to be human itself means that we find this order of things a problem and are rebelliously disposed towards it. And yet this order still stands over against us and makes its claims upon us. When man is least on guard against God he finds his natural ordering reasserting itself and carrying him in directions against which his self-will revolts.

The order of things that God has made is *there*. It is objective, and mankind has a place within it. Christian ethics, therefore, has an objective reference because it is concerned with man's life in accordance with this order. The summons to live in it is addressed to all mankind, because the good news that we *may* live in it is addressed to all mankind. Thus Christian moral judgments in prin-ciple address every man. They are not something which the Christian has opted into and which he might as well, quite as sensibly, have opted out of. They are founded on reality as God has given it. In this assertion we can find a point of agreement with the classical ethics of Plato, Aristotle and the Stoics which treated ethics as a close correlate of metaphysics. The way the universe *is*, determines how man *ought* to behave himself in it. And Christians need have no problem understanding how there can be, in societies and cultures untouched by Christian influence, a recognition of moral principles which are true, simply because they know that such cultures stand within a created order of things and may be expected to demonstrate this fact in many ways.

It has been a characteristic of classical Christian thought to understand ethics in relation to a 'human nature'. Consider, for example, from the Eastern church this exchange in Maximus Confessor's *Disputation with Pyrrhus* (*PG* 91:309):- '*Pyrrhus*: What, then? Are virtues natural? *Maximus*: Certainly they are natural. *P*: But if they are natural, why are they not present equally in all who share the same nature? *M*: They are present equally in all who share the same nature. *P*: But why is there so much moral inequality among us? *M*: Because we do not all do what is natural. If we all equally did what was natural according to our human origin, there would be evident among us not only the one human nature but one human virtue admitting of no "more" or "less".' The Western Christian reader, conditioned to detect the scent of Pelagianism, may be tempted to respond to such talk with Augustine's retort to Pelagius: 'Enough of the constitution of human natures! Our concern is with their restoration!' *De sanandis non de instituendis naturis agitur* (*De natura et gratia* 11.12). And it is true that Maximus does nothing to suggest that sin is more than random individual defect, and so is open to a Pelagian interpretation. But that weakness is no reason to ignore the common tradition of both East and West which stresses the reality of a human nature, with its proper virtues and excellences, which is given in creation, a nature which, as Adam's descendants, we fail to instantiate adequately and which therefore is our judge. Augustine himself spoke constantly about such a nature, and indeed he could hardly otherwise have thought

17

seriously about its restoration. 'Any and every unrighteous man must be the object of our hatred in respect of his unrighteousness and the object of our love in respect of his humanity; that by reproving the fault in him which rightly earns our hatred, we may liberate that in him which rightly earns our love, that is to say the human nature itself, and set right every fault in it' (*Contra Faustum* XIX.24). There is, of course, a difference between speaking in this way of a 'human nature' and speaking as we have done of a 'created order' within which man takes his place. The one is more centred on man, the other on the universe of created beings. But the difference is less than may appear, for the concept of a human nature is actually inseparable from the concept of nature as such. Without 'nature' around it in which it can take its place, 'human nature' can be nothing but an insubstantial phantom, visible only through some ectoplasmic formula such as 'radical freedom'.

This contention sets us against the main thesis of Alisdair MacIntyre's influential book *After Virtue*: 'If a premodern view of morals and politics is to be vindicated against modernity, it will be in something like Aristotelian terms or not at all' (p. 111). For MacIntyre's critique of voluntarist 'modernity' (which shares much with that common among the American students of Heidegger, most notably Leo Strauss) we have great sympathy; but his polarization of the options in these terms is wayward and historically unjustified. MacIntyre can understand Stoicism only as a deviance from the best classical teleological tradition, as an odd anticipation of modernity. Its conception of 'life according to nature' (*to kata physin zēn*) strikes him, for reasons that are hardly more than hinted at, as an antithesis rather than a complement to a teleological belief in the good for man (pp. 157f.). Christianity is ambiguously related to the Stoic-Aristotelian alternative, at one moment a 'Judaic' ally of the Stoic morality of law (p. 159), at another a fellow-traveller with Aristotelian teleology. Its usefulness in the latter role apparently dates from the twelfth century and not before (pp. 159ff.).

Against this we must insist that the earliest tradition of Christian moral thought, owing comparatively little to Aristotle, was formed, nevertheless, in a realist mould. Its classical influences were both Platonic and Stoic, more Platonic on balance; but it is easy to overestimate the significance of the formal debt to these sources and ignore the obvious, that it derives its substance predominantly from the reading of the Bible. And the Bible provided it with something very much more than a series of naked commands, which is all that modernity, from which at this point MacIntyre has not emancipated himself, can make of the Jewish Torah. It is partly to stress the existence of this authentic Christian tradition of moral thought, as well as from personal predilection, that I shall refer so often in what follows to Augustine. My use of mediaeval writers, on the other hand, will be mainly to trace the roots of *modern* thinking. (That is *my* debt to the Heideggerians, who have constantly pointed to the Middle Ages as the watershed from which flows the modern mind: see, for example, Hans Jonas's article 'Jewish and Christian Elements in Philosophy' in his *Philosophical Essays*, pp. 21–44). It is arguable, however, that the thought of Thomas Aquinas is best understood as a continuation of the patristic tradition, only secondarily as an Aristotelian revision of it, and very subordinately as a theatre of war between voluntarism and realism.

There is, however, another side to the matter which has to be asserted equally strongly. In speaking of man's fallenness we point not only to his persistent rejection of the created order, but also to an inescapable confusion in his perceptions of it. This does not permit us to follow the Stoic recipe for 'life in accord with nature' without a measure of epistemological guardedness. The very societies which impress us by their reverence for some important moral principle will appal us by their neglect of some other. Together with man's essential involvement in created order and his rebellious discontent with it, we must reckon also upon the opacity and obscurity of that order to the human mind which has rejected the knowledge of its Creator. We say that man's rebellion has not succeeded in destroying the natural order to which he belongs; but that is something which we could not say with theological authority except on the basis of God's revelation in the resurrection of Jesus Christ. We say that this, that or the other cultural demand or prohibition (the prohibition of incest, for example, or of racial discrimination) reflects the created order of God faithfully, but that too is something which we can know only by taking our place within the revelation of that order afforded us in Christ. It is not, as the sceptics and relativists correctly remind us, self-evident what is nature and what is convention. How can we be sure that the prohibition of incest is not yet another primitive superstition? How can we assert confidently that Bantu and Caucasian races belong equally to one human kind that renders cultural and biological differentiation between them morally irrelevant? The *epistemological* programme for an ethic that is 'natural', in the sense that its contents are simply known to all, has to face dauntingly high barriers. But we are not to conclude from this that there is no *ontological* ground for an 'ethic of nature', no objective order to which the moral life can respond. We may only conclude that any certainty we may have about the order which God has made depends upon God's own disclosure of himself and of his works.

Creation and redemption each has its ontological and its epistemological aspect. There is the created order and there is natural knowledge; there is the new creation and there is revelation in Christ. This has encouraged a confusion of the ontological and the epistemological in much modern theology, so that we are constantly presented with the unacceptably polarized choice between an ethic that is revealed and has no ontological grounding and an ethic that is based on creation and so is naturally known. This polarization deprives redemption and revelation of their proper theological meaning as the divine reaffirmation of created order. If, on the other hand, it is the gospel of the resurrection that assures us of the stability and permanence of the world which God has made, then neither of the polarized options is right. In the sphere of revelation, we will conclude, and only there, can we see the natural order as it really is and overcome the epistemological barriers to an ethic that conforms to nature. This nature involves all men, and indeed, as we shall see later, does not exclude a certain 'natural knowledge' which is also a part of man's created endowment. And yet only in Christ do we apprehend that order in which we stand and that knowledge of it with which we have been endowed.

The false polarization of which we complain has its latest expression in the Roman Catholic debates between advocates of a 'faith-ethic' (*Glaubensethik*) and those who urge the case for an autonomous morality on which all men of good will can agree. (See J. V. MacNamara's *Faith and Ethics* for a helpful account of this rather unhelpful disagreement.) On the one hand an ethic which, in its concern for Christian distinctiveness, acknowledges no roots in a universal human nature and is therefore implicitly voluntarist in its foundation; on the other, an ethic which allows no critical distance on the moral commonplaces of our culture because it refuses to admit an authoritative perspective in revelation. Are Catholic advocates for the faith-ethic content, we may wonder, to appeal to such moral distinctiveness as may be wrung from the characteristic peculiarities of the Christian ethos such as prayer, virginity and community discipline? And are Catholic autonomists content to overlook the extent to which our modern civilization is marked, not by cheeful agreements among men of good will, but by the profoundest moral disagreements? Has either school seriously reflected on the implications of the fact that the Vatican (in common with other Christian voices) is in flat disagreement with Western liberal culture on abortion, a matter that bears upon the very meaning of the *humanum* which all men share?

It cannot be long, I suppose, before some Roman Catholic moralist discovers that a voluntarist faith-ethic consisting of ecclesial conventions and house-rules and an autonomous natural ethic without obligation to revelation, so far from being competitors, do in fact make very comfortable bed-fellows. Then, with this tension duly 'overcome', the Roman Catholic contribution to public debate will be nicely conformed to the philosophy of the Church of England in the matter – if, that is, the Church of England has generally accepted the principles expressed in its document *Putting Asunder* (1966) on the reform of the divorce law. Briefly they are these: when the church contributes to public debate on matters of concern to secular society at large, it should forget that it is the church of Jesus Christ and should address society on terms common to all participants. The attempt to be distinctively Christian belongs only to the pursuit of internal discipline among the faithful. It is worth observing how the Mortimer Commission reached this conclusion, which, if it were taken seriously, would put an end to the prophetic ministry of the church once and for all. It began, quite properly, with a theology of secular law based on Jesus' words about the Mosaic divorce law 'for the hardness of your hearts', and concluded that it was appropriate for Parliament, as for Moses, to provide for the divorce and remarriage of hard-hearted subjects of the Queen. 'If *per impossibile* the Christian minority today had power to impose on the nation a matrimonial law satisfactory to itself, to use the power would surely be unjust as well as socially disruptive'(14). So far so good; but this, we notice, is a *theological* conclusion about law based upon a *theological* premiss in revelation. The Christian church has distinctively Christian reasons for not wanting a divorce law conformed to the Christian ethic of marriage. But the Commission confused this theological argument with another. 'Hardness of heart', they suppose, includes 'conscientious incredulity' *among the legislators.* Christians must distinguish 'between those dictates of the law of nature which are apparent to all men of good will and those which seem clear to themselves but not to others'(13). They also note that 'legislators have been sceptical of metaphysics, regarding law as concerned only with what can be agreed independently of men's diverse religions and philosophies'(15). They do not ask whether the church, too, can conscientiously regard law in this way. They do not ask whether the distinction between self-evident moral truths and those known only to Christians corresponds to a real distinction in the truth itself or is merely a shadow cast by changing patterns of moral blindness. They simply propose to accommodate themselves to these secular perspectives in order to ensure that they are listened to. 'It is right . . . for Christians to cooperate with secular humanists . . . in trying to make the divorce law as equitable as it can be made. Since *ex hypothesi* the State's matrimonial law is not meant to be a translation of the teaching of Jesus into legal terms . . . the standard by which it is to be judged is certainly not the Church's own canon law and pastoral discipline. Any advice that the church tenders to the state must rest not upon doctrines that only Christians accept, but upon premisses that enjoy wide acknowledgment in the nation as a whole'(17). The confusion of the Commission's two arguments appears from the failure of the third sentence in this quotation to follow from the second. Just because a divorce-law cannot be a simple translation of Jesus' teaching on marriage, it does not follow that all the church's discussion of the subject has to be based on non-theological premisses. If anyone doubts this, let him consider how the matter might work out in relation to disarmament and deterrence. Jesus taught us not to return evil for evil, but to turn the other cheek; but in a world of wickedness there is need for institutions and sanctions of justice, and we cannot simply convert Jesus' teaching into international policy. All the premisses there are theological, and they will have their proper place in any authentically Christian discussion of the subject. But suppose we then observe that most of our fellow-countrymen are not interested in international justice anyway but only in national self-interest: does that then entitle us to conclude that any statement Christians make will argue solely from national interest and avoid such theological esoterica as the duty of one nation to care for the interests of another? One can understand this second argument only as a rather cynical counsel for rhetorical effectiveness: if the church wants to be heard, let it speak only words that it knows will be welcome to its hearers! We can certainly not appeal to the doctrine of Natural Law to stand between us and the moral disaster to which such a policy must undoubtedly lead.

The Spirit and Christian freedom

The evangelical character of Christian morality appears in its relation to the resurrection of Christ from the dead. But even so it does not appear fully until we add a word which, had we been following Saint Paul directly, we should have placed first. From the resurrection we look not only back to the created order which is vindicated, but forwards to our eschatological participation in that order. Of that final enjoyment we have a present anticipation through the Pentecostal gift of the Holy Spirit.

Returning to the Epistle to the Galatians we find 'the Spirit' in opposition both to 'the law' (3:2; 5:18) and to 'the flesh' (3:3; 4:29; 5:16–26) as the true basis for Christian ethics. The law, as we have seen, is inadequate, as it appeals simply to the immanent power of the subject, 'the flesh', and offers no gospel of subjective participation in its good order. Even if it is possible to view the giving of the law as good news, as a manifestation of the grace of God (and Paul is not unwilling to admit that this is so, 2:21), it is good news that remains firmly in the realm of the objective, apart from me. Thus, whether I face it confidently and aggressively or despairingly and with a sense of burden, I am 'under the law'. This is no merely contingent false motive that may or may not tempt a man in the direction of Pharisaism; it is the inescapable fact about anyone who confronts the deed of God, even the gracious deed of God, with only his own resources to respond to it. For man's false relation to the natural moral order is not merely a matter of ignorance; it is also a matter of impotence. 'When we were children, we were slaves to the elemental spirits of the universe' (4:3). These 'elemental spirits' (*stoicheia*) are actually identified with the law given by the hand of angels on Mount Sinai (3:19–25), and yet at the same time they are the 'beings that by nature are no gods', to which even the formerly pagan Galatians were in bondage (4:8–9)! How can Paul so daringly associate the revealed morality of Old Testament faith with the superstitious idolatry of paganism? Because the order of creation, whether in a pure or an impure form, can encounter us only as a threat. It can do nothing to reconcile rebellious man to itself, nor can it interpret itself to his confused reason. Hence its tyrannous, arbitrary and sometimes frankly misleading character. Only when man can respond to God by the power of God is he 'not under the law' and so able to fulfil it (5:14,18). It is as the working of God, the 'fruit of the Spirit', that Paul characterizes Christian ethics (5:22–24).

The resurrection of Christ, viewed in isolation, might appear to be two removes away from ethics. First, it is the promise, but not the fulfilment, of a world-redemption yet to be completed; the order there renewed and vindicated in principle still awaits its universal manifestation. Secondly, it involves a 'world-order' and a 'mankind' which it is all to easy to view in a non-moral way. What, after all, is more unlike me than this 'mankind' who figures so large in theological statements? I see 'mankind' as apart from myself, even though I am a part of it; and even when I do see myself as a part of mankind, I objectify myself and make 'myself' other than myself in order to do so. But salvation does not consist merely in the objective reality of a renewed order of things apart from myself. It does not consist even in my 'knowing' of that reality, if this 'knowledge' is still qualified by an alienated detachment from its object. The Pentecostal gift means that the renewal of the universe touches me at the point where I am a moral agent, where I act and choose and experience myself as 'I'. It means that in the redemption of the world I, and every other 'I', yield myself to God's order and freely take my place within it. There is a transition from the objective to the subjective mode. And in that transition, marked by mention of the believer's 'freedom', the eschatologically awaited world-redemption has an anticipated reality already present.

We can describe this Christian freedom, in the first place, in traditional terms, speaking of the removal of psychological barriers which prevent us from responding to the challenge of God's deeds. In classical Reformation terminology, it is liberation from 'the bondage of the will'. In the New Testament, especially in the writings of Saint Paul, we often find the gospel contrasted with the law precisely on the ground that it offers a subjective deliverance from the incapacity to obey (*e.g.* Rom. 8:3). The demand of the law merely enhanced the impotence of the subject (Rom. 7:7–13). Faced with God's summons the human will was rendered a nerveless paralytic. But the Spirit is the indwelling power of God, effecting in us both the will and the action that is according to God's good purpose (Phil. 2:13). Man is given the freedom to respond as a moral agent to what God has done for him. So far from God's intervention reducing the scope of his free will, it is the precondition for it, at least in so far as that will has to confront, not a conveniently reduced demand which it feels it can cope with, but the real challenge of the divinely created order. Only in the power of 'God who works within you to will and to do' can we respond to the command, 'Work out your own salvation'.

But this traditional presentation, though true, is insufficient. It fails to integrate the subjective and the objective aspects of salvation, so that it could seem as if Jesus Christ, in himself, had nothing more to contribute to our freedom than Moses did, the difference being simply that the Holy Spirit follows in Jesus' steps, not in Moses', making obedience a practical proposition. Saint Paul did not tell the Galatians that now, in the power of the Spirit, they could keep the circumcision and food laws of the Old Testament without being overwhelmed by the burden of them. Nor did Saint Peter conclude that the Gentile Christians were perfectly able, in the power of the Spirit, to bear the yoke 'which neither our fathers nor we have been able to bear' (Acts 15:10). If they had, their gospel would have been a gospel of the Spirit alone. It is perfectly logical that successive revival movements, from the Montanists on, by emphasizing the inward moral power of the Holy Spirit unchristologically, should have ended up bound into the most terrible legalism. As soon as we credit the Spirit with giving us some power or freedom that is not that of Jesus Christ, we commit ourselves to the same path. To overcome this misunderstanding we must show how the freedom realized in *our* subjectivities by the Spirit is the same freedom as that which Jesus first achieved in *his* subjectivity – 'objectively' from our point of view. The gift of subjective freedom must already be an aspect of our being-in-Christ, not merely a precondition or a consequence of it. Before the Spirit gives us this freedom it is Christ's freedom. In the second place, then, we must characterize Christian freedom as participation in Christ's authority within the created order, the authority by virtue of which, according to Saint Paul, we are no longer slaves but sons. That means not only that we can do now what we could not do before, but that we may do now what we were not permitted to do before. The apostles understood very well what kind of authority Christ exercised when he said 'the Son of man is lord even of the sabbath' or when he 'declared all foods clean' (Mk. 2:28; 7:19).

Christian ethics, then, is distinguished from obedience to the law of the Old Covenant not only by its subjective moral power but by its content, because the believer shares in the authority realized in history by Christ himself. The *paidagogos*, as Saint Paul tells the Galatians, which guided the human race through its infancy by means of the inhibitions of the Mosaic law, has now been pensioned off. The coming of Christ is the coming of adult sonship for mankind, which puts him in a different relation to the natural order, no longer subservient but humbly and proudly in command (Gal. 3:23 – 4:7). Not that the created order has changed, or was ever anything other than what God made it, but that in Christ man was able for the first time to assume his proper place within it, the place of dominion which God assigned to Adam. Thus Christian freedom, given by the Holy Spirit, allows man to make moral responses creatively. He has the authority to designate the character of the reality which he encounters, not merely to adhere to certain designations that have already been made for him. As a moral agent he is involved in deciding what a situation is and demands in the light of the moral order. As a moral agent in history he has to interpret *new* situations, plumbing their meanings and declaring them by his decision. This kind of authority is not a challenge to the authority of God; it is a restoration of Adam's lordship in the natural order, the lordship by which he calls things by their names (Gn. 2:19). Under 'the law' he was told what the names were, and the possibility of a deeper understanding, either of the law itself or of the situations it addressed, was denied

24

him. Now by the Holy Spirit there is the possibility of creative discernment, 'the mind of Christ' (1 Cor. 2:16).

And yet this characterization of freedom, too, is inadequate – indeed, it is perilously misleading – if it is left to stand on its own. For it may be taken to mean that the Holy Spirit, in conferring such authority upon man, has, as it were, withdrawn authority from the rest of the natural order which confronts man, and has left him to make what he will of it. It is plainly the concern of those who, under the name of 'situation ethics' or whatever other title, have advocated a Christian morality without rules, that the creativity of the moral life should be vindicated. But creative freedom conceived in this way can only break down into mere improvisation, dominion become domination. This degeneration follows immediately when man's authority is not accompanied by respect for the order in which he exists and over which he rules. How can creativity function with its eyes closed upon the universe? For man does not encounter reality as an undifferentiated raw material upon which he may impose any shape that pleases him. In refusing to admit that human freedom is ordered by generic rules, 'normless' ethics has, in effect, refused to address man's freedom to the ordered reality of the world which confronts it, preferring to assume that the universe is still waste and void, awaiting the cry of the human voice, 'Let there be . . .' – and of course we can have no idea what is to follow! Such creativity is certainly not the creativity of human love. Only God expresses love by conferring order upon the absolutely orderless, and he has contented himself with doing it but once.

We can detect behind this destructive train of thought the influence of Anders Nygren's famous characterization of Christian *agapē* as an imitation of the divine, in effect a totalitarian exercise in *creatio ex nihilo*: 'Agape creates value in its object' (*Agape and Eros*, p. 210). But *agapē* cannot exercise its own creativity independently of God's creativity, which has gone before it and given the universe the order to which it attends. To imagine otherwise would be a new form of delivery back to 'the flesh', no less imprisoning for the fact that the fetters of autonomous isolation were forged in the false confidence that they would be tools of freedom.

And so we must complete our account of Christian freedom by saying that the Spirit forms and brings to expression *the appropriate pattern of free response to objective reality*. Saint Paul designates this response in general terms as 'love' (Gal. 5:6). The legalism which demands circumcision and the equally imprisoning rejection of legalism which opposes circumcision with uncircumcision are both overcome by 'faith working through love' (Gal. 5:6). Love is the overall shape of Christian ethics, the form of the human participation in created order. It is itself ordered and shaped in accordance with the order that it discovers in its object, and this ordering of love it is the task of substantive Christian ethics to trace. Again we must add that the love which the Spirit enables is the same love as that which was historically realized in the humanity of Christ. It was the mark of love within Christ's Lordship that, so far from overthrowing the given order of things, he rescued it from the 'emptiness' into which it had fallen (Rom. 8:20–21). His redemptive love thus fulfilled the creative task of Adam, to call things by their proper names. His authority over nature and his salvific concern for the true being of nature go together inseparably. And so it is that as man is given by the Spirit to share Christ's authority, he cannot do so without love, both for the created order in general and for the particular beings, human and other, which stand within it in various problematic relationships. Love does not bear the dominating and manipulative traits that have been given to it in some attempts to characterize the Christian ethic. It achieves its creativity by being perceptive. It attempts to act *for* any being only on the basis of an appreciation *of* that being. Thus classical Christian descriptions of love are often found invoking two other terms which expound its sense: the first is 'wisdom', which is the intellectual apprehension of the order of things which discloses how each being stands in relation to each other; the second is 'delight', which is affective attention to something simply for *what* it is and for the fact *that* it is. Such love is the fruit of God's presence within us, uniting us to the humanity of God in Christ, who cherishes and defends all that God the Father has made and thought.

The task of this essay is to describe the shape of Christian moral thought theologically, showing how it responds to, and is itself an integral part of, the Christian gospel. In its course we shall retraverse more slowly the course we have followed in this introductory chapter. In the first section we shall be concerned with the objective reality proclaimed in the gospel, the achievement of salvation in the death and resurrection of Christ; and from this central evangelical point of reference we shall look back to what is reaffirmed there, the order of creation, and forward to what is anticipated there, the kingdom of God (chs. 2,3). We shall then reflect on the moral epistemology that is implied in ethics founded on these proclamations (ch. 4). In the second section our attention will turn to the subjective reality proclaimed in the gospel, the presence of the Spirit in believer and church. Here we shall discuss first the meaning of moral freedom (ch. 5), and then, at greater length, the correlative idea of authority, when it will be unhappily unavoidable that we must expound the concept of authority in general terms before speaking explicitly of the moral authority of Christ to which the Spirit bears witness (chs. 6,7). The section will end with a brief discussion of the dialectic of freedom and authority within the

Christian community (ch. 8). In the third section we develop the theme of these last paragraphs on love as the form of the Christian moral life. In contrast to the deductive movement of thought which marks the first two sections, we shall here move 'from below': starting with the fragmented and differentiated moral responses to reality which are expressed in codes of moral rules, we move to the idea of moral character, which unifies an individual's many moral choices, but which is still differentiated (chs. 9,10). From there we come to the fundamental relations of love to God and man which give unity also to the varieties of moral character (ch. 11); and finally, in an eschatological chapter, we speak of the judgment and justification of God, which gives point to all morality, while at the same time it relativizes its pretensions in the light of divine forgiveness (ch. 12).

Part One

The objective reality

2

Created order

In proclaiming the resurrection of Christ, the apostles proclaimed also the resurrection of mankind in Christ; and in proclaiming the resurrection of mankind, they proclaimed the renewal of all creation with him. The resurrection of Christ in isolation from mankind would not be a gospel message. The resurrection of mankind apart from creation would be a gospel of a sort, but of a purely gnostic and world-denying sort which is far from the gospel that the apostles actually preached. So the resurrection of Christ directs our attention back to the creation which it vindicates. But we must understand 'creation' not merely as the raw material out of which the world as we know it is composed, but as the order and coherence *in* which it is composed. To speak of the resurrection of creation would be meaningless if creation were no more than so much undifferentiated energy. Such a proclamation can have point only as it assures us that the very thing which God has made will continue and flourish. It is not created energy as such that is vindicated in the resurrection of Christ, but the order in which created energy was disposed by the hand of the Creator.

It is true, of course, that to speak of this world as 'created' is already to speak of an order. In the first words of the creed, before we have tried to sketch an outline of created order with the phrase 'heaven and earth', simply as we say 'I believe in God the Creator', we are stating that the world is an ordered totality. By virtue of the fact that there is a Creator, there is also a creation that is ordered to its Creator, a world which exists as his creation and in no other way, so that by its existence it points to God. But then, just because it is ordered vertically in this way, it must also have an internal horizontal ordering among its parts (assuming,

31

what we know to be the case, that it is not an undivided monad). It forms, over against the Creator, a whole which is 'creation'; and if there is any plurality of creatures within it, they are governed by this shared determinant of their existence, that each to each is as fellow-creature to fellow-creature.

Out of these two fundamental directions of created order we form the concepts of order as 'end' and 'kind', of 'teleological' and 'generic' order. Absolute disorder (if we may be permitted to imagine something that God's very existence prohibits) would be a plurality of entities so completely unrelated that there would be no 'world' in which they existed together, no relation that would enable them to be thought together. One thing would exist, and another thing would exist; but they would be unconnected universes. In the two planes of order as end and kind we discern two relations in which different things may exist together and be thought together. They may be related by a *directing* of the one thing to the other: A 'is ordered to serve' B, and B is A's 'end' (to use for the moment the Platonic form of expressing the teleological relation). Or they may be related by a *reciprocity* of each toward the other: there is some respect in which A is 'like' B and B 'like' A, so that they stand alongside each other as members of a 'kind'. These relations do not yet presume any extension in time; they are not yet relations between happenings, like, for example, the relation of cause and effect. They belong to the world as it were stopped still in its tracks; they are given in the fact of creation itself. Without these twin concepts we could not think of a 'universe'. If some A and some B were related neither teleologically nor generically in any respect whatsoever, there would be two unconnected universes, which is to say, no universe at all.

We can speak of *ta panta*, the universe as a whole. Its plurality of hierarchical grades, its distinctions between heaven and earth, between spiritual and material reality, are held under control. The community of all natures is not permitted to explode in fragments. *Synestēken*, 'it holds together': thus Saint Paul, in the great cosmic Christology of Colossians 1:15–20. Two verbs and three prepositional phrases express the structure of that universe and its coherence. The two verbs: 'were created' and 'to reconcile'. The wholeness of the universe depends on its being a created universe, and thereafter on its being reconciled, brought back into the order of its creation. These are the fundamental cosmic events, the framework of its history; and to them attaches the first prepositional phrase, *di' autou*, 'through him'. The Son of God's love, in whom we have redemption, is the *means by which* these two cosmic events, the creation and reconciliation of all things, take place. Both of them? So the apostolic church maintained, thinking back, no doubt, from the later to the earlier, yet not hesitating to affirm the earlier as necessary to the later. 'Through him', then, expresses the causal and temporal ordering by which cosmic order is a happening and not merely a concept; it comes to pass by 'the blood of his cross' and his becoming 'the first-born from the dead'. But the Son effects not only the *temporal* realization of cosmic order. Order as such holds together *en autō* and *eis auton*, 'in him' and 'for him'. 'For him' expresses the teleological order of creation: it is 'for him' who is its end. But in verse 20 that phrase refers us clearly to the Father, while equally clearly it refers us in verse 16 to the Son. God is the end of all creation; but so therefore is the Son who is the 'image of the invisible God'. 'In him', on the other hand, does not refer to the Father. Only of the Son can it be said that 'in him all things hold together'; for this phrase suggests the identification of the Son with creation, as creature as well as the Father's image. Is he, then, merely one creature among others? Certainly not: as the Redeemer, as the visible presence of the invisible God who is creation's end, he must be, even as creature, 'the pre-eminent one', the *archē* (who thereby levels all other *archai*, v. 16), the 'head' of the renewed creation taking shape in the church, the 'first-born'. These expressions convey his supremacy *in* creation; for in creation, too, there is a teleological ordering *eis auton*, a direction of the whole to its head and captain. And this 'for him' depends on the other 'for him', the one which is not paralleled by an 'in him', the directing of all creation to its God. Yet *this* 'for him' *is* related to an 'in him'. In so far as 'in him' suggests supremacy, it is the supremacy of the representative, a supremacy based on affinity. He is creation's head only in so far as he stands alongside it as the creature, the first-born from the dead who leads creation on the path from death to life, the path which only it, and he with it and at its head, can walk.

The only pure teleological relation, unqualified by any generic equivalence, is that between the creature and its Creator; only there is there an ordering-to in which there is no element of ordering-alongside. But within the created order there is a complex network of teleological and generic relations. Creatures which have generic equivalence as creatures may be ordered to one another teleologically: vegetables and men are both creatures, but vegetables are ordered to men as food for their nourishment. Rocks and vegetables are both creatures, but rocks are ordered to vegetables as the foundation for the soil in which they are to grow. Some forms of generic equivalence, on the other hand, allow of no natural teleological ordering within them. Christianity has always seen the relationship of human beings to one another in this light, and repudiated claims for a natural hierarchy among them, the idea of a slave-race created to serve a master-race, for example, or (though not without occasional unhappy ambiguities) of woman created to serve man. But the absence of a teleological order between two beings does not mean that they are associated in a generic equivalence of such strength as that which unites the human race. Between some created beings there are merely contingent relationships, which involve no significant ordering, either to or alongside. There is no teleological order in either direction, for example, between fire and fish, and they are members of no common kind; yet there is still the loose generic bond which arises from their both being creatures, and they are tied into the web of generic and teleological order by their relations with other beings.

Other categories of reality, too, and not only material entities like rocks and vegetables, fish and fire, are ordered by kinds and ends. Operations have their generic and teleological relations, which is why the subject is of importance to moralists. Speech is ordered to truth, and marriage to fidelity. But in thinking about operations the Aristotelian tradition of classifying kinds hierarchically, as sub-species within species and species within genus, is a bad guide. In morality it is more the rule than the exception that particulars belong to more than one unconnected kind and are ordered in several different sets of likenesses at once. This is what gives good moral thinking its often acknowledged 'open-textured' quality; we never know in advance what combinations of generic features may be displayed by any situation on which we will deliberate or reflect. It provides the stuff of cliff-hanging moral dilemmas: the attitude which looks like compassion from one point of view looks like disloyalty from another; the action which most expresses justice also suggests a contempt for human life. The taxonomic paradigm which often dominates the discussion of kinds can be no more than a highly simplified and stylized representation of what is meant by generic relations in morality.

One further clarification of these important concepts is necessary before our discussion can proceed. There have traditionally been two ways in which teleological order has been presented. The Platonic formula is that A is ordered-to-serve B: the vegetable creation is ordered-to-serve the animal, the animal ordered-to-serve the rational, and reason ordered-to-serve divine truth. The question of the end of each being is also the question of what other being transcends it on the scale of ontological dignity. By contrast the Aristotelian formula can speak of the end of each being without raising questions of transcendence at all. A is ordered-to-flourish as A: the vegetable creation to grow luxuriantly, the animal creation to move with strength and vigour, the rational creation to think. The virtue of the Aristotelian conception is that it allows us to think of teleological order as a purely *natural* ordering, an ordering within the created world which does not beg questions about what lies outside it. When Plato speaks of the human mind as ordered-to-serve divine truth, he clearly allows cosmology to include theology and soteriology. This risks eroding the hard edge which separates Creator from creation and imposing an over-simplified pyramid-shape upon cosmology. Scholastic Christianity, under Aristotelian influence, tried to guard against this danger by distinguishing sharply between the 'natural' and the 'supernatural' ends of man. In so doing, however, it also intended to protect what is true in the Platonic conception. One cannot speak of the flourishing of any kind without implicitly indicating a wider order which will determine what flourishing and frustration within that kind consist of. An acorn flourishes by becoming an oak; but why should this be a more successful thing for it to become than pig's food? We have to choose between a purely anarchistic answer, based on an ultimate competition between all species, and an answer which points to the value for *other* beings of there being oaks and not just acorns. So it is, when we speak of the flourishing of a human being, that we raise the question of the wider order within which the content of human flourishing is determined. And there arises the possibility that the answer will point to a 'supernatural end', to a reference point outside the network of kinds and ends in nature, which nature as a whole is ordered-to-serve and which determines what the flourishing of the natural order is to be.

Any attempt to think about morality must make a decision early in its course, overt or covert, about these forms of order which we seem to discern in the world. Either they are there, or they are not. This decision, which will shape the character of the whole moral philosophical enterprise, forces itself as much upon secular as upon Christian thought. Secular man can observe the same indications of order as anyone else. He can see that vegetables are ordered to serve animal life as food, and he can see that human beings stand in a generic equality alongside one another. And so secular man, if he becomes a thinker, has the same decision to make. On the one hand he may interpret these relations of order as part of a universal world-order, a network of interrelationships forming a totality of which mankind himself is a part. If he does so, he steps, despite himself, on to theological ground, and will find himself required to specify rather carefully how he conceives the relation of cosmic order to the presence of mind and reason within it. Alternatively, renouncing the pretensions of 'metaphysics', he may turn altogether away from the apparent objectivity of order. Dismissing the immediate and pre-critical supposition that order could be 'perceived', he will maintain instead that it was 'imposed' upon the raw material of experience by the will-to-order within the observing mind. For moral philosophy this means that all our moral beliefs, such as that every human being is the equal of every other, are not 'beliefs' at all but mere 'commitments', claiming no correspondence with reality. They are the ways in which the will projects the patterns of the mind upon the blank screen of an unordered world.

In the one case we have the old road of traditional idealism, with all its theological overtones, leading us to the classic debate between theism and pantheism. In the other case we have the new and familiar road of English-speaking empiricism, which leads, if the traveller is vigorous and deter-

35

mined, to the loss of all ordered relations within the universe. Hume's sceptical dissolution of the cause-effect nexus and of inductive inference represents the tendency of the anti-metaphysical option. But what of the claims of Hegelian idealism to have overcome this alternative? Do we not have, in Hegel's ontologizing of epistemology, a way of saying that our categories of kind and end, though they are seated within the human mind, are nevertheless real by virtue of their contribution to the world-historical whole? No: the reality that is conferred on them by this historicist overview is reality as something *else* than as the kinds and ends that we thought we discerned. The kind, once it falls victim to the doctrine that the reality of a notion is the history of its thought, is no longer a kind at all, but a particular phase of the intellectual history of the world. The end is no longer a given ordering-to, that invites and allows freedom of response, but a manifestation of the irresistible thrust of historical necessity. Thus in effect Hegelian idealism, too, abolishes the principles of order, though so long as it maintains its world-historical perspective this abolition is not immediately apparent, since the intellectual events into which they have been converted are events on a sufficiently large scale to create the illusion of permanence. Once follow the conservative tendency of English idealism to convert the world-historical into the history of individual thought, and the positivist possibilities of the movement are immediately apparent. The positivist revolution in English-speaking philosophy which took everybody by surprise half a century ago was as much a mutation of the Hegelian idealist tradition as Hume's thought was of Berkeley's.

For a Christian believer it would seem that there could be little hesitation over this decision. For only if the order which we think we see, or something like it, is really present in the world, can there be 'evangelical' ethics. Only so, indeed, can there be a Christian, rather than a gnostic, gospel at all. The dynamic of the Christian faith, calling us to respond appropriately to the deeds of God on our behalf, supposes that there is an appropriate conformity of human response to divine act. It supposes that divine initiative and human obedience are two movements, distinct though not independent, both of them free; that free human response is not overwhelmed by the necessity of the divine deed on the one hand, and that the divine deed is not reducible to the exercise of human decision on the other. Moral fact and moral response are two. The divine and the human agents both have reality and both have freedom, even though the human reality and freedom are not at ontological parity with the divine, but depend upon the divine from first to last. Thus in speaking of the order which God the Creator and Redeemer has established in the universe, we are not speaking merely of our own capacities to impose order upon what we see there. Of course, we can and do impose order upon what we see, for we are free agents and capable of creative interpretation of the world we confront. But our ordering depends upon God's to provide the condition for its

36

freedom. It is free because it has a given order to respond to in attention or disregard, in conformity or disconformity, with obedience or with rebellion.

Saint Basil distinguished two kinds of order, one 'natural' (*physikē*) and the other 'deliberative' (*kat' epitēdeusin*) or 'artificial' (*technikē*). The one is 'the order of creatures established according to the creative principles', the other is 'the order in artefacts, sciences, social conventions, enumeration *etc.*'. Eunomius the Arian has refused to speak of order in the Godhead, because 'order is at the behest of the one who imposes it'. But this argument shows that 'he has either never realized, or else has purposely concealed the fact that there is a form of order which does not arise from our disposition but goes with the natural sequence of things' (*Adversus Eunomium* I.20). This may have inspired Augustine to think in the same way, contrasting the *ordo naturae* with 'another way of assessing things, according to the use which each has for them' (*alius pro suo cuiusque usu aestimationis modus*). 'Reason', acting in a situation where it can judge freely, detached from need or desire, can weigh 'what each object is according to the scale of reality'; 'necessity' thinks of 'what means should be adopted to what end' (*De civitate Dei* XI.16). What emerges very clearly from Augustine's discussion is that the order of human disposition, so far from being necessitated by the natural order, may stand in a questionable, even a contradictory relation to it. Man is free to say his Yea or Nay in action to what reason, given the liberty of detached judgment, observes to be the case. This conception, at any rate, will not be vulnerable to the tired objection that a doctrine of natural order is incompatible with historical contingency in general and with the theory of evolution in particular. Let us imagine, as an exercise in not-too-fanciful science-fiction, that biological technique succeeds in 'directing' the course of evolution in such a way that human reproduction is managed entirely and universally *in vitro*, that pregnancy becomes obsolete among humans, and that sexual union comes to serve no end other than the cementing of affection. Now when we speak of a 'natural ordering' of sexual love to procreation do we mean to predict that human artifice can never achieve such a thing? No: natural order does not form an impregnable barrier which man can never choose to breach; it merely establishes the conditions upon which such a breach can be made. It will still be the case, even if we succeed in diverting reproduction through other channels, that human sexual love is ordered also to procreation. This is an unchanging principle of order which will continue to be a principle of order even when human beings refuse to procreate, even, let us add, when human beings have passed from the scene altogether. This does not entitle us to say that procreation can never be separated from sexual love. It entitles us to say only that if it is, then sexual love will be frustrated of its natural purposes. Parents in that age, whatever their biological fertility, will be among the barren so pitied in the Old Testament.

But bound up in the decision for or against a coherent Christianity, there is the decision for or against humanism. For if we are to give any content to the term 'humanity', we must do so in a context where we can understand it as a kind and relate it to the wider order in terms of its end and the ends of other beings. Humanism is dependent on such a context. It is possible for humanism to refuse the mighty answers of the Reformed catechisms, 'Man's chief and highest end is to glorify God, and fully to enjoy him for ever', because creation *is* contingent and man's place in it *can* be understood solely in terms of his 'natural' rather than his 'supernatural' end. But it is not possible for humanism to refuse the *question*, 'What is the chief and highest end of man?' For without some answer to that question it has lost, not only the grounds for respecting this human species (thus leaving itself engaged upon a pointless self-worship), but also, as we shall see, the very reason to understand humanity as a unitary species at all, rather than as a chance objectification, or 'tragic thrownness', of being.

The theological doctrine of mankind, offered us with supreme poetic magnificence in the eighth Psalm, shows him set within an order which he did not make, joyfully accepting his privileged place within it. He has been set over all the works of God's hand, and is 'lacking a very little of God'. But his place as ruler is distinguished from that of God as Creator. The universe, with humanity at its head, acknowledges not humanity but God as its Creator. It is God's majesty that is praised in the heavens and not man's. Man's own acknowledgment of God as his Sovereign (his ordering-to-serve) is what shows that his rule is not usurpation but obedience. From within the universe (ordered-alongside) this insignificant and mortal creature is called, by God's 'remembering' of him, to fulfil a high function in it (ordered-to-flourish). Such a picture does not by any means imply that the rest of the created order finds the whole of its teleological fulfilment in serving *him*. It, like he, is ordered primarily with a 'supernatural' ordering, to praise God. But man's ordering-to-flourish as its ruler is a necessary condition for the rest of creation to fulfil its own ordering. His rule is the rule which liberates other beings to be, to be in themselves, to be for others, and to be for God. And this he does by the rational speech with which he articulates the praise of God to which the whole creation is summoned. The bulwark against chaos is established 'out of the mouths of babes and sucklings'.

The attack upon kinds: the freedom of God

And yet there are theological reservations voiced about the linking of moral obligation to the natural generic-teleological order. In the natural order as we have described it ends and kinds are interdependent, so that the ordering-to of any particular being is a function of its ordering-alongside as a member of a kind. Natural ends are discerned generically, so that a morality which corresponds to them will be generic. That is to say, its judgments will be made about kinds of things and situations, and about particulars only as instances of a kind. Kinds are independent of particularizing features of time and place; they order beings in one time and place alongside beings in others, discerning likenesses among them that may be represented equally well in any time and place. If morality, then, is tied to natural teleology, and teleology to generic order, morality too must transcend time-place particularizations. An action of kind X must be good in any time or place, regardless of who does it, when or where. Of course, kind X may be very carefully specified. Small differences of circumstance may make moral distinctions between kinds X^1, X^2, X^3 and so on, which may demand great subtlety and discrimination; but it remains the case that when the necessary distinctions have been made, the moral judgment applies to the kind and not just to the particular. And this causes great difficulty for some theological thinkers who sense that a generic morality is irreconcilable in principle with the Christian belief that morality is the demand of God's will, which must ⬅ be free and unbound. Generic morality, as they see it, ties God's will down to an eternal and necessary structure over which he has no more power to command. The Christian understanding, on the other hand, requires that God be free and his deeds contingent; that is, the works of a free God are works that might have been done otherwise, since God was under no necessity to do them as he did.

In the first place the objector is concerned that we should think of the world *as a whole* as contingent. It is not acceptable to think of God as being under a necessity to create the world as it is, not even a necessity arising from within his own being. For although we may perhaps dare to speak, by way of analogy and hesitantly, of a divine love that 'had' to express itself in creation, as soon as we go beyond that to suggest that it had to create this world and not some other one, we say in effect that the 'creation' is not a creation at all, but an emanation, a reflection of the inner law of God's being, sharing its necessity and thus, in some sense, sharing its divinity. We have taken the first step towards pantheism, and blunted the edge of the doctrine of creation. However, there is no reason why this proper theological concern should not be fully accommodated within a teleological and generic understanding of created order. In speaking of kinds as independent of time-place particularity there is certainly no need to attribute to them an eternal transcendence such as belongs to God himself. Kinds are not independent of the temporo-spatial universe. No claim is made for their existence 'before creation'. They are simply, by virtue of their role as ordering principles within the temporo-spatial universe, independent of any *particular* time-place determination. They are not particulars; they are universals. Certainly, as we know, within the Platonic tradition of thought about universals there has been a tendency to regard them as divine. This tendency was reflected in some interpretations of Christianity by giving them the status of divine thoughts, so that there was a generic equivalence between the order of the universe and the divine mind. But in rejecting this form of the doctrine of kinds one is not compelled to reject kinds altogether. Our contention that the relation of the creation to the Creator is teleological, but not in any way generic, has properly safeguarded the absolute contingency of the creature and the freedom of the Creator.

It is characteristic of Protestant thinkers to claim that the freedom of God was inadequately respected in pre-Reformation Christian thought. T. F. Torrance may be taken as typical, when he complains that 'there lay deeply entrenched in the high mediaeval theology the idea that God is impassible and changeless, and that all created things have existence only as the objects of the eternal knowing and willing of God, so that their creaturely existence is directly grounded in the eternity of God'. And although medieval theology avoided thinking of the world as an emanation of God, 'it held on to a (modified) notion of a hierarchy of being, embracing both the lowest and the highest being, which seriously blurred the Biblical distinction between the Creator and the creature, and introduced into its doctrine of God an unfortunate ambiguity' (*Theological Science*, p. 59). We need not quarrel with this moderately-phrased judgment on its own terms. No doubt medieval theology was as much subject to ambiguity as our own is, and no doubt the doctrine of *analogia entis* is entirely open to dangerous misconstructions which obscure the distinction between Creator and creature. However, this kind of characterization of the high medieval theology hardly does justice to the astonishing insistence on the freedom of God which marked, not merely the late-medieval voluntarism of Duns Scotus and William of Ockham, but the whole scholastic tradition from Peter Lombard. Lombard decisively rejects Augustine's thesis that God's omnipotence is limited by his reason. The world is limited by God's will, not his reason; and God's will is not limited by anything. *Potest aliud velle quam vult*: 'his will may be other than it is'. *Potest*, notice, not *potuit*! God *can* will other worlds than this, not merely *could have* willed! Those who try to limit God's power by arguing that God cannot do otherwise than he does, because he cannot do other than what is good and just, fail to see that anything God did would be good and just if he did it. Many things that are not good and just are not so simply because God has not willed them (I d.42, 43).

Bonaventure, who shows himself inclined to restrict some of Lombard's statements in the interests of maintaining God's rational consistency, is nevertheless prepared to endorse the main thrust of the position: God could make another world better than this. It would not be *this* world, unless the improvements were merely matters of accidental characteristics (*e.g.* size), but God could make it, and could have made it. The argument that God would have made things as excellent as they could be in the first place, an argument which Augustine really believed, is dismissed with dispatch: Of course there must be a limit to any given world; but that does not imply a limit to the creative power. It makes no sense to ask *why* God did not do something better, for the only answer is, 'Even so he willed it' (*Commentary* on I d.44). And Saint Thomas Aquinas, who earned Torrance's wrath by flirting with the idea that the world might be eternal, nevertheless speaks entirely in line with this. God is limited by the logic of non-contradiction, but by nothing else. We cannot possibly say that God's wisdom 'required' that things should be as they are, for God's wisdom and God's power are one. Whatever God did would have been *conveniens et iustum* if he were to do it. God has the 'absolute power' to do even things which he has foreknown and foreordained that he will not do. These things cannot be done, because God has decided against them; but that does not mean that God cannot do them (*Summa Theologiae* I.25.3,5). Omnipotence, in other words, is the power to do what might have been done, and is not alienated by actual decision. God does not 'bind himself' by disposing of his power one way and not another. So we see that even Thomas Aquinas' identification of will and reason in God can be put to the service of a fundamentally voluntarist perception of divine omnipotence.

But the theological objector's concern for God's freedom is not limited to concern for the contingency of the created world as a whole. It also intends to maintain God's freedom to act and to command as an agent *within* the temporo-spatial universe that he has made. We cannot be content to say that God has made his dispositions once and for all, so far as this world is concerned, in the creation of an order of kinds and ends, that he made these dispositions freely, and that he is at liberty to make any other world than this whenever he chooses. We must also insist on his freedom within this world to do more than merely reiterate the changeless summons of the generic order once given. And so the theological objector goes on to argue that morality must respond to the agency of God in history, and not rest solely upon the uniform structures which stand apart from history. But as soon as he says this, he appears to be committed to denying the generic character of morality; for any command or principle that changes in history thereby becomes a particular, a mere item in the history of ideas. The demand that morality must change with God's acts in history therefore puts the axe to the root of the doctrine that morality is generic.

Thus the objection sides with the more radical voluntarism which has been traditionally traced to the late-medieval thinkers, Scotus and Ockham. I am in no position to pronounce on the merits of a more recent interpretation which finds greater continuity between Ockham and the older medieval tradition (see, for example, H. Junghans, *Ockham im Lichte der Neueren Forschung*), nor to say whether his thought can be made consistent with itself on the point. But it does seem clear that once the decisive step has been taken to relate the Natural Law exclusively to the will of God, and obedience to the will of man, then even the natural order becomes a matter of divine 'statute' (to use the term that Scotus introduces into the discussion of Lombard's 44th distinction – *Ordinatio* I d.44). For Ockham it appears that the deformity of acts contrary to Natural Law rests on their 'circumstantial' opposition to 'divine precept' (II *Comm. in Sent.* q.15). Once this position is reached it is only a matter of time until the conclusion is drawn that the changing of the divine precept, which Ockham views, perhaps, as merely an abstract possibility, has in fact happened in the course of salvation-history. It can hardly be more than theological conservatism if Ockham continues to make the distinction between God's *potentia absoluta* and his *potentia ordinaria* correspond to that between his operations outside this world-order and those within it. The logical bond between the world-order and the prevailing disposition of *potentia ordinaria* has been severed by the thesis that moral obligation is purely a relation of will to will, obedience to precept.

Let us be clear at the beginning that there are elements in this position which no theology can ignore without forfeiting its claim to be Christian. Christianity is committed, in the first place, to a view of divine providence which expects it to act 'arbitrarily'. We should not be dismayed by this term, meaning simply that God exercises *arbitrium*, the right of decision in matters where there is no reason for him to do one thing rather than another. For example, the decision that someone should die at a certain time, or another person be born: these are not decisions which we can demand that God justify. It is pointless to say 'It isn't fair' – and that not because God truculently exempts himself from the canons of fair behaviour, but because such canons are inappropriate to judge the nature of such events. In the second place, Christianity is committed to recognizing a special exercise of such divine freedom in individual vocation. Only in so far as God's decisions may be arbitrary can they include particular demands addressed to particular individuals. Only in so far as he is not limited to the generic address to mankind as a whole can he call me in a way that is uniquely my own. If God were not free to do this, the differentiation of one individual biography from another would be purely a matter of chance; but the Christian doctrine of vocation teaches us to understand it in terms of particular callings received as individual gifts from God. And vocation, of course, is only one aspect of God's dealings with individuals. Election, grace and conversion all depend on God's right to command particularly, to address individuals in ways not susceptible of universalization.

Thirdly, Christianity is committed to the meaningfulness of history as the stage on which mankind's salvation has been wrought. 'Salvation-history' means change and innovation; it means that God can do a 'new thing'. Consequently we must not proceed on the assumption of a uniform pattern of divine activity in all ages, for it is central to Christian belief that there is a difference between God's self-manifestation before and after the coming of Christ. It may even seem that the difficulty which so exercised the church Fathers about the morality of the divine commands to the patriarchs can be firmly set on one side. For salvation-history means nothing unless it means that God has made himself known to Abraham in his era differently from the way in which he has made himself known to us in ours. However, in this very example we see the problem with this line of thought. For if it were in truth the case that morality depended entirely on the particular commands of God for particular persons, no-one would ever have found the commands given to the patriarchs difficult in the first place. But the difficulty has been felt by every sensitive reader of the Old Testament. The assistance given by the concept of salvation-history is not to remove altogether our sense that the morality of the patriarchs was problematic, but to give us a way of understanding why God should have dealt with the ancients in a morally concessionary, and thereby problematic, fashion. We do not believe that it was *as* right for Abraham to use Hagar as a concubine as it is now for us to disapprove of concubinage. What we believe, if we make a moral judgment on the matter at all, is that we can, in the light of history, make allowances for Abraham's concubine. But that is precisely to defend a generic criterion of morality. For 'making allowances' is nothing other than specifying more exactly what circumstances might differentiate our situations from Abraham's, an undertaking which is meaningless unless he and we alike can be set together within the same field of moral judgment.

Furthermore, however insistent we are upon the possibility of individual vocation, we do not usually confuse vocation with moral duty. Of course, there is a moral duty that we should follow our vocations – but that is a *generic* duty, not a particular one! It would be wrong to say of any action which I might find myself 'called' to do that such an action was 'morally obligatory'. It is not morally obligatory, for example, to live in Toronto. I may at one time of my life have been called by God to live there, and I was, of course, under an obligation to obey God's call. The fact that it was then my vocation made it contingently obligatory for me; but it was not, and is not, an obligation in itself. But anyone who thought that he was bound to love his neighbour in the same way that I was bound to live in Toronto, simply because he was called to it – 'That is my calling, I cannot answer for anyone else!' – would evidently have no idea what categorical moral obligation was. Morality is that to which one is summoned, not particularly, like the summons to become a priest or to marry a certain person, but by virtue of being mankind in God's world. As Kierkegaard unforgettably demonstrated, there may be conflict between the vocational and the ethical, between God's call to Abraham to sacrifice Isaac and the moral principle forbidding it. Conflicts of this kind could not arise if there were no difference in principle between morality and vocation; they would merely be uncertainties about what one's vocation was. But we can hardly be satisfied with any resolution of such conflicts that in effect does no more than deny that they can arise.

Such a conflict is strikingly attributed to Jesus himself, whose vocation first appears in paradoxical tension with his duty to his family in the story related by Saint Luke (2:41–52) of his journey to the temple at the age of twelve. Unlike the conflict described by Saint Mark (3:21,31–35), in which Jesus' family appears officious, this incident enables us to appreciate the tension; we can well sympathize with Mary's protest, and the justice of her claim is tacitly acknowledged in the event as Jesus returns with his parents to Nazareth 'and was obedient to them'. In speaking of a 'tension' between the vocational and the generic demand, we need not assent to the view apparently held by Kierkegaard (in *Fear and Trembling*) that there is no resolution possible within the sphere of moral thought – that what is demanded at the vocational level is 'a religious suspension of the ethical'. Because the vocational demand, which is not generic, is sanctioned by the generic principle that one should heed one's vocation, the conflict is resolved like any other conflict between *prima facie* moral claims. As conflict and as resolution, it is no different from, let us say, the decision whether to donate a certain sum of money to the relief of the starving or to the rehabilitation of prisoners. What makes it distinctive, however, is that the conflict cannot be fully understood by anyone except the agent, since the character of one of the claims is susceptible only of private discernment.

Finally, there would be no 'problem of evil' to trouble us if the good were exhaustively accounted for in terms of God's arbitrary dealings in providence. We may agree that the concept of 'fairness' is inappropriate to such providentially disposed events as someone's death; but that does not prevent us from experiencing a sense of tension between the order of morality and the eventualities of history as a whole. The question whether the God who rules history is good can be, and is, put. And when Christians point to the cross and resurrection of Christ as the resolution of that problem, they admit that there is a tension which demands resolution. The 'problem of evil' is the problem of the inscrutability of providence in the light of the moral order. The cross affords us that interpretation of providence which allows us, not yet to see the good perspicuously within it, but to be certain that we shall ultimately see it. But the problem has arisen because our knowledge of the good (imperfect as it is) and our perceptions of providence (imperfect as they are) are two, not one. We have not learnt the meaning of goodness by reading it off God's arbitrary decrees, off the death of this man and the birth of this other. We have learnt it from the regularities of the created order. The vindication of God is the vindication of those regularities in the face of the mysterious course of history; it is the demonstration that the God who rules the world is the same as the God who made it, and that the outcome of history will affirm and not deny the order of its making.

There is, then, an irreducible duality between the freedom of God to act particularly in history and the generic ordering of the world which is reflected in morality. For history to be meaningful history, and for God's freedom to be gracious freedom, there must also be order which is not subject to historical change. Otherwise history could only be uninterpretable movement, the denial of what has been in favour of what is to be. The fact that temporal movement is comprehensible as 'history' points to the prior fact that temporal movement is not the sole manifestation of God's work. He who is unchanging, with 'no variation or shadow due to change' (Jas. 1:17), is the author, not only of change itself, but of the order which makes that change good.

The attack upon ends: the polarity of will and nature

Up to this point we have been discussing an objection to the idea that morality is concerned with the *generic* order. Teleological 'ordering-to', which is effected by the will of God, should be disembarrassed of any association with generic 'ordering-alongside', it has been argued, in order to protect the freedom of God to act historically and particularly. We have responded that this freedom of divine *arbitrium*, though essential to a theology of providence, is not the same operation of God's will as that which we discern behind the moral law; and that the latter, belonging not to history but to creation, expresses the regularities of the generic order. We now have to consider an objection from the other side, which aims to disembarrass the generic ordering of moral thought from what are felt to be insupportable teleological implications.

Two convergent concerns motivate this attack upon ends. On the one hand there is a long-standing objection made in the interests of scientific thought to the idea that kinds are determined by 'final causes'. The belief in final causes, it has been maintained since Francis Bacon, was the great impediment to the search for a scientific understanding of the relationships among natural phenomena. Only when thought could escape the inhibiting influence of a teleological philosophy could it examine the universe in a way that was open to the contingency of relations, not presupposing that it would find a unifying purposiveness but prepared to find exactly what it did find. On the other hand there is the objection made by thinkers of the Enlightenment to the idea that the moral will can be determined by a teleological order discerned within nature. Only when purposiveness is imposed upon nature by a free and unconditioned will, it was argued, can that purposiveness be moral. These objections, with their different concerns, converge upon a programme of interpretation which we may call 'the polarity of will and nature'. On the one hand scientific thought is anxious to free nature from immanent purposiveness; on the other, moral philosophy wishes to free the will from any purposiveness in nature. It suits both of them to assign purposiveness exclusively to the human will, and to dissociate it from nature. But both retain a strong interest in discerning the generic order within nature, the scientific because of its concern with observable regularity, the ethical because of its belief in consistency as a criterion of justice.

(1) It is indeed quite striking how insistent were the eighteenth-century champions of a 'voluntarist' morality (if we may attend to their side of the case first) that moral judgment, though independent of any teleological order in nature, must nevertheless respect generic relations. Hume's 'moral sentiment', with the aid of which he hoped to dispense with 'incomprehensible relations or qualities which never did exist in nature', could be evoked 'only when a character is considered in general, without reference to our particular interest' (*Treatise of Human Nature* III.1.2). Kant made the doctrine famous as the 'categorical imperative': 'Act only on that maxim whereby thou canst at the same time will that it should become a universal law' (*Groundwork* 421). This principle was of crucial importance to the voluntarist programme of moral thought; since there would be no way of distinguishing the moral affections from other affective impulses, feelings and desires, unless the former were bound to respond to all like things in like ways, that is, consistently, and so justly.

Hume's use of the word 'general' marks the connection of moral thought to the question of kinds (*genera*), which were discussed in the English philosophy of his time under the name of 'general ideas'. Our adjective 'generic' follows him as closely as possible – given the fact that in modern speech 'general' is unsuitable, since it has come to mean 'unspecified' or 'undifferentiated'. Some recent moral philosophers (notably R. M. Hare) have intended to mark the same point by building on the Kantian 'universal', understanding it as an allusion to the medieval designation of kinds as *universalia*. With these champions of 'universalizability', who deserve gratitude for keeping the question of generic order alive in recent discussion, we would profess no difference other than a terminological one. The difficulty with 'universal' is that Kant intended far more in speaking of a 'universal law' than simply to abstract a generic rule from its particular applications. As 'universal' the law was also objective, necessary and *a priori*; it abstracted from empirical differentiations of every kind. It becomes, then, difficult to distinguish the universal law from the categorical imperative which requires obedience to it. There is only one law, and that of stark formal simplicity. It constitutes the foundation

46

of practical rationality, and thus also of sociality; so that, as 'universal', it achieves a secondary political force, being not only 'valid for every rational being as such' (*Groundwork* 413), but eligible for the sovereign legislative will in the 'kingdom of ends'. Thus it abstracts also 'from the personal differences of rational beings and likewise from the content of their private ends' (433).

Hegel attempted to correct the formalism of Kant's universal by distinguishing an 'abstract' from a 'concrete' form. The former constituted the bare foundation of 'contentless' individual self-consciousness, the latter the differentiated organic complexity of social order, which provides the subject with the context of public intelligibility for his actions (*Philosophy of Right* 34–40, 119–128). Neither pole of the Hegelian universal expresses the generic intelligibility of differentiated actions independently of their conformity to the structures of society. Its association of differentiated order with the universality of the state and the absolute universality of world history bequeathed to modern thought a fruitless opposition between a concept of law as social normativity and an irrationalist subjectivism. When the distinctive character of generic order is clarified, however, there is still a place for speaking of 'universality' in relation to ethics. Ethics is dependent on a 'universe', a world of meaning which created beings of every epoch hold in common, which provides the matrix of their order and intelligibility.

But is it possible to acknowledge generic determinations in nature without also acknowledging teleological determinations? The difficulty of separating the two can be illustrated by comparing the first two of the three forms which Kant gives to his categorical imperative. From the first form, in which we are bidden to act only so that our maxim could become a universal law of nature, we are led to the second form, which tells us: 'So act as to treat humanity, whether in thine own person or in that of any other, in every case as an end withal, never as a means only' (*Groundwork* 429). We shall ask, as many critics have asked, whether this second formula really is, as it is claimed to be, a form of the first. Why has Kant singled out the kind 'humanity' for this universal respect? The answer he offers is: 'Rational nature exists as an end in itself. Man necessarily conceives his own existence as being so.' But of course man does not necessarily conceive his own rational nature as making him part of *humanity* – Kant is quick enough to make the distinction himself at other points. And there is no saying where any individual, left to his own rational self-consciousness, may draw the lines of his generic identification with other beings. He may decide that his rational nature puts him among a small class of Enlightened, or that it makes him one of those who are born to rule, or even qualifies him as the sole bearer of a unique subjectivity. Neither the genus 'humanity' nor any other genus is a necessary posit of the 'relation of the will to itself so far as it is determined by reason alone'(427). If we are to defend the claim that humanity is an 'objective end', in a sense that the class of the

47

Enlightened, of those born to rule, or of unique subjectivity is not, we shall have to appeal to some teleological determinant situated outside the rational will itself.

It is a mistake to suppose that the notion of justice can be reduced to the formal rule of generic consistency. For 'justice', in the moral sense in which we customarily use the word, already presupposes certain preferences among the kinds. It is not compatible with a policy of justice, for example, that the less reasonable among mankind should, however consistently, be made to serve the interests of the more reasonable. It is not that such a policy could not be implemented with perfect consistency, but simply that it is based on a rival and incompatible teleology to that which justice implies. In requiring that like things should be treated in like ways, it has already made some judgments as to what likenesses are significant and what are irrelevant for morality. These judgments are teleological. Without them generic consistency amounts to no more than loyalty to an arbitrarily chosen class or set. But morality, as expressed in the principle of justice, needs more than infinitely interchangeable sets; it needs the organization of these sets in terms of their relative importance. This organization is what lies behind the traditional doctrine that some generic relationships enjoy an ontological status as 'natural kinds'.

(2) This response, of course, does not meet the parallel objection, the one made on behalf of the sciences, which will certainly welcome the dissolution of natural kinds, with their teleologico-generic determinations, into an infinitely various series of possible generic equivalences. For scientific thought proceeds by self-conscious abstraction, in which the more obvious determinants of kind and end are forgotten in order that the object of investigation may be hypothetically included in other, less obvious classes. To take an example: the science of economics has deliberately forgotten that vegetables are food and motor cars are artefacts, in order to discuss the growing of vegetables and the manufacture of motor cars under a single classification as 'industry' and the results of these labours as 'products'. In forgetting the teleological determination of vegetables for animals to eat, it forgets also their 'kind' as food. It forces them into less obvious classifications, in order to view them in less obvious ways and achieve some knowledge of them which was not obvious knowledge. It goes without saying that such an abstraction is a perfectly legitimate stratagem of thought. The very fact that some scientific hypotheses prove fruitful in terms of their experimental results shows that there was unsuspected knowledge to be had about unsuspected generic relations. If we are not to dismiss the whole of scientific civilization as an illusion, and if we are not to resort to the scepticism of the pragmatists and say that it is true because it works, we can only conclude

that, when a hypothesis consistently works, it is because it, or something not unlike it, is true. But the question is whether the refusal of 'final causes' which led to the discovery of new generic relationships was actually necessary to it. Granted the historical sequence, that voluntarist discomfort with Aristotelian teleology at the end of the Middle Ages bred the new experimental cast of mind, does that mean that natural teleology is false, or merely that abstraction from it was a helpful ascesis for the scientific mind?

We can lay this question alongside a similar one about the role of nominalism. Undoubtedly the nominalism of figures such as Ockham was no less important to the birth of the experimental spirit than the voluntarism which he shared with Duns Scotus. The theory that generic equivalence had no objective ontological standing, but was the imposition of the mind upon a universe of particulars, certainly encouraged the desire to experiment with new generic orderings. Yet in the long run science found nominalism an enemy to its project; for science is interested in nothing if not regularities, and nominalism must deny that the regularities which science purports to observe are real. Scientific endeavour has been sustained not only by the sense that it may *dare* to think new thoughts about the world order (important as that has been), but also by the conviction that its thoughts, when supported experimentally, can actually declare (with whatever limitations) something of the character of objective reality. The denial of real regularities could never be more than a goad, driving it to discard the obvious and straightforward relationships in search of hidden structures of greater complexity. If the denial were taken absolutely seriously, science would lose its peculiar *raison d'être* and be absorbed once again into the category of simple speculation from which it once sprang forth. Perhaps the crisis of scientific self-understanding which is a mark of our own day may be due precisely to the revival of a very radical nominalism within the context of historicist idealism. Science may have needed to flirt with nominalism in its youth, in order to pluck up its courage, but as marriage-partners the two are incompatible.

The proposal to think reality without ends, 'voluntarism', must be viewed in the same light as the proposal to think it without kinds, 'nominalism'. It is an artifice of thought. Like the nominalist artifice, the voluntarist artifice yields evil consequences if it is mistaken for a statement of cold truth. Abstraction from teleology makes it impossible, in the first place, to know the universe whole. At best, of course, knowledge of the whole must be knowledge of a mystery. Because we stand within the universe, and not outside it to view it as God views it, we can only move out towards that whole knowledge, as a limit towards which our mind strives. But such a term of mental striving is essential if knowledge is to be knowledge. Knowledge which admits discontinuity as anything other than a challenge to be overcome has in principle abandoned the task of being knowledge, which is the perception of differing fields of vision as one universe. But such fragmentation is positively embraced by the abandonment of teleology, which means the abandonment of the desire to discern relations between kinds. The issue here is not simply the supposed dissonances between the 'scientific world-view' and faith, nor between the sciences and the humanities. Fragmentation is the hallmark of scientific knowledge itself, which has become balkanized into a multitude of 'sciences' laying conflicting claims upon the same territory of experience. The various theories of 'aspects of reality' which have been adduced to save the conception of science as a unified undertaking can do little more than underline the fact. Knowledge of the world without ends can never become a unified knowledge.

Karl Rahner has written suggestively of the problem posed by the plurality of the sciences, which he describes as the problem of 'gnoseological concupiscence', drawing an analogy with the conflicts among the voluntary impulses of the soul according to Thomistic psychology (*Theological Investigations*, XIII, p. 90). Scientific pluralism 'can never be fully eliminated or overcome in a higher synthesis' (p. 101). Nevertheless, each science has within it an 'aggressiveness' in respect of the others which 'impels it towards the totality of human knowledge' (p. 84). 'Each particular science', therefore, 'is in a state of self-alienation.' No knowledge can rest in the fact of pluralism, but must recognize in other forms of knowledge a factor common to it and to them – the 'human factor' – which establishes the love-hate relationship expressed in the very fact of interdisciplinary dialogue. It is the task of theology, when it engages in such dialogue, to draw attention explicitly to this 'human factor', which belongs to each science and yet transcends it (p. 88), for theology is concerned with 'the transcendence of man as such' (p. 96). It therefore acts as the 'guardian . . . of "gnoseological concupiscence" ', protecting against 'the mortal danger, inherent in every science, of according itself an absolute value and of supposing that the key which it carries . . . will fit every door' (p. 90). A regrettably large part of this conception is left unclear. How seriously are we to take the background to the term 'concupiscence' in the doctrine of original sin? Did the Fall of the sciences into pluralism occur prehistorically in Adam, or rather recently with the collapse of neo-scholasticism at the end of the nineteenth century (*cf.* XIV, pp. 29ff.)? Is the constant emergence of new sciences and the self-transformation of old ones controlled by historical necessity, or is it the result of an undetermined free play of the experimental spirit? Rahner's characteristic 'tip-and-run' method of discussion does not allow us answers to these questions.

In pursuit of them we may turn with especial interest to the thought of the Dutch philosopher Herman Dooyeweerd, whose reflections on the plurality of the sciences, very far from being occasional observations, are deeply integrated into the structure of the 'Philosophy of the Cosmonomic Idea' which he inherited from Abraham Kuyper and brought to an austere pitch of theoretical systematization and terminological complexity. (For what follows see especially his *New Critique of Theoretical Thought*, I, pp. 545–566.) He attacks with resolution the 'prejudice' that the special sciences can be independent of philosophy, arguing that the way any science is conducted will reflect the dominant motif of some philosophical presupposition. A special science could be independent of philosophy only if, *per impossibile*, 'it could actually investigate a specific aspect of temporal reality without theoretically considering its coherence with the other aspects' (p. 548). It is, in truth, nothing more than nominalism to imagine that this can be done. Scientific thought proceeds by abstracting questions of 'universal functional coherence' within a specific 'modal law-sphere' and ignoring the 'typical structural differences' which are displayed in concrete reality. Experimental method is 'essentially a method of isolation and abstraction', directed to the solution of theoretical questions which the scientist himself has formulated (p. 561). For example, theoretical jurisprudence discusses many different kinds of law governing different kinds of institution: states, churches, trade unions, international relations, *etc.* But it cannot tell us what the difference between a state and a church is; it can tell us only what their systems of law have in common by virtue of their common function within their different institutions (pp. 552f.). What has happened under the influence of the 'humanistic science-ideal' is that this functional abstraction has been absolutized. Empirical phenomena themselves do not justify the abstraction; for it is only in the opposition between logical thought and non-logical aspects of experience that the division of these fields of study can arise (p. 565).

These observations on scientific procedure may lead us to expect that Dooyeweerd, like Rahner, will see the plurality of the sciences as a kind of inescapable wound at the heart of knowledge. But, on the contrary, Dooyeweerd can tell us, give or take one, how many sciences there ought to be. There should be one corresponding to each of the 'modal aspects' of reality which the cosmonomic philosophy discerns; that is to say fifteen (p. 3): number, space, motion, energy, organic life, feeling, logical thought, historical development, language, social intercourse, economy, art, justice, morality and faith. (But only thirteen are enumerated in *The Christian Idea of the State*, p. 35, and fourteen in *Roots of Western Culture*, p. 41.) Dooyeweerd's equivalent to 'gnoseological concupiscence', which is the phrase 'the carnal mind' drawn from Colossians 2:18, does not apply to plurality as such, but only to the absolutizing of some one modal function, the pretence of some science to hold the *archē* of all meaning. As well as the responsibility of every science to think itself philosophically in a correct relation to the others, and so to Christ the root of restored reality, Dooyeweerd also maintains the sovereignty of each science within its own sphere (otherwise, its 'modal irreducibility'), a principle which *justifies* a high degree of scientific pluralism, disciplining it only by the overall organization of the cosmonomic idea. It may be doubted whether Dooyeweerd really intends that each science shall be open to the others, except in so far as that is implied by the subordination of each to Christ as the common *archē* (II, pp. 331–337). Quite apart from the 'tensions and antitheses' which, because of the carnal mind, beset the disclosure of the different modal aspects, there remains, in Dooyeweerd's view, a certain necessary impermeability of each aspect to the other, a certain formal distance in their relations which ensures that while each special science is destined to encompass, and be encompassed by, the cosmonomic philosophy, no special science has the possibility of encompassing any other (II, p. 76). Does this arise, we may wonder, because Dooyeweerd reduces the intermodal teleological relations to a purely temporal order of succession (I, pp. 28–30)?

In the second place, abstraction from teleology creates a dangerous misunderstanding of the place of man in the universe. For it supposes that the observing mind encounters an inert creation – not, that is, a creation without movement, but a creation without a point to its movement. Thus the mind credits to its own conceptual creativity that teleological order which is, despite everything, necessary to life. All ordering becomes deliberative ordering, and scientific observation, failing as it does to report the given teleological order within nature, becomes the servant of *techne*. Of course, man continues to eat vegetables; but he no longer knows that he does so because vegetables *are* food, and comes to imagine that he has *devised a use* for them as food. And so he looks for other uses for them, which will seem to him to have as much validity as that one which was, if he could only have remembered it, given in nature. That vegetables exist as food for other animals than himself will not impress him – unless, of course, the continued existence of other animals too falls within his deliberative purposes for the world, in which case both vegetation and animal life will continue to hold their value as a feoff from himself. Thus arises the irony of our own days, in which the very protection of nature has to be argued in terms of man's 'interest' in preserving his 'environment'. Such a philosophy offers no stable protection against the exploitation of nature by man, since he can discern nothing in the relations of things to command his respect. And, of course, this unprincipled domination must extend itself to include his own psychosomatic nature, all that is not itself the devising mind, so that humanity itself dissolves in the polarization of the technological will and its raw material. Man's monarchy over nature can be healthy only if he recognizes it as something itself given in the nature of things, and therefore limited by the nature of things. For if it were true that he imposed his rule upon nature from without, then there would be no limit to it. It would have been from the beginning a crude struggle to stamp an inert and formless nature with the insignia of his will. Such has been the philosophy bred by a scientism liberated from the discipline of Christian metaphysics. It is not what the Psalmist meant by the dominion of man, which was a worshipping and respectful sovereignty, a glad responsibility for the natural order which he both discerned and loved.

3

Eschatology and history

'As it is, we do not yet see everything in subjection to him.' So the author to the Hebrews appears to dismiss, almost abruptly, the great vision of Psalm 8, the vision of man set in authority over the rest of creation, lacking a very little of God, crowned with glory and honour. The order which the psalmist believed that he beheld in the world around him the writer to the Hebrews declares to belong to 'the world to come'. It is not realized – yet. It is not something that we can already count on. 'But', he goes on, 'we see Jesus, who for a little while was made lower than the angels, crowned with glory and honour because of the suffering of death' (Heb. 2:5–9).

In reading the eighth Psalm as a prophetic utterance about 'the world to come', the writer is not guilty of ignoring its obvious sense as cosmology. He is not attempting to *replace* the psalmist's doctrine of creation with an eschatology which will better suit his own Christological interests. Rather, he sees in Christ, and in the order of the world to come, the vindication and perfect manifestation of the created order which was always there but never fully expressed. The elusiveness of that order in our experience did not mean that it had no kind of existence. It existed from the beginning in God's creative conception. The God who 'in bringing many sons to glory [made] the pioneer of their salvation perfect through suffering' was the very one 'for whom and by whom all things exist', the first and final cause of the ordered cosmos (2:10). The 'pioneer of [man's] salvation', who brought humanity to its proper place by his humiliation and exaltation, was the one 'through whom [God] created the world', who shares the Creator's eternal transcendence over his creation (1:2,10ff.). The answer to the question 'What is man that thou art mindful of him, or the son of man, that thou carest for him?', a question about the created order, is given in the triumph of him who bore the title 'Son of man'. In his conquest over death and in his glorification at the Father's right hand we see man as he was made to be, not subject to the angelic forces of sin and mortality which presently oppress him, but able for the first time to take his place in the cosmos as its lord. The triumph of the Son of man prepares the way for the future triumph of his 'brethren', mankind as a whole. But this eschatological triumph of mankind is not an innovative order that has nothing to do with the primal ordering of man as creature to his Creator. It fulfils and vindicates the primal order in a way that was always implied, but which could not be realized in the fallen state of man and the universe.

The relation of the thought of Hebrews to that of the Psalm is, of course, complicated by the phrase 'Thou hast made him little less than God', where the author's Septuagint version translates *elohim* (god) as *aggelous* (angels). He is convinced that the Psalm did not intend to suggest that man was destined to be less than angels: 'It was not to angels that God subjected the world to come ... In putting everything in subjection to him, he left nothing outside his control' (2:5,8). Therefore he deals with the phrase about the angels by interpreting the expression 'little' in a temporal sense: 'for a little while'. This enables him to see Christ's incarnation and glorification as the sign that mankind's subordination to angels is provisional and temporary: 'We see Jesus, who for a little while was made lower than the angels, crowned with glory and honour.'

If our currently accepted translations of *elohim* do justice to the sense of Psalm 8:5, then plainly the author was prevented by his translation from understanding that text exactly. Nevertheless, he clearly understood its intention, and in taking the interpretative liberty of assigning a temporal significance to 'little', he restored the balance which the translator had destroyed. He did not wrest the Psalm to make a Christological prophecy out of it; up to the end of his verse 8 ('we do not yet see everything in subjection to him') he followed the intention of his text in speaking of mankind as a whole. The temporary subjection of mankind to angels belonged to the Rabbinic 'present age', the age of sin and suffering. The 'future age' would see the renewal of the created order as God intended it to be. Although we do not see the glory of mankind, we do see the glory of Jesus in his passion and exaltation. That is the guarantee: the pioneer of salvation has been made perfect through suffering, and he calls the rest of humanity his 'brethren' and his 'children' (2:11–13).

When we describe the saving work of Christ by the term 'redemption', we stress the fact that it presupposes the created order. 'Redemption' suggests the recovery of something given and lost. When we ask what it is that was given and lost, and must now be recovered, the answer is not just 'mankind', but mankind in his context as the ruler of the ordered creation that God has made; for the created order, too, cannot be itself while it lacks the authoritative and beneficent rule that man was to give it. In speaking of the redemption of all creation, of course, we must not allow the idea to float free in independence of 'the revealing of the sons of God', for which, according to Saint Paul, it waits (Rom. 8:19ff.). We cannot speculate on what 'redemption' will imply for the non-human creation. And yet Scripture speaks of such a redemption. For redemption is what God has done for the whole, and not just for a part of that which he once made.

At the same time, however, we must go beyond thinking of redemption as a *mere* restoration, the return of a *status quo ante*. The redemption of the world, and of mankind, does not serve only to put us back in the Garden of Eden where we began. It leads us on to that further destiny to which, even in the Garden of Eden, we were already directed. For the creation was given to us with its own goal and purpose, so that the outcome of the world's story cannot be a cyclical return to the beginnings, but must fulfil that purpose in the freeing of creation from its 'futility' (Rom. 8:20). This fulfilment is what is implied when we speak of the 'transformation' of the created order. Thus there is an important place in Christian thought for the idea of 'history', using the term as it is widely used in philosophy and theology to mean, not mere events on the one hand, nor their narration in an intelligible story on the other, but their inherent significance and direction which makes them intelligible and narratable. The Christian understanding of this idea is, of course, only to be reached through a Christian understanding of the end towards which events are directed, that is, through eschatology.

The eschatological transformation of the world is neither the mere repetition of the created world nor its negation. It is its fulfilment, its *telos* or end. It is the historical *telos* of the origin, that which creation is intended *for*, and that which it points and strives *towards*. Eschatological transformation rules out all the other conceivable eventualities which might have befallen creation, all those ends to which God did not destine it. In the first place it rules out that threatened end of all things which is implied by the Fall: corruption and disintegration. It rules out also the gnostic possibility that creation is to be repudiated or overcome in the name of some higher good. It rules out the possibility that the temporal extension of creation forms a random and meaningless flux. Eschatological transformation resolves the unanswered question of creation, the question of what its temporal extension means. This question would be unanswered even in an unfallen world and to an unfallen mind; the sealed scroll of history is painfully inscrutable even to one who has gazed devoutly and joyfully on the order of creation in all its wholeness. But given the fact that the world is fallen and is perceived only by fallen minds, it is for the one who redeems it to unloose the scroll and to reveal 'what is to happen soon'.

Nowhere, perhaps, is the relation of created nature and history more luminously expressed than in the diptych of visions which opens the main section of the book of Revelation. In chapter 4 we are shown a classic Old Testament vision of creation. Around the throne of God there is a rainbow marking the covenant of cosmic order; there is the council of angels, the natural forces of lightning, thunder and other 'sounds', and four forms of created animal life, all joining in an unceasing hymn of praise. God is present to the world: the symbol for his presence which is dear to John the Seer is that of a multitude of eyes, the eyes which range through the whole earth according to Zechariah (4:10). But God's presence here is not in his divine Spirit, which remains withheld before the throne as seven burning torches; it is a purely immanent presence in the vitality of creation itself. The heavenly hymn tells us of the finality and completeness of God's creative act of will. But then in chapter 5 we see that the Creator holds a sealed scroll in his right hand, which represents the puzzle of history, a puzzle so terrible that it reduces the rejoicing prophet to tears. How can we enter into the joy of creation when we do not know the meaning of creation's history? It is hidden from us until the Lion of Judah, who is also the slain Lamb, unseals its meaning. In him the presence of God in the world, the eyes, becomes personally embodied; and in him that presence is also the presence of the divine Spirit, no longer withheld. In him, then, history can be led in its destined course to its destined end.

At the conclusion of John's great vision we return to creation once more, with 'a new heaven and a new earth', a vision of creation transformed. Where initially the sea of chaos had lain subdued to a glassy stillness before God's throne, now 'the sea was no more' (21:1). The very possibility of disruption, once held back by God's creative decree, is altogether vanished. A redemption that is *merely* restoration cannot observe that transformation; which is why Origen, whose eschatology was influenced by the cyclic concepts of Platonism, was plagued by those questions which did so much damage to his reputation about further falls and redemptions in the aeons to come. Origen was on surer ground when he followed Clement of Alexandria and Irenaeus of Lyons in popularizing the idea that redemption was 'divinization'. Certainly this idea has to be understood properly, without any suggestion that it involves the 'dehominization' of man or the 'uncreation' of the created world; but it does succeed in conveying the truth that man is summoned to a destiny that is not given immediately in his creation, a 'higher grace', as Athanasius put it, 'to reign eternally with Christ in heaven' (*Contra Arianos* II.67).

The resurrection of Christ, upon which Christian ethics is founded, vindicates the created order in this double sense: it redeems it and it transforms it. For the resurrection appears in the Gospels under a double aspect, as the restoration of Jesus from the dead and as his glorification at God's right hand. When the resurrection is distinguished from the ascension (as it is by Saint

Luke and indirectly by Saint John – *cf.* 20:17) it looks backwards. It is a recovery of the lost: the man Jesus is given back to his circle of friends to gladden their hearts. Death, the enemy of mankind, is conquered; God has reinstated the descendants of Adam as 'living soul' by sending them the last Adam, the 'life-giving spirit'. From this aspect the emphasis of the resurrection narratives is upon the physical reality of the restored body: Jesus eats and drinks and is touched, to show that he is not merely a spiritual phenomenon. The elements of mystery in his appearances arise from the lost powers of true humanity; they elude the normal human limitations because such limitations were in the first place alien to humanity. When, however, the resurrection is presented alone without the ascension (as it is by Saint Mark and Saint Matthew) it looks forwards. Already Christ is transformed; the physical has been assumed by the spiritual, the man of dust by the heavenly man. The resurrection appearances are encounters with divine power and authority. Humanity is elevated to that which it has never enjoyed before, the seat at God's right hand which belongs to his Son. The important thing is not which of these two aspects of the resurrection we emphasize at any moment, but that it does properly have both aspects; origin and end are inseparably united in it. The humanity of Adam is carried forward to its 'supernatural' destiny precisely as it is rescued from its 'sub-natural' condition of enslavement to sin and death. The vindication of that humanity in Christ's resurrection includes both its redemption and its transformation.

Contemporary theology has suffered from a tendency to ignore the ascension of Christ, no doubt out of a sense of the cosmological questions it raises as well as out of a once-fashionable tendency to discount the witness of Saint Luke and Saint John in favour of that of Saint Mark. Consequently the resurrection has borne the whole weight of the 'forward-looking' emphasis on the exaltation of Christ, so that correspondingly its 'backward-looking' significance as the return of Christ from the dead has been lost sight of, a development that suits very well certain preoccupations that we shall address shortly. Even Karl Barth was prepared to write at one stage: 'The empty tomb and the ascension are merely signs of the Easter event, just as the Virgin Birth is merely the sign of the nativity' (*Church Dogmatics*, III/2, p. 453). Happily he made amends later, stimulated, perhaps, by polemic engagement with Bultmann, and distinguished the resurrection and ascension as 'two distinct but inseparable moments in one and the same event': the resurrection is Jesus' 'coming from' perdition and death, the ascension is his 'going to' heaven and the Father (IV/2, pp. 150ff.). Barth is quite right to stress the *unity* of these two moments as moments of one event, the event of man's 'justification' (Rom. 4:25). It is also correct – indeed, it is simply responsible to Saint Mark and Saint Matthew, as well as to some passages of Saint Paul – to focus our attention *primarily* on the resurrection in attempting to comprehend the twofold event as one, for the ascension is an unfolding of the significance of the resurrection, and is included, as it were, in its scope. But that is far from saying that the ascension is 'merely' a sign, like the empty tomb. The ascension is properly part of our confession of faith in the creed, the empty tomb is not.

So it is that Christian ethics, too, looks both backwards and forwards, to the origin and to the end of the created order. It respects the natural structures of life in the world, while looking forward to their transformation. This can be seen, for example, in the First Epistle of Peter, which starts with a general characterization of the Christian life in terms of 'hope', which is set 'fully upon the grace that is coming to you at the revelation of Jesus Christ', and then elaborates a special ethics in terms of respectful submission 'for the Lord's sake' to every institution of human life, especially the institutions of government, labour and marriage (1 Pet. 1:13; 2:13ff.). There is no conflict here between what might be thought of as the 'radical' character of the general outlook and the 'conservatism' of the specific counsel. A hope which envisages the transformation of existing natural structures cannot consistently attack or repudiate those structures. Yet the 'conservatism' (if it is proper to use the word) includes a sense of distance, which springs from a sharp awareness of how much the institutions need redemption and how transitory is their present form.

Natural ends and history

This insistence on the integrity of the created order, even in the light of its transformation, forces us to define an important area of controversy. The turn of modern thought towards what is usually called 'historicism' is now all-pervasive. In Western theology historicism has had an uneven influence: having made its initial impact towards the end of the last century through the disciples of Hegel, it suffered a major rebuff in that famous theological revolution which followed the First World War; but in recent decades it has become dominant again, partly as a result of Christian attempts to come to grips with the categories of Marxism, partly through the belated influence of Teilhard de Chardin's evolutionary cosmology. The heart of historicism can be expressed in the thesis that all teleology is historical teleology. The concept of an 'end', it is held, is essentially a concept of development in time. Nothing can have a 'point', unless it is a historical point; there is no point in the regularities of nature as such. What we took to be natural orderings-to-serve and orderings-to-flourish within the regularities of nature are in fact something quite different: they are orderings-to-transformation, and so break out altogether from nature's order. The natural exists only to be superseded: everything within it serves only a supernatural end, the end of history. That may be conceived as the kingdom of heaven; it may be conceived as the communist paradise; or (as especially in liberal historicism) it may be simply an undefined term of self-justifying change, receding infinitely like the horizon as we approach it. But in each case natural order and natural meanings are understood only as moments in the historical process. They are to be dissolved and reconstituted by that process, and their value lies not in any integrity of their own but in being raw material for transformation.

An articulate attempt by Wolfhart Pannenberg to discover historical teleology in certain strains of Socratic and Aristotelian thought ('Appearance as the Arrival of the Future' in *Theology and the Kingdom of God*) may be taken as typical of the historicist programme. Pannenberg is concerned principally with the relation of appearance to reality, which he wishes to suggest is essentially the relation of present to future. At the centre of his argument there is a short paragraph (pp. 137f.) on which we focus our attention. The Platonic concept of 'form' incorporates not only the Parmenidean *archē*, but also Socratic *aretē*. But 'an element of futurity is contained in the notion of the good. Insofar as everyone strives for the good and the useful . . . it is clear that no one already finds himself in its possession; rather, he hopes to attain unto it. Thus, in the essence of the good, as that which is striven for, there is something future.' This argument, so central to the case and so scantily elaborated, actually *imposes* a historicist concept of good-as-project upon classical categories which know nothing of such a concept. 'The good' is said to be a historical category because it is the object of striving and striving occurs within time. But although we who live in time, strive in time, as we do everything else in time, it is by no means essential to the notion of striving that it should be in time. The sunflowers in a painting strive for the sun, even in that timeless moment which the artist has caught on the canvas. 'Striving' is given in the bare teleological orientation itself. So far from Plato's 'Idea of the Good' containing an element of futurity, that element is introduced only as we respond to it by formulating a project in history to accord with it.

The essential thing to observe about the difference between natural and historical teleology is that natural ends are generic, historical ends particular. In created order one is destined to some fulfilment because it is the appropriate fulfilment for beings of one's own kind; but historical destining is a unique and unrepeatable destining of events to a single goal. Pannenberg is aware that in explaining 'the good' as a historical category he has to overcome the 'universality' (*i.e.* generic character) which characterizes our thinking about it. He argues that universality is purely a construction of the human mind with no basis in reality, except in the phenomenon of *repetition* (pp. 141f.). 'Innumerable new events "repeat" earlier ones, although they always bring forth something new. The element of change remains unobservable in the overwhelming majority of events; thus from a sufficiently broad perspective, one can speak of a repetition of *the same* structures in an indefinite multiplicity of events.' Pannenberg really wants to tell us that such sameness is illusory; but in order to explain how we come to conceive of generic equivalences he is forced to allow it some substance. For what, after all, *is* a repetition if it is not the occurrence of a new event with some generic relation to an earlier one? How can anything be 'the same' as anything else unless it bears some 'likeness' to it? And it is precisely on the basis of such likenesses that we can discern natural as well as historical ends, the purposes which things share with other things as well as those which are uniquely their own.

It may be thought that the chief objection to historicism is that it has potentially revolutionary implications. This is a mistake. Historicism can take on a revolutionary form, and has played a large part in fashioning modern conceptions of revolution. But Leo Strauss (to whom we owe a masterly critique of historicism in his *Natural Right and History*) always stressed the important part played in its development by the conservative reaction at the time of the French Revolution (pp. 13f.). It was precisely in shrinking from the revolutionary possibilities of universal principles that moral thought took refuge in the 'concrete' reality of a tradition. Eternal truths could criticize and overthrow established traditions; in their place must be asserted the immanent truthfulness and capacity for self-criticism of all living historical traditions. Existing institutions were not to be defended on the grounds that they met some universal standard of justice (for such a line of argument was too dangerous); they were to be defended as the outcome of history. Springing from historical process, they constituted a mediating good, which would, and of its own immanent dynamism could, pave the way to whatever further goods history had to offer.

We cannot object to the idea that history should be taken seriously. A Christian response to historicism will wish to make precisely the opposite point: when history is made the categorical matrix for all meaning and value, it cannot then be taken seriously *as history*. A story has to be a story about something; but when everything is story there is nothing for the story to be about. The subject of a story must be something or someone of intrinsic value and worth; if it is not, the story loses all its interest and importance as a story. The story of what has happened in God's good providence to the good world which God made is 'history' in the fullest sense. But when that world is itself dissolved into history, as all the characters of Joyce's *Finnegan's Wake* are dissolved into prose, then history is left without a subject, so that we have no history any more, but only (to use the word which most perfectly expresses the sterility of the conception) 'process'. And then again, the story of the world as Christians have told it has its turning-point in the saving act of God in Jesus Christ. Through that crisis it is uniquely determined towards its end. But when every determination to every end is understood equally as a determination to the end of history, the critical moment of the story is lost, the turning-point forgotten. We will develop these two criticisms in turn.

(1) That which most distinguishes the concept of creation is that it is complete. Creation is the given totality of order which forms the presupposition of historical existence. 'Created order' is that

which is not negotiable within the course of history, that which neither the terrors of chance nor the ingenuity of art can overthrow. It defines the scope of our freedom and the limits of our fears. The affirmation of the psalm, sung on the sabbath which celebrates the completion of creation, affords a ground for human activity and human hope: 'the world is established, it shall never be moved'. Within such a world, in which 'the Lord reigns', we are free to act and can have confidence that God will act. Because created order is given, because it is secure, we dare to be certain that God will vindicate it in history. 'He comes to judge the earth. He will judge the world with righteousness, and the peoples with his truth' (Ps. 96:10,13).

Classical Christian theology took trouble to distinguish between the ideas of 'creation' and 'providence'. The continued sovereignty of God in and through the perilous contingencies of history was assured by the order which was God's primary gift in creation. The modern faith in 'continuous creation' is merely the latest form in which forgetfulness of this dialectic between order and contingency betrays itself. Very much less edifying than Psalm 96 are the hymns offered by contemporary collections to celebrate the modern faith:

> Creation's Lord, we give you thanks
> That this your world is incomplete.

God's loose ends, it appears, are man's opportunity! But, true to the spirit of liberal progress, the author disowns any interest in completion anyway:

> Since what we choose is what we are,
> And what we love we yet shall be,
> The goal may ever shine afar, –
> The will to win it makes us free.

(This was written at the turn of the century, in the first heyday of historicist theology. But I quote it from the Hymn Book of the Anglican and United Churches of Canada, a collection published in 1971. That fact is an interesting straw in the wind. At a time when Pannenberg is rehabilitating Troeltsch in academic theology, there are corresponding rehabilitations going on in our popular piety!)

An adequate understanding of the sabbath would have armed us against this. The sign which celebrates the completeness of creation looks forward also to the fulfilment of history. Does the eschatological meaning replace, or annul, the reference to creation? The question is faced at Hebrews 4:3–11, where the author quotes together Psalm 95:11 ('They shall never enter my rest') and Genesis 2:2 ('God finished his work which he had done'). God's works have been completed since the beginning of the world, he tells us. What remains is for us to *enter* that sabbath rest which has been waiting for us all this time, as it were, unoccupied. Disobedience prevented those 'who were formerly evangelized' (the Jews of the Old Covenant) from entering, so that God has appointed another day of entry. Whoever does enter ceases from his labours as God once ceased from his (Heb. 4:10). For the author to the Hebrews, then, the completion of creation, so far from being put in doubt by the thought of a yet-to-be completed history, is the only ground on which we can take the latter seriously. Historical fulfilment means our entry into a completeness which is already present in the universe. Our sabbath rest is, as it were, a catching up with God's. For a perfect visual representation of the completeness of creation, let me refer to William Blake's water-colour 'God Blessing the Seventh Day'. The figure of God sits centrally, his hands extended in blessing. From behind his throne emerge angels, the powers of creation, whose extended hands form, to surround the Creator and themselves, a circle, that which is complete in itself, save that above and beneath the Creator it forms itself roughly into a crown and a footstool. But from the circle of creation there radiates light, which appears to stream out *towards* the observer, so that history appears to be formed as the perfection of creation projects itself into another dimension.

If we can, and must, speak of the completeness of God's work in creation, we can, and must, speak equally of the incompleteness of his work in the providential government and redemption of history. Saint John reports Jesus as saying, with regard to a miracle performed on the sabbath, 'My Father is working still, and I am working' (5:17). Yet what is the Father's work, to which Jesus' own miraculous work on the sabbath bears witness? It is the vindication of creation from death, the manifestation of its wholeness. As the Father 'raises the dead and gives them life', so does the Son (21); and the Son can do nothing else, nothing of his own, but only what he sees the Father doing (19). The issue of Jesus' sabbath miracles is precisely whether he may 'make a man's whole body well' (7:23); that is to say, whether history may manifest the true meaning of the sabbath, the completeness of God's creation and its coming vindication.

When we refer to creation as the 'presupposition' of history, we give a logical expression to what is said metaphysically by speaking of creation as history's 'origin' or 'beginning'. Of course, 'origin' is the language of analogy. We cannot give conceptual content to the idea of an origin of history, as we can to the idea of an origin of a stream. Nevertheless, we have to think of history somehow, and if we are going to think of it as a kind of stream (which we do whenever we speak of its 'direction', 'movement' or 'end'), we are forced to formulate our metaphysical understanding in one of two equally inconceivable ways: either it is a stream with a source, or it is a stream that has flowed from eternity. In choosing between these two, we have to decide what we think about the extent of historical possibility. The patristic church correctly discerned that to think of the world as infinitely extended in time carried the heretical suggestion that history contained all possibilities immanently within itself. (This suggestion was no less implied in the cyclical conceptions which were current in the classical world: the cyclical concept implies that even sameness and regularity can be generated out of temporal movement, and it was no mistake that Nietzsche, in carrying historicism to its limits, found himself drawn back to this idea.) To defend the finitude of history as the object of God's creative decree, the early Fathers spoke of creation as absolute origin, *ex nihilo*. The possibilities of history were defined by the terms of the gift of being which God conferred upon the world. To put the same point in the language of another theological era, creation is a 'covenant'.

The finitude of historical possibility has still to be defended against the repeated but misconceived attempts of theologians to account for creation as the first phase in the process of history. (If the most recent attempts of this kind have all been prompted by the theory of evolution, the earliest, paradoxically enough, are those which now oppose them with an interpretation of the 'days' of Genesis as literal twenty-four hour periods.) Whatever scientific researchers may believe they are able to tell us about the prehistory of the universe, they can tell us nothing about 'creation' in the theological sense, because creation is not a process which might be accessible through the backward extrapolation of other processes. Creation as a completed design is presupposed by *any* movement in time. Its teleological order, expressed in the regular patterns of history, is not a product of the historical process, such that it might be surpassed and left behind as history proceeds further towards its goal. It is the condition of history's movement, a condition to which, in one form or another, history will always bear witness.

Historicism, with its incapacity to distinguish natural from historical teleology, will always tend to confuse the goodness of natural structures with sin and disorder. For if all teleology is historical teleology, and the natural structures have no integrity as totalities within themselves, then actual good and evil alike stand together under the judgment of historical fulfilment, as 'imperfect'. With creation cut loose from its beginnings and treated merely as another name for history, the beginnings are left without positive characterization; they are merely the unfinishedness from which the end calls us forward. And with sin no longer defined against the criterion of a good natural order, and with only the future as its judge, evil has no definite characterization either. It, too, is merely the historical imperfection from which we are to advance. But one type of imperfection is very much like another. Thus historicism betrays resemblances, both to the old gnostic dualism which called creation evil, and to the idealism which denied the reality of evil altogether. The characterization of history as process replaces the categories of good and evil with those of past and future. Instead of the Christian threefold metaphysic of a good creation, an evil fall and an end of history which negates the evil and transcends the created good, we have in historicism a dualist opposition between a historical 'from' and 'towards', in accordance with which all the traditional language of good and evil is reinterpreted.

(2) There is a simile for human history which has been popular with Christian writers of many periods since Irenaeus used it in the second century. The course of God's dealings with mankind is compared to the growth of a child from infancy to maturity. The effect of this simile is not only to make past history comprehensible under the description of growth, but to make future history inherently predictable as the development and enhancement of the course in which things have so far run. The simile thus serves an apologetic purpose; it seeks to commend the eschatological intervention of God in terms of the natural strivings for progress which any reasonable man can recognize as constituting the highest in human endeavour. It is this, rather than its 'optimistic' tone, which identifies it as one of those elements in ancient thought which have encouraged modern historicism. For there are optimistic forms of historicism, but also pessimistic ones; just as there are revolutionary forms, but also conservative ones. But what they have in common is the confidence that history will declare its own meaning. 'The ways of God', as Leo Strauss put it, 'are scrutable to sufficiently enlightened men' (*Natural Right and History*, p. 317). This is implied by the understanding of natural teleology as historical. For the natural ends of things are certainly scrutable; and if we really believe that in discerning the end for which something exists we discern the direction of history, then we must conclude that the direction of history is something about which mankind, even with only a moderate degree of enlightenment, knows a very great deal indeed.

Gone, then, is the mystery of God's dealings, the inscrutability of historical events which reduced the prophet to tears. And gone is the decisive role of Christian proclamation, 'to make all men see what is the plan of the mystery hidden for ages in God who created all things' (Eph. 3:9), in making known, that is, 'the unsearchable riches of Christ' (verse 8). When the Reformers laid down their criteria for the Christian doctrine of redemption as *sola gratia, solo Christo*, they intended to safeguard precisely the point that is lost in historicism: the fulfilment of history is not generated immanently from within history. For to speak of 'grace alone' is to say more than that God is at work within history: it is to speak of a work 'from outside'. It is to insist that, in transforming the world that he has made, God is not merely responding to necessities intrinsic to it, but is doing something new. The transformation is in keeping with the creation, but in no way dictated by it. This is what is meant by describing the Christian view of history as 'eschatological' and not merely as 'teleological'. The destined end is not immanently present in the beginning or in the course of movement through time, but is a 'higher grace' which, though it comes from the same God as the first and makes a true whole with the first as its fulfilment, nevertheless has its own integrity and distinctness as an act of divine freedom. 'Behold! I do a new thing!' The dangerous but exciting term 'divinization', by which the Greek tradition has spoken of man's salvation, expresses this truth, that man's destiny goes beyond all that is comprehensible within the immanent possibilities of his being. It is a measure of how far apocalyptic historicism has swept the field, that even this paradoxical term, which appears so committed to thinking the unthinkable, has been put to service to express the *expected* outcome of man's onward march of self-transcendence!

Contemporary historicist theologians who seek support for their position in Irenaeus (*Adversus Haereses* IV.38) are not mistaken. Nevertheless, there are elements even in Irenaeus' thought which show him to be on guard against the misleading tendencies of this passage: especially the idea that redemption 'recapitulates' creation (III.18), the distinction between the 'image' and the 'similitude' of God (V.6), and the concept of men's 'becoming gods' which is to be found at the heart of IV.38 itself. The subsequent patristic tradition was on sure ground when it took this last notion more seriously than it took his speculations about the childhood and maturity of the race. An important passage from Basil (*De Spiritu Sancto* 16.38) illustrates how important it became for the Nicene theologians to stress that 'perfection' (*teleiōsis*) was 'from without' (*exōthen*). Basil is discussing the creation of the angels, who, of course, have no history of salvation as we do, and therefore no Pentecost, but are among the 'works of creation from the beginning'. For them, too, existence depends upon the Holy Spirit as well as upon the Father and the Son. They are created by the Father as their 'first cause', the Son as their 'artificer' and the Spirit as their 'perfecter', to whom is assigned their 'stability' in holiness (*teleiōtēs, stereōsis*). But to speak in this way of holiness as a part of the angelic creation may seem to imply that perfection is immanent to the natural constitution of angels. At all costs Basil must correct this impression: 'The powers of heaven are not naturally holy, for otherwise they would be no different from the Holy Spirit . . . Holiness is from outside their being and confers (*epagei*) perfection upon them through the communion of the Holy Spirit.' Even of the angels, to whom we can hardly know how to attribute a 'history', it must be said that perfection is contingent upon the sanctifying work of the Spirit and 'conferred' upon their created nature from outside it.

Only if historical ends are understood in this eschatological way can we understand also the claim that 'Christ alone' brings the world-order to its fulfilment. For if the destiny of the world is immanently present within its natural orderings, then it must be present in it universally. In which case the best that can be said of Christ, and of the saving history which is centred upon him, is that he represents and, by anticipating its full flowering, reveals the immanent tendencies that are already present in world history as a whole. But that is not an adequate confession of the apostolic faith. Certainly, we must not champion 'saving history' so zealously that the kingdom of God ceases to be the destiny and purpose of *all* history, and appears relevant only to a narrow band of special activity within it. Yet Christian universalism must still make the distinction between that point in history which confers destiny and purpose on the whole and that whole which has destiny and purpose conferred upon it. The birth of Christ and the birth of John Smith are both destined by God to fulfilment in the kingdom of heaven. But the birth of John Smith is so destined, not by its own intrinsic tendency but through the birth of Christ. It does not carry its historical *telos* with it, but receives it from that one saving event. Traditionally this has been expressed by saying that God is active in the birth of John Smith in providence, and in the birth of Christ in salvation. Our complaint against historicism is that it has made every act of providence by definition an act of salvation. All happenings have taken on a Messianic character.

It must be conceded at once that some representatives of the new Christian historicism show themselves alert to the concerns which we have voiced. Jürgen Moltmann, in particular, offers considerable satisfaction in this regard, as the following sentences from his essay *Hope and Planning* indicate: '(Christian hope) must remove itself as much as possible from the stormy God of history, from the God of fate and chance. Theologically, this means that we must again learn to differentiate between the promise of God and the providence of God. The promise of God is not based on the providence of God, but rather the providence of God serves the fulfilment of the promise of God. The deterioration of Christian hope began . . . with the disintegration of the promise of the God who makes history into a general providence of God over history . . . The promise of God became merely the expression, the revelation, of the divine planning-mentality for history. The human spirit of planning could then be understood as the image of the divine, and that led to natural reversal which made "providence" simply a hypostatized ideal of the still undeveloped human capacity for anticipatory disposition' (*Hope and Planning*, p. 184). I must admit that I am simply puzzled to know how a thinker who can make this point with such sharpness can then go on to maintain, in the same essay: 'Both hope and planning have their foundation in suffering and in dissatisfaction with the present' (p. 178), and even, 'Hope invokes itself in an evolutionary contradiction to present reality' (p. 194). Do these sentences still speak of that 'Christian hope' which has its grounding only in the resurrection of Christ? Or has that turned out, after all, to be only one species of a broader genus 'hope', which we speak about in particular for reasons of confessional loyalty while all the time subordinating it to the more general phenomenon?

If we base our hope on the resurrection of Christ, it is impossible to say that it is 'founded' in 'dissatisfaction', for our dissatisfaction with the present is overwhelmed by the glorious vindication of creation which God has effected in Christ. But if we do regard hope as founded in dissatisfaction, then we certainly also regard it as founded in the immanent possibilities of history. We may grant that 'hope' is concerned with possibilities which are not *predictable*, which from every calculation must appear 'impossible'. 'Hope reaches out further over against historical possibilities and can even be characterized as a "passion for the impossible",' Moltmann says (p. 194), but then immediately explains that last phrase: 'the not yet possible'. Not *yet* possible! There speaks the truly committed planner, who regards the 'human capacity for anticipatory disposition' as still undeveloped! For even the possibility of convulsive, revolutionary transformation – the 'evolutionary contradiction' – is still a possibility which belongs immanently to history. Far-sighted people will take it into account, so that 'hope' will be differentiated from 'planning' only in degree.

The very heart of historicism is illuminated in an observation by Hannah Arendt in her essay 'The Concept of History' (*Between Past and Future*, p. 68), when she comments upon our modern habit of dating all chronology as AD and BC. 'The decisive thing in our system is not that the birth of Christ now appears as the turning-point of world history . . . but rather that now, for the first time, the history of mankind reaches back into an infinite past to which we can add at will and into which we can inquire further as it stretches ahead into an infinite future. This twofold infinity of past and future eliminates all notions of beginning and end, establishing mankind in a potential earthly immortality. What at first glance looks like a Christianization of world history in fact eliminates all religious time-speculations from secular history.' To this essay I acknowledge a special debt for my own understanding of the problem, as well as to George Grant's *Time as History*.

Historicist ethics

The importance of this controversy for a treatment of Christian ethics can be simply stated. Classical Christian thought proceeded from a universal order of meaning and value, an order given in creation and fulfilled in the kingdom of God, an order, therefore, which forms a framework for all action and history, to which action is summoned to conform in its making of history. Historicism denies that such a universal order exists. What classical ethics thought of as transhistorical order is, it maintains, itself a historical phenomenon. Action cannot be conformed to transhistorical values, for there are none, but must respond to the immanent dynamisms of that history to which it finds itself contributing.

There is a strong sympathy between this denial and the subjective answer to the question of the last chapter: Is cosmic order really present in the world, or is it imposed upon reality by the human mind? It would not be impossible, certainly, for a historicist to return a consistently realist answer to this question, basing himself strictly on evolutionary natural history and relating morality to the phase of biological evolution to which mankind has now come. It would, however, require a great deal of self-discipline. Natural evolution moves so slowly that a thinker who wishes to make a positive contribution to moral discussion must find himself impatient at the snail's pace of any moral change that can be derived from it. We are used, therefore, to seeing evolutionary moralists sidestep from natural history into social anthropology, so that moral values are associated, in the manner most congenial to historicist thought, with human *culture*, a decision which implies a subjective answer, whether rationalist or voluntarist, to the question. For although cultural moral values may be objective from the point of view of the individual agent, in so far as his culture is objective to him, they are, nevertheless, the products of the human thought, to be numbered among the cultural artefacts of the human race. A morality which itself 'has a history' can only be an aspect of that to which historical change is proper; and 'nature', as we are often told (evolution notwithstanding), 'has no history'. Historicism comes in many forms, some inclining to be definite and some to be agnostic about the ends which human cultures serve. Yet there is a predominant idealist strain in historicist thought that has given considerable currency to the idea that the end of history is for history to become 'conscious of itself'. That is to say, the emergence of historicist philosophy is itself the end which history serves. Mankind is to know that he is a historical being, and to take conscious control of the processes of history. To use a term which has become popular in some theological circles, the end of history is the 'hominization' of the world: all events are to fall under the conscious direction of human culture, so that the world itself becomes, so to speak, a human artefact.

From this there follow radical changes in moral thought in two areas in particular: mankind's relation to nature, and the individual's relation to society.

(1) In man's dealings with nature historicism invariably promotes a strong tendency to intervene and manipulate. The logic of this is simple: the ends of natural life which human action should respect are no longer understood to be given objectively in nature itself, but to be conferred upon nature by the interpretation of a human culture. But that culture serves its own historical end. In so far as that end is to become consciously directive, intervention becomes a necessity. It is not, however, that it can never be right to let alone. Rather, 'letting alone' has itself come to be understood as a special form of 'intervention', and a case has to be made for this form of intervention rather than another. The burden of proof has shifted, so that it has to be borne by those who would let alone rather than those who would intervene; and they have to discharge their burden by arguing, in quite alien terms, that letting alone would be the most effective *form* of intervention in this case. To see how letting alone can also be a form of intervention, consider the phenomenon of the 'wilderness park', well known on continents that have seen a rapid expansion of human civilization in the last century. An area of previously unbroken wilderness is

marked out on a map; a fence is built round it, a gate gives access to it, and a road, with car-parking facilities, brings traffic to the gate. Inside it professional gamekeepers 'manage' the stocks of wildlife and ensure the maintenance of a properly balanced wilderness ecology. Thus even wilderness becomes hominized. True, the bush is still as thick and the bears are still as wild as ever they were before; but the thickness and the wildness now no longer confront mankind as an independent good. They flourish as man's work of art, existing only to serve that route of cultural fulfilment that he has mapped out for himself.

But it is not only with non-human nature that historicism proves systematically interventionist. Man's relation to his own natural constitution is radically affected by the historicist point of view. And here we will take as our paradigm a natural institution of which the New Testament has a good deal to say, the institution of marriage. Jesus taught (as Saint Matthew reports) that 'he who made them from the beginning made them male and female, and said, "For this reason a man shall leave his father and mother and be joined to his wife, and the two shall become one flesh" ' (Mt. 19:4–5). In attempting to understand him Christians have classically believed that in the ordinance of marriage there was given an end for human relationships, a teleological structure which was a fact of creation and therefore not negotiable. The dimorphic organization of human sexuality, the particular attraction of two adults of the opposite sex and of different parents, the setting up of a home distinct from the parental home and the uniting of their lives in a shared life (from which Jesus concluded the unnaturalness of divorce): these form a pattern of human fulfilment which serves the wider end of enabling procreation to occur in a context of affection and loyalty. Whatever happens in history, Christians have wished to say, this is what marriage really is. Particular cultures may have distorted it; individuals may fall short of it. It is to their cost in either case; for it reasserts itself as God's creative intention for human relationships on earth; and it will be with us, in one form or another, as our natural good until (but not after) the kingdom of God shall appear.

A historicist account, on the other hand, must argue that this 'natural good' is not given transhistorically in nature at all, but is the product of cultural development peculiar to a certain time and place. (In developing the argument it will presumably lay stress on the variety of patterns of erotic relationship which have been maintained in other cultural milieux than that of classical Christianity. It is worth observing that not all variations are relevant to the discussion: there are numerous cultural variations which do not affect the basic structure of marriage; and there are others which do, but which raise problems for the culture that sufficiently demonstrate their unfittingness for human fulfilment.) By making

marriage an item of cultural history in this way, historicism necessarily raises a question about it. However well it thrives today, it
is moving towards some kind of metamorphosis. Historicism makes
all created goods appear putatively outmoded. So that if there are
currents of dissatisfaction evident in a society's practice of
marriage, such as might be indicated by a high divorce rate or a
prominent homosexual culture, they will be treated with great
seriousness as signs of the evolution for which the institution is
destined. Even if they do not represent the direction in which that
evolution must eventually move, they will be welcomed because
they bring the question of marriage and its alternatives to the level
of conscious choice, and so assist in the transformation of natural
relationships into cultural projects, as history 'becomes conscious
of itself'.

But classical Christian thought, too, believed in the transformation of marriage; and this gives us an opportunity to contrast the
historicist conception with one that is, in a fuller sense, 'eschatological'. Jesus taught (again according to Saint Matthew) that 'in
the resurrection they neither marry nor are given in marriage, but
are like angels in heaven' (Mt. 22:30). Humanity in the presence
of God will know a community in which the fidelity of love which
marriage makes possible will be extended beyond the limits of
marriage. To this eschatological hope the New Testament church
bore witness by fostering the social conditions which could support
a vocation to the single life. It conceived of marriage and singleness
as alternative vocations, each a worthy form of life, the two together comprising the whole Christian witness to the nature of affec-
tionate community. The one declared that God had vindicated the
order of creation, the other pointed beyond it to its eschatological
transformation. But the coexistence of the two within the Christian
church did not mean a loss of integrity to either. Each had to
function as what it was, according to its own proper structure.
The married must live in the ways of marriage, the single in the
ways of singleness. Neither would accommodate in itself or evoke
in the other an evolutionary mutation. Marriage that was not
marriage could not witness to the goodness of the created order,
singleness that was not singleness could tell us nothing of the
fulfilment for which that order was destined.

The key to Paul's famous discussion in 1 Corinthians 7 is his rejection
of the concept of an ascetic marriage, a kind of half-way house between
marriage and singleness: 'The husband should give to his wife her conjugal
rights, and likewise the wife to her husband' (3). His own single state he
would gladly commend; but it is a matter of individual gift (*charisma*, 7).
Rash and ill-judged asceticism will only lead to sexual sin (*porneia*, 2).
Paul's subsequent recommendation of singleness must be understood in
the light of this opening statement (1–7). It addresses those who are in

some doubt about their gift: there is a presumption in favour of singleness, but personal emotional circumstances should be the determining factor. (The metaphor 'to burn' (*pyrousthai*, 9) means to be frustrated in love – in love *with* somebody, that is, as generally in classical erotic literature, and not, as modern commentators vulgarly suggest, merely to be over-sexed.) After the section addressed to the married concerning circum-stances of divorce (10–16), Paul expounds the general principles of vocation (17–24). One's vocation is the circumstance 'in which' one is called (*i.e.* to follow Christ). In terms of the conditions it affords for obedience, it is neutral; therefore there is a presumption against changing it. This advice is then applied to the unmarried (25–35): first, there is a presumption for singleness because there is a presumption against a change of state in either direction (26–28); secondly there is an eschatological presumption for singleness, since the last days (the 'impending distress' of 26, RSV mg.) will impose constraints upon all natural structures (29–31). The freedom of the single person to wait unhindered upon the Lord's coming is enviable. But this is not a moral principle, and as a general orientation it is not intended to 'lay any restraint' or 'put a halter round the neck' (35*).

The concept of alternative gifts is clearly present also, if less explicitly, in Saint Matthew's account of Jesus' teaching (19:10–12). The saying 'It is better not to marry' is not for all, but for those to whom it has been given. (The RSV translation of this verse, which identifies the 'saying' (*logos*) as the 'precept' against divorce in the previous verses, is misleading.) Such as are given this course of life are not only those whom chance or violence have made incapable of marriage; they are those, too, who have imposed this form of self-denial upon themselves in view of the eschatological kingdom. These verses show more awareness than the Pauline passage of the ascetic implications of singleness; they lay less stress on its superiority. But the structure of the thought is entirely compatible: singleness is intelligible as a vocation because of the *eschaton*, and the decision between singleness and marriage is made on the basis of an individual gift.

The degeneration of the patristic and medieval tradition of teaching on singleness sprang from the loss of this understanding that one's state is a gift. Thus the choice between marriage and singleness became character-ized, in despite of Paul's disclaimers, as a moral choice; and although the Western church preserved a reference to Paul's 'he does not sin' by means of the doubtfully intelligible distinction between precept and counsel, this inevitably implied the disparagement of marriage. The development of monasticism as a force of spiritual revival in the fourth and fifth centuries was finally responsible for associating singleness with a higher spirituality, and this soon came to mean that it was a condition for certain forms of ministry in the church.

(2) If historicism fails in its treatment of nature for lack of a concept of creation, its social thought fails equally for lack of a strong eschatology. Eschatology has been profoundly important in shaping the Western tradition of politics (which in modern times has become the 'liberal' tradition). The opposition in Western theology between the City of God and the earthly city has enabled

political thought to avoid theocratic conceptions of government, which, by claiming to express the rule of heaven on earth, must unify the earthly and the heavenly into a single totalitarian political claim. Western theology starts from the assertion that the kingdoms of this world are *not* the kingdom of our God and of his Christ, not, at any rate, until God intervenes to make them so at the end. If we ask why not, the answer must surely be that their judgments cannot reconcile the world; thus they can neither be perfectly true nor perfectly merciful. Their sovereignty can be only a relative sovereignty; and the believer, who knows himself subject to the absolute sovereignty of God's reconciling judgment, keeps his spiritual 'space' in relation to them, just as they keep a certain 'space' of their own in relation to the judgments of God. This does not mean (as it has sometimes come to mean in degenerate forms of the tradition) that the secular state can be independent of God and his claims, or that the pious individual can cultivate a private existence without regard for the claims of his society. It means simply that earthly politics, because they do not *have* to reconcile the world, may get on with their provisional task of bearing witness to God's justice. And it means that the individual, because he is not absorbed by the claims of his earthly community, can contribute to its good order that knowledge of man's good which he learns from his heavenly calling.

Paul Ramsey's article 'The Uses of Power' (in his collection *The Just War*) laments the loss of classical Western politics which has followed on the loss of transcendence. Mankind's knowledge of his heavenly citizenship provided him with an 'ultimate reconciliation' of the 'ambiguities of sacrifice'. In the light of that ultimate reconciliation one could offer his life for the sake of his nation, which could afford only a 'proximate reconciliation', that is, some earthly good of justice which was worth an immortal man's dying for. But in a world where all values are immanent, too heavy a demand is made upon earthly politics to provide the meaningfulness and justification for an individual's life. Ultimate reconciliation for a man's death this worldly city can never afford. 'So modern secular man is unable any longer to look into the heart of the tragic ambiguity of all earthly sacrifice, the meagreness of every political achievement and the transience of the common good men serve by means of political power' (p. 17). No earthly good can be worth dying for unless there is a heavenly good that is worth living for. So cultural and economic activities and 'all other non-violent sources of political change' are put in place of politics, with its concern for justice, law and order, based upon the foundations of power. Force is banned, and liberal man becomes 'post-political', refusing to avail himself of the only weapons of earthly justice that there are.

Our complaint that historicism loses sights of the distance between God's kingdom and man's may seem paradoxical, since

it is often said on behalf of the historicist approach that it has
restored the kingdom of God to a position of importance in
political thought. But its use of eschatological categories is characteristically to *legitimize* the immanent tendencies of history rather
than to *criticize* them. If there is no locus of value outside history,
then history must provide its own critical movements from within,
so that the kingdom of God becomes a form without content, an
empty 'end' which will receive its definition from the history which
has led up to it. Thus historicism represents a return to totalitarian
thinking, in which the whole content of the claim of the good is
mediated to man through his developing social culture. This is
not to suggest, of course, that historicism is bound to a *state*-
totalitarianism, in which the institutions of government are identified as the bearers of cultural value. Contemporary thought,
Marxist as well as liberal, has on the whole learnt very well from
the disasters to which this identification has led. But even without
it, and allowing for a more diversified dialectic and a multiplication
of revolutionary initiatives, we are still faced with a totalitarianism
which allows the critic no ground of rationality unless he is the
voice of a 'movement'. To criticize the culture as a whole is
unthinkable; one can only speak *for* the culture *against* the culture,
as the representative of a new strand in the culture which will
fashion its future. To this implausible disguise, then, moral criticism
resorts in modern liberal society, presenting itself partly as sociological prediction, partly as threat. The critic must describe the
future of the culture in a way that justifies his concerns; and he
must show that he speaks for a constituency sufficiently large or
sufficiently determined to make his predictions come true!

Liberal historicism, in order to remain liberal, has to cultivate
movements of social dissent. This is not the place to speak of
the intellectual roots, part Christian part rationalist, of the liberal
political thought of the West, nor of the logical and historical
necessities which have driven it to assume a historicist form. It is
enough to observe that once liberalism is clothed in historicist garb,
it has to pinch itself, as it were, to find out if it is still alive.
Only the passionate antitheses of resentment and refusal remain to
convince it that cultural history is more, after all, than the
triumphal progress of an all-encompassing state. Protest, rather
than administrative evolution, must be the engine that propels
history forwards on its way, the tool with which we fashion the
raw material of past and present experience into the artefact of
our own future. Despite the sincere determination of many theologians to assert a Christological foundation for this conception,
it is impossible not to feel that here, as with the crowd before the
praetorium, what is really happening is the replacement of Christ
by Barabbas. It was not by solidarity with man's frustrated rebel-
liousness that Christ 'led captivity captive'. In the zealot's demand

for a political convulsion there was a measure of anthropocentric self-confidence which had in its turn to be repudiated and carried to the cross. Neither the earlier state-totalitarian historicism nor the more recent liberal culture-totalitarianism has understood to what an extent the search for justice, whether by administration or by protest, is interwoven with partiality and escalating destructiveness. Not in the immanent turbulence of social movements is hope to be found, but in the revelation of divine justice at Calvary. Only under the criticism of Christ's cross can the destructive dialectic of unrighteous order and disordered anger be exposed, and the provisional and humble service of justice be maintained.

'By faith Abel, though dead, still speaks,' wrote the author to the Hebrews (11:4*), alluding to Genesis 4:10, where Abel's blood 'cries out from the ground'. The reason he still speaks is that God did not heed the cry: he did not exact from Cain the full satisfaction that nature demanded. Rather, he sent him to live 'in exile from the ground', in a civilization alienated from nature and protected from its judgments. The 'mark' which protects him is the artificiality of his civilized arts – including most especially the arts of justice, for every judgment passed in Cain's city will leave Abel still crying out. Society's justice will never be true justice, but always justice and guilt intertwined in a self-renewing cycle of injury and restitution. Offended society cries out for satisfaction, and is covered with guilt when it takes it. The hanged man defiles (Dt. 21:22–23), not by reason of his own guilt, for which his death has made satisfaction, but by reason of the guilt of those to whom the satisfaction has been given. In the simple profundity of Cain's story there is the most searching expression of mankind's perpetual disquiet about his own civilization and its dependence upon violence. We cannot look to civilization to satisfy nature's claim; for always in doing justice it does injustice as well. It was the great contribution of Reinhold Niebuhr, earlier in this century, to understand this as clearly as anyone has done, and to restate for modern liberal society the theological truths which long since gave the Western political tradition its rationale.

But 'the sprinkled blood [of Jesus] speaks more graciously than the blood of Abel' (Heb. 12:24). It puts to rest the cry of outraged innocence which Cain's civilization could never silence. Abel was not vindicated, but Jesus was; and by his vindication put an end to the unfinished business of nature's justice. But where Abel's vindication would have meant the destruction of Cain's race, Jesus' vindication meant a new beginning for it. Abel was innocence in controversy with guilt; Jesus was innocence in identification with guilt. 'God . . . sending his own Son in the likeness of sinful flesh and for sin . . . condemned sin in the flesh' (Rom. 8:3). He took the place of the hanged man, which was also the place of his executioners, under condemnation; he took the place of Abel in vindication. He represented both innocent Abel and guilty Cain, and reconciled them to each other and to God. His resurrection satisfied nature's claim on behalf of the innocent, and God's on behalf of the guilty. That is why Christian theology speaks of the death and resurrection of Christ as an act of justice (*dikaiōma*, Rom. 5:18). For it is the true fulfilment of God's justice to reconcile the world, not a fulfilment that natural justice could have anticipated or demanded, but not a fulfilment either that denies or overturns natural justice. Jesus did not appeal *against* divine justice when he prayed 'Father, forgive them . . .' (Lk. 23:34). He demonstrated a divine justice that was more complete and more satisfying than any that eye had yet seen or ear heard of. It is the task of Christian eschatology to speak of the day when that justice shall supersede all other justice.

4

Knowledge in Christ

Morality is man's participation in the created order. Christian morality is his glad response to the deed of God which has restored, proved and fulfilled that order, making man free to conform to it. In the last chapters we have spoken of created order and its fulfilment; in the section which follows we shall speak further of man's participation in it. This chapter provides a pause for reflection. In it we are to consider the epistemological question which is raised by speaking of a 'created order' in this way. It looks forward to the next section, in that moral knowledge is also part of the *subjective* disposition with which we respond to God's work, inseparable from the freedom and obedience to which it summons us. Yet knowledge is also, and perhaps more importantly, a function of its object; and our epistemological pause follows quite properly on what we have learnt about the *objective* reality to which human morality responds. If we attempt to think at all about created order, we find ourselves asking epistemological questions which are not about us, but about it. How is the order of the created universe available to our knowledge, seeing that we belong to it, and cannot rise above it to survey it like God? What kind of knowledge can this be that has the order of creation as its object?

Our epistemological pause, we may add, quite properly *follows* on what we have learnt about the created order and its fulfilment, for epistemology is a reflexive, not an absolute, intellectual operation. We are not attracted by the first chapters of many treatises on ethics, which begin by telling us what ethics is in an abstract way, and wondering whether knowledge as such has any place in it; having demonstrated that it does, they then go on to ask what kind of knowledge is germane to it. Such a procedure cannot escape the reproach of having allowed its conclusions to dictate its theoretical starting-point; for there is no *neutral* account of what moral thought is, from which such sceptical questions can successfully be raised and answered in a spirit of pure enquiry, without either faith or unbelief. And if the outcome is the highly satisfactory conclusion that, after all, *theological* insight is germane to moral thought, we can be impressed with this only as a triumph of apologetics, which is to say, a legitimate, but essentially rhetorical, turning of the logical order of things upon its head in order to counter the arguments of unbelief. Inasmuch as the conclusion was present in the starting-point, it was the source of the starting-point; inasmuch as the starting-point has made genuine concessions to non-theological conceptions of ethics, these concessions will be reproduced in the conclusion, combating and perhaps frustrating its theological ambitions. A supposedly neutral starting-point, a simple assertion of what moral thought is, can only have been derived from some experience of moral thinking in life; but that will have been informed by a wider set of dogmatic convictions, whether believing or unbelieving.

We have learnt a great deal from the arguments of T. F. Torrance on this point, and especially from the fine opening chapter of his *Theological Science*. 'In scientific theology', he writes, 'we begin with the actual knowledge of God, and seek to test and clarify this knowledge by inquiring carefully into the relation between our knowing of God and God Himself in His being and nature . . . It is in the course of this inquiry that we raise the question of the possibility of the knowledge of God – that is to say, in inquiring how God is actually known, we inquire also how far He may or can be known. In this procedure we have to reject as unscientific any attempt that begins with the question "How can God be known?", and then advances to the question, "How far is this actual?" ' (p. 9). We need express reserve only about Torrance's use of the adjective 'scientific' as a term of approbation for the reflexive approach to epistemology. What kind of a commendation is this meant to be? Does it presuppose that the natural sciences are the norm for all disciplined knowledge? It would be pardonable to suspect so, given Torrance's unbounded enthusiasm for the philosophical aspects of Einstein's discoveries; but he disavows it, and we must take his disavowal seriously. Are we, then, to suppose that there is some universal *Wissenschaft* which dictates method to all forms of enquiry? But that is precisely to reinstate the absolute epistemology which he has worked so hard to banish! We would do better to replace the epithet 'scientific' with 'realist' – and even then avoid using it as a term of commendation, as though this *a posteriori* epistemology were to be justified on *a priori* grounds!

Let us begin with a sketch of what this knowledge must be like.

It must, in the first place, be knowledge of things *in their relations to the totality of things*. To know cosmic order is, in a sense, to know the totality of things – not, that is, to know everything that exists, which must be the prerogative of God, but to know what we do know as part of a meaningful totality. We must grasp the 'shape' of the whole, in so far as it gives meaning to the particular objects of our knowledge. But this 'apprehensive' knowledge of totality is a distinctive form of knowledge, which in an earlier day would have been called 'philosophy' and is sometimes now called 'metaphysics'.

In the ancient period Western culture organized all its knowledge under the general direction of 'philosophy' in this sense. It purported to apprehend the shape of the universe as a whole and to place particular objects of knowledge within the overall picture. It had not yet effected the differentiation of knowledge into empirical 'science' on the one hand and 'religion' on the other. About this differentiation, and about the etiolated philosophy which in modern times attempts to mediate between the two, we may well have mixed feelings. We should not romanticize classical metaphysics or attempt to exculpate it from the charge of 'suppressing the truth' which Saint Paul brings against idolatrous world-views (Rom. 1:18). We may reasonably think that some separation between the realms of the empirical and the *a priori* afforded the only way out of the *impasse* of superstition. Yet the fragmentation of knowledge in the pursuit of investigative science suggests a sceptical despair about the very possibility of knowing things in all their aspects and in their relations to other things; while the abstraction of religion from empirical reality represents a flight of faith into the subjective and the irrational.

To recover the 'sense for the whole' or 'for the Universe' from the fragmentation of analytic reason was one of the most worthy preoccupations of the romantics, and in theology especially of Schleiermacher. 'The sense strives to comprehend the undivided impress of something whole; it will perceive what each thing is and how it is; it will know everything in its peculiar character. But that is not what they mean by understanding . . . They seek to grasp nothing in and for itself, but only in its special aspects, and therefore, not as a whole, but only piecemeal . . . They think, indeed, that they have the true and real world, and that they are the people who grasp and treat all things in their true connection. Would that they could but once see that, for anything to be known as an element of the Whole, it must necessarily be contemplated in its characteristic nature and in its fullest completeness!' (from the third of the *Speeches on Religion*, pp. 127–130). The romantic tendency, however, was so to exalt the sense of the whole as *feeling*, that it would rarely challenge the claims of empiricism to represent *knowledge* as forcefully as that. The sense for the whole must be a 'glimpse', a 'ray penetrating', a 'miracle'. Thus the romantic critique came to terms too readily with its adversary, and accepted the separation of religion, as feeling, from both theoretical and practical reason.

Thus romantic theology bequeathed us a wholly unbiblical contrast of faith and reason, in place of the New Testament contrast of faith and sight. When the author to the Hebrews (11:1*) wrote that 'faith is the reality (*hypostasis*) of what we hope for and the substantiation (*elenchos*) of things unseen', he allowed nothing to modern irrationalism. 'By faith we understand (*nooumen*) that the created order was fashioned by the word of God, so that what is seen does not originate in the world of appearances.' The principle that governs the constitution of the world, which for this author is the principle which governs also the course of history, is open to understanding. It may be comprehended by a faith which can reach behind appearances that are not self-interpreting and discern the origin of things in the realm of the unseen. Faith is thus the *appropriate* stance of reason before the mysteries of world-origin and novelty in history. After this, can we listen quite comfortably to Schleiermacher saying, 'Though you allege that nature cannot be comprehended without God, I would still maintain that religion has nothing to do with this knowledge . . .' (from the second *Speech*, p. 35)?

In the second place, this knowledge, because it is knowledge of the whole, must be *from within*. It must be, to use in its strict sense a rather overworked term, 'existential' knowledge, which can occur only as the subject participates in what he knows. Knowledge of the universe never takes shape at an observer's distance; it is not knowledge-by-transcendence. We may, of course, know particular objects in this way, from a relative distance; that is what makes the natural sciences possible. But the more encompassing the object of observation is, the more difficult it is to isolate and transcend; that is what makes it inevitable that the natural sciences, when they approach the limits of cosmic order – its beginnings, its ultimate constituents, its spatial limits – turn back into philosophy again. We expect scientific knowledge to 'comprehend' or 'contain' its object, whereas in this knowledge the object contains us. Such knowledge must always have an incomplete character; even though it is knowledge *of* the totality, it is not total or exhaustive knowledge, nor ever could become so. The whole can be known only as a mystery which envelops us, into which our minds can reach only with an awareness that there are distances and dimensions which elude us.

The sceptical Koheleth (Ecclesiastes), who can appear so negatively disposed to the ideals and concerns of the Wisdom tradition, is in fact simply anxious to place human wisdom firmly in its existential context and rebuke its pretensions to transcendence. 'When I applied my mind to know wisdom, and to see the business that is done on earth, how neither day nor night one's eyes see sleep; then I saw all the work of God, that man cannot find out the work that is done under the sun. However much man may toil in seeking, he will not find it out; even though a wise man claims to know, he cannot find it out' (8:16–17). Wisdom, like any other goal that man may set himself, does not take one outside the world of flux and change. It, too, is a temporal activity, and like all such activities will yield in due time to its contrary. When Koheleth commends wisdom, he does so in terms that are suitable for commending a human activity: it is 'better than might' (9:16), it 'excels folly as light excels darkness' (2:13), it can afford protection to the wise man's life (7:12), it makes his face shine and the hardness of his countenance change (8:1). Yet it is quite wrong to imagine that it exempts one from the contingencies which befall us all in an essentially meaningless sequence of history. Koheleth has no perception of a revealed meaning in history; it is simply a series of contradictions and reversals, as the famous passage on 'time' makes clear (3:1ff.). We aspire to achieve an Archimedean point from which we can comprehend it all, and our aspiration is vain. 'He has put eternity into man's mind, yet so that he cannot find out what God has done from the beginning to the end' (3:11). It does not matter whether we take *'ôlam* as 'eternity' in a strictly time-transcending sense, or merely as sempiternal extension: ' . . . a sense of time past and future, but no comprehension of God's work from beginning to end' (3:11, NEB). Either way man's wisdom does not afford him a total purchase on the cosmos and its history; he can reach out towards apprehension only from within.

This principle has an important bearing on the question of how we know generic order, the order of 'kinds'. As universals, of course, kinds are perceived only through the particulars that instantiate them, and this fact has permitted empiricist philosophies to pose an oft-repeated dilemma. Our knowledge of kinds, it is argued, cannot be a true knowledge of universals, since we do not have the universe of instantiating particulars before us. Our pretended knowledge of kinds, then, cannot be more than an inductive inference based on hitherto observed regularities, a merely provisional construction of the mind which may be revised in the light of unforeseen contingencies. This argument is built upon a truth which certainly demands recognition. Our conceptions of kinds, and of the differentiating features which determine them, are always open to clarification in the light of new particulars. For example: in the last few years there have come into existence a few human beings who, as a result of *in vitro* fertilization techniques, have three biological parents, the genetic mother and father on the one hand and the mother who bore the pregnancy on the other. This new kind of human genesis (however it may be deprecated) is now a fact; and it requires of us completely new clarifications of thought as to what 'parenthood' consists in. On the other hand, we would be unable even to embark upon these clarifications unless we already *knew* what parenthood was. We could not even observe the regularities between one instance of parenthood and another unless we had already apprehended elements of generic order which connected them. For a 'regularity' is not a particular occurrence, like the birth of a child; it is a relation between two or more particular occurrences. One does not observe a regularity between two occurrences without observing the relation between them, which is to say, their generic ordering. The empiricist dilemma, then, either proves more than it pretends to, or less. It either proves that *no* generic order, not even regularity, is really 'observed', but is all a construct of the mind;

or else it proves merely that our *conceptual* knowledge of kinds is a provisional construct of the mind based on our actual *discernment* of kinds in the regularities of events, which is true, but not what was intended.

Behind the dilemma lies a failure to comprehend how the knowledge of created order, knowledge 'from within', differs from the knowledge of particulars 'from above'. The popular term 'universal' contributes to this misunderstanding, in that it suggests that generic knowledge is simply a quantitatively complete knowledge of particulars. Order is not known by accumulation of particulars, but immediately – without, that is, a process of discursive inference – through the historical sequence of particulars. Such knowledge is not exhaustive knowledge. It is 'universal' knowledge in the sense that it is the knowledge of things as a whole, in their cosmic relations to one another, but not in the sense that it has seen every particular there is to see, nor even every *relevant* particular there is to see. It is, by its very nature and not by accident, *provisional* knowledge, in that it is subject to continuing intellectual refinement in the light of new particulars, in the course of which the elements of order, perceived at first in the roughest outline, come to be understood with increasing subtlety and discernment.

In the third place, such knowledge must be knowledge *from man's position* in the universe. It is not enough to say that it must be 'from within'; for not every position within the order of things is a position to which knowledge is accessible. Knowledge is the characteristically *human* way of participating in the cosmic order. Man takes his place, which is the place of 'dominion', by knowing the created beings around him in a way that they do not know him. According to the creation story of Genesis 2, it is man who gives the animals their names. Such a relationship to the rest of creation belongs to him in order that he may fulfil his own part in the universe by discerning and interpreting what he sees about him. Knowledge is the root of his authority over his fellow-creatures, as it is also the root of the communion which each human being enjoys with his fellow-humans. Just as we must dissent from the idea that knowledge always implies transcendence over its object, so we must dissent from the idea that the knowing subject may be anything, anywhere. To know is to fill a quite specific place in the order of things, the place allotted to mankind.

But that means that the exercise of knowledge is tied up with the faithful performance of man's task in the world, and that his knowing will stand or fall with his worship of God and his obedience to the moral law. We cannot speak of knowledge as belonging to man's place in the universe without remembering that this place has not been faithfully occupied, that man has refused the role assigned him by his Creator. Knowledge will therefore be inescapably compromised by the problem of fallenness, the defacement of the image of God, and by the fallen creature's incapacity to set himself right with good will and determination. Mankind remains mankind, of course, however much he has tried to be something different; but he is not the mankind that he was intended to be, but fallen mankind. He is still a creature whose part it is to think and to know; but his knowledge is not that communion with the truth of things that it should be, but misknowledge, confusion and deception. He continues to observe generic and teleological order in the things around him; but he misconstrues that order and constructs false and terrifying world-views. So it is that, according to the Scriptures, his fallen condition is most typically and characteristically expressed by the sin of idolatry. Idolatry is the distinctive corruption of philosophical knowledge. Animals, plants and stones cannot become idolaters, because to them it was not given to know the order of things. Nor (if this abstraction could ever have existence) could the robot whose knowledge was confined to the purely empirical and 'scientific'; for he would lack the apprehensive intellectual capacities which make knowledge human. (A scientist, on the other hand, can be an idolater, precisely because his work depends on these capacities; without imagination he could not *inquire* into anything!) Only the creature whose task it is to live by the truth of the whole can suffer the fate of living in an illusory universe constructed by his own mind. How, then, we must ask, if true knowledge of the whole is co-ordinated with obedience, can there be such a knowledge available to disobedient man?

In the fourth place, a negative feature: such knowledge must be *ignorant of the end of history*. Whatever apprehension of created order may belong to man by virtue of his place within that order, the shape of history belongs to the secret counsel of the Lord of history. The creature must walk blindfold along the road of time, and may see only when he turns to survey that portion of the road which has already been traversed.

Any philosophy of history which takes some other starting-point than simple revelation is doomed to end up trapped within one or another form of natural determinism. It can give no account of the future except by extrapolating regularities from the past. There are, of course, many possible regularities for it to choose among, so that there are many different types of philosophy of history. Some are cyclical, singling out the repetitive character of the natural processes and extending the principle of repetition explicitly to include larger patterns of events; in which case they are, in the end, quite overtly philosophies of nature. In the modern period Nietzsche affords the most striking example of historicist thought which has turned in this direction. More characteristic of modern philosophies of history is a unilinear scheme. But even this can be developed only by extrapolating other constituent patterns in nature, so that these theories, too, whether evolutionary, utopian or cataclysmic, are still covertly philosophies of nature. (Evolutionary philosophies, like that of Teilhard de Chardin, which take the natural sciences for their starting-point, illustrate this very clearly.) To be truly 'history', history must be shaped by the unique, by that which cannot be guessed from the scrutiny of natural repetitions. This is not to disallow the historian's interest in discerning intelligible causality in past history; it is simply to point up the difference between historical understanding and transcendent observation of a closed system, such as will allow us to make predictions. To understand the end of history, therefore, cannot be the work of philosophy; it will be a disclosure of prophecy if it is to happen at all. The finger of God must point to the place in history where the meaning and direction of the whole is to be found, and his voice must proclaim it: 'This is my beloved Son, with whom I am well pleased.'

But the search for a philosophy of history (which did not begin, as is sometimes suggested, with the Judaeo-Christian idea of history as revelation) bears witness that the question about the end of history is a matter of anxiety. And naturally so; in the fallen condition of the universe the created order is constantly put in question by the events of history, so that we have no assurance that the good which we have been given to know, and may still presume to know even though our knowledge is misknowledge, can and will sustain itself. Thus the unresolved character of history touches us not speculatively but existentially. The question of the end of history is urgent because it is the 'problem of evil'. Perhaps thinkers need never have troubled themselves about the end of history had Adam not set in motion a train of happenings which threatened the good order of creation itself. As it is, Adam's children must find out, though they have no means of doing so, where the course of events is tending, for without that knowledge they cannot tell whether such knowledge of the good as they possess is a real ground of hope or the last trace of a joy that is about to be engulfed in novelty. To face novelty with confidence, they must be sure that what they have truly known as good in the past cannot be invalidated by what they may yet have to know. As it is, their knowledge of the good is at risk, and any bend in the stream of history may reveal things which cannot be known together with what they have known hitherto. The history of the world may divide into two irreconcilable universes, and the future make war with the past. Perhaps the historicist vision, when stripped of its vacuously optimistic progressivism, is the truest vision of things apart from revelation; for it does not pretend to assure us, on the basis of the past, that such a falling-apart cannot and will not happen. Indeed, it may sometimes raise the nasty suspicion that it actually has happened, and that our rational access to the past is now completely blocked by some apocalyptic event, such as the French Revolution, which has cut reality in two!

'Why do the righteous perish?' This is the form in which the question is put throughout the Old Testament, a form which attends to evil as event (rather than as substance) and which seeks a teleological rationale in the action of God to 'vindicate' those who are unjustly afflicted. 'He will make your righteousness shine clear as the day and the justice of your cause like the sun at noon' (Ps. 37:6, NEB). Those who say that the Old Testament offers no resolution of the problem of evil simply have not understood the way in which it addresses the problem. It offers a historical resolution, precisely because it understands evil as a historical problem.

It must be granted that to some Old Testament authors it appears that an answer can be given within the terms of natural process, that a cyclical series of events will ensure that right succeeds to wrong as surely as spring gives way to summer. Thus Psalm 37 promises that 'like grass [the wicked] soon wither, and fade like the green of spring' (2, NEB); and the author of Psalm 73, when he enters into the sanctuary of God, sees how the feet of the unrighteous are set in slippery places: 'in a moment how dreadful [is] their end, cut off root and branch by death with all its terrors' (19, NEB). The natural cycle of events is sufficient, as it would seem to these preachers, to vindicate the justice of things, though we would misunderstand them badly if we did not see that it is only the faithfulness of God's activity which allows them to think of a 'natural cycle' in this context. Dissatisfaction with this answer is evident both in Job and in Ecclesiastes. The poet of Job attends with a seriousness which has never been equalled to the difficulties raised for the cosmological answer by the psychology of suffering itself, with its overpowering burden of resentment at the appearance of arbitrary injury. His resolution of the tension between the two perspectives, the sufferer's and the cosmologist's, is to emphasize the inscrutability even of the natural order – not repudiating the connection of justice and nature outright, but casting over nature too the same veil of divinely-sustained mystery which the sufferer conceives to enfold the questions of justice. Ecclesiastes, on the other hand, adopts from the start a radical scepticism about human ends and their attainment, declaring that it is the mysterious privilege of God to award happiness where he will – not as a function of human success, but as an epiphenomenal crown set upon the otherwise meaningless and circular pursuit of natural ends. Both the confidence of the cosmological answer and the questionings of its critics are taken seriously by the prophets, who are the first to express the question in terms of the ultimate direction of history. They teach us to hope for a final clarification, which will go beyond the inequities of natural reprisal and redress, and will deal not only with the apparent prosperity of the wicked but even with the multitudes of the innocent dead. When Saint John of the Apocalypse saw the martyred souls beneath the altar crying 'How long?' (Rev. 6:9–10) he saw the question as the Old Testament had left it (*e.g.* Dn. 12:2–3): outstanding injustice awaits the final intervention of God to judge the world and to give life to the dead. The same prophet marvellously expressed the limitations of a purely cosmological theodicy in the diptych of chapters 4 and 5. It is the opacity of history, the sealed scroll in the hand of the Most High, that reduces John to tears; it is the revelation of the Lion of Judah, who is also the Lamb, which affords to all creation the joy of having history, and with it the problem of evil, made intelligible.

What, then, must such knowledge of created order be, if it is really to be available to us? It must be an apprehensive knowledge of the whole of things, yet which does not pretend to a transcendence over the universe, but reaches out to understand the whole from a central point within it. It must be a human knowledge that is co-ordinated with the true performance of the human task in worship of God and obedience to the moral law. It must be a knowledge that is vindicated by God's revelatory word that the created good and man's knowledge of it is not to be overthrown in history. Such knowledge, according to the Christian gospel, is given to us as we participate in the life of Jesus Christ. He is the point from which the whole is to be discerned, 'in whom are hid all the treasures of wisdom and knowledge' (Col. 2:3). He is the obedient man. And he is the one whose faithfulness to the created moral order was answered by God's deed of acceptance and vindication, so that the life of man within this order is not lost but assured for all time. True knowledge of the moral order is knowledge 'in Christ'.

Exclusive knowledge

The phrase 'in Christ' must not be etherealized in defiance of the incarnation. It does not speak solely of a universal Logos, but of the Logos made flesh in the first century AD, crucified under Pontius Pilate and raised again on the third day. We are asserting that true knowledge is to be had in this place and no other; it is an exclusive claim which must disallow some pretensions to knowledge as well as allow others. The object of this exclusive knowledge, on the other hand, is inclusive: it is the whole order of things created, restored and transformed. This polarity between an exclusive knowledge and an inclusive object of knowledge, between revelation in the particular and created order in the universal, must be carefully defended.

This is why we have avoided using the classic term 'Natural Law' in the course of our exposition of created order, and will continue to avoid it, despite points of strong sympathy between our account and the more realist versions of Natural Law theory. The Western tradition of Natural Law has been unable to avoid an ambiguity in which universality has been attributed not only to being but to knowledge. Thus in Thomas Aquinas's exposition, to which, in some degree, all subsequent Natural Law thinking refers back, the 'first principles' are (like the axioms of propositional proofs) *per se nota*, 'self-evident'. 'The good is the first object which the practical reason, which is ordered to action, apprehends. For every agent acts to an end, which has the meaning of "good". So the first principle of practical reason is founded on the meaning of "good", which is: "the good is what all things seek after". This, then, is the first precept of the law: "the good is to be sought and done, the evil to be avoided"; all the others precepts of the Natural Law are based on this' (*Summa Theologiae* II–I.94.2). It is true that Thomas Aquinas can give a careful account of how the 'secondary principles' of Natural Law may be lost sight of *vel propter malas persuasiones . . . vel etiam propter pravas consuetudines et habitus corruptos* (94.6). Nevertheless, this epistemological caution should not obscure the fact that for Thomas the primary principles are authenticated by their universal self-evidence alone. As John Finnis insists in his eloquent defence of Thomist theory, they 'are not inferred from speculative principles . . . they are not inferred from facts . . . they are not inferred from metaphysical propositions about human nature . . . nor are they inferred from a teleological conception of nature or any other conception of nature. They are not inferred or derived from anything' (*Natural Law and Natural Rights*, pp. 33f.).

Renaissance and Counter-Reformation thinkers made a serious attempt to separate out the ontological from the epistemological universality of Natural Law, and to subordinate claims for natural knowledge to a very secondary position. This attempt is marked by a revealing preference for the terminology *ius naturae* ('Natural Right') rather than Thomas Aquinas's *lex naturae* ('Natural Law'). 'Law' carries with it the subjective implication made clear by Thomas, that it is *aliquid per rationem constitutum* ('something constituted by reason'). In speaking of 'Right', one can suggest something more objective, an *ipsa natura rationalis* ('rational nature itself'), to which an act may display a 'conformity or disconformity' (*convenientia aut disconvenientia*). Thus Grotius (*De iure belli et pacis* I.1.10), who then proceeds to speak of two ways in which natural right may be known (12): *a priori*, from the direct observation of conformity or disconformity with nature, and (but with little security or certainty) *a posteriori*, from what is universally believed in all nations. This clarification of Natural Law theory in an ontological direction Finnis disapproves (p. 45) under the curious denomination, 'rationalist'. Is not that term more naturally applied to a tradition which roots the first principles of moral action in *reason*? At the Enlightenment it was rationalism in this sense, and not the realist version of Natural Law propounded by Suarez, Vasquez and Grotius, that prevailed. (We need not dissent from the judgment that these thinkers were also, in other respects, voluntarists, and in that way prepared the ground for Hobbes to overwhelm them.) True to the principle that epistemology is a function of political theory, the Enlightenment established universal consensus as the measure of any future law of nature – which has the curious effect in our own day of driving Natural Law thinkers in search of support from the findings of comparative anthropology!

In the great theological attack upon Natural Law which was spearheaded earlier this century by Karl Barth, we can only regret that the ontological and epistemological issues were never properly differentiated. In his pursuit of an uncompromised theological epistemology Barth allowed himself to repudiate certain aspects of the doctrine of creation (such as 'ordinances') which ought never to have fallen under suspicion. Emil Brunner, for all his unclarity over the epistemological issue, deserves credit for having understood this. Barth, indeed, treated Natural Law as a tradition to which many undesirable features of moral theology were attributable, regardless of whether or not they were logically or historically homogeneous with it. It was under this rubric, for example, that he criticized legalism and casuistry. All this left him with a formal account of the theological basis of ethics which, depending exclusively on the divine command – interpreted in the existentialist way as particular and unpredictable –, was far too thin to support the extensive responsibility for moral deliberation which he would claim in practice and sometimes even defend in theory. Furthermore, his approach to the doctrine of creation, which had to be subordinated ontologically to Christology, had disturbing results in a series of frankly Apollinarian Christological conceptions. Yet for all that, the *epistemological* positions of this greatest of twentieth-century theologians remain fundamentally important for Christian ethics.

However, the constant tendency in Christian thought for this polarity to collapse does at least remind us of the truth that knowledge is grounded in being, human knowledge specifically in human being, and Christian knowledge in Christ's human being. What we have already said about knowledge belonging to man's place within the universe requires us to take the connection between knowledge and being further. To speak of an exclusive knowledge is to make this narrow point in the human race the sole point from which the vocation to human knowledge can be fulfilled. This can only be arbitrary unless the same point is also the sole place from which the vocation to human *being* is fulfilled; but that is what the doctrine of man's fall and redemption tells us is the case. The claim for exclusive knowledge, then, is an epistemological implication of the fallenness of man, a theme which previous generations handled in terms of the loss, or defacement, of the image of God.

Knowledge of the natural order is moral knowledge, and as such it is co-ordinated with obedience. There can be no true knowledge of that order without loving acceptance of it and conformity to it, for it is known by participation and not by transcendence. In disobedience our perceptions of it assume false and strange shapes. Yet even in our confusion and error we remain, by the merciful providence of God, human beings. We are not so visited with the fruit of our moral disorder that we find ourselves converted, like Odysseus' sailors, into swine. In this sense it is true to say that the image of God is 'defaced' but not 'lost'. We remain beings for whom knowledge is the mode of their participation in the universe. Even in confusion and error we do not simply cease to know; we do not become swine for whom knowledge is not a possibility. The ignorance, error and confusion which are attributable to us are all *failures* of knowledge, disasters which can befall only those beings which actually do know. For non-knowing creatures falsehood is no danger. We will speak more truly of 'misknowledge', rather than of simple lack of knowledge. Furthermore, even in the disorder consequent upon the Fall the universe, in the merciful providence of God, does not cease to be the universe. Disorder, like misknowledge, is attributable only to things which are in their true being ordered. And the universe, though fractured and broken, displays the fact that its brokenness is the brokenness of order and not merely unordered chaos. Thus it remains accessible to knowledge in part. It requires no revelation to observe the various forms of generic and teleological order which belong to it. An unbeliever or a non-christian culture does not have to be ignorant about the structure of the family, the virtue of mercy, the vice of cowardice, or the duty of justice. Nor does such a one have to fail entirely to respond to this knowledge in action, disposition or institution.

So much must be said about moral knowledge as a natural function of man's existence. Nevertheless, such knowledge is incomplete unless the created order is grasped as a whole, and that includes its relations to the uncreated. If the Creator is not known, then the creation is not known *as creation*; for the relation of the creation to its Creator is the ground of its intelligibility as a created universe. If one term of that relation is obscured, the universe cannot be understood. There is no principle of self-contained cosmic intelligibility, in relation to which the existence or non-existence of a Creator may be regarded as a separate question and postponed to another day. The very contingency of the universe points us beyond itself towards the transcendent Creator on whom its intelligibility depends; so that Paul can say that the invisible God is seen through the comprehension of the things which he has made (Rom. 1:20). Yet creation would not be creation, nor contingency contingency, if it simply revealed God unambiguously to us. This knowledge of God, Paul goes on, is something from which we can turn away, refusing to glorify God as God. And in that case the universe confronts us as something which might have been understood but has in fact been misunderstood, giving rise to various kinds of idolatry in which the creature is regarded as absolute.

But this means that the order of reality is not truly known at all. Order cannot be known piece by piece, but only as a whole. A form that is conceived incompletely must be perceived wrongly. If Schubert's Unfinished Symphony were the only evidence for the symphonic form that we had, we would not have a *partial* knowledge of what a symphony was, we would have a completely false idea. Therefore we cannot speak of the various partial ways in which the universe is accessible to knowledge simply as 'partial knowledge' and leave it at that. If we know the value of the family, and do not know its relation to individual freedom, then we have misunderstood even the family. If we grasp the importance of compassion, but cannot relate it to justice, then even our compassion has become a vice rather than a virtue. Knowledge of the moral order is a grasp of the total shape in which, if anything is lacking, everything is lacking. Thus Saint Augustine in the *City of God*, with an inconsistency that is only apparent, explains the success of the Roman empire in terms of traditional Roman virtues and, at the same time, denies that they are virtues at all, since there is no virtue without true religion. Such misknowledge may take the blatant form of idolatry, or its modern non-religious equivalent, ideology, in which a part is allowed to interpret the whole; or it may, more doubtfully, take the ascetic and sceptical form of a self-consciously fragmented knowledge which disavows metaphysics. Either way it is not knowledge of the created order.

From which we conclude that revelation in Christ does not *deny* our fragmentary knowledge of the way things are, as though that knowledge were not there, or were of no significance; yet it does not *build on* it, as though it provided a perfectly acceptable foundation to which a further level of understanding can be added. It can only expose it for not being what it was originally given to be. This is the sense, then, in which it is true to say that the image of God in man was not merely 'defaced' but 'lost'. We are not to think of revelation as conferring upon man a knowledge of created order which he never possessed before (though it is true, as we have said, that it confers a knowledge of the shape of *history* which he never possessed before), for knowledge is, and always has been, man's mode of participation in the universe. Rather, revelation catches man out in the guilty possession of a knowledge which he has always had, but from which he has never won a true understanding. It shows him up, not as a swine which has no capacity for knowledge, but as a man who has 'suppressed the truth' in unrighteousness (Rom. 1:18). The Christian moral thinker, therefore, has no need to proceed in a totalitarian way, denying the importance and relevance of all that he finds valued as moral conviction in the various cultures and traditions of the world (whether these be 'Christian', 'non-Christian' or 'post-Christian'). He has no need to prove that anything worth while in them has arisen historically from Christian influence. But neither can he simply embrace the perspectives of any such culture, not even – which is the most difficult to resist – the one to which he happens to belong and which therefore claims him as an active participant. He cannot set about building a theological ethic upon the moral *a priori* of a liberal culture, a conservative culture, a technological culture, a revolutionary culture or any other kind of culture; for that is to make of theology an ideological justification for the cultural constructs of human misknowledge. He can only approach these phenomena critically, evaluating them and interpreting their significance from the place where true knowledge of the moral order is given, under the authority of the gospel. From that position alone can be discerned what there is to be found in these various moral traditions that may be of interest or of value.

In the thirties Barth spoke against those German theologians who felt themselves bound to shape their theology in response to the great new cultural fact of their time and place, the sudden and passionate yearning for national identity among the German people. The issue can be seen most clearly in his comments on Emmanuel Hirsch (*The German Church Conflict*, pp. 28ff.). Hirsch wrote: 'If we in theology and Church are too small for [God's] hour, if we cannot . . . risk ourselves to the inrushing "new", to our own folk in this living movement, then we are cast out.' It was this deference to the 'inrushing new', this interpretation of a major cultural movement as God's hour, that Barth had to contest. 'Hirsch wants to build the church on this rock and this rock only. It is from this viewpoint that he construes her preservation, her renovation, her task.' Does this mean that theology cannot respond to the cultural crises of its day? Barth himself, of course, was doing just that. But it responds from its own 'Christian centre . . . the Word of God, or Jesus Christ, crucified and risen', who 'stands as Lord'. It was a matter of authority. Neither the 'German hour' nor any other hour could become important for theology under its own momentum or on its own self-interpretation. It would have only that importance and significance which the Lord of the Church assigned it. Theology could not allow itself to speak *from* it, but only *to* it, as the exposition of the Word of God drove it to articulate critical reproof or exhortation.

To approach the debate, as most theological students do, by way of the exchanges between Barth and Brunner, is to risk missing its primary importance, as well as experiencing some puzzlement over the intensity (intellectual as well as emotional) with which a rather narrower disagreement could be pursued. Nevertheless, Barth was right to say that the principle that theological authority is to be found solely in Christ could admit of no more or less. And he was right to object that Brunner conceived the theologian as divided between two tasks, proclamatory and apologetic, in only one of which he was beholden solely to the authority of Scripture. If on reading Brunner's *Nature and Grace* we find, as many have, that Barth's *No!* strikes us as unsympathetic, we may redress the balance by studying Brunner's political thought in *Justice and the Social Order*. For there we cannot fail to observe how unquestioningly he treats the authority of that coalition of classical and biblical elements of thought which, on his account, constitute our modern notion of justice. But does this place him in a different position from that of the early Temple with his theology of Christendom? Or from Tillich, with his 'correlation' of the 'questions' of our existence and the 'answers' of the Christian message? It is hard to see how such an approach can become more than a work of ideology, in which the gospel is proved to be 'at home' in our favoured cultural setting, whatever it may be. It is not nothing, of course, that these men all knew well enough to make a better cultural choice than Hirsch.

But is that a theological matter, or are we merely to congratulate them on being Swiss, English and German Socialist respectively, and on exercising correspondingly wiser political judgments? What has now become painfully clear is that the theological tradition which springs from such thinkers is unable to deal convincingly with those liberation-theologies which most blatantly subject the theological enterprise to the sectional perceptions of a single cultural group ('black' theology, 'feminist' theology, *etc.*). It can show embarrassment at them, or it can be patronizingly interested in them; but it cannot now complain at being excommunicated, and assert the universality of theology, since all the time it has understood the theological task as a discreet exercise in cultural accommodation.

Two objections are commonly raised to this account of authority in Christian moral thought. Either would be serious if it could be sustained. In the first place it is argued that we have left ourselves no room to say anything about the character of moral thought as a corporate enterprise of *learning*, which must respond to the new challenges of historical experience. In the second we are charged with neglecting the role of *compromise* in moral understanding.

Moral learning

If the moral instruction which the church received from the apostolic age (or the individual believer from catechetical training) could be conceived as an inventory of items of knowledge, we would then have to decide: can the church (or the believer) add to that inventory or not? If moral knowledge were accumulated as items of information may be accumulated, or if it were 'possessed', as scientific knowledge-by-transcendence may be possessed, then knowledge gained by the church since the apostles (or by the individual since his catechetical class) could be only *new* knowledge, which could only be admitted, or refused admission, as a *supplement* to what had originally been known. If moral learning consisted in the accrual of new items of moral knowledge, then each new area of moral concern which confronted the church (or the individual) would demand an absolute choice: either acquire some understanding which was not given in the faith you received, or refuse to learn altogether!

But moral learning is not like that. (Nor, indeed, is theological learning as a whole; it was precisely this misunderstanding that gave rise to the discredited 'two-source' conception of Scripture and tradition, with the consequent Protestant reaction against the 'innovations' which tradition had made.) Moral understanding is a grasp of the whole shape of things. If a set of moral conceptions has at any time to be supplemented by major additions – let us suppose that a culture discovers for the first time the importance of treating human beings as 'persons', or awakens to the possibility of injustice by economic domination – then something more has happened than a simple *accrual* of moral wisdom. There is no empty space in a moral outlook which unlearnt moral truths may come in to fill. To learn radically new moral truth is to change the shape of the whole outlook. One cannot *add* moral truth to moral truth; one can only *repent* false perceptions of the moral order and turn to truer ones. The fact that moral illumination does, in its fundamental form, involve conversion – having to unlearn as error what one thought one knew as truth – should alert us to the inadequacy of the accumulative model to express our experience of moral learning.

This might lead us to imagine, on the other hand, that simple moral learning, as opposed to repentance, cannot take place at all; that we can know only by a series of crises in which we repent and are forgiven, without any connected development in our moral understanding. Some Protestant traditions have embraced this idea as a radical way of freeing themselves from justification by works. But it is a mistake, for it implies a scepticism about the very possibility of finding moral understanding in Christ. For in this conception nothing is actually *communicated* in the crisis except a new beginning; there is nothing to guide the believer more effectively through his next period of moral action than through his last. (Converted into ecclesiology, this conception makes all tradition suspect; the church's course is by no means 'from one degree of glory to another', but merely a series of revivals from defection.) There is a mode of learning, which is not accumulation on the one hand, not merely a sequence of repentings on the other. There is 'sanctification' (as the Reformation terminology had it) as well as 'justification', which does not, nevertheless, defy the fundamental principle of grace, that when Christ was given, everything was given. We can know *better* what we already know *in outline*. Moral 'learning' is all the time 'thinking'. It is the intellectual penetration and exploration of a reality which we can grasp from the beginning in a schematic and abstract way, but which contains depths of meaning and experience into which we must reach. For an analogy we may think of what it is to study a great picture; beginning from the first superficial glance, which takes in the picture whole but as yet entirely without insight, and going on for a lifetime, always discovering 'new' things, which are yet not new but were there in the picture from the first.

We must qualify the analogy, of course, by admitting that the 'new' steps which are taken in moral thought (which are not radically new) are occasioned by 'new' events in history, which may indeed be radically new. We have mentioned already the example of *in vitro* fertilization. It is a thing which has never happened in the history of the world before our time, that a person has had three biological parents; that fact requires us to speak of parenthood in new ways. A technical innovation, therefore, is the occasion for our asking new questions about parenthood and developing new concepts – by analogy, no doubt, with existing ones, but none the less innovatory for that. This may seem to imply that the historical situation created by technical progress exercises authority over our moral thinking. We may even say, 'This development poses new moral questions', or 'No thought about parenthood can evade the challenges presented by *in vitro* fertilization'. But this is only a rhetorical performance. If a moral 'issue' has arisen about this new technique, it has arisen not because of questions the technique has put to us, but of questions which we have put to the technique. If we find this development morally, as opposed to technically, important, we do so by virtue of that knowledge of the moral order which we have brought with us. We did not learn from the scientists that it raised moral issues, nor did we learn from them what the moral issues it raised were. It has become the object of moral enquiry by virtue of a dynamic of thought which, simply as a technical innovation, it could not have initiated and cannot control. And any answers we may reach about this development will be dictated (if it is genuinely a *moral* enquiry) not by the sheer facticity of the development but by what has always been the case about parenthood, which we have now to rediscover and rearticulate in a new context. We may, of course, yield before the sheer facticity of the development and so get our answers wrong, leaving a more difficult task of thought for our successors. But wrong or right, we must pretend at least to be answering the moral question, the question which both arises and finds its answer within the circle of moral discourse. Those scientists who summon us to discuss these new techniques, on any other terms than these, are apparently not seeking a moral discussion at all, but merely a social legitimation for what they have achieved.

Conflict and compromise

If moral learning is, as we describe it, the exploration of an order which we grasp from the beginning as a whole, then it must begin (at least for any sinful human being) with the initial conversion of the mind in repentance. And to proceed with seriousness it must be constantly renewed in repentance as well. But repentance implies not only the acknowledgment of truth, but the acknowledgment of falsehood. It makes a distinction between them and sets them in conflict – a conflict which begins in the only possible place, with the falsehood of one's own thoughts and actions, but which cannot be restrained from taking issue with falsehood in the world, if only because self and world are mutually determining by their interaction. Moral learning, then, founded in conflict, cannot be what it is often portrayed as being: a taking into self of the changing perspectives of each world-situation, the forging of successive syntheses in a dialectic of tradition and experience. It can only be the drawing and redrawing of the line of separation, giving that formal intention of repentance its infinitely complex substantiation in the discernment of the world-order in truth. Not that this makes it anything other than *learning*. So long as we exist as beings in history, the ground we traverse will be, in some sense, new ground, and we will find in created order the illuminative power to interpret new situations. But there can be no interpretation which does not find the known within the unknown; and in moral learning we expect to see emerging through all the new shapes and forms that we encounter the same determining patterns, and the same opposition of true and false, that we first sought to discern and understand when we repented. The thought that false order can take no new forms, that having been recognized, described and labelled it will, like the toothless giants of Bunyan's second *Progress*, trouble our pilgrimage no more, is a dangerous deception. Moral knowledge 'in Christ' can never graduate beyond Jesus' conflict with Pharisee and Sadducee, a conflict to be discerned and traced anew at every turn in the way.

In Saint John's Gospel the form of this constantly present challenge to true knowledge is characteristically called 'the world'. The subtlety and suggestiveness of this expression rests upon its ambivalence: on the one hand, 'the world' is the organization and commitment of evil to oppose the good; but on the other it is still nothing less than that which God has made and loves, 'his own' to which he came but which would not receive him. The conflict in which Jesus engaged and which led to his death was not the conflict of dualist myth between two independent realities, the ultimate principles of good and evil, but a conflict between the true and false forms of the one reality. (Only such a conflict, or course, could lead to a decision; for only as the false and true forms of one reality can good and evil find themselves in competition for the same world-space; the war of good and evil in Manichaean myth never ends, because it is a sham war.) The death of Christ shows us the outcome of the encounter between the true human life and the misshapen human life, between the order of creation as God gave it to be lived and known and the distorted and fantastic image of it in which mankind has lived.

The outcome of the encounter is that the false excludes the true. The true participation of man in creation is brought abruptly to an end as the Son of man is put to death, deprived of the basic form of participation which is the precondition for other forms, his physical life. We should not allow our shock at this wrong outcome to be dulled by what we know of its subsequent putting-right. We confess that God reversed the crucifixion of the Son of man and vindicated the true against the false; but that does not alter the fact that the corrupted order had in itself the tendency and the capacity to destroy the uncorrupted, and so to defend itself against all correction or amendment. We confess, too, that even in this destruction of the true by the false there lay in the counsel of God a deeper mystery, the mystery of representative judgment, so that man's rebellion did not outrun the divine purpose even for the three days that Jesus lay in the tomb. But that does not alter the fact that it proved impossible for the true to live alongside the false within the one world. The meaning of the cross *in itself*, the meaning which is presupposed by all further meanings which it assumes in the light of the resurrection, is that joyful and obedient participation cannot continue freely in the world but must conflict with disobedience and so be driven out. Apart from the further word of God in the resurrection, this hopeless word must be the last word. When that further word is spoken, however, when the Son of man is vindicated and even his sufferings are shown to have served the divine purpose of setting right man's wrong, that penultimate word is not simply forgotten. We are not invited now to live in the created order as though there had been no cross. The resurrection body of Christ bears nail-prints, and the life of those who follow him means taking up the cross. The path to full participation lies through being excluded.

Discipleship, then, involves us in the suffering of exclusion from various forms of created good which are our right and privilege as Adam's restored children. This exclusion may be at the hands of others, who do not wish us to participate in those forms of life except on their terms; or it may be that our own fallen humanity does not equip us as it should to participate in these goods without compromise. Thus, to take an example of the one case, an individual or group may find itself barred from exercising a proper and fitting measure of political authority by others who presently exercise political authority. Or, to take an example of the other case, an individual may be ill-endowed psychosexually to enjoy the fulfilment and responsibility of sexual life in marriage. Temptation to compromise arises when the barrier is not an absolute barrier but a conditional one. Access to political power is available, on certain terms; sexual satisfaction is also available, in certain forms. What is required is simply a compromised witness to the order of creation. Not necessarily a very major compromise, perhaps. We may observe how conscientious people can strike some quite tough bargains with the world as they struggle to preserve the greatest measure of integrity compatible with securing the goods they desire. The fallen order of things often displays something of the grandeur and beauty of its created nature, and there is no reason why compromise should always be, as the cliché has it, 'squalid'. The point is simply that striking bargains with the world is not the *imitatio Christi*. Christ's followers are called to bear his cross, to 'mortify' those aspects of their own nature which are inclined to compromise 'upon the earth' (Col. 3:5, AV). They are called to accept exclusion from the created good as the necessary price of a true and unqualified witness to it.

Our initial response to the complaint that we do not allow a place for compromise must therefore be an unyielding one: there is no place for compromise – not, at least, in its primary and most obvious sense. We are not invited to strike bargains when we respond to the claim of the created good upon us; the price of our doing so is the loss of a clear knowledge of the good. This response is, however, open to some clarification. There are two features of moral deliberation to which the designation 'compromise' may be applied in a secondary sense (though it would be better to find another term.) These features are essential to moral thought, and so lend plausibility to the case for compromise in its primary sense.

(1) In moral deliberation we attempt to fit our action to the conditions in which we have to act. This is what has traditionally been called 'casuistry'. The general moral rules which we have learnt or formulated must be adapted to recognize the specificities which define the moral field more precisely. The situation in which we must act may quite probably include features which are in themselves deplorable and which impose unwelcome constraints upon our actions. Thus we may speak, in a secondary sense, of having to 'compromise' between the ideal and the actual. (This expression is still highly imprecise, since it is not a case of finding a *middle* way at all: the 'actual' does not constitute an opposite pole of attraction to the 'ideal'. It is a matter of finding the *right* qualification for one's general rule of action, which will recognize the *truth* about the circumstances in which one has to act. It is what we often, and more wisely, call 'realism' – though not in its technical philosophical sense.) It is an old and damaging confusion – recognized in Paul's earliest correspondence with the church at Corinth (1 Cor. 5:9–10) – to suppose that compromise in this secondary sense implies compromise in the primary sense, so that an uncompromising witness would seem to require an uncompromised world as its setting. Moral integrity is taken to imply a disinvolvement with the ambiguities of society, and so to be quite impracticable. Faithful witness is an abstract ideal, which can take no form in the world as it is; compromise, therefore, is the law of our being, and no-one, not even Jesus himself, can get by without striking bargains. But this is not what Christians have traditionally said about the moral witness of Jesus. It is precisely the mark of his *faithful* witness that it shines as light in the darkness, where it is needed. Faithfulness, when conceived on the model of his faithfulness, is a possibility in any situation, however desperate the context or limited the choices. Every moral decision will be a decision between faithfulness and compromise. And that is why all

that is implied in 'casuistry' – careful discernment of situations, discriminating case-by-case deliberation, *etc.* – is not to be dismissed as though it were a mere coming-to-terms with evil, for it is precisely what faithfulness requires. If decision were merely a matter of choosing between competing forms of compromise, there would be no reason to take the discernment of situations half so seriously.

(2) The forging of compromises does have a legitimate place in Christian moral thought when it addresses one special area of concern, namely the definition of norms for the conduct of public life. About this we shall have more to say later. When we discuss what we shall require of one another in our community life (even in the special community of the church), we cannot do other than fashion an oblique and indirect witness to the created order. The necessary privacy of many areas of obligation forbids us to know with clarity what is, and what is not, the cross that is laid by God upon another person; so that our social demand cannot cut as deeply upon any individual as does the immediate demand of the cross of Christ. There is a virtue of moderation which must be practised by legislators, as well as a virtue of realism. Some traditions of Christian moral thought have presented this political task as the central task of Christian ethics, conceiving of the church's moral teaching either as a kind of cultural pedagogy which shapes expectations and norms for society at large, or, more narrowly, as legislation for the special discipline and government of the community of faith. In such traditions, where ethics has chiefly to do with community norms, it is clear that compromise is of its essence. But devising norms for public life is only a subsidiary concern of Christian moral thought (though not an unimportant one). Its primary concern is existential, not legislative. And it has not done its work unless it has learnt that the cross of Christ may demand a self-denial which no social norms, not even those of the church, can demand. That moment of self-denial, when we prefer to forgo the created good which is our right rather than enjoy it on terms of compromise, is also a moment of knowledge, at which the good becomes clear and conspicuous to us as rarely ever besides.

Part Two

The subjective reality

5

Freedom and reality

Our argument up to this point has traced the way in which Christian moral thought must respond to objective reality – the reality, that is, of a world-order restored in Christ, the reality which the gospel declares. But a further task lies before us if we are to show that Christian ethics are evangelical ethics. For we cannot simply take it as read that the redemption of the world is in fact good news for us moral agents. Why should it not mean, after all, that our moral agency is now proved to be pointless and futile, since we are caught up in a restoration which has proceeded quite independently of us? Why should it not mean that God, having vindicated his new and perfect humanity in Jesus Christ, will be content to leave us old and unsatisfactory humans on one side? Or why should it not mean that such an act of kindness on God's part requires of us a superhuman effort in response, an effort in which we are thrown back entirely on our own resources, and to which it must be probable that our moral agency will not prove adequate? The answer to such doubts is the apostolic proclamation of the Holy Spirit. If ethics are to be evangelical, they must conform to this part of the apostles' message too. We have to speak of God at work within us, applying and confirming God's act in Christ for us. We have to show that the redeemed creation does not merely confront us moral agents, but includes us and enables us to participate in it. This is the point of the 'transition from the objective to the subjective mode' of which we spoke in chapter 1.

The heart of that inadequate approach to moral teaching which has gained the name 'Pelagianism' in the church (although not every form of it corresponds exactly to what Pelagius himself thought) is a misunder-

101

standing about divine initiative and human response. While wishing quite sincerely to emphasize the importance of the divine initiative, the reality of grace and the absolute dependence of man upon it, Pelagius supposed that the human response lay outside the sphere of that divine initiative, as an independently grounded reaction to it. The more emphatically the gracious deed of God was stressed, the more remarkable the initiative of grace was made to appear, so much the more awe-inspiring, in Pelagius' eyes, was the responsibility thrown upon man to respond appropriately. God does everything except infringe upon our freedom by taking over the response that we must make to him. The reply of Western Christianity to this view, a reply most influentially articulated by Augustine, is simple: there can never be a moment when the divine initiative pauses and waits, as it were in expectation, to see what man will do. Even man's 'response' is still God's initiative, and, so far from this undercutting the freedom of man, it is the only possible ground on which man can be free. 'God is at work in you,' says Saint Paul (Phil. 2:13), 'both to will and to work for his good pleasure.'

In using the words 'objective' and 'subjective' in a trinitarian context to differentiate the proper works of the Son and the Spirit, we follow a lead given by Karl Barth, though well aware (as he was) of the mistaken impression which this pair of terms can convey. They may remind us all too easily of the Idealist polarization of 'subjectivity' and 'objectivity', in which object and subject lose their primary relational sense – their concern with the *vis à vis* – and become overweighted with psychological and ontological implications. To speak of God as 'subject' in this tradition is not simply to regard him as the agent of some action, but to place him in the realm of Mind, Spirit or Personality, which is to be valued above the merely objective realm of Things. If our words are read in that way, we can hardly prevent the suggestion of an affinity between the psychological and the divine, thus losing sight of the difference between the Spirit and simple human inwardness. It is important, then, to spell out at the beginning what we intend by this reference to the 'subjective mode', and this can be done by way of two complementary assertions: first, that the Spirit makes the reality of redemption, distant from us in time, both *present* and *authoritative*; secondly, that he evokes our *free* response to this reality as moral agents. We will attempt to give a schematic outline of these complementary assertions directly; a fuller exploration of them will occupy us for the next four chapters.

(1) The Spirit makes the reality of redemption *present* to us. The restoration of created order is an event which lies in the past; its universal manifestation belongs to the future. Yet on these two points, the resurrection of Jesus Christ from the dead and his parousia, the whole of our life is made to depend even now, as each moment of it successively forms our present. We have not said

that the Spirit makes the timeless and transcendent God present to us. A theologian can certainly say that with a good conscience, and we may rejoice that it is true. But such an assertion can follow only from the New Testament's assertion that we are crucified and raised with Christ and reign with him in glory. The nearness of God to our present existence is always nearness 'in Christ'. A doctrine of the Spirit which would avoid the perils of Montanism will turn first to this 'in Christ'. But the events of Christ's death, resurrection and parousia are past and future to us. Any sense in which they can be said to happen now (in the disciple's *imitatio Christi*, in conversion or in the sacraments) must be secondary to the fact that they happened, and will happen, then. We speak of the Spirit when we make the transition from 'then' to 'now', when the remembered past and the unthinkable future become realities which shape our present. The work of the Holy Spirit defines an age – the age in which all times are immediately present to that time, the time of Christ.

We say further: the Spirit makes the reality of redemption *authoritative* to us; for authority is the mode in which this past and future reality is also present. There are other ways, immanent and non-authoritative, by which past and future events enter into the present and affect it. Events have consequences which endure, sometimes in the form of lasting institutions or pervasive habits of thought. Events can be anticipated, and excite us to action in expectancy and hope. But the redemptive moment, or moments, of Christ's passion and triumph act upon our present in quite another way. They are God's final deed, the *eschaton* in which history is given its meaning; and as such they stand equidistant from all moments of time and determine what the reality of each moment is. 'Authority' and 'reality' are inseparable aspects of the presence of God – a point to which we shall return at greater length in the next chapter.

Whatever our reservations about Kierkegaard's appeal to 'subjectivity', we can learn much from his concept of the believer's 'absolute contemporaneousness with Christ'. In the section entitled 'Come Hither!' in *Training in Christianity*, he begins with the reminder that the one who said 'Come unto me' lived eighteen hundred years ago in conditions of humiliation. Is he not now in glory? Yes, but heaven is not open to us. 'From the seat of his glory he has not spoken one word.' Therefore we encounter him, if at all, only through the conditions of his incarnation as an object of faith (pp. 26f.). Can we learn anything about Christ from history? Kierkegaard's negative answer is easily misunderstood, when it is made the servant of a quite different problematic, that of historical scepticism. By 'history' he tells us that he means 'world-history', the total course of events; and by 'learning about Christ' he means learning about *Christ, i.e.* as an object of faith. Christ does not belong immanently to the course of events; he is a paradox. We cannot infer from any possible course of events that a certain man was God. The 'consequences of Christ's life', by which Kierkegaard means especially the history of Christendom, prove nothing relevant (pp. 28–34). Hegel's world-historical individual is 'note-worthy' only because his life had 'noteworthy consequences', not in himself. 'But the fact that God lived here on earth as an individual man is infinitely noteworthy . . . How could it be noteworthy that God's life had noteworthy consequences?' (p. 34). The misfortune of a world-historical Christendom is that it has 'done away with Christianity' (p. 39), *i.e.* with faith, as encounter with the absolute. 'In relation to the absolute there is only one tense: the present.' But it is the unique character of *one* past event – the eschatological event, as we would say – that it can be present, and so part of 'reality' (which Kierkegaard defines narrowly as present reality). 'Every man can be contemporary only with the age in which he lives – and then with one thing more: with Christ's life on earth; for Christ's life on earth, sacred history, stands for itself alone outside history' (pp. 67f.).

The term 'authority' warns us that when redemption is present to us it does not encounter a vacuum. It exercises its authority over an existing reality. It encounters an apparent structure of order which is presented within the world, criticizing it and transforming it. It brings true reality to bear upon the appearances of reality which our world (that segment of the whole which shares our moment in history with us) presents to us. The effect of this is twofold: our world is judged, and it is recreated. The unreality of its existing coherence and continuity is exposed; and there is introduced a new series of events which present a truer coherence and continuity. There are within Christian moral thought a large number of pairs of contrasts which reflect, in one way or another, this double aspect of moral authority. Among the general moral concepts we see it in the distinction between the reflexive and the directive conscience, in the contrast of deontic and teleological ethics, and, most fundamentally, in the opposition of reason and will. In the specifically theological concepts we see it in the contrasts between repentance and moral learning, between justification and sanctification, and between conversion and instruction. The Holy Spirit brings God's act in Christ into critical opposition to the falsely structured reality in which we live. At the same time and through the same act he calls into existence a new and truer structure for existence. He gives substance to the renewed creation in Christ, giving it a historical embodiment in present human decisions and actions, so that it becomes partly visible even before its final manifestation. We speak of two *aspects* of the Spirit's work, not of two works. It is perilous to draw too sharp a line in particular items of experience between repentance and moral learning, between justification and sanctification, between conversion and instruction. When did we ever not have to repent while we learnt? When did obedience not go hand in hand with the need for forgiveness? When did we not find worldliness at the heart of the church we thought to instruct, and belief surprising us in the world we thought to convert? Yet the distinction is fundamental to our understanding. When the opposition of death and resurrection is collapsed, neither death nor resurrection remains. A moral authority which does not both judge and and recreate is not the authority of Christ, but a purely natural authority, to follow which is to be conformed to the world.

We sum up the first assertion by referring to the words of Jesus' farewell discourse in John 16:8–11: 'And when he [the Counsellor] comes, he will convince the world concerning sin and righteousness and judgment: concerning sin, because they do not believe in me; concerning righteousness, because I go to the Father, and you will see me no more; concerning judgment, because the ruler of this world is judged.'

The work of the Holy Spirit is presented here in three steps which correspond to three moments in the work of Christ: the crucifixion, the resurrection (with the ascension) and the parousia; these three are seen in turn as three judgments: the world's judgment on Christ (unbelief), the Father's judgment on Christ (exaltation), and Christ's judgment on the ruler of the world. Each of these three moments of judgment is included in the one act of God by which creation is redeemed and fulfilled. It is the Spirit's office to make them impinge immediately upon the reality which constitutes 'the world', to 'convince' it. The repudiation of Christ, as the Spirit performs his office, becomes *our* repudiation of him; his exaltation is the life that is offered to *us*; every decision that *we* make now takes on importance as a pre-echo of that final decision in which the false spirits reject, and are rejected by, God. Sin, righteousness and judgment become present and authoritative to us; they determine the meaning of the life that we are given to live, and we are made to participate in the redeeming work of God. This office the Holy Spirit performs 'when he comes'. Not in the age of Christ himself (that is, when the drama is still being played out), not in the course of sacred events which are enacted for us; but in *our* age, the age after Pentecost (as Saint Luke would present it), the age of Christ's exalted absence (in Saint John's conception), 'when he comes'. This age is the age of the secret presence of God, Father and Son, to the believer and the believing community (14:22–23), the age of the apostolic witness to Christ (15:27), of martyrdom (16:2), of eschatological expectation (16:13), of prayer (16:24). It is in this age that we need the divine ministry which makes a 'then' into a 'now'.

We have quoted the RSV translation of the Greek verb *elengxei*, 'he will convince'. The revisers of 1880 chose 'convict'; the NEB, with expansive prodigality, indulges itself in no fewer than four verbs, 'confute', 'convince', 'convict' and 'show'. What is meant is what used to be contained in the English verb 'convict', and is still, barely, contained in the noun 'conviction'. It means, to make someone recognize something in such a way that he is seen to have been at fault before. It is to bring about a discovery of truth which judges even as it enlightens. The Spirit's office of conviction, then, is a critical office, but is not an office of final judgment, or condemnation, but is set in a missiological context. The apostolic ministry, enabled by the Spirit, addresses the world, the world which God loved and sent his Son to save, and proclaims that its ruler is judged (*i.e.* finally), the spirit which has shaped its rebellion. But the world, in being 'convicted' of that judgment, is not judged finally, but has an opportunity to be the rebellious world no longer. Are we to contrast this missiological service of the Spirit with the ecclesiological service, of which we read a few sentences later (again, with special reference to the apostles' ministry), that 'he will guide you into all the truth' (16:13)? Only to the extent that the ministry to the world is typically critical, that to the church typically constructive. But it is always understood that criticism leads to reconstruction, conviction opens into guidance. Even at the moment of criticism, the moment of confrontation and illumination, it is not only sin, but also righteousness and judgment that are given as 'conviction'. There is already present in that moment the call to live life in a continuing sequence of decisions which will embody Christ's exalted life and anticipate his final triumph over this world's ruler.

(2) The Spirit evokes our *free* response as moral agents to the reality of redemption. This assertion makes it clear in what sense 'subject' and 'subjective', once the misleading Idealist implications have been set on one side, are the appropriate terms to use of the Holy Spirit's work. He confirms and restores us *as moral agents*, which is to say, *as the subjects of our actions*, not as divorced subjectivity which subsists in its own self-awareness. In confirming us as subjects, he teaches us how, within this age of eschatological judgment, we may act. To do this he does not take over our subjecthood; he enables us to realize it. In a sentence of critical importance for theological ethics Saint Paul wrote: 'God is at work in you, both to will and to work for his good pleasure' (Phil. 2:13). This sentence, too, may sometimes be misunderstood, as though the apostle were speaking of an absorption of man's work into God's by virtue of a qualitative inwardness. But the willing and the working (as the Greek syntax makes clearer than the English) are man's willing and working. Human willing and working are made possible by the divine work 'within', which brings the free human agency to expression. God is present to man-as-subject, God the Holy Spirit attesting God the Son and evoking human attestation of him in human will and deed.

Need we add, then, that the Holy Spirit's work is not restricted to individual human agents, and so goes beyond what is normally thought of as subjectivity? Communities, too, act as subjects; and if they are to act in such a way that the sin, righteousness and judgment manifest in Christ shapes their acts and attitudes, it will be only by the Holy Spirit's work. This is what makes the life of the church possible, both as a Catholic whole and in its many local manifestations, official and unofficial. The relationship of ecclesiology to the doctrine of the Holy Spirit is too well established to need any elaboration here. We need only voice a caution against a misunderstanding, analogous to those Idealist misunderstandings which we have rejected, which treats the Holy Spirit as a kind of global personality or communal subjectivity into which the several subjectivities of the members are taken up. It is no more acceptable to speak of the church as possessing a semi-divine subjectivity than it is to speak of an individual believer doing so. There are, as we know, conceptual difficulties in the idea of a communal agency; but the doctrine of the Holy Spirit is not to be regarded as a short cut to solving them. If communities can be agents and subjects (though without being persons, or possessing personality), then they are human agents, just as much as individual agents are. The Spirit enables this agency in the case of the church and its dependent communities just as he does in the case of believing individuals. He is not ambiguously 'I' and 'Thou' to the church, but always 'Thou' to it, as it is to him. He addresses it, 'Set aside for me Paul and Silas', and it addresses him, 'Come, Holy Ghost, our souls inspire!'

The effect of the Holy Spirit's presence to man-as-subject, individual or communal, is *freedom*. It is this freedom that makes Christian ethics meaningful, and indeed demands it. For freedom is the character of one who participates in the order of creation by knowledge and action. That man is free implies that he can know and act; thus moral enquiry is a meaningful undertaking for him. The proclamation that he is *set* free carries with it a further implication, that man's freedom has been, and so can be, alienated. Moral enquiry is therefore demanded in the face of this dangerous possibility.

In saying that someone is free, we are saying something about the person himself and not about his circumstances. Freedom is 'potency' rather than 'possibility'. External constraints may vastly limit our possibilities without touching our 'freedom' in this sense. Nothing could be more misleading than the popular philosophy that freedom is constituted by the absence of limits. There is, to be sure, a truth which it intends to recognize, which is that the 'potency' of freedom requires 'possibility' as its object. For freedom is exercised in the cancellation of all possibilities in a given situation by the decision to actualize one of them; if there were no possibilities, there could be no room for freedom. Nevertheless, there do not have to be many. Even in deciding whether we will accept an inevitable situation cheerfully or resentfully, we exercise our freedom in choosing between alternative possibilities of conduct. Where the popular philosophy becomes so misleading is in its suggestion that we can maximize freedom by multiplying the number of possibilities open to us. For if possibilities are to be meaningful for free choice, they must be well-defined by structures of limit. The indefinite multiplication of options can only have the effect of taking the determination of the future out of the competence of choice, and so out of the category of meaningful possibility for freedom. For example, a decision to marry depends upon marriage becoming possible within the limiting structure of one's existing relationships. If that limiting structure were withdrawn, and one had all the conceivable partners in the world immediately available, one could not freely choose to marry any of them. The empty space for freedom must be defined if one is to move into it. Furthermore, the decision to marry itself cancels out both marriage and singleness *as possibilities*, by actualizing marriage as a new limit to which one has bound oneself. The empty space must be cancelled when one does move into it. Decision depends upon existing limits and imposes new ones. Limit is the very material with which freedom works. When the Holy Spirit makes a person free, that freedom is immediately demonstrated in self-binding to the service of others: 'You were called to freedom . . . In love be one another's slaves!' (Gal. 5:13*).

But although any choice which cancels out possibilities by actualizing one of them is a 'free' choice, it is not a matter of indifference for the exercise of freedom which possibilities one will choose to actualize. Certain existentialist thinkers, following the ancient Stoics, have commended suicide as the action which most supremely vindicates man's inalienable freedom in the face of constraining circumstances. Indeed suicide may be a free act, but it is not an act that affirms freedom. For freedom as there exercised encompasses its own annihilation, not in the necessary cancellation of the empty space of possibility by the creation of new limit, but in the destructive and defiant attack upon the nature of the free agent himself, who is permitted thereafter to make no more free choices. For although human freedom operates by the cancellation of possibilities, it is ordered to its own continued exercise. It is not merely a means to an end, which can then disappear. The end of man itself, described from the point of view of man's functioning, can be called 'perfect liberty'. Freedom is a teleological structure, in which freedom-given serves freedom-to-be-achieved. '*For* freedom Christ has set us free,' says Saint Paul; 'stand fast therefore, and do not submit again to a yoke of slavery' (Gal. 5:1). This further submission to slavery would, of course, be the result of a false exercise of freedom: 'do not use your freedom as an opportunity for the flesh' (5:13). Freedom can alienate itself and produce unfreedom. This is why the gospel speaks of the 'bondage' of sin and of freedom 'restored' by the Holy Spirit's indwelling, bringing man into union with the free humanity of the risen Christ.

The alienation of human freedom does not mean that mankind can be subject to necessity in the same way that creatures not originally created for freedom are subject to necessity. Man does not become like a stone or a plant. We might wish to say that fallen man is 'unfree' in a more radical sense than stones or plants which have never alienated a freedom that they once possessed; but we would have to say, too, that he can never be simply *without* freedom as they are without freedom. Created to exercise free choice, mankind is bound to the terms of creation and remains, even in a state of alienated freedom, a race of free agents. Nevertheless, fallen man does not live freely; for, as a free agent, he is bound to the choices he has made for unfreedom. His bondage, quite unlike the passivity of a tree or a stone, is brought upon him by his own free refusal of certain possibilities which would have allowed him the continued exercise of his freedom. Unfreedom, for him, is a galling and condemning state of affairs.

What, then, are these possibilities which he refused? They are the possibilities of recognizing and rejoicing in the objective reality of the good. The sin by which man has bound himself is the determination to live fantastically, in pursuit of unreality. But freedom can be exercised only in relation to real possibility. Fallen man remains, of course, a being who goes through the motions of free decision, but he lacks that relation to the realities of the universe which could make such decisions effective for 'perfect liberty'. Clearly the restoring of man's freedom must involve his awakening once again to the reality of God's creation as it is revealed in Christ. The work of the Spirit as 'witness' to the objective deed of God in Christ, and his work as 'life-giver' who restores freedom and power to mankind enthralled, are not two distinct works but one. For man's thrall is precisely that he has lost touch with reality.

Our two assertions, then, bring us to a common point. The *authority* of redemption lies in its power to determine the present reality of the world with which we have to do. Our *freedom* as agents depends upon our acting in accord with reality. *Reality* is the point on which both freedom and authority rest, and at which they complement each other. When we speak, then, of the 'subjective reality' from which Christian ethics proceeds, we are speaking of this point: the bearing of reality upon the acting subject, its presence to him as authority and his fulfilment within it as a free agent. The 'subjective reality' is, as is by now obvious, no different reality from the 'objective reality'. It is the one reality, the reality of a world redeemed, which is both apart from us (in Christ once for all) and immediately engages us (through the Spirit here and now). Our present task is to explore this active engagement with reality, which we continue to do through its complementary aspects as freedom and authority; in this chapter we continue with some further exploration of the alienation of freedom.

Alienation and conversion

Free human engagement in the ordered reality which God has

made and restored is described by Saint Paul in a single Greek word, *hypakoē* (Rom. 1:5; 6:16). It is difficult to find a satisfactory translation for it. It means 'obedience', which is a practical idea; but its derivation from the noun *akoē*, 'hearing', is still very much alive in Paul's mind, which requires that a cognitive sense also be understood. Perhaps the best we can manage is 'attentiveness'. Paul speaks of the 'attentiveness of faith', and in that phrase is contained the whole of our response to God, from hearing, understanding and assenting, to willing and acting. But James, in a well-known passage, raises an issue about this response which Paul's phrase does not envisage: 'Be doers of the word, and not hearers only, deceiving yourselves' (Jas. 1:22). Here there arises the thought that *hypakoē* may be split into two distinct elements, 'hearing' and 'doing'. This thought arises out of the experience of sin, which is a failure of *hypakoē*; it fails precisely when its two elements are not co-ordinated, when hearing is not doing. What in the operation of divine grace is one, falls into two parts in human sin.

The celebrated controversy (which is now generally admitted to be no controversy at all) between Paul and James, on the question of whether man is saved by faith alone or by faith and works, resolves itself in this way. James is conscious of the possible fissuring of man's response to the gospel into a mere intellectual assent apart from existential commitment (2:14–26). Paul, on the other hand, never advocated a mere intellectual assent: his contrast between 'hearing with faith' and 'works of the law' was intended to make quite a different point (Gal. 3:2). The phrase *akoē pisteōs* (Gal. 3:2,5) should be interpreted in the light of *hypakoē pisteōs* at Romans 1:5; 16:26 (*contra* W. F. Arndt, F. W. Gingrich, *A Greek-English Lexicon of the New Testament*, 4th ed., *s.v. akoē* 2b). Paul's 'faith' is always the unified response of mind and will, 'faith working through love' (Gal. 5:6). Correspondingly, the cognitive content of *hypakoē* should not be ignored: it appears clearly enough in the phrase 'obedience (or attentiveness) to the truth' (*hypakoē tēs alētheias*) at 1 Peter 1:22.

Saint Augustine's interpretation of the Holy Trinity, built on the analogy of the human mind in its relationship to truth, depends upon the point which is here being made. Knowing and willing must be entirely proportionate and coextensive, to establish the consubstantiality of the Son and the Spirit and the procession of the Spirit from the Son. Without passing judgment on the adequacy of this analogy for the doctrine of the Trinity, nor upon the understanding of the *imago Dei* which it implies, we can learn from the psychology simply in its own right. The fallen and corrupted human mind, thinks Augustine, is the mind which knows something without loving it, or without loving it proportionately; which loves something without knowing it sufficiently to justify its love; which understands without willing, and wills without understanding; but such conditions only betray the fact of the mind's disorder. The mind in perfect possession of the truth loves as it understands and understands as it loves. Reason and will are at one. (See especially the ninth book of *De Trinitate*.)

We start at this point in order to emphasize that the problem of the relation of 'reason and will', as it has come to be thought of in Western moral philosophy, springs out of a malfunction of the moral life and does not belong within its normative morphology. The disjunction of hearing and doing, or of reason and will, is sin. It is the failure of man to make the response that is appropriate to him as a free rational agent. In such a failure man himself seems to disintegrate into dissociated powers, into a rational self on the one hand, which has a cognitive relation to reality, and a voluntative self on the other, which consists of affections, emotions and decisions. This is the psychological aspect of the alienation of freedom. In the effective operation of the Spirit, to know is once again to will, or, to speak more theologically, to believe is to love. That is why we can speak of the work of the Spirit as witness and life-giver, his ministry to the reason and to the affections, as complementary aspects of one work and not as two.

The possibility and the limits of this disintegration are represented for Western culture in Milton's portrayal of Satan in *Paradise Lost*. Satan's absolute and irreparable rejection of God becomes, in Milton's treatment, a representation of what man is ultimately capable of doing – not within the confines of time, of course, but eschatologically. As such Milton's portrayal interprets the ultimate significance of sin. The famous line which Milton puts on Satan's lips, 'Evil, be thou my good!' perfectly captures the double movement of the soul which is the essence of the Satanic gesture: in the first place, the convulsive turning of the will to evil in place of the good which is its natural orientation; in the second place the veiling of the reality of evil under the guise of good. The moment of brilliant light which enables Satan to address evil as evil, even while he embraces it, is replaced by the darkness in which the evil is addressed and embraced as good. In the will's convulsive embracing of evil the reason must find a point of rest. It cannot rest in the reality of the chaos which the will has embraced, but must create for itself a new order, a fantastic order without objective reality or substance, formed around the new orientation of the will, a parodistic imitation of reality which it calls 'my' good. Thus reason and will part company only for an instant of self-destroying freedom, in which Satan looks to evil and says, 'Be thou . . .!' From then on reason is enslaved to this new orientation of the subject, obligated to form representations which will justify it.

The movements of the soul which are seen in the myth in their eschatological finality are, of course, entirely familiar features of moral experience. There is, on the one hand, the experience of yielding to temptation: knowing some course of action to be right, the agent proceeds, conscious of guilt, freely to do the opposite. 'The man who knows the good he ought to do and does not do it is a sinner' (Jas. 4:17. NEB). This is the movement which moral philosophy since Aristotle has analysed as 'incontinence' (*akrasia*), the paradoxical triumph of the appetite over reason. On the other hand there is what we call the 'rationalization' of our decisions, in which we revise our moral convictions to justify our past performance. There can be, of course, good reasons to refine and correct moral opinions in the light of experience; so that not every modification of an agent's moral principles is rationalization in the sense that we condemn it. But human beings do rationalize; the reason and the will, once they have been torn apart in the moment of yielding to temptation, demand to be reconciled. The consciousness of having acted irrationally must be assuaged, even at the cost of reason's grasp on reality. And so it is that, in the free exercise of the will to sin, man deprives himself of his freedom, for he cuts off his cognitive access to the created order. He cuts himself off from the earth on which he must have a purchase if his agency is to amount to more than a flailing of limbs.

The redemptive work of the Holy Spirit involves the restoration of our access to reality. But this restoration cannot be wrought upon the reason alone, in isolated separation from the will. That would be merely to recreate the dividedness of will and reason which accompanied the moment of temptation. In fact, since man does not, within the co-ordinates of time, effect the two movements of his rebellion with the eschatological completeness of Satan, dividedness continues to be part of his experience. He lives in guilt, which may, perhaps, be a reassuring sign that he has not yet entirely sold his soul to the devil, or may, alternatively, be a terrible anticipation of divine judgment, but is certainly not in itself a work of grace. That work must involve also a detachment of the will from its self-chosen orientation; man must be freed to cease willing his own past. But as willing his own past is, in itself, a natural thing to do, a guarantee of the coherence and integrity in our purpose that is indispensable to our fulfilment as moral beings, that 'freedom' is, in one sense, death. If we cease to reinforce the fundamental choices of our past with the continuing affirmation of our will, we abandon altogether that 'I' which we were in the way of realizing; it becomes to us the 'old man' who, as Saint Paul says, is crucified with Christ. Repentance cannot be the mere realignment of a will that retains a fundamental continuity with its past; it involves a moment of self-annihilation.

But neither can this self-annihilation of will take place in isolation from the cognitive realm. If it did, it would not be a repudiation of the arbitrariness of its own past convulsion. It would merely add a new convulsion, equally arbitrary, to the old. If the will merely turns in repudiation upon its own past, as earlier it turned against the objective order, it is no more than a continuation of the pattern of wanton self-assertiveness. Sin has its own vain regrets, its own self-hatred, every bit as wilful as self-confidence

112

and pride. The systematic negation of reality can lead to a self-negation which has nothing to do with repentance as Christians know it. To repudiate arbitrariness, we must regain contact with that which is not arbitrary. Repentance must go hand in hand with faith, which is the proper stance of reason when it attends to an object which it cannot transcend or contain. It is a form of cognition, though a unique form as its object is unique. And as the knowledge of good, whether created or uncreated, cannot be had without commitment, it is a form of cognition which depends in its turn upon the reorientation of the will, as the reorientation of the will depends upon it. Conversion, then, is not something in which either the will or the reason has a leverage upon the other, by virtue of a residual connection which either can claim with objective good. It is an event in which reason and will together are turned from arbitrariness to reality, an event which is 'miraculous' in that there are no sufficient grounds for it, whether rational or voluntative, within the subject himself. Repentance and faith do not come in that order as a matter of logical necessity; neither is it a logically necessary sequence when we reverse the order and speak of 'faith working through love'.

Can there be repentance without faith? The question is put with extraordinary poignancy at the conclusion of Thomas Mann's great novel *Doctor Faustus*, as the first-person narrator draws together his reflections on the fate of the hero, the composer Leverkühn, and his anguish over the hell into which Nazi Germany has sold itself. Leverkühn's last work, the cantata 'Faustus' Lament', rejects, we are told, the thought of being saved, 'not only out of formal loyalty to the pact with the devil and because it is "too late", but because with his whole soul he despises the positivism of the world for which one would save him, the lie of its godliness' (p. 490). And yet 'he dies as a bad and as a good Christian: a good one by the power of his repentance, and because in his heart he hopes for mercy on his soul; a bad one in so far as . . . the Devil will and must have his body' (p. 487). What this means for Germany appears in the last paragraph of the book (p. 510): 'Germany, the hectic on her cheek, was reeling then at the height of her dissolute triumphs, about to gain the whole world by virtue of the one pact she was minded to keep, which she had signed with her blood. Today, clung round by demons, a hand over one eye, with the other staring down into horrors, down she flings from despair to despair. When will she reach the bottom of the abyss? When out of uttermost hopelessness – a miracle beyond the power of belief – will the light of hope dawn?'

The question which Mann's novel poses for us can be understood in two ways. In the first place it can be taken as a problem arising entirely within unbelief: how is one to repent who has nothing to believe in? How can there be rebirth without a gospel? If Mann thought that any currently proclaimed gospel was adequate to deal with the self-invoked damnation of his people, he was not acknowledging the fact. His was the problem of religious man with nothing really certain to believe in but damnation;

all else was 'the positivism of the world for which one would save him, the lie of its godliness'. From this point of view the hope for mercy was nothing but the self-evidently vain hope of the truly damned; the plight was nothing other than the plight of there being no divine mercy. But behind this problem arising within unbelief we can recognize a different problem, which is rather a question put to faith itself: how can true faith be characterized except as faith in miracle, absolutely beyond looking for or counting on, miracle that snatches man out of the very reality of hell itself? Faith that is faith indeed and not merely prudentially pious calculation cannot dare to think itself or propose itself or describe itself for fear of falsity. It can only be observed as the possibility of miracle reflected through the mirror of the impossibility of human self-redemption. 'No, this dark tone-poem permits up to the very end no consolation, appeasement, transfiguration. But take our artist paradox: grant that expressiveness – expression as lament – is the issue of the whole construction: then may we not parallel it with another, a religious one, and say too (though only in the lowest whisper) that out of the sheerly irremediable hope might germinate? It would be but a hope beyond hopelessness, the transcendence of despair – not betrayal to her, but the miracle that passes belief' (p. 491). Such hope in sheer miracle (which dare not call itself, in the stricken silence, faith in the resurrection) is nevertheless not hope that is quite apart from faith.

Conscience and autonomy

The consciousness of guilt, in which our moral reason disapproves of what we are, nevertheless, freely willing to do, offers a paradigm of how reason and will can, in the absurdity of sin, be torn apart. This characterization, however, is only a schematic one. Guilt is also, as Saint Paul describes it in Romans 7, a dividedness of the will against itself, in which our true affections, as well as our judgment, are offended by the 'other law within [our] members'. Modern thinking about the guilty conscience has stressed its emotional component as self-repudiation, where the ancients stressed its rational component as self-criticism; both interpretations have some justice, such is the complexity of the phenomenon. The word 'conscience' comes from the Graeco-Roman world, where it meant 'self-consciousness', especially that uneasy awareness that one has of oneself when one knows one has done something wrong. Primarily with this meaning it was introduced into the New Testament, and so into Christian moral thinking, by Saint Paul. But in medieval and modern usage it has acquired a new sense, and has come to be used not only for the guilty moment of self-awareness but for the whole faculty of moral understanding and self-direction. This shift in meaning marks an important, and largely damaging, development in moral psychology, in which the separation of reason and will comes to be treated as normative. This in turn generates a conception of freedom as autonomy, the agent's independence of reality.

In the ancient world the words *syneidēsis* (in Greek) and *conscientia* (in Latin) meant 'consciousness', and especially a consciousness in which two or more people shared (*cf.* 1 Cor. 10:29, which should perhaps be translated: 'I do not mean your own self-consciousness, but the consciousness which you share with the other man'). More narrowly they mean consciousness of oneself, usually in the experience of guilt, which the ancients liked to portray dramatically as having a secret witness to all one's actions. When the ancient world spoke (as in the much-quoted line attributed to Menander) of conscience as 'a god to all of us', it had in mind not a legislative deity but an avenging one, like the Furies in classical myth. From this point the meaning of the word broadened out, as moral self-consciousness became a general psychological category for the seat of moral agency in the soul. This last development is especially marked in Latin, where *conscientia* became a synonym for 'heart'. In the New Testament this complete range of meaning is represented, so that there is no one English word which can do duty for *syneidēsis* every time it appears there. (See C. A. Pierce, *Conscience in the New Testament*, whose general conclusions are secure, though his detailed exegesis of texts is not always satisfactory.)

But nowhere in the New Testament (nor indeed in the classical world as a whole until a later period) does *syneidēsis* mean a faculty of *moral direction*. Later moral theology (followed by some more recent biblical studies) was accustomed to read this idea back upon texts which did not contain it, and especially upon Paul's two discussions of the morality of eating meat sacrificed to pagan deities (1 Cor. 8 and 10; Rom. 14). These two discussions, we must note, are somewhat divergent in their emphasis. The later discussion (Rom. 14), conducted without any use of the word *syneidēsis*, is altogether simpler, focusing clearly upon the need for faith in any doubtful or controversial action. 'He who has doubts is condemned, if he eats, because he does not act from faith' (Rom. 14:23). It is a warning against what we might call 'inauthentic' action, done under community pressure. A sense of conviction is a necessary condition (though Paul would hardly have thought it a sufficient condition) for any action to be acceptable to God. The argument in 1 Corinthians is more complex, and is directed to a different point: the peril of the weak believer who, by 'habituation to the idol', is likely to eat sacrificed meats with actual idolatrous intent. 'If someone sees you, the enlightened one, present in an idol's temple, will not his *syneidēsis*, since he is weak, be fortified to eat of the sacrifice?' (1 Cor. 8:10*). It is wrong to read this as though it were simply an anticipation of the Romans argument, warning against inauthentic decisions accompanied by scrupulous doubts. Paul is rather concerned with the *consciousness* which is 'habituated to the idol'; that is to say, the weak brother is really superstitious, and cannot help taking such beings seriously, so that if he became involved in a pagan feast he would approach it 'as an idol-sacrifice', *i.e.* with an idolatrous mind.

The idea of a directive conscience emerges clearly only with the later Greek fathers, where it is a development of speculations about natural law. Chrysostom (*De statuis* 12,13) speaks of conscience as making knowledge of good and evil 'self-taught'; it 'rings in the ears, teaches and instructs'; it is the depository of the law, which is therefore already familiar to us when we hear Christ's teachings; it 'suggests what ought to be done'.

This is to think about conscience in a new and very different way. Yet it is still left for medieval thinkers to take the decisive step which shapes the modern conception of conscience: to identify it with the power of moral reason as such.

When conscience becomes a category for all moral understanding, we may suspect that dividedness has come to be seen as the natural condition of moral knowledge. Why should this be? It arises on the one hand from the characteristic medieval concern to ensure the freedom of the moral agent. Freedom is associated with the will. The will, therefore, comes to be thought of as the ontological ground of personal agency, the 'real me' who is the subject of all my acts. For reason, it appears, is bound to objective reality, and therefore cannot be free as moral agents are free. It arises on the other hand from the classical interest in the forcefulness of conscience, its power to impose tortures upon the soul, which derives in fact from its emotional components but was widely interpreted as evidence of the natural authority of reason. Such an interpretation reinforces the tendency to see reason, together with the external world, as 'not-I', distinct from and set over against the will which is the seat of my personal agency. The perceptions of reason thus come to be placed among the *circumstances* of the subject's agency. From the concern to vindicate freedom, then, and the concern to exalt the inherent authority of reason, there flow the objectification of reason and its alienation from the acting subject. The psyche is fragmented. The subject is no longer a reasoning-willing subject, but a will which has at its disposal the services of a reason; while the reason exercises an authority over the subject's activity which should properly belong only to external reality. Thus arises in the West a moral psychology in constant oscillation between rationalism and voluntarism, all the time unable to establish a satisfactory relation between the agent and the real world.

This conception may already be detected behind an important discussion in Thomas Aquinas (who, anxious as always to qualify prevailing voluntarist conceptions, is unethusiastic about it). When he asks himself two questions, 'whether an errant conscience creates an obligation' and 'whether an errant conscience constitutes an excuse', we can see that he is confronting an idea of moral agency in which the conscience (or reason) stands over against the moral subject, either as an external authority which imposes obligations upon him or as an unfortunate circumstance which excuses him from blame. The question of a mistaken conscience is understood by analogy with the misguided commands of a ruler or with the accidental weakness of a faculty such as sight or hearing. Thus the will alone is the true moral subject who is 'obliged' or 'excused'. In answering these questions Thomas does his best to undo the damage done by the way they have been put. He reminds us that the will is incapable of doing any thinking on its own apart from the reason; he insists that every act of will apart from reason is disruptive of moral agency; and he recalls that there is such a thing as culpable error of the reason. But the way the questions have been framed make it too hard for him. Once the issue has been conceived in terms of the conscience's 'obliging' or 'excusing', the objectification of reason is complete.

The key questions of *Summa Theologiae* are II-I.19.5 and 6: *utrum ratio errans obliget* and *utrum voluntas concordans rationi erranti sit bona.* We may note that he immediately rephrases the questions in terms of conscience, treating *ratio* and *conscientia* as synonymous for the purposes of this discussion. The first question is answered positively, though not without a certain evasiveness. Rather than state outright that one is obliged to follow an errant reason, he converts the question into another form which is said to be equivalent: *utrum voluntas discordans a ratione errante sit mala*, 'whether an act of will is bad when it goes against a mistaken reason'. To this he can answer 'yes' directly. The theory that it is bad for the will to be at variance with an errant reason only in matters of indifference is answered by the wise observation that the will has no independent knowledge of right and wrong. It is absurd to think of the will as a subject which can weigh the dictates of the reason against other considerations and find them wanting: 'If one knew that the dictates of human reason ran contrary to God's precept . . . one's reason would not be entirely in error.' The second question is phrased in the form 'whether an act of will is good when it follows a mistaken reason', and then converted back into the original form, 'whether an errant conscience constitutes an excuse'. To this Aquinas will not say 'yes'. Certainly, there is such a thing as ignorance which is in no respect voluntary, and a conscience affected by such ignorance must plainly be followed. But there is ignorance, as Aristotle taught, which is 'indirectly voluntary', such as 'ignorance of the law of God which one is bound to know' (*cf. Nicomachean Ethics* 1113 b – 1114 a), and this does not serve to excuse a wrong act. 'It is possible to go back on the error, since the ignorance is vincible and voluntary.'

And so Thomas Aquinas implies that if you have a mistaken conscience, anything your will does will be sinful. It is possible to see in this paradoxical conclusion simply a cautious reluctance to draw the obvious conclusions from the way the question has been argued. Thus Eric D'Arcy (*Conscience and its Right to Freedom*) argues that Thomas' successive discussions of the issue show him edging nearer and nearer to the view that ignorance is culpable only if it is voluntary; yet he will not quite let go of the classical idea that ignorance of certain things is culpable in itself. Thus he is almost a modern, wanting only the courage to carry through the separation of reason and will to its necessary conclusion, which, for D'Arcy, is the rationalist rather than the voluntarist conclusion, namely the unquestionable authority of the subjective moral reason. And indeed Thomas has opened himself to this interpretation. He has said that 'the principle of good and evil in human acts derives from the act of the will . . . the end of the act is the object of the will and not of the other faculties'

117

(19.2). He has identified the 'inner act' with an act of the will (18.6). Yet perhaps it may be truer, as well as more charitable, to suggest that Thomas understood his paradox as an indirect challenge to the separation of reason and will which was implicit in the form of the question. In his discussion of how acts are 'commanded', we may observe, he refused to separate the will and the reason as originators of action (17.1); and he maintained that the object of any act of will must be presented to it by the reason (19.3). Furthermore, in his earlier discussion of conscience (I.79.12 and 13) he was most unready to reify the conscience (which he thought of, dividing it into two parts in the mediaeval way, as habit and act), and he well understood that to speak of conscience 'binding' was to use a metaphorical expression which actually referred to something that the agent himself does in applying his knowledge to his action.

Without any of the caution that Thomas displayed, moralists of the seventeenth and eighteenth centuries simply gloried in the absolute authority with which conscience, displaying, as they thought, its rational character as well as its divine institution, presided over the vacillations of the will and the ambiguities of judgment. It was, in Butler's famous words, that 'superior principle ... which distinguishes between the internal principles of (the) heart ... which, without being consulted, without being advised with, magisterially exerts itself ... and which, if not forcibly stopped, naturally and always of course goes on to anticipate a higher and more effectual sentence' (*Sermons* 2). If anyone was tempted to chafe under the rule of this guide which had been assigned him by the author of his nature, he was told simply: 'That your conscience approves of and attests to such a course of action is itself an obligation' (3). Moralists of this tradition were, in effect, setting up conscience as an arbitrary tyrant, as was evidenced by the copious observations on conscientious disorder which interested pastoral writers such as Jeremy Taylor. The tribute that had too often to be paid to the categorical authority of subjective moral reason was the paralysis of indecision or the frenzy of exaggerated scruple.

The eighteenth-century reaction to this, anticipating the emergence of voluntarism as the dominant force in modern moral philosophy, was to deny the competence of reason to pass moral judgments and to attribute them instead to 'affection' or 'sentiment'. 'Morality', as Hume said, 'is more properly felt than judg'd of' (*Treatise of Human Nature* III.1.2). Here first arose the modern presumption that strong conscientious conviction is emotional rather than rational in its source. For to suppose any one feeling rather than another uniquely authorized by reason was, this school of thought maintained, to fall victim to an illusion. Moral judgments could not be 'reasonable' or 'unreasonable' in the ordinary sense, since they did not deal in claims of truth and falsehood. By appealing to the affections in this way these thinkers hoped to reassert freedom of moral agency against a conception of moral reason which had become oppressive. In so doing they opened up the 'fact-value distinction' which was to be of such weighty importance for modern thought. With no chain of reason (by which was meant *deductive* reason) to connect factual judgment with practical decision, the agent was left to value things on his own responsibility, without the world to help him.

But that meant that he was thrown back on a sheer act of will. Modern voluntarism, with its ponderous talk of responsibility and of making the world by our decisions, has a very different sound from the early attempts to free moral agency from the constraints of reason, but it is their natural outcome. For if it were left simply in the sphere of feeling, morality would appear to be nothing more than a spontaneity of mood and emotion. What distinguishes moral attitudes from mere impulse, and gives them a higher claim to our respect, is precisely that they are not spontaneous but deliberated. Yet how can there be deliberation without a train of reason? The modern substitute for moral deliberation in the traditional sense (*i.e.* the attempt to bring action into conformity with the good) is a kind of extended and meditative foresight which accompanies decision and transforms it into a solemn act of will. The 'responsible' agent is the one who, while still taking his decision for no objective reason, has nevertheless peered anxiously into its likely consequences and implications and, as we say, 'knows what he is doing' – which, after all, is the only thing that there is left for him to know!

It is the most curious feature about the separation of reason and will in Western thought that each, as it is cut off from the other, takes on the characteristics of the other. The rationalists' conscience 'commands', while the voluntarists' moral sentiment is forced to learn to think. In Kant's profound distillation of the modern ethos we see how voluntarism and rationalism can become, in effect, indistinguishable, while the Western programme of agent-autonomy is carried to its height. Kant's 'rational will' derives from reason its ability to think generically and to respect universal moral laws, and from will its independence from all laws that it has not legislated for itself. It binds itself to universal principles, but without acknowledging any indebtedness to external reality. Its rationality lies in its adherence to a purely formal order. In satisfying the champions of conscience and the champions of freedom simultaneously, it shows the extent to which the aspirations of both parties were the same. Each had it in mind to vindicate freedom as autonomy, that is to say, in terms of an authority for action which belonged entirely to the moral agent himself and was not derived from external reality.

It was exactly this project which lay behind the elaboration of the consciousness of guilt to become an all-embracing principle of

119

moral understanding. Conscience, it seemed, was a power within the soul which could generate its own forceful moral judgments without any dependence upon the world outside. This other-worldly self-sufficiency was in truth never more than an illusion created by the memory of past perceptions of moral order; the forcefulness, while not an illusion, was due to emotional rather than rational factors. The project was misconceived from the beginning. Moral freedom can never be established on a basis of self-sufficiency and independence of the world. Freedom, if it is freedom to act *within* the world, must itself be *of* the world. Man's status as agent is part and parcel of his created being in the world, and his acts depend for their significance on their context in the world's history. Man has, therefore, nothing to fear from the world-order within which and into which he acts. He has only to fear being cut off from it. For God has given him his freedom at the same time as he has given him a world in which to be free.

We return, then, to the presence of external reality as the essential condition for the exercise of freedom. Reason has its importance only as the agent's means of purchase upon reality, and not in itself: the authority attributed to reason is more properly understood to belong to reality. We speak of 'authority'. The real world *authorizes* man's agency in general by being the context of its exercise, and his particular acts by being the context in which they have a point. Our next task is to explore this notion of authority further, and to show how it is the appropriate conception by which to understand the presence of reality to the agent's freedom.

6

Authority

We have promised to speak of how the Holy Spirit makes the reality of redemption (that is, of Jesus Christ) authoritative to us. That small segment of reality, elect and chosen of God, shapes all the reality that we encounter, so that to be in touch with reality in any form we have to be in touch with that reality. We ought, therefore, from a formal point of view, to proceed immediately to that central focus of our discussion; and whatever remained to be said about other authorities, we ought to say it afterwards in the light of what had first been said about the authority of Christ. I am proposing, however, to take a less rigorous course. It will, I hope, make for an easier exposition when we discuss Christ's authority in the next chapter, if we have first said something about the question of authority in general and more specifically about divine authority. For the concept of authority with which we shall be dealing is not exactly that in modern intellectual currency, so that it is advisable to clarify it, as best we can, directly.

A typical modern use of the term 'authority' may be quoted from John Finnis (*Natural Law and Natural Rights*, p. 234): 'A person treats something as authoritative, when he treats it as . . . a reason for judging or acting in the absence of understood reasons, or for disregarding at least *some* reasons which are understood and relevant.' Overlooking the hint of nominalism in the way the definition is formulated, we may accept this as a serviceable account of one *kind* of authority, the only kind, perhaps, that a legal or political theorist needs to interest himself in. *Political* authority may very well be thought of as a reason for acting without reasons; but it is not the only kind of authority there is, and should not be taken as the typical case. When we come to speak

121

of the authority of God, whether in itself or mediated through the authority of Christ, we are speaking of a kind of authority for which political command offers only a partial and imperfect model. And because the modern age has tended to construe all authority as political authority, the notion of divine authority has become increasingly puzzling to it, though there are other kinds of authority familiar to us in experience which could provide complementary analogies.

def'n

Authority is the objective correlate of freedom. It is what we encounter in the world which makes it meaningful for us to act. An authority, we may say, is something which, by virtue of its kind, constitutes an immediate and sufficient ground for acting. If someone listens to music, joins a club, or reads philosophy, his action requires no explanation. Beauty, community and truth are sufficient grounds for action in themselves. They make action undertaken in relation to them immediately intelligible. If there were nothing in the world which invited our action, if all that freedom could achieve was an irruption into a system that was closed against it, then the very existence of free agency would become problematic. This is the dilemma that is recognized by determinist philosophies. But its solution is not to doubt the reality of free agency, but to describe the world in such a way that freedom can be seen to have a place within it. And since freedom is not indeterminacy or randomness but purposive action, that means describing the world as a place in which actions may have ends, that is to say, as a teleological system.

Authority is one aspect of the teleological structure of the universe. It is not the whole of it, since there are ends which are not ends-of-action, and not every end-of-action is an authority. There are subjective ends-of-action (we may call them 'goals') which particular agents may adopt for particular actions and which will vary from person to person and from occasion to occasion. Someone may listen to music in order to be able to converse with a music-loving friend; may join a political movement in order to overthrow a government; or may read philosophy in order to improve concentration. It is not such ends as these which concern us when we use the term 'authority', but those which give the actions their generic intelligibility. We speak of them as 'grounds' of action because they give rise to the generic forms which human action takes. Thus one kind of 'end' is at the same time a 'beginning'. As well as being the object towards which action strives, it is the authority which has called the form of action into being. The term 'authority' in this sense recalls the Greek word *archē*, which means at once both 'beginning' and 'rule'. It is in this sense that we can properly understand the New Testament supposition that the universe contains *archai* and *exousiai*, 'rules and authorities'.

These terms belong to the angelological conceptions of the Pauline New Testament. They are grouped with *dynameis*, 'powers' (Rom. 8:38; 1 Cor. 15:24; Eph. 1:21; 1 Pet. 3:22), with *kyriotētes*, 'lordships' (Eph. 1:21; Col. 1:16), with *thronoi*, 'thrones' (Col. 1:16) and with *angeloi*, 'angels' (Rom. 8:38; *cf.* 1 Pet. 3:22). Our interpretation is not angelological, but it is one proper use, which neither precludes nor requires other uses, of this biblical pattern of thought which is flexible enough to take different forms and perform different tasks. These are not the strongly personal celestial messengers, familiar to us from the book of Daniel and the Lucan infancy narrative, who announce themselves by their names. Nor are they the representatives of national identities which emerge at some points in the Old Testament (*e.g.* Dt. 32:8; Ps. 82). These authorities are only vaguely defined as beings which may encourage or inhibit human action. They are part of the created order (Col. 1:16), and their destiny is to be ordered under the rule of Christ (Col. 2:10; *cf.* Eph. 1:21; 1 Pet. 3:22). Yet they are tumultuous and tyrannous adversaries in this condition of darkness, against whom we wrestle (Eph. 6:12). They were responsible for Christ's death (1 Cor. 2:8), humiliated by him on the cross (Col. 2:15), and are even, as rebels, to be 'brought to nothing' (1 Cor. 2:6; 15:24). The nearest to precise identification of their role that we find is at Romans 13:1–2, where Paul speaks of *exousiai* explicitly as political authorities. This has suggested to some that this text lies outside the group and does not refer to the angel-*exousiai* at all. But we do not have to choose between an angelological and a political interpretation of Romans 13:1–2. The point of angelology is precisely to give a framework of understanding in which such a phenomenon as political authority can be talked about.

Saint Paul wrote, 'There is no authority except from God' (Rom. 13:1). Taken in isolation this statement is susceptible of two quite divergent interpretations, and upon the divergence a great issue hangs. Does Paul mean that all authority is an aspect of the operations of God? A powerful tradition of thought within Christian culture, one closely associated with Christian Neo-Platonism, has inclined to believe that every movement of the human soul is, at nearer or further remove, inspired by the one divine mover. God's authority, his capacity to summon man to desire and action, is mediated through a diversity of created objects, upon which man's affections are ostensibly fixed; but all the time it is really God lurking behind these objects, not the objects themselves, that alone has power to quicken movement in the soul. The created order itself is capable of inspiring love or striving only as God operates secretly through it, breathing life into its otherwise inert form. Thus the whole history of human desire and action is the history of man's confused and often misdirected response to God's call. As a description of man's pilgrimage to his supernatural end this is, of course, extremely compelling; but its focus is so sharply transcendental that it overlooks the reality of creation as the context in which man's pilgrimage is conducted. The created order contains 'authorities' which have their own relative finality; it is not only the divine that has the power to quicken action. Certainly, the authorizing power of created beings derives from the fact that in truth they are God's handiwork. They owe their power, as they owe their being, to his creative gift and to his continual affirmation of that gift in sustaining providence. There is no authority except *from* God. Nevertheless, that gift was really given. Authority really is vested in creaturely existence. God, in creating, has effected not only other beings, but other powers, yet without in any way diminishing his own sovereign being and power. Only because this is so can Paul proceed from the divine source of authority to speak at once of a plurality of authorities: 'The authorities that exist have been instituted [placed in their order] by God.'

Natural authority and the authority of truth

We start, then, from the observation that created beings can evoke free action from us. Many characteristic features of human society arise because some human beings have this power over others. The young accept the recommendations of their elders. Those who have physical beauty or charm of speech influence other people. Forceful personalities gather a following. Widely-held opinions are more likely to win new adherents than those held by only a few. Customary practices are maintained because they are customary. We acknowledge influences, too, from non-human sources: an experience of beauty in nature can prompt us to contemplation or prayer, to painting or to writing poetry. The forms in which we may encounter and respond to authority are very many; but the underlying factors which command us and compel us, the 'authorities' themselves, are few and recurrent. We may mention four: beauty, age, community and strength (a word which includes the whole range of natural virtue, from might to wisdom) have the capacity, as we encounter them in individuals, in human institutions and in the natural world, to inspire and order our actions in distinctive ways. And to these four instances of 'natural authority' within the created order we must add a further striking instance of an authority which would be classed as 'natural', according to medieval thinkers, 'in a relative sense', which is to say that it belongs to the natural order as it is encountered under the conditions brought about by Adam's sin: the authority of injured right to command our resentment and vengeance, the authority which shapes our structures of justice and government.

Is this to cast our net too wide? It may be said that we should not include just *any* immediate and sufficient ground of action in our conception of authority, but only those grounds which are afforded us in a social context through human speech. What sense does it make, we may be asked, to compare the artist's response to beauty in the natural world with the young person's response to the counsel of his elders? Are we not in danger of replacing the unduly narrow modern conception of authority with one that is so expansive as to be without interpretative force? There is a measure of justice in this objection, in so far as it reminds us that the focus of any concept of authority must be the capacity of one human being to command the obedience of another through speech. However, as we explore what it is that makes speech authoritative, we discover precisely those forces at work which influence us also by other means. The only virtue which belongs intrinsically to speech is truth; but any account of authority must explain how speech can be authoritative quite apart from its truthfulness. To account for authority, therefore, is to describe a borderland between culture and nature, where culture draws upon, and is shaped by, natural forces. Speech becomes the vehicle through which these natural authorities summon us, and in summoning us shape our social life.

To the demands of such authorities we may respond critically or uncritically. There is, of course, as we have said, a prima facie intelligibility about any response to natural authorites. The person who listens to music or joins a club acts quite 'reasonably', in one sense, regardless of whether he or she reflects critically upon what she does. However, to achieve any kind of *moral* awareness she has to expose her responses to critical examination: is listening to music a cover for idleness? Does the club have worthy aims? and so on. Such questions do not challenge the validity of the natural authorities of beauty and community absolutely; but they do suppose that in our responses to them we must evaluate their various claims in any situation and weigh them against others. Natural authority is not unconditional; it is subject to the review of a higher authority which can presume to order and criticize it. The higher authority, to which any form of critical reflection turns, is the authority of truth.

The authority of truth, though itself natural in the sense that it is inherent in the created order, differs from what we have called the 'natural authorities' in that it is not encountered as part of our *immediate* experience of the world. We become conscious of it only as we attempt to comprehend the world as an ordered whole. Its authority belongs to the order of things as a totality, whereas those other authorities belong to differing elements within it. Reflection in obedience to truth is reflection about the relations of things. Such reflection takes on the specific character of moral reflection when it is directed to discerning how our response to natural authorities (as well as to the immanent necessities of our existence, the animal drives to eat, sleep, mate and defend ourselves) may be ordered appropriately to the relations of things, to discerning the good of human action which conforms to the truth of the created order. The authority of truth, correspondingly,

125

can be called 'moral authority' when this context of moral reflection is in view.

We become aware of the authority of truth, as we become aware of other authorities, by meeting it concretely, presented to us by some particular situation, person or thing. People and things 'have' moral or intellectual authority, just as they have authority of other kinds. A moment of magic beauty in Holyrood Castle inspired Mendelssohn to compose his Scottish Symphony; a moment of intellectual illumination reading Cicero's *Hortensius* inflamed Augustine with the love of wisdom and set him on his life's career as a thinker. But at this point the similarity ends. The compelling moment of beauty attracts us to itself in its uniqueness, whereas the moment of illumination sets us on a search which leads away from itself towards the truth as a whole. For Mendelssohn the opening bars of his symphony could be successful only as they recaptured and enshrined *that* moment; the *Hortensius*, on the other hand, would do its work for Augustine by enabling him to think critically for himself and so, by implication, to think critically also about Cicero. The only authority that a particular person or thing may derive from the truth is a didactic authority which is self-effacing and points beyond itself. The Idealists of the last century made this point by contrasting the 'concreteness' of art with the 'universality' of science. That is why our attachments of loyalty to individual wise men or particular books of wisdom are more problematic than our loyalties to favourite works of art, men of power or cultural traditions. Of course, such attachments may be delightful and enriching, as, for example, when we retain our reverence and affection for an inspiring teacher; but when that happens other elements have entered into his claim upon us which must not be confused with the claim of truth itself. When a wise man or a tradition of thought comes to be thought beyond reach of critical question, he or it is dishonoured. The translucent didactic authority to which it could once lay claim in the service of the truth has been replaced by an authority that is immediate and opaque. This changeling may be the authority of tradition, or it may be the authority of strength – for wisdom itself is a form of strength which can command its own natural deference among mankind quite apart from critical appreciation, as we see from the role of 'technocrats' in political life. But either way the fundamental stance of the thinker *vis à vis* the truth, critical and open to criticism, will be betrayed by the seduction of the wrong kind of authority. The difficulty which this principle raises for our understanding of the authority of Christ is a matter to which we must return in the next chapter.

All this can be regarded simply as a reformulation, from the point of view of the acting subject, of the positions we maintained in chapter 2. There is given in creation an order of kinds and ends, within which our actions, too, attain their intelligibility. Our task as moral agents is to participate in this order, understanding it and conforming to it in what we think and do. The point of re-stating these contentions in terms of 'authority' is not to add something to them, but rather to deny that anything needs to be added. Natural Law thinkers of the Renaissance and Counter-Reformation showed themselves under the sway of voluntarism when they asked what it was that gave the natural order its authority, and replied that it was authorized by the command of God. The creation thus appeared to them to be an inert thing, meaningless for human action until assigned by divine command a significance that it did not otherwise have. Our aim is simply to contradict this. The created order carries its authority for action in itself, because agents, too, are a part of the created order and respond to it without being told to.

But from here we have to take a step in parallel to that which carried us from chapter 2 to chapter 3. What follows when we admit that the created order is in disarray, that our perception of it is blinded by sin, and that we find its history aimless and mystifying? What is implied when we experience the natural authorities of creation as 'elemental spirits of the universe' (Gal. 4:3) which threaten and enslave us? Then it is that we have to learn how to speak distinctly of a divine authority in revelation, which is not to be confused with the immediate authorities of nature, nor with the authority of truth which is always in danger of being misrepresented by us. To this divine authority we turn next. But before we do so, though by way of digression, it is necessary to make some remarks about political authority, which will serve three purposes: to complete our general account of authority, relating it more clearly to modern accounts; to show how the interpretation of divine authority has been influenced by the political model; and to prepare the way for some later observations on the authority of the church.

Political authority

Political authority is a complex phenomenon which owes something both to the immediacy of the natural authorities and to the critical reflectiveness of moral authority. Attempts have often been made to interpret it exclusively under one or the other of these two categories, always unconvincingly. On the one hand, political authority certainly owes something to two elements of natural authority, might and tradition (which are forms of strength and age respectively). When law cannot be enforced, losing the authority conferred by might, it becomes a dead letter which people do not obey. When law is changed too often and too drastically, losing the authority conferred by tradition, it forfeits public respect, so that people obey it cynically and without conviction. From this some thinkers have thought it plausible to conclude that the authority of law derives exclusively from 'power', *i.e.* from an established structure of forceful domination. But this is to overlook an important feature of the relation between authority and might. Although it is true that the possession of might is an indispensable condition of political authority, so that one who cannot enforce cannot command, it is also the case that an excessive dependence on might will destroy authority. One who will *only* enforce, cannot command either. Violent regimes lose authority, however much additional support they may claim from tradition. For true political authority to flourish, there must be a stronger motive of obedience than is furnished by fear of sanction and habitual conformity. People obey political authority because they think they ought. It exercises a moral authority which can command a critically reflective obedience.

This very consideration, on the other hand, has tempted other thinkers to assimilate political to moral authority. This is the inclination of those natural-law theorists who stress the didactic role of positive law as society's moral tutor, and would like to conclude that an unjust law is no law at all. Their accounts, too, are unsatisfactory, inasmuch as they obscure the difference between obeying the law because we ought to do so, and obeying it because what it requires of us is what we ought anyway to do. The law does lay claim to a moral authority; but that authority is not in the first instance the authority of such wisdom and justice as it contains, but of a general obligation of society to the law as such. But how could there be such a general obligation binding us to the authority of political institutions if they were no more than structures of power? For the law to command our presumptive moral assent, it must embody a further claim, the claim of injured right to be avenged. For any institution to exercise political authority, it must at least have a formal commitment to righting wrongs. A law may be unjust without ceasing to be a law; but if a system of law were to abandon altogether its obligations to justice, then, indeed, it would cease to be law, and would merely be 'lore' or 'lordship'.

The distinctive form of authority which we call 'political' is, then, at its simplest, a concurrence of the natural authorities of might and tradition with that other 'relatively natural' authority, the authority of injured right. When these three authorities are exercised together by one subject, then they are endorsed by a moral authority which requires that we defer to them. They are exercised together when the first two are put at the disposal of the third; that is, when one whose possession of *might* is in accord with the *established order* of a society takes responsibility for the *righting of wrongs* within that society. The moral principle which requires deference to political authority amounts, in effect, simply

128

to this: the threefold cord should not be broken. We should not only obey an institution which unites these three authorities in itself, but we should make every effort to sustain it. For justice, in the relative sense in which it is appropriate to speak of it in human communities, can be realized only by this triad of authorities in combination.

We can see why this should be so if we understand justice as *public right action*. Each of the three terms, 'public', 'right' and 'action', is safeguarded by one of the three constituent authorities which political authority unites. Tradition safeguards the sphere of *public* life; for the substance of any community, that which its members hold in common, is determined by what they can 'pass on' from one to the other. Resentment of injured right is the form in which concern for *right* lays hold upon us at the instinctual level. Might, the power to coerce, is the guarantee that *action* can be effective. None of the three can effect justice on its own, nor any two without the third. Resentment of injured right must express its concern in effective action, which is to say, it must become vengeance; but vengeance cannot be just unless it renounces its character as purely private satisfaction and allows itself to become the matter of public judgment. Might, when it has not surrendered its coercive operations to the control of the public interest, is a damaging aggression upon community life; but the public interest itself is arbitrary and tyrannous unless it gives first place to the righting of wrongs. Tradition is a restrictive imposition upon the freedom of the individual spirit unless it is a tradition of concern for right, in which offences against freedom are resented; but even a tradition of concern for right must remain, as so much tradition-alism does, the merest nostalgia if it is not also a tradition of effective community action. Political authority, then, cannot take form without these three elements: sufficient might to govern, sufficient identification with the tradition of the community to govern legitimately, and sufficient commitment to righting wrong to govern, within the relative possibilities open to human powers, justly.

But from all this we may draw an important inference: it is possible for a community to live pre-politically, without a political authority that commands moral respect. Smaller communities, both natural and voluntary, do so all the time, and count it a virtue that they are not politically organized. But even in the wider community of those who are associated neither by blood nor by common projects the combination of might, tradition and the concern to right wrongs does not have to occur. This was the perception expressed, albeit clumsily, by those 'social contract' theories of government of the seventeenth and eighteenth centuries which assigned the origin of political institutions to a mythical agreement among the members of society. The myth was clumsy because in representing the community's will to have government as a self-conscious device, it confused morality with planning, and represented the whole sphere of political existence, even communal existence, as the invention of man's will. Christian thought, in attributing the origin of authority to divine providence, can recognize the extent to which the political will in any community disposes of an already existing matter. Nevertheless, the political will is important, and societies that do not maintain it risk being governed immediately by the turbulent claims of might, tradition and vengeance in competition with each other.

Yet, even at its best, public right action can bear only an indirect relation to the demands of truth and goodness considered absolutely. Justice in human communities is only relatively just. It is not mistaken to think of political authority, by positive law or by other means, as 'applying' the principles of natural law to social life; for 'applying' is a sufficiently broad term to cover any kind of conscientious attempt to make action correspond to the demands of right. But this 'application' is something rather different from what is involved in individual moral decision. An individual moral agent, who has come to understand one or another aspect of the moral law with new clarity, may publish and act upon what he has learnt as best he can, and, if what he has said proves very unpopular and he suffers the fate of Socrates, he may, no doubt, find a Plato to celebrate his martyrdom and give his message a wider and more effective circulation. But the political leader, though obligated to the same moral truth as the individual agent is, must hazard not only his own survival but the survival of political authority in his society upon his attempts to respond to it. He is constrained by the limited possibilities for action in the public sphere, limitations arising from its dependence upon tradition and might, and for him it is a matter of principle, not merely of expediency, not to strain those possibilities to their breaking-point. So political order is necessarily arbitrary – not only in the harmless sense that it involves decision over matters where there is no clear reason for doing one thing rather than the other, but in the more problematic sense that its correspondence to the demands of right is compromised. The recognition of this fact about political existence is a characteristic feature of Christian political theory. Athens thought of Solon as a wise man, Israel of Moses as a mouthpiece of divine law. But for Jesus Moses was an artificer of compromise: 'For your hardness of heart Moses allowed you to divorce your wives, but from the beginning it was not so' (Mt. 19:8). The exercise of political authority is the search for a compromise which, while bearing the fullest witness to the truth that can in the circumstances be borne, will, nevertheless, lie within the scope of possible public action in the particular community of fallen men which it has to serve.

Authority

Divine authority

If the law requires me to pay taxes to support government programmes which I think immoral, I may still be obliged to pay the taxes of which I disapprove. This is one of the paradoxes of political authority: its moral claim is to a degree independent of the moral claim of its particular demands taken on their own. Thus it seems to provide a paradigm for an authority which transcends moral authority. Confronted by political authority, moral judgment declares itself overruled. Of course, moral judgment does not prescribe unlimited deference to political authority: it may be right to do what the state commands without suppressing our critical opinions of it, and even in the matter of doing there are evidently limits beyond which it would not be right to go. Nevertheless, though restricted, the paradigm is significant. Political institutions can confront us with a morally arbitrary demand which it is morally obligatory to obey.

This paradigm sheds light on one important facet of the authority of God. It is an authority which can transcend the judgment of our moral reason. It stands above our consciousness of moral obligation, and yet demands, as a matter of moral obligation, to be obeyed. In the face of divine command our reason declares its own authority suspended. It tells us to obey that which is beyond the scope of thought. Thus there is an encounter between the divine command and human rationality, in which the very faculty with which we ourselves think critically finds itself an object of higher criticism. This encounter, in which divine authority appears as transcendence overwhelming immanence, was the theme of those theological voluntarists of the Middle Ages who located the source of moral law in the arbitrariness of the divine will. To encounter divine command is to encounter that which is more fundamental than all reason: it is to encounter the ultimate *fiat* to which no questions may be put. Reason itself directs us to understand that all our rational perceptions of morality are hypothetical, dependent on the form in which it has pleased God to give this *fiat* to us. Standing before the burning bush, reason knows that it must take off its shoes: here is that which puts an end to thought, and simply demands that we worship and obey.

On the other hand, the same political paradigm may suggest something quite different. The concession to political authority is, after all, strictly circumscribed: like Galileo, we mutter under our breath as we make our act of conformity. And that means that sovereignty properly belongs not to law but to truth, for only a perception of the truth can lead us to whole-hearted action. The marvel, we may say, is not that the community can demand conformity; the marvel is that conscience can secretly transcend that conformity and pass judgment upon it in the light of truth.

131

And this application of the paradigm illuminates another facet of divine authority. If it is to command us as absolute authority, it must command us as supreme reality. Authority presupposes a foundation in being, and, just as truth prevails over the natural authorities because it is the truth of reality as a whole, so divine authority will prevail only because it belongs to that first reality in which truth is grounded. This tradition of thought, in which divine authority appears as reality proving itself against unreality, characterized those theological rationalists who located the source of the moral law in the divine reason.

If this medieval argument continues to exercise a fascination, it is because it concerns a question that is basic to all theological ethics, namely, the relation of the divine command to the order of creation. How does God's word engage our obedience when it would seem that our obedience is totally committed to the authority of created order as it is present to our reason? The tradition of theological rationalism clearly inclines to a continualist answer: God speaks *through* the order which reason perceives. The tradition of theological voluntarism prefers a discontinualist one: God's command *cuts across* our rational perceptions and relativizes them. Both these answers can claim to be grounded in the witness of the Bible. To speak only of the Psalms, the divine authority of Yahweh as King is celebrated in two contrasting ways, in terms of the *security* of the created order which manifests his irrevocable decree – 'Thou didst set the earth on its foundations, so that it should never be shaken' (Ps. 104:5) – and in terms of the *instability* of all created things before his presence as judge – 'The mountains melt like wax before the Lord' (Ps. 97:5). An adequate statement about the divine authority will include true perceptions from both sides, just as the corresponding statements about created order and history in chapter 3 needed to accommodate both the inherent teleology of creation and its historical destining to transformation.

Left to itself each of these traditions has shown a tendency to degenerate into humanism. The rationalist tradition, beginning from its commitment to trace an ontological continuity between the secondary authorities of creation and the primary authority of God, was drawn in the direction we have identified as Neo-Platonist, to present the structures of creation as no more than mediating agents for the divine reason. This did not necessarily imply a crude pantheism: it could remain very well aware of the difference between created being and uncreated being. Nevertheless, the voice with which creation summoned mankind was taken to be a faithful reproduction of God's voice. That was the case particularly, as we have seen in chapter 5, with the voice of man's own moral reason, God's representative or vicegerent, as it was claimed, within created human nature: *vox conscientiae vox Dei*. Of course, this offered some security of tenure to the perceptions of reason, where the tension-ridden universe of the voluntarists might seem to deliver man over to sceptical despair. But this security was won at the cost of a falsification. The security that rationalism offered was a dogmatic security based on the assumption that certain very fundamental rational perceptions must be immune from criticism. But reason can be rational only when it is critical, not merely critical of vulgar *idées reçues* but critical also of its own apparently unchallengeable principles of operation. It has a security of tenure, certainly, but that security is based upon the objective reality of the world-order in which it has its place and function. It is not based upon a secret corner of purely formal knowledge in which the usual review of thought in the light of reality may be suspended. Because reason knows the cosmos from within, as an embracing mystery which surrounds it, it knows that it can never be uncritical of any of its own perceptions, not even the strictly formal ones, and that it must always be open to the possibility of revelation from the standpoint of transcendence. Such openness is very different from reason's conceiving *itself* to be an angel of revelation. When reason presumes to occupy that role, it compromises its own integrity by forgetting its self-critical responsibility to objective truth.

Christian rationalism appears at its very best in Thomas Aquinas' well-known treatise on law (*Summa Theologiae* II-I.90–97). The *lex aeterna*, which is *ratio divinae sapientiae secundum quod est directiva omnium actuum et motionum*, 'the rational order of divine wisdom inasmuch as it directs the acts and motions of everything' (93.1), is reflected in the world as *lex naturalis*, the 'sharing in the eternal law by intelligent creatures' (91.2); and this in turn is developed and applied in society as *lex humana*, in which the human reason proceeds 'from the precepts of natural law as from common and indemonstrable principles . . . to making more specific arrangements', *ad aliqua magis particulariter disponenda* (91.3). Nothing could be clearer than that *lex aeterna* presupposes the free and omnipotent decree of God in creation, and so the complete contingency of creation. It is not a law of God's own being, but a law by which he orders the created world to its given destiny (93.4). There is, therefore, no hidden 'divinization' of the world through its ordering by natural law. The sheer givenness and unquestionableness of the divine *fiat* is preserved. Nevertheless, as this *fiat* takes form as the divine *ratio* for the government of the world, it does become accessible to human *ratio* (when properly instructed) through the medium of the world-order. Thus the mystery of omnipotence, while fully acknowledged, is, as it were, banished to the very limits of speculation, so that it cannot impinge upon our reading of the divine mind in nature's book. This gives reason a certain security of purchase upon the divine purpose.

In the treatment of Natural Law the implications of this security become evident. It is restricted in the first instance to truths *per se nota*. While allowing that this category must include much more than the frankly self-evident axioms which define the conceptual structure of morals – *e.g., bonum est faciendum et prosequendum*, 'the good is to be done and sought after' (94.2) – he does not avoid giving a false prominence to the rational *a priori* at the expense of the objective and empirically observable regularities of the natural order. This narrowly defined sphere of natural law, when properly understood, is credited with the authority of the divine *fiat*. The force of formal rational self-evidence has thus become conflated with the force of the divine word. Already we see on the horizon the whole project of rationalism from Descartes onwards, the exaltation of the formal rule of thought to the status of divine law in relation to which all else is criticized.

The voluntarist tradition, on the other hand, was concerned to make a sharp distinction between the authority of the divine command and any authority that man might discern within the order of creation. It did not have to deny that creation did have an order, that that order did derive from the command of God, and that there was a congruence between nature and the moral law. Thus Scotus and Ockham could continue to speak of 'natural law'. But the point of central importance was the immediate contingency of morality upon the declared will of God. It was not derived from God *through* the created order; hence arose Ockham's famous contention that God could make it right for us to hate him if he so willed, the ultimate reversal of the proper order of creature to Creator. The point of this contention, of course, was to draw attention to the fact of sheer authority demanding sheer obedience. But the problem had to arise: once the divine command is abstracted from the ordered universe, what content is left to the idea of authority itself? If we rule out every claim that might *support* the authority of God's will – he created us, he sustains us, he redeems us – as guilty of impudent *lèse majesté* and derogating from its unmediated demand upon us, how, then, is God's will more 'authoritative' than any other alien will that may try to force itself upon us? If nothing that our minds can comprehend is in the slightest degree relevant to recognizing the authority of God's will, how is that authority to be recognized? An initial concern to isolate sheer authority and sheer obedience must end up paradoxically by abolishing both authority and obedience in an immediate clash of wills. Ultimately man can do nothing but resent God's will, as he resents any other alien imposition, and shake it off if he can. The voluntarist journey ended with a vacuum of authority, an empty chamber swept and garnished ready for the idea of rational autonomy to enter as soon as Kant had mended the breach between reason and will. With this notion the voluntarist and rationalist paths met at the antipodes.

All the main themes of voluntarism emerge in high relief in a breathtaking passage from Ockham's Commentary on book II of the *Sentences*, q.15. We can leave it to historians to decide how representative this *reportatio* from early in the thinker's career really is; it is sufficient for us that these thoughts were thought, and were expressed as they are here. The question before Ockham was a characteristically medieval one, 'whether a bad angel is always engaged in bad acts'. He is not greatly interested in the question as such; but it affords him the occasion to propound the theory that there can occur within the will of a created being an act which is immediately caused by God alone. In this case the act is the act of willing-not-to-be-punished, *nolere poenam*, which the angel would presumably stop doing if he could, since his resentment at the punishment constitutes the pain of it, but which is, at the same time, manifestly a disposition of his will. From this, he claims, we can reach an understanding of how God confirms the righteous and hardens the hearts of the wicked. In the blessed the act of seeing God and of loving him is caused immediately by God alone. It is an act in the will, and therefore free; but it is in no way caused either by the agent's will or by his reason. Similarly with the damned: God, as a total cause, causes 'whatever is absolute' in the act of hating and rejecting himself, *i.e.* he causes the hatred and rejection of himself *as such*, considered apart from those aspects of hating and rejecting God which make it sinful (for then God would be an agent of sin). 'For God can cause any thing as such, apart from any other thing that is not the same as that thing', *Deus potest omne absolutum causare sine omni alio quod non est idem cum illo absoluto.* But how can hatred and rejection of God be considered apart from their sinfulness? The third of several objections which Ockham envisages being made to this idea is based on Aristotle's claim that certain acts are evil simply as such; it is impossible to talk about them without talking about them as evil, *statim nominati habent maliciam annexam et difformitatem.* To this he replies that hatred of God and other sins are evil merely circumstantially, by virtue of being performed by someone who has been forbidden by God to perform them: *odium Dei furari adulterari habeant malam circumstantiam annexam et similia de communi lege quatenus fiunt ab aliquo qui ex praecepto divino obligatur ad contrarium.* If they were commanded by God, they would be meritorious. And in that case we should have a different moral language: we should not call such acts by their present names, 'theft', 'adultery', 'hatred', *etc.*, because such names carry the connotation that they are forbidden, *nec nominarentur furtum adulterium odium etc., quia ista nomina significant tales actus non absolute sed connotando vel dando intelligere quod faciens tales actus per praeceptum divinum obligatur ad oppositum.* The fourth objection is based on the seeming contradictoriness of supposing that the created will could earn merit by keeping such amoral commands as these. To which he replies that there is nothing contradictory in thinking that a given act may be performed rightly by one agent when it would be wrong for another, the difference being only that the one was commanded to perform it, the other prohibited.

The most striking feature of this discussion is, of course, the strong claim for the freedom of God's will, which cuts morality loose from its moorings in the created order of things. We should not, however, overlook a secondary feature which is, if anything, even more pregnant with consequences for the future. In the face of the naked will of God, the human subject is himself reduced to being only a naked will, or 'cause' (*causa*).

This gives us the clue to understanding how the theological voluntarism of the Middle Ages could prepare the way for the very untheological voluntarism of later ages. When agents have become simple 'causes', it ceases to matter whether they are human or divine.

The value of the voluntarist emphasis lay in its perception that the dialectic between reason and revelation rests not on an accidental deficiency of human reason but on the aboriginal metaphysical fact that human reason is not transcendent. Thus human judgments are always, and as such, susceptible to divine criticism. Human reason itself, by its own critical self-understanding, tells us this, and points to its own supersession. In the divine-human encounter trusting obedience is the only appropriate reaction, and the only properly self-critical reaction on man's part. The risk of Abraham cannot be avoided. But once its dangerous tendencies have been thus corrected, rationalism too can instruct us. If obedience is to be 'trusting', it must be hopeful. The disciple who obeys the divine word in defiance of his own limited perceptions of right is genuinely trustful only if he believes that the paradox is not an ultimate contradiction in reality. He must hope to see the moment of critical confrontation finally resolved by the elevation of his reason to grasp God's action as a coherent whole. Otherwise he is acting not in faith but in cynical despair. 'Faith is the assurance of things hoped for, the conviction of things not seen' (Heb. 11:1). Rationalism was not wrong to promise an ultimate scrutability in the divine purpose; it was wrong only as it attempted to empty that promise of its eschatological character and hurry forward to a premature fulfilment by the route of a reductive immanentism.

The voluntarist was also right to stress that God's freedom to innovate was not adequately described in terms of a *lex aeterna*, a blueprint which could not be changed but could only be successively realized. God's action can encompass novelty, that which is itself unpredictable except in terms of God's own declaration of his intent: 'Behold, I am doing a new thing' (Is. 43:19). God cannot suffer under constraint, even from his own past dispositions. On the other hand, God's freedom also implies his self-posited faithfulness. When we say that God 'bound himself' in the covenant of creation, we use a paradoxical metaphor, certainly, but what we say is not meaningless. It means that God's freedom is exercised in congruence with itself. It is not randomness, turning idly back upon itself and cancelling out its own creative deed, but redemptive transformation, which respects and exalts that which has gone before. Rationalism was correct to predicate coherence of God's deeds. 'He cannot deny himself,' says the apostle (2 Tim. 2:13), not thereby setting a limit upon God's power, but declaring that God's unlimited power includes also the power to be consistent with itself.

136

The authority of the divine word is encountered concretely in the authority of Jesus, who taught, according to Saint Mark, 'as one who had authority, and not as the scribes', and evoked the response, 'What is this? A new teaching with authority! He commands even the unclean spirits, and they obey him' (Mk. 1:22,27). The authority of God's word as Jesus proclaimed it was partly evidenced by its very novelty. It was 'not like the scribes', but cut across the expectations and traditions of teaching within the Jewish community, claiming no precedents. It impinged critically upon the existing conceptions of right which the community's reflections upon past revelation had established. But at the same time the divine authority was proved by its capacity to bring order to chaos in a way that was immediately recognizable. Jesus' 'mighty works' were significant of God's presence not merely because they were mighty, but because they were works of healing and exorcism. The new teaching vindicated itself by vindicating and restoring the old creation.

Deontic and teleological language

By way of postscript to our digression we may comment on a question that has troubled thinkers of recent generations perhaps more than it should have done, that is, the relation between 'deontic' and 'teleological' forms of moral language. The question has some rather strange features, not the least odd being the persistent discussion of two forms of language when there are, apparently evident to all, not just two, but many forms in which moral judgment can be expressed. We can say that we 'ought' to do something, that we are 'obliged' to do it, that it is 'right' or that it is 'good'. We can use a wide range of evaluative adjectives, calling it 'noble', 'fine', 'charming' or 'just'. We can simply instruct someone to do it – an operation which may be performed in a number of different grammatical ways. Furthermore, each language has its own distinctive range of expressions, and there is often a difficulty of exact translation from one language to another. Rhetorical considerations as well as philosophical ones may dictate the choice of expression: there are courteous ways of saying things and abrupt ways, formal ways and informal. Why, then, do philosophers continue to remark on two kinds of moral language when there are so many?

The polarity certainly has its source in the antithesis of voluntarist and rationalist understandings of morality. Deontic ethics has its source in the voluntarist conception that morality is a matter of command and obedience. (The word 'deontic', coined from the Greek *deon*, points to the prominence of 'ought' and its equivalents.) It suggests that morality is a kind of burden laid upon us, which cuts across our natural aspirations and purposes. It is important to distinguish this idea from the notion that moral judgments are 'prescriptive' – a term which is more conveniently and commonly used, as in contemporary 'prescriptivism', to draw attention to the action-directing function of all moral speech, of whatever kind. It is also important to distinguish it from the Kantian idea of 'heteronomy' – for the whole thrust of Kantian ethics was to insist that the 'ought' gave access to the only truly autonomous moral judgment, which was 'the free submission of the will to the law', and that nothing could be more heteronomous than conduct arising from the spontaneous movement of the subjective inclinations. The point, rather, is that the moral claim is encountered *apart from any perceptions about the subject's fulfilment or welfare* which might compromise the absolute obedience which it elicits for its own sake. 'Teleological' ethics, on the other hand, derives from the ontological conception of God as the *summum bonum*, in which it was the task of moral reasoning to recognize and respond to the ordered structures of being and good. 'Teleological' is not meant to be understood narrowly, as speaking only of a calculative, consequentialist morality, but in the way that we have ourselves used it, pointing to any kind of propriety or order within the world. There are, of course, consequentialist interpretations of teleological ethics. Utilitarianism is an offspring from this rationalist root, and shows its ancestry by its confidence in a self-evident and unarguable idea of happiness which does in fact, and should self-consciously, govern all human conduct as an end.

It is sometimes suggested that faced with this dichotomy we have only two possibilities open to us. We can claim, on the one hand, a strict interchangeability between these two forms of moral language; on the other, we may suppose that they point objectively to two different kinds of morality. The latter course, which has proved the more popular in recent discussions, can itself lead in two ways. It can suggest a grading of the two kinds as higher and lower, a measure which will probably indicate a Kantian kind of preference for the 'ought'; or it can result in a simple pluralism (which amounts, so far as I can see, to reconstructing ethics as a *sociological* study – for I do not know what it could mean to say that there were irreconcilably conflicting kinds of moral claim abroad in the world *simpliciter*). However, it would appear that the alternative is wrongly posed in the first place. We are not compelled to think the two languages *interchangeable* (if that means without loss of sense) in order to say that they point to the same objective moral reality. There is evidently a difference in sense between saying that one 'ought to' do something and saying that it is 'good'. Yet any actual moral claim can be expressed either in terms of obligation or in terms of the good; and it would be merely doctrinaire to insist that in choosing the second form of expression one must fail to appreciate its true moral force. What the two languages do is to draw our attention to different and complementary aspects of moral claims as we encounter them. The deontic language emphasizes the critical relation of moral authority to natural authority and of divine authority to all created authority. We say 'ought' when we need to stress the contradiction between this overriding claim and what we should otherwise have thought or felt. Although it is mistaken to claim that only the conception of obligation qualifies thought as truly moral, this mistake conceals a truth: for it is certainly the case that we think morally only as we think critically, and the force of the 'ought' is to stimulate us to do that. On the other hand, the teleological language draws attention to the rationality of moral and divine authority. It drives us to express, as best we can, the meaning of that authority within the ordered universe, even when that expression is the expression of a hope for a resolution that we cannot yet comprehend.

Kant, for all his commitment to deontic ethics and his dependence on the notion of law, understood that the distinctive character of the 'ought', its expression of the 'imperative', arose from the relation of constraint between the objective law of reason and a will not subjectively determined to it. A holy will, like the divine will, would not encounter the law as imperative or as 'ought' (*Groundwork* 413f.). The strong antithesis between the concepts of happiness and duty is the constant theme of the 'Analytic' section of the *Critique of Practical Reason*, where classical ethics is subjected to criticism for its approach to moral law by way of the controlling concept of the *summum bonum*, which inevitably, Kant argues, left their moral thought heteronomous and at the mercy of the principles of happiness and pleasure (*e.g.* 64f.). However, in the 'Dialectic' section the notion of the 'highest good' is reinstated in Kant's ethics as the object, though not the motive, of the pure practical reason, and we learn that the Christian eschatological hope of the kingdom of God, complete with the idea of happiness, is, together with the immortality of the soul, a necessary 'postulate' of practical reason.

We may say, then, that the tension between the two moral languages reflects a necessary dialectic in the perceptions of moral agents for whom moral insight is still a task and not yet an achieved fact. In moments of grace we may be given the perception that our duty and our fulfilment are one and the same, and we may speak of that unity in hope and faith; but we cannot ask that we should never be challenged to further thought and conscientious struggle by an awareness of the divergence of inclination and duty.

7

The authority of Christ

It is not the Holy Spirit, but God the Father, who has conferred authority upon Jesus. And that authority has not been conferred through the quickening of our hearts or the acknowledgment of our lips. It was conferred, quite apart from us, without our faith and without our obedience, when God raised Jesus from the dead. So when we say that the Spirit makes the reality of what God has done in Jesus 'authoritative to us', we are speaking not of how the authority of Christ comes to *be*, but of how, originating apart from us, it comes to *claim* us, of how we 'enter' the kingdom of heaven. The work of the Spirit, who does not speak 'from himself', is to bear witness to the kingdom, making its reality present to us as he elicits our faith, and making its authority bear upon us as he elicits our free obedience.

'When the Spirit of truth comes, he will guide you into all the truth; for he will not speak on his own authority, but whatever he hears he will speak, and he will declare to you the things that are to come. He will glorify me, for he will take what is mine and declare it to you. All that the Father has is mine; therefore I said that he will take what is mine and declare it to you' (Jn. 16:13–15). The content of the Spirit's ministry to the church (and we may extend it to the church as a whole, although the context refers it primarily to the witness of the apostles) is the truth: the whole of it, because in Jesus all truth, the truth of world-order and the truth of world-history, is summed up. The Spirit is not given to *create* the new reality, since in the exaltation of the Christ the new reality has been given its decisive form; but he is given to bring that new reality to bear upon the old, to 'speak what he hears' (*i.e.* the Father's decree concerning the Son) and to 'declare what is to come' (*i.e.* the universal manifestation of the kingdom of God at the fulfilment of history). Thus he is to 'glorify'

Jesus, which is not to usurp the Father's prerogative in exalting him, but to give what the Father has done a universal resonance in the praise offered by a redeemed and obedient creation. 'All that the Father has is mine.' To speak of divine authority after the resurrection of Christ is to speak of the authority of the exalted Christ. There is nothing else left to say, no codicil or postscript in which the Spirit might address us with a divine claim that did not refer us to Christ's rule.

When the church has forgotten this, it has strayed in one of two directions: towards an excessive admiration of spontaneity, on the one hand, and towards an excessive reverence for tradition on the other. Of course, the Holy Spirit in the New Testament is seen to work also through spontaneity, in prophecy and ecstatic utterance; yet the attitude of the apostolic church to spontaneity is cautious. Such manifestations are valuable as a sign of the presence of the supernatural in the midst of the church; yet they do not represent the normal condition of receptivity to God, and they require especial scrutiny. We must, says Saint John, 'test the spirits to see whether they are of God'. And the criteria for recognizing the workings of God's Spirit can be summed up in one comprehensive principle: 'Every spirit which confesses that Jesus Christ has come in the flesh is of God, and every spirit which does not confess Jesus is not of God' (1 Jn. 4:1–3). Admiration for spontaneity and reverence for tradition are, of course, aspects of the same failing: a refusal to bring this Christological principle of criticism to the manifestation of spirits, present or past, within the church. What, after all, is tradition other than spontaneity in slow motion? The Montanist movement of the second and third centuries illustrates archetypically the church's double temptation to value spontaneous innovations in themselves and then to build them into a new law. Needless to say, the church cannot do *without* either spontaneity or tradition; nor, when they faithfully attest Christ, can spontaneity and tradition have any other source than the Holy Spirit of God. The point is simply that they are not self-authenticating.

God the Father has conferred authority upon Jesus; what we call the kingdom of God is also the exaltation of the Son of man. Starting from this central point of reference, we may draw two conclusions about our experience of divine authority.

In the first place the authority of God is not incommunicable, interior and removed from public view, but is located in the public realm in an event of history which may be told. In speaking of divine authority we may never simply mean an inner prompting, a compulsion of which we can give no account, 'a reason for acting in the absence of reasons'. For God's command will always prove itself to us in terms of *that* reason, the public reality of Jesus' life, death and exaltation. The voluntarist tradition of thought, by exalting the command of God above all reason, deprived it of speech and thereby relegated it to the sphere of private and interior compulsions, making it a matter of personal vocation rather than shared moral obligation. When I cannot say why God commands me to do this rather than that, I can equally not say that he

141

commands anyone else to do it. I can only point inarticulately to a sense of inner necessity which grips me without gripping the world of ordered meanings in which I conduct my life. But by authorizing a public event, the meaning of which is open to speech and thought, God has made a wider claim on us than can ever be experienced as individual vocation. He has made a moral demand, which gets its grip upon us by getting a grip upon the ordered world in which we participate, a demand which can be described and discussed in generic terms. Jesus said to the man who wanted to bury his father: 'Leave the dead to bury their own dead; but as for you, go and proclaim the kingdom of God' (Lk. 9:60). If this saying can affect us in any way, even to the limited extent of making us feel uncomfortable, it is because it cannot be only a private communication between God and that particular man – which would have no significance for us and no place in the gospel. Whatever its immediate reference to his particular calling, there are implications for the ordering of God's claim upon all of us. It points to the kind of demand which God's presence in the world makes upon every human agent. We may allow for the element of particularity in the way it encountered that man, and yet learn something about what it is for anyone at any time to be a disciple.

In the second place, God's authority, located as it is in a man's life and in his victory over death, may oppose the natural authorities in their rebellion and disorderliness, but is not opposed to the created order as such. It does not override our obligation to the truth in a 'teleological suspension of the ethical' such as Kierkegaard described, though it may criticize our perceptions of it. It promises to vindicate the authority of creation, and requires 'blind' obedience only in the sense that what we think we know of that creaturely authority must be open to challenge if we are to grasp its shape comprehensively. When Jesus said, in relation to one of the most solemn obligations that the ancient world recognized, 'Leave the dead to bury their own dead', that was not merely a strong assertion of the transcendence of the kingdom. If the kingdom were purely transcendent, if it did not impose a true order upon our worldly obligations, then we would be without guidance as to how to live in the world. We would be poised between world and kingdom as between life and death; but that is to say we would in practice adopt an unreformed worldliness, for the transcendent kingdom, having no point of purchase upon our life in the world, would become merely a rhetorical consideration. But because the kingdom is life and not death to us, it can reorder our worldly claims, and under its authority we can discover a positive ethic for life in the world, one which has a place, among other things, for obligations to parents – though burial is not among the most pressing of them. We should not, then, be tempted to set Jesus' 'radical' ethic of the kingdom against the practical this-worldliness

142

of the apostolic churches, as we see it, for example, in the so-called Household Codes of the epistles. Such an opposition not only goes beyond the written record, but is misconceived in principle. In its apparent determination to avoid all minimizing applications of Jesus' words, it refuses to take them seriously *as ethics* at all, because it allows them no purchase upon the ordering of human life. All that his words are permitted to do is arouse our expectancy (rather in the manner of a Zen riddle) that at any moment we may confront an irruption of divine authority in a form about which nothing definite can be said.

What these two conclusions point to is the foundation of Christian ethics in the incarnation. Since the Word became flesh and dwelt among us, transcendent divine authority has presented itself as worldly moral authority. It comes to us not as a *mysterium tremendum* which simply destroys all worldly order, but as creation restored and renewed, to which God is immediately present in the person of the Son of man. The teaching and life of Jesus must be *morally* authoritative if we are not to be thrown back upon the gnostic gospel of a visitor from heaven who summons us out of the world. We cannot regard the divine command, in Helmut Thielicke's distressing phrase, as 'extraplanetary material'. For though the redemption of the world had to be wrought from outside it by God's gracious intervention, it had still to be the redemption of the world. The meaning of Jesus' life and teaching must be a worldly meaning, a reality of human existence which can command our lives in the world and reorder them in the restored creation.

In exploring the importance of the incarnation for the authority of Christ we need to establish a set of equivalences which are often confused. Moral authority is the authority of order, the created order of kinds and ends in which all created beings participate. It is 'universal' in the sense which we indicated in chapter 2; that is, it supposes a universe of meaning which created beings inhabit in common. The authority of divine transcendence, on the other hand, is beyond world-order, and can only appear to us as an unaccountable and mysterious breach in the world-order. Encounter with divine authority must be a unique event, irreducibly particular, incapable of comparison with any other. When we speak, then, of divine authority presenting itself as moral authority, we mean that the particular (transcendent) has assumed universal (worldly) significance. The moment of divine irruption is more than an irruption: it is the foundation of a renewed order. 'The very stone which the builders rejected has become the head of the corner' (Mk. 12:10). So Christ's particularity belongs to his divine nature, his universality to his human nature. As the one whom God has sent he is irreplaceable; as the new man he is the pattern to which we may conform ourselves. As the divine conqueror he triumphs over the false authorities of the fallen world; as the Son of man he exercises authority over the redeemed world. As the Lord of time he confers unique significance on each moment, fashioning time into history; as a participant in time he stands in relation to other moments in time as they stand in relation to each other and to his moment. This is to reverse the conceptual schema of most modern idealism, by which the universal is understood as the divine and the particular (or rather 'concrete') as the human. Incarnation (without the definite article) has meant that the meaning of the whole has been focused in a representative one. Which is why *the* incarnation has effectively been forgotten in modern idealist thought, since it is not difficult to show how any concrete being may, given the right conditions, be an 'incarnation' of universal meaning in *this* sense. But universality is a property of worldliness. What is remarkable, and what only *the* incarnation can tell us of, is not the representation of universal order in any one being, but the coming within universal order of that which belongs outside it, the one divine Word which gave it its origin and which pronounces its judgment.

Our task, then, is to describe the form of divine and moral authority as they meet in Christ. We may distinguish three questions, which are interrelated but not to be confused. The first concerns Christ's *irreplaceability* as a moral authority. The second is how moral authority can also have the character of *good news*. The third asks how moral authority can be *historical*.

These three questions are all present, though with differing emphases, in the 'Foundations' of Helmut Thielicke's great *Theological Ethics*. Our first word about Thielicke's enterprise must be one of appreciation. Not content to cross the *pons asinorum* of Lutheran theology and simply assert the dependence of ethics on the 'prior fact' of justification (p. 51), Thielicke gives positive content to the idea that ethics must be evangelical by directing us to three elements in Christian proclamation which shape the 'mystery' of Christian ethics. It is an eschatological mystery, he tells us, which rests on the 'irresolvable tension between time and eternity, between this aeon and the coming aeon'. It is a Christological mystery, resting on the tension between deity and humanity in Christ. And it is a sacramental mystery, resting on the tension between the sign and the thing signified, 'as the body of the Lord is hidden under the signs of bread and wine'. We could hardly refuse to be grateful for such a resolve to conduct theological ethics theologically. Who else, we may wonder, has announced an intention of grounding Christian ethics on the doctrine of the two natures in Christ (pp. 44–47)?

Yet we observe with some unease the repeated references to 'irresolvable tension'. The notion belongs appropriately to the first of Thielicke's three doctrinal foundations, the eschatological. Its uncomfortable transference to the second and the third (when did Christians speak of the incarnational paradox as a 'tension' between God and man in Christ?) betrays the fact that for Thielicke the eschatological motif is dominant. That in itself could be constructive, if it were recognized that in the ambiguous coexistence of the new age and the old we have to do with two *worldly* realities, each with a comprehensible and communicable form. Yet the insistence on tension is so strong that the new age loses its comprehensibility, and hence its worldliness (*n.b.* the surreptitious reference to time and *eternity* quoted above, as though that were a synonym!) and becomes merely a transcendent mystery, alien and critical.

The consequences of this become apparent when Thielicke discusses Jesus' moral teaching. Two chapters (chs. 17,18; pp. 332–382 in the English edition) are devoted to the interpretation of the Sermon on the Mount. They are based upon Luther's conception that the 'radical' teaching of Jesus is in opposition to the structures of this world's order, and their purpose is to rule out any minimizing interpretation of the text which will allow for a 'compromise' between the radical demand and the world. Luther's doctrine of the Two Kingdoms, suitably reformulated in eschatological terms, commends itself as a way of expressing the unresolved tension between them. The Sermon on the Mount, Thielicke believes, contains 'the law of the coming world' (p. 349), and addresses us as unfallen, or, alternatively, as already belonging to the kingdom. Its task is to 'unsettle' (p. 336), to 'compel us to understand this aeon as the zone of relativities and for that very reason as the fallen aeon' (p. 357). The orders of this aeon are only 'emergency orders', and ethics is an 'emergency discipline; peaceful coexistence between the two aeons is ruled out' (p. 381). 'Behind us stands the cherub with the flaming sword which smites in all directions, and before us stands the Last Day, beyond which alone lies unbeclouded vision' (p. 382). It implies no intention to belittle Thielicke's achievement in giving eschatological categories this impressive existential immediacy if we ask whether this really resolves anything for Christian ethics. In the end we have only the uncomfortable sense that the Sermon on the Mount is, after all, not relevant to our lives in the world except in so far as it reminds us of their provisionality. It is in this context (p. 487) that we read of the divine command as 'extraplanetary material'. It is no answer to say that 'the Sermon on the Mount does not overlook the reality of the world; it protests against it' (p. 486), for protest, in itself, is formless. Thielicke is finally led to say that 'the Christian too always acts in the form of compromise' – with the simple difference that he knows what he is doing, to use a favourite phrase, '*coram Deo*' (p. 487).

What, then, of an *evangelical* ethics? Thielicke's gospel sounds troublingly like a gospel of deliverance *from* the world rather than *of* it. The gnostic leaning is, of course, held firmly in check by its eschatological framework: the new aeon, too, is 'the world' in its renewed state. But since the new aeon can assume no form in this aeon except the formless form of protest, we are left, in effect, to be guided by the emergency orders. This becomes quite apparent in the four chapters devoted to the relation between Gospel and Law (chs. 5–8; pp. 51–146), which involve a defence of 'the continuing significance of the Law for believers'. 'The fact that the Law continues to have significance even for the justified ... assures that existence, as existence *coram Deo*, is in fact a history' (p. 124). It 'is obvious in the light of the fact that our Christianity is never something complete and finished but is constantly in process of becoming' (p. 126). To which we must object, not that moral law has no place in the Christian life (we shall find a place for it ourselves), nor that life in Christ can break out of its ambiguities and incompleteness before the parousia, but that life in Christ must not be denied its own worldliness, its own (but with safeguards) 'law'. Given the opposition of law and gospel in the Reformation traditions we can only understand Thielicke's thesis as meaning that the Christian life has to be lived under some other authority than the authority of Christ.

Is not the heart of the problem, then, a weakness in the understanding of the incarnation? Is there not, after all, a doubt as to whether the divine authority really has assumed a worldly form? We may focus the question like this: Did the Sermon on the Mount, with its 'extraplanetary' demand, actually take on form in the human life of Jesus of Nazareth? And is this form, however imperfectly, reflected in the lives of the apostles and the saints? If so, have we any right to restrict its significance to a purely transcendent protest, and to deny that it has given us a pattern for life in the world? The chapter on 'the christological character of the *imago dei*' (ch. 10; pp. 171–194), with its uncompromising denials of *imitatio Christi*, does not provide a satisfactory answer to these questions.

Irreplaceable authority

As the one whom God has sent, Jesus is irreplaceable; as the new man he is the pattern to which we may conform ourselves, the bearer of a moral authority which belongs to the true order of human life in the world. These two conceptions are not easy to think together. The incarnate divine presence is an event bounded by definite references of time and place which constitute God's final utterance to mankind 'once for all'. We may draw from it general conclusions about God's dealings with mankind in every time and place, but that is because this event is the ground of such dealings, not because it exemplifies them. But moral authority cannot be located in a particular person or event except as an example of the universal pattern. Socrates' death at Athens in 399 BC may be said to carry moral authority in that it commands our admiration and inspires us to emulate the philosopher's integrity and courage. But it does so by directing our attention to the virtues of integrity and courage as such, which are aspects of a moral order that is not particular to any time and place. Socrates' death carries authority because it witnesses to those virtues; any other person's death, comparable in significant respects, could witness to them quite as effectively. The authority of a witness is interchangeable in principle. Furthermore, as the purpose of bearing witness is to bring the observer to equality of perspective with the witness himself, the moral authority of a particular witness is in principle self-effacing; it aims to open the observer's eyes to the moral order and so make itself, as mediator, redundant. What follows when we apply such a concept of moral authority to Jesus is apparent in the famous observation of Kant (*Groundwork* 408):

'Even the Holy One of the Gospels must be compared with our ideal of moral perfection before he is recognized as such.' The 'holy one' becomes another example of a moral order which has its validity quite independently of him.

One common approach to resolving this difficulty has been a direct appeal to Jesus' identity with the Logos, or Word of God, through whom all things are made. Socrates, it is said, points away from himself precisely because he knows himself to be only a witness and servant of the moral order. In this respect he is like John the Baptist, whose task is to point to one greater than himself. But in Jesus we meet the moral order itself revealed as incarnate. The self-effacing character of moral authority arises from the non-identity of the witnesss and the object of witness; but in Jesus the witness and the object of witness are one. Thus in Jesus' teaching we find a direct self-commendation which is comprehensible only because of who he is. This approach has one very clear merit. It resolves to establish a concept of Jesus' moral authority which arises directly from Christological proclamation. In declining to accept the dilemma on Kant's terms and preferring to start directly from those of Saint John, it commends itself as an approach with theological seriousness. However, we may then remember that the difficulty was not entirely conjured out of nothing by Kant, but was reached (in our discussion at least) from a perfectly theological concern to ground the moral order in creation; and then we may wonder, simply on theological grounds, whether this approach is adequate. Does it not have a flavour of monophysitism about it? In its use of the Logos-concept as a bridging-notion between God and creation, is it not hinting that the moral order is not a *created* order at all, but an expression of the character of divinity? If so, it must be open to the objections raised in the last chapter to the Neo-Platonic tendency to swallow up created authority in the divine. If, on the other hand, its proponent wished to avoid the suggestion of monophysitism, and yet retain the idea of Christ as the concrete embodiment of the Logos which shapes creation, would he not stand before us as a rank Arian, dividing the Word from the Godhead? In our view the solution is not to be found this way, nor are Saint John's words about the Word through whom all things are made (Jn. 1:3) to be given this Stoicizing interpretation, which makes the shape of the universe a direct imprint of the character of the immanent Word.

In contrast to this monophysite resolution to the problem we may wish to propose a diphysite one, which will attempt to preserve intact the creatureliness of the moral order. It will distinguish two aspects within Jesus' authority, his 'moral authority' in the strict sense, in which he confronts us as a teacher and as an object of imitation, and his authority as the divine Word by whom God proclaims the redemption of the created order. When

God declares, in the resurrection of Jesus, that he will sustain, redeem and transform that which he has made, his word is *about* the moral order but is not part *of* it. Rather, it has the character of the underlying divine *fiat* which holds the moral order in being. If, as an experiment in thought, we were to abstract Jesus' moral authority from the authority of this divine word, we might say about him everything that we might say about Socrates. We might say that any comparable example or teacher would do as well; that his moral authority is self-effacing; that if it is true that we should forgive our enemies, then it is as true on Saint Francis' lips as on Jesus', and that simply from the point of view of morality it makes no difference from whom we learnt it. The point at which Jesus is irreplaceable is not here. He is irreplaceable because in his resurrection the moral order was publicly and cosmically vindicated by God. Saint Francis may teach morality as well as Jesus, but only Jesus has revealed God's final redemptive word about morality.

Such an approach has certain clear advantages. It discourages, in the first place, ill-founded attempts to discover a uniqueness in Jesus' teaching where uniqueness need not be discovered. When we find in the teaching of sages earlier than Jesus or independent of him thoughts that are comparable to his, we need not make great efforts to demonstrate his originality. It is not, for example, a striking service to Christology to insist that Jesus was the first to propound the Golden Rule in its positive rather than its negative form; nor will we recognize the divine presence more clearly when we learn that no rabbi before him combined the quotation of Deuteronomy 6:5 with that of Leviticus 19:18.

In the second place, this approach has the advantage of clarifying an important distinction in the hermeneutics of Christian faith and obedience. The Christian faith which the Holy Spirit evokes in us is faith in Jesus as the one sent by God in historical particularity. If some Christian community, possessed by a desire to make the creed more relevant, were to substitute the name of some well-known contemporary dictator for that of Pontius Pilate, the rest of the church would express justifiable anxiety that this community had not grasped the uniqueness of Jesus' death, but mistakenly supposed it to be a mere example of the general relationship between persecuted and persecutor. If, on the other hand, a community under persecution were to address its tormentors with the words with which Jesus addressed Pilate (Jn. 19:11), 'You would have no power over me unless it had been given you from above', it would be an admirable instance of the *imitatio Christi*. What is the difference? If the one historical transposition is illegitimate, why not the other? The point is surely that Jesus' words to Pilate point to a generic principle that is not in itself historically particular, but becomes so only circumstantially when addressed by Jesus to Pilate. It is a perfectly valid application of the principle to apply it to any comparable situation. In this respect the hermeneutic principles which apply to Jesus' moral teaching are exactly comparable to those which apply to the teaching of Socrates. But no equivalent transposition could be made with Jesus' identification of himself as the Son of man, which is not moral teaching, and not of universal application as moral teaching is.

However, someone could reply that exactly the same distinction could be made in the case of Socrates' teaching. On the one hand there are universal principles, *e.g.* that one should not flee when condemned unjustly by the laws of one's own country; and on the other there are stories about himself, *e.g.* that his *daimon* gave him no warning on the day that he was condemned. Propositions about particular events and persons are logically incapable of generic application; it is this, and not anything to do with their status as revelation, which makes the historical statements of the creed different from Christian moral teaching. Consequently, the question of whether Jesus' moral teaching is included in the irreplaceable revelation of divine authority cannot be settled merely by separating out the universal from the particular. To try to settle it that way is to beg the question against the incarnation. For a diphysite Christology, too, can undermine the incarnation if its divisive movement of thought is not corrected by a unifying one. If we allow our experiment of thought to stand without qualification, our conclusion may simply be that as a moral teacher Jesus has no special authority at all. And this is by no means a hypothetical conclusion, but has been rather strongly in the air in circles which have proclaimed his life, death and resurrection as saving event while treating his moral teaching and example with a studied lack of interest. Having distinguished the two aspects of Jesus' authority, then, can we learn to think of that authority once again as the one and undivided authority of the Son of God? Is there an analogue to the Christological doctrine of the hypostatic union?

We may approach this question in two stages, epistemological and ontological. At the epistemological level we may point out that a certain irreplaceability belongs to moral authority even where there is no question of divine uniqueness. When Kant urged that 'the Holy One of the Gospels must be compared with our ideal of moral perfection before he is recognized as such,' he made, it must be said, rather niggardly allowance even for the purely human moral authority which we may ascribe to such a one as Socrates. Is it not the case that Socrates showed us aspects of the moral law which we could not have appreciated without him? Kant seems to have envisaged such an *a priori* immediacy of the moral law to the mind that any kind of disclosure was unnecessary. And if that were the case, no individual teachers would possess moral authority at all, for moral authority would never be alienated from the moral law itself. It is possible to speak altogether too abstractly about the interchangeability of moral witnesses and the equality of perspective between teacher and taught, overlooking the fact that they are the goal, rather than the presupposition, of moral authority. Moral authority arises where there is no equality of perspective and no alternative witness, but where someone exceptional is needed to show people things which, however universally true these may be, they are not capable of recognizing otherwise. We may characterize Jesus' moral authority by analogy with that of the great teachers if we remember that it cannot be outgrown short of an eschatological fullness of vision. And in that context we need not be afraid to speak even of an equality of perspective with the Son of God, in that the New Testament refers to our 'adoption as sons', and to Christ as 'the first-born among many brethren' (Rom. 8:23, 29).

But at the ontological level we must say something stronger: Jesus is not only a witness to the restored moral order, however indispensable; he is the one in whom that order has come to be. God has willed that the restored creation should take form in, and in relation to, one man. He exists not merely as an example of it, not even as a prototype of it, but as the one in whom it is summed up. To participate in the new creation is, not provisionally only but for ever, to participate in Christ – in an equality with him, certainly, since we have been adopted into his relation to the Father, yet never interchangeably. And so we may speak of his authority quite satisfactorily in terms of the 'concrete universal', though the thought that lies behind that phrase has been turned upon its head. It is not that concreteness has become susceptible of universal meaning, *finitum capax infiniti*, but that in the renewed creation order the universal meaning which lies behind all our moral perceptions has been given a concrete and irreplaceable embodiment, one who is designated by God to bear its authority in himself: 'This is my Son, my Chosen; listen to him!' (Lk. 9:35).

To sum up this train of thought we may refer simply to Hebrews 2:10 – 3:6. 'It was fitting that he, for whom and by whom all things exist, in bringing many sons to glory,' (shall we say 'authority' for *doxa*?) 'should make the pioneer of their salvation perfect through suffering.' In what follows the author explores the implications of this term 'pioneer' (*archē-gon*), its implications of similarity and generic equality on the one hand, and its implications of transcendence on the other. First, equality: 'For he who sanctifies and those who are sanctified have all one origin. That is why he is not ashamed to call them brethren.' 'He had to be made like his brethren in every respect,' he goes on (17), 'so that he might become a merciful and faithful high priest in the service of God.' This 'apostle and high priest' we are to 'consider' (3:1). How are we to consider him? As one like ourselves, who has been a faithful witness to the order in which we live, 'faithful to him who appointed him, just as Moses also was faithful in God's house'. The comparison with Moses does for the author's argument what the comparison with Socrates has done for ours: it requires a qualification, to show how Jesus has an *irreplaceable* authority which cannot be attributed even to the most faithful of God's witnesses. 'Yet Jesus has been counted worthy of as much more glory than Moses' (again, shall we say 'authority'?) 'as the builder of a house has more honour than the house . . . Now Moses was faithful in all God's house as a servant, to testify . . .' while Jesus is the founder of the new order. Of course, the author acknowledges, God himself is the founder of all things, and certainly the founder of the new order; but he has founded it in Jesus. In this house Jesus will always be the son (6), and we shall be 'his house if we hold fast our confidence and pride in our hope'.

Evangelical authority

The burden of morality arises from its arbitrariness. Overcoming the burden, proclaiming the good news of liberation, is a matter of overcoming arbitrariness. In the last chapter we touched briefly on how the voluntarist characterization of divine authority may make God's command appear as an alien imposition, which can only be resented. Now we must notice quite a different possibility for the voluntarist tradition, one which was expressed supremely in the thought of the Reformation. Arbitrariness is not the prerogative of the divine command. It belongs essentially to political authority, but also (as Luther magnificently understood) to reason itself, to the extent that reason has become abstract and out of touch with reality. Even a realist understanding of the redeemed world-order can be arbitrary if it is not related to the existential situation of the agent. It may direct mankind to the achievement of his true good, and yet, if it does not address his need as a sinner, it may be no more than a repetition of the curse. In speaking of 'the Law', which was Saint Paul's name for that phase of Jewish experience which was dominated by the Mosaic social order, the Reformers rightly believed they had found a category for understanding the burdensomeness of morality as such, which is to say, of any socio-moral order which bore down oppressively upon the moral agent because of its arbitrary relation to his plight. Given such a social order as that, the transcendent arbitrariness of the divine command, which cut across all order, was not oppressive but liberating. Because it took no form except that of criticism, it could only set the agent free. The simple transcendence of divine authority, then, lay at the heart of the Reformers' gospel.

When the apostle contrasted 'the law' and 'the gospel', he was pointing to the dialectical tension in Israel's history between the experience of God through *promise* and the experience of God through *command*. The law represented a phase in God's dealings with his people in which their primary character as blessing, first made evident in the promises to Abraham, was provisionally obscured through the Mosaic order, in which they are seen as ambiguously open either to become blessing or to become curse. The law was thus a particular historical phase of Israel's experience of God; but the Jewish experience of history is seen to represent a universal existential situation in which an individual at any point of history may find himself before Christ has become a saving reality in his own experience. To experience moral command as 'the law', then, is to encounter it *as though* from a point in the history of salvation at which God has not yet given the total blessing which he has promised his people. Law supposes that God's complete saving purpose is still an object of hope. But the promise of completion is conditional, and depends upon the faithful performance of the command. Command, therefore, becomes a hurdle which one must overcome in order to experience blessing. Law is *command as reciprocal bargain*, the breach of which promises disaster. In these circumstances command evokes anxiety, but not anxiety for the future of the community so much as for the individual. The divine promise assures us that Abraham's seed will be preserved for salvation through a faithful remnant; but that offers no ground of confidence to the individual, for whom the question 'Am I to be among the chosen?' is not answered either in promise or in law. Thus the anxiety which the command promotes isolates the individual, with his unresolved destiny, from the community which is to inherit God's promises. Inescapably, then, the law confronts the individual supremely as a *demand for community-adherence*. Its content is dominated by ritual observance, that aspect of public righteousness by which the individual is claimed by his conformity for membership of the community. It reaches the individual, not directly as God's word to him, but 'mediated through angels' (Gal. 3:19*), that is, through the created authority of the community. Against this authority, vested in prophets, priests and kings, he can claim no rights. They are beyond the criticism of one who is not himself a prophet, priest or king, who has no anointing and no share in the Spirit of God, but who can obey the command only as it reaches him through God's representatives.

The passage of 2 Corinthians (3:4 – 4:6), in which Paul contrasts the ministry of Moses with that of the Christian apostle, is of great importance. The key to the passage is given in the repeated assertions of the apostle's confidence (3:4, 12; 4:1), a confidence based on divine accreditation (3:5–6) and on the eternal validity of the gospel message (3:11), which results in a complete frankness and directness of communication (4:2). In contrast to this stands Moses. His message is one of condemnation rather than justification, of death rather than of the Spirit of life (3:7–9), and its significance is merely provisional, as is symbolized by the fading of the splendour from his face after he comes down from the mountain in Exodus 34 (3:7, 11, 13). His ministry, therefore, has a certain style about it which is appropriate to his message; that style is represented by the veil, a symbol of concealment and dissimulation which is the very opposite of the openness characteristic of the Christian apostle (3:13). To understand the climax of the passage it is necessary to punctuate 3:13–16 as follows: (a) a light pause, and no more, after *katargoumenou* (13) makes it clear that the hardening of the Israelites' minds was a necessary result of the Mosaic concealment. The dispensation of Moses was intended to hide the glory of God from the mind of man by a system of law and worship. (b) A parenthesis, beginning with *achri gar* (14) and concluding with *epi tēn kardian autōn keitai* (15), illustrates the effect of this hardening from the resistance of the Jewish community to the gospel in Paul's own day. (c) A new sentence, beginning with *hēnika de ean epistrepsē* (16), does not continue the discussion of the Jews in Paul's day, but resumes the exposition of Exodus 34. The subject of *epistrepsē* is Moses (thus NEB correctly, against most English versions). We may therefore paraphase the whole: 'We differ from Moses (who was cautious and not confident) in that he veiled his face to conceal from the Israelites the steady diminution of the radiance. They were left in ignorance of it. To this day, indeed, when the Old Covenant is read, that same veil remains in place. It is never revealed (to the listening Jew) that in Christ the Mosaic radiance has been done away with. To this day, I say, when Moses is read, the veil obscures the Jews' understanding. But when Moses turns back (from addressing the people) to face the Lord, the veil (we read) is taken off. The Lord (of whom the text speaks) is the Spirit; and where the Spirit of the Lord is, there is (not caution and dissimulation, but) freedom.' The dispensation of concealment at the foot of Mount Sinai gives way to an exchange between Moses and the Lord at the summit, in which all concealment is set aside. There, indeed, there is an immediate and direct communication of God with mankind, a communication into which Israel as a whole was not admitted. But we Christians are admitted to it, because 'the Lord of whom this passage speaks' (17, NEB correctly) is the Spirit, who is now given to all believers and not to the lawgiver alone. The whole of Christian communication (in which, we must observe, Christian ethics is included) takes place at the summit of Mount Sinai and not at its foot, 'with unveiled face' (18), so that the glory of the Lord is manifest to all without concealment.

The Lutheran tradition, which of all theological traditions has most strongly cherished the Pauline dialectic of law and gospel, has usually found it difficult to accept that an *ordered* moral demand can be, in and of itself, evangelical. The antithesis between Moses and Christ has been widened to encompass a total opposition between order and transcendence. The liberating activity of God is marked by its insusceptibility to characterization in terms of order, while order, even the order of creation, has been classed with law rather than with gospel, and so assigned a purely provisional and transitory significance. The implications for understanding Jesus' moral teaching have been variously understood. We shall address only the recurrent claim that they represent a continuing dialectic between gospel and law, and that the believer is claimed by both gospel and law when he responds to Christian moral teaching.

In Luther's own thought we can already see how much Christian moral teaching is understood in terms of a continuing presence of law. Often, it is true, not all moral teaching is understood this way, but only teaching about our social duties as members of families, as employers, as subjects and as magistrates. Thus, for example, in his exposition of the Sermon on the Mount Luther lays great stress on the contrast between the *attitudes* which are taken to be the concern of the Beatitudes and the formal *structure of responsibilities* which is imposed upon us by our situation in the world (*WA* 32:304ff.) On other occasions it would seem that all morality is included, as in the breath-taking passage from the 1531 *Commentary on Galatians* (*WA* 40:446f.), where the distinction between law and faith is equated with that between the active and contemplative lives. For Luther's successors this continuing role of law was expressed by the addition of a 'third use' to Luther's account of the 'theological' and 'civil' uses of the law (*e.g.* Melanchthon, *Loci Communes: de lege divina*, CR 21:405f., and Calvin, *Institutes* II.7.6ff.; *cf.* Luther's *Commentary on Galatians*, 1531, on 3:19, *WA* 40:478ff.). The third use was the 'didactic' use, which was the law's role in instructing the believer in righteousness. The historical question, whether Luther anticipated such a third use in his polemic against the antinomians, is not of great importance to us. The significant thing is that in this discussion the moral law, whether or not it is allowed to instruct the believer, is all the time the Mosaic law, the 'law' which was opposed in Saint Paul's dialectic to the 'promise' and the 'Spirit'. Thus a normative Christian ethic, whether it is admitted or denied, is regarded either way as something unevangelical, a *preparation* for the gospel at best.

Hence our objection when Helmut Thielicke finds it necessary to justify the presence of an 'imperative' in Christian ethics by speaking of 'the continuing pedagogic significance of the Law for believers' (*Theological Ethics*, I, pp. 126ff.). In our state of pilgrimage, he tells us, our liberation from the law is not complete. 'As surely as we must insist that the believer is radically and totally liberated from the law, so surely must we also put the question of whether we are such believers, to what "extent" we are, and whether it is practical to throw away our crutches before we can really walk.' Which would seem to mean: we must hesitate in unbelief and doubt! Our objection is not to the idea that there is in the believer's experience something comparable to the oppressive discipline of the Mosaic order, a 'mortification' of 'your members which are on the earth' (Col. 3:5, AV), but to the suggestion that this is the *sole* significance of normative Christian ethics. Thus every creative and redemptive summons from God must be introduced, as it were, with an apology for the fact that it is not good news. But the command of God is not to be dismissed as an unevangelical *praeparatio evangelii*. It is not a crutch; it is a life-giving command, 'Rise, take up your bed and walk!'

Karl Barth's famous reversal of the usual order in his anti-Lutheran paper 'Gospel and Law' should be seen as an attempt to bring German Protestant ethics back into the catholic mainstream of Christian moral understanding. Yet we cannot be content while the term 'the law', with its necessary Pauline overtones of preparation for, and opposition to, the gospel, remains the usual term for prescriptive moral teaching. I have felt free to use the term 'moral law', understanding the adjective to differentiate Christian moral teaching from '*the* law'. 'Law' on its own should, in my view, by restricted to two spheres of reference: (a) positive community law; and (b) that special case of positive community law which had such rich theological significance for Paul, namely the law of the Mosaic community.

Jesus' moral authority is evangelical in the fullest sense, since the moral order which he proclaims is the kingdom of God, the theme of his message of salvation. It is a moral order in which the arbitrariness of sinful man's relation to God's purposes has been overcome and done away with. When Saint Matthew introduces Jesus' teaching with the programmatic summary, 'Repent, for the kingdom of heaven is at hand' (Mt. 4:17), he shows quite clearly how the moral challenge belongs with the eschatological message. The well-known sermon in which he collects so much of Jesus' moral teaching begins with the announcement that the poor in spirit are to possess the kingdom, the sorrowful are to be comforted and the meek are to inherit the earth. The call to practise a righteousness which exceeds that of the scribes and Pharisees cannot be heard apart from this setting. It is, on the whole, an exaggerated piety that insists too much upon the impossibility of Jesus' teaching in the Sermon on the Mount. Certainly, it is too much for us to keep these moral precepts consistently, short of eschatological transformation, as it is too much for us to keep any serious moral programme consistently. The mere challenge of morality itself points us to the limits of our capacity to live well and to our need for world-redemption. But world-redemption is precisely what Jesus' message announces, and it is that that should command our attention and belief before anything else.

Certain features of Jesus' message are of special importance in characterizing his moral teaching as gospel, providing the basis for Paul's perceptions about how his coming reversed the situation which obtained under the law. In the first place there is the message that *God mercifully forgives our sins*, which more than anything else transforms the terror which we feel before the ambiguous blessing and curse of the law into trusting confidence. It is not, of course, that there is no mention of the forgiveness of sins in the Old Testament, both within the context of covenant faithfulness and as part of the national eschatological hope. But in Jesus' message this theme assumes a controlling immediacy, which allows Paul to contrast the gospel with the law as a life of faith as opposed to a life of works. If the Father welcomes home the prodigal son, life in the Father's fellowship is not conditional upon a consistent moral or ritual achievement. In the second place, the alienation and insecurity of the individual is overcome by *the teaching of the Abba prayer*, in which the disciples are summoned to share Jesus' own relationship to the Father and the complete assurance which it implies. Thirdly, the mediatorial role of community institutions is countered by *the criticism of externalized morality and religion*, a theme which occupies a central place in the Sermon on the Mount itself. This criticism affirms the individual agent, in his secret chamber and apart from all observing eyes, as the recipient of God's moral demand; he is not merely a comforming member of the community which God addresses. These two latter elements are taken up by Paul in terms of the contrast between law and Spirit. It is the Holy Spirit who bears witness with our spirit, addressing us at the seat of our individual agency and teaching us to pray the Abba prayer with Jesus (Rom. 8:15–16). And it is the Holy Spirit who breaks down the Mosaic mediatorial community-structure, which concealed God as much as it revealed him, and who creates a different relationship of freedom and openness within the Christian community.

Are we to say that this has nothing to do with 'moral' authority? Such a terminological decision would be purely captious; for to live addressing God as our Father, trusting him for the forgiveness of sins, and not hiding from our responsibility to him behind the performances of the community, this is precisely to live in the order for which mankind and the world were made. We may even speak of an 'evangelical moral law' – a 'law of Christ', as Saint Paul put it (Gal. 6:2) – for although the phrase has a self-conscious element of verbal paradox about it given the opposition of law and gospel, the paradox serves precisely to show up how the arbitrary socio-religious weight of Mosaic law was *not* that summons to fulfilment which is given by God's grace. Danger arises only when this contrast is forgotten, when attempts are made to reconstruct the 'evangelical law' on the model of the Mosaic, assigning to the Christian community and its institutions a role analogous to that of the community-structure of Israel. To the criticism of this development we shall return in the next chapter.

Historical authority

Historical ends, as we observed in chapter three, are particular, while moral ends are generic. From this it follows that, since historical ends defy analogy and attach to events only as those events are thought of as unique, historical ends have nothing to do with the *worldliness* of events. There are only two ways by which we may come to understand time as 'history': either by believing that *God* has conferred upon particular moments of time a unique significance that is not derived simply from their likeness to other moments, or by believing that *man*, in constructing his own narrative interpretation, has done so. For example: a wedding has a certain significance and point simply by being a wedding like other weddings, capable of evoking our generic response to the place of marriage in human life; but when we think that any wedding has a unique significance, because it is the wedding of *this* couple and not of any other, then we have seen in it some meaning that does not arise from its place in the world-order, and we must speak of it either in theological or poetic terms, either of divine vocation or of some heroic world-shaping transcendence. Historicism is at odds with moral thinking, because its conception that all ends are of this unique kind necessarily does away with the very structure of worldly meaning which gives morality (as opposed to theology or poetry) its point.

The coming of Christ has, before it has any other meaning, a historical one: it is a word of God which confers upon the totality of events their shape and point as 'history'. 'God', the writer to the Hebrews proclaimed, echoing a parable of Jesus' own teaching, has 'in these last days spoken to us by a Son' (Heb. 1:2; *cf.* Mk. 12:1–12). The word spoken 'in these last days' makes a history out of the 'many and various' utterances of the past which would otherwise have had no shape and direction. Here history is given a climax and, with the climax, all that preceded is formed into history. Christ's authority is 'historical' because it confers a unique meaning on the shape of world events. But from that it follows that it confers a unique and unrepeatable significance to each event, as it is seen to be a part, whether major or minor, of that total history. No deed of man can claim any longer to have autonomous intelligibility. Thus the prophets of Israel, from reading the events of their own land as a history shaped by God's purposes for his people, came to speak also of affairs far distant from Israel's borders, since Israel's calling gave them a measure for interpreting all events everywhere, making one 'history' of all the deeds of men upon the face of the earth.

Historical authority can draw together in one narrative, to serve one historical end, contradictory movements. A story can encompass a change of mind, or a disagreement, and still remain a story with a single point, not in itself contradictory or divided. The dying thief can acknowledge Christ upon the cross, and in that moment of repentance bring all his life of brigandage to its fulfilment, not merely its last few hours. Historical authority can reconcile, where moral authority can only judge. We must expect to find, then, within the world-history which Christ shapes around himself, moral incompatibilities that are reconciled historically. When we read, for example, of the conquest of Canaan and the terms of the ban, we will understand the Christological significance of these events only if we suspend the moral question which we immediately wish to put to them. The Christian reading of the Old

Testament has been constantly baffled by a failure to understand this. The moral question has pushed itself forward, either in indignant protest or (worse) in sophistic justification. Like the elder brother of the prodigal son, Christians reading the book of Joshua need to learn how to ask other questions before the moral ones: the history of divine revelation, like the waiting father in the parable, is not concerned only with justifying the good and condemning the bad. This Old Testament history is concerned only to reveal the impact of the divine reality upon the human in election and judgment. We may wonder, of course, as we read the book of Joshua, what attitude this God of jealousy and wrath will take to the worldly order of things; and that question will be answered for us only as we follow the story of his self-revelation forward to its climax in Jesus Christ. The demand which this part of the story makes upon our faith is not that we should struggle to reconcile in moral terms the form of creaturely order which is shown us by Christ in Gethsemane with these unbridled acts of war, but that we should accept what is, perhaps, the greater scandal: a reconciliation in the history of divine revelation which can embrace even such a contradiction to the moral order. In God's self-disclosure something had to come *before* the vindication of the moral order: the transcendent fire of election and judgment had to be shown in all its nakedness, in all its possible hostility to the world, if we were to learn what it meant that in Christ the Word of God became flesh and took the cause of the world as his own cause. This 'had to' refers to an order of self-disclosure which was necessary if we were to understand the import of the incarnation, and not to any necessity imposed on God. The incarnation must never be taken for granted, as though it concerned a God who was, quite naturally and in the course of things, at home in the world. Before we could learn of God as vindicator of the moral order we had to learn something even more basic.

But when that has been said, the Christian gospel does proclaim that God has made himself at home in the world, that the Word has become flesh. The created order has been vindicated in a way that was never anticipated in the book of Joshua. The story which comes to its climax in Christ is not only the story of divine election (as the book of Joshua understood it) but (as the primaeval history of Genesis understood it) the story of the election of mankind in Adam and of the world-order in which Adam was created. The moral questions, then, are only suspended, to allow the theological questions priority; they are not forgotten. We are not mistaken to think that Joshua was morally unworthy of Gethsemane, any more than the elder brother was mistaken to think that the prodigal was unworthy of his father's compassion. There is, in Jesus' own references to Elijah, more than a hint of criticism of the holy war conceptions which that prophet attempted to restore (*e.g.*

Lk. 9:52–56) – yet Elijah has his place with Moses on the Mount of Transfiguration. A Christian understanding of the authority of Christ, then, conceives that it presents a moral challenge to all ages. Moral incompatibilities are not finally overlooked, but are set right. To be among the chosen of Israel's God means, in the end, to be conformed to the order of worldly life which God has created. To believe in the anointed one of God means also to believe in the moral order which Jesus has shown and vindicated to us. Such a belief, Christians have generally maintained against the Marcionite and anti-Jewish strands of thought in the church, does not imply disbelief in the amoral disclosures of God by ritual, cult and violence; but neither does it imply the permanence of the contingent social institutions of the Jewish past which have given expression to the moral order. It means belief that Christ turns these fragmentary utterances of God's voice, in warrior triumphs and legislative order, into a history which culminates in the divine manifestation and vindication of created order. Thus all the time, in one sense, the story of the Old Testament was the story of that order; and in reading the Old Testament as Christians we may expect to see this story, too, emerge from its pages.

This hermeneutic principle has been acknowledged in the church at least since Justin Martyr, who distinguished within the Mosaic law two, or possibly three, categories of command: 'that which was ordained for piety and the practice of righteousness' and that which was 'either to be a mystery of the Messiah or because of the hardness of heart of your people' (*Dialogue with Trypho* 44.3; *cf.* 18.1). In its twofold form the distinction became a commonplace in patristic hermeneutics. 'Who does not know?' begins the author of the Pseudo-Augustinian *Speculum 'Quis Ignorat'* (5th century) 'that within Holy Scripture . . . there are propositions to be understood and believed . . . and commands and prohibitions to be observed and acted upon . . . ? Among the latter some have a meaning hidden in sacramental ritual, so that many commands given to be obeyed by the people of the Old Testament are not now performed by Christian people . . . Others, however, are to be observed even now.' With Thomas Aquinas (*Summa Theologiae* II–I.99.3ff.) the distinction is established in its threefold form (*iudicalia, caeremonalia, moralia*); in which it is taken up by the Reformers, Melanchthon (*Loci Communes*, CR 1:201), Calvin (*Institutes* IV. 20.14ff.) and Cranmer (*42 Articles*).

It is surprising to observe the disrepute into which the tradition has fallen in recent times, for all our modern preoccupations with hermeneutics. Three observations may help to clarify its usefulness. (1) It purports to be a Christian hermeneutic of Old Testament law. The need for such a hermeneutic arises because the Council of Jerusalem declared that most observances of the Mosaic law were not binding on non-Jewish Christians (Acts 15:19–29) and because Jesus taught that the Deuteronomic divorce law was written 'for the hardness of your hearts' and did not represent God's primary intention for marriage (Mk. 10:5–9). It is not pertinent to object that no such distinction among the laws is conceived of in the Old

Testament itself, for that is precisely the point. The distinction arises only as Christians ask how the Old Testament law can be read thoughtfully outside the social and religious context to which it first belonged. The patristic church was, however, encouraged to think along these lines by their awareness that in the prophetic period a certain critical distance on the law had already been assumed: Ezekiel's saying, 'I gave them statutes that were not good' (20:25) is quoted in this context both by Justin and by Irenaeus (*Adversus Haereses* IV.15f.). (2) The distinction does, however, interpret the law in categories that are clearly germane to what the Mosaic system was, in fact, about. It is not an alien imposition to say that the Old Testament corpus of laws was concerned with morality, with pre-moral religious ritual and with political jurisdiction all at once. It may be a distinctively Christian judgment that the pre-moral ceremonial law does not bind Christians while the moral law does; but it is a perfectly sympathetic interpretation of the Mosaic order to say that it has concerns that are pre-moral as well as concerns that are moral. (3) It was appropriate that the fundamental shape of this distinction should be twofold, as its concern was to characterize the twofold authority of Christ, historical and moral, fulfilling and completing the history of Israel on the one hand, vindicating the universal moral order on the other. The recognition of a third category has the force of acknowledging that not everything that is historically particular to Israel is marked by an absence of moral concern. The Old Testament witness to the moral order itself is bound up in historical and arbitrary social forms. This, then, marks the end of naive attempts to apply the principle in a classificatory way, such as that of the *Speculum 'Quis Ignorat'* with its proposal, misconceived as well as tedious, to make a list of all the moral commands of the Bible. To confess that this is impossible does not make the principle less valuable to us. Its contribution is to identify the different *concerns* which shape Old Testament law, and to relate these concerns theologically to Christ; so that even though any text may reflect more than one of these concerns, we have criteria for assessing its relation to the moral order without ignoring its particular socio-religious setting and function.

Since this is the story which the Scriptures tell, the authority to which they point is a universal moral authority. Not every event which shapes other events into history must necessarily have a moral authority; not every story of divine election must necessarily command other times and places than its own. It is because the story of Jewish election is also the story of created order that Gentiles may respond to it. It is because the redemption which Jesus brought was a redemption of the world that he may command the form of our lives within it. If there were no world in common between us and our redeemer, then, were he never so divine, he could not redeem our world but only snatch us out of it into some other.

Every generation of Christians has its fashionable form of scepticism; and the fashion of our own is to doubt the possibility of a moral authority which can command the modern world from a historical situation in the first century AD. (We are not concerned here with limited *historical* doubt as to whether it is possible to distinguish Jesus' teaching from what the early church made of it, but with the *systematic* doubt that any first-century teaching, of whatever provenance, could command twentieth-century mankind.) Those who urge this doubt upon us are moved by various considerations. Some are impressed by the cultural foreignness of first-century Palestine; for not only is the Graeco-Roman world itself less familiar to us than it was to our fathers, but the land of the Dead Sea Scrolls does not fit into it quite as simply as it once seemed to. Others are struck by the novelty of our modern moral deliberations, newly focused as they are by the conditions of a mass society and the technological domination of nature. But neither of these considerations can account for the force with which these doubts assail modern Christians. Cultural foreignness, which we meet in our contemporaries almost daily, is not a final barrier to understanding, but a warning against shallow understandings. Novelty in the moral questions we confront is not peculiar to our modern society, but a feature of moral thinking in every age; again, it is a stimulus, not a barrier, to the comprehension of old and new within one moral field. The root cause of our scepticism lies not in these complications of moral thought which are, nevertheless, finally unproblematic, but in the conception of time as history, with its denial to past events of any significance other than their contribution to subsequent developments. Historical understanding makes it necessary to construe the word 'past' as meaning 'alien'; it forbids us to meet a historical figure on his own terms, allowing us only to place him in his context, which means, in effect, to distance ourselves from what he would say to us.

Whatever may be said in favour of these doubts, it cannot be what is often thoughtlessly said, that they pay respect to Jesus' humanity. For they deny him, and the apostolic writers with him, what would seem to be a necessary correlate with humanity, which is membership of a common world with other human beings about which they can communicate. The tendency of these doubts is to destroy the community of intelligibility between our speech and his, so that we may know his words only historically, as an event of the past, and not as a communication about the world with which we could enter into discussion. Their underlying concern, of course, is not with the divinity of Jesus Christ, but rather with the divinization of mankind as the creator of his own history. The community of past and present is destroyed in the interests of a doctrine of historical transformation, in which fulfilment is seen to lie by way of the negation of the past. The other-worldliness of our modern scepticism is the self-conscious anti-worldliness which is characteristic of the concern with modernity and progress.

The subjective reality

The 'historical hermeneutics' which have enjoyed a wide popularity under the influence of H.–G. Gadamer can best be understood as the attempt of a conservative historicism to mend the breach which radical historicism has created. They are therefore doomed, in my opinion, not to get to the root of the problem. The meeting of two alien 'horizons' may all too easily be celebrated precisely as an achievement of historical transcendence, without ever paying respect to the fundamental truth that past generations occupied the same world as ourselves and can speak with us about it. Is it sufficient to say that the modern horizon will be 'fused' with the ancient? How can such a fusion be anything other than a selective absorption of the ancient by the modern in accordance with the laws of its own metabolism? The lack of a common object of discourse delivers us over to our pre-understandings. To supply this lack is not, of course, to prejudge any questions about the authority with which any ancient writer will speak of the world, or whether he will tell us the truth about it. It is simply to insist that there is a common world about which questions of truth can be raised between us and him; so that moral authority can challenge us, and evoke our free response, even across the gulf of centuries.

8

The freedom of the church
and the believer

We return to the theme of freedom, the freedom to act in such a way that our freedom itself is affirmed and sustained, the freedom to achieve our supernatural end, which is the perfect liberty of the kingdom of God. It is Christ, the pioneer of renewed creation, who evokes this freedom in us, as the Holy Spirit makes the authority of his eschatological triumph subjectively present and immediate to us. But we return also to the observation that freedom does not belong to us only as individual agents. Our communal action, too, is made free by the work of Christ, who is the first of a community of brothers. Human freedom consists not only in the power to act alone, but in the power to act together, as a co-operating fellowship. Our humanity is destined, as the seer of the Apocalypse presents it, for the shared life of a city, a fulfilment, redeemed and transformed, of the collective existence of ancient Israel, the 'new Jerusalem, coming down out of heaven' (Rev. 21:2).

Among the fundamental questions of ethics which Augustine quotes from Varro at the beginning of *De civitate Dei* book XIX is the question *de sociali vita: utrum sic tenenda sapienti, ut summum bonum, quo fit homo beatus, ita velit et curet amici sui, quemadmodum suum, an suae tantummodo beatitudinis causa faciat quidquid faciat'* (XIX.1.3) – 'whether the wise man should so regard the social life as to value and pursue the final good as highly in his friend's case as in his own, or whether all his action should be conceived as a pursuit of his own happiness alone'. The Christian answer is: 'when they wish to say that the wise man's life is a social one, we agree – and say it much more clearly than they do' (*nos multo amplius adprobamus*, following G. Combès' French translation, 5). 'Much more clearly', because in its pagan form the question about the social life, as Augustine has already observed in reporting Varro, is not strictly a question about the final good at all. According to Varro the final good can be identified *prior* to raising the question 'whether the wise man should have a companion or not' (1.3). But for the Christian the community, rather than the wise man, is the *subject* of ethical reflection: 'How ever could the City of God . . . either take its beginning or advance upon its journey or achieve its proper ends, if the life of the saints were not a social life?' (5). Thus Christian thought undertakes to resolve an outstanding difficulty in classical ethics. On the one hand there was the tradition of Platonism, shaped by the martyrdom of Socrates, for whom the call of the good meant a solitary and tragic opposition to society; on the other there was the tradition of Aristotle, for whom the fulfilment of human good always presupposed a supportive social context, yet without, in the end, being any less an individual good, achieved by the philosopher standing, as it were, on the shoulders of society at large. Neither, thinks Augustine, takes the collective subject of ethics seriously enough, because neither knows of the City of God, which eschatologically transcends the tensions between infinite individual aspiration and the limitations of collective structures.

It has been traditional to speak one-sidedly of the church's *authority* in morals, an expression which is in itself unexceptionable and indeed necessary, but which can be understood correctly only when it is treated as a derivative implication of the church's *freedom* of moral action. What we have to discuss, when we touch on the relation between collective and individual, is not a dialectic of individual freedom and collective authority, but a dialectic of two freedoms, in which both community and believer are authorized to be free human agents. For the church, too, is mankind acting. It hears God's word addressed to it, it enters the kingdom of God by faith, and it begins to be conformed to its life. It hears God's word and does not merely speak it. It is mankind, and not an angel. Certainly, the church does proclaim the kingdom and is, therefore, in its secondary movement, the kingdom's messenger; but it can be so only because it has first heard the message and obeyed.

This rejection of what we may call 'angel-ecclesiology' could appear at first sight to be a typically Protestant gesture, belittling the authority of the church and exalting the freedom of the individual. The matter, however, is more complicated than that. For although it is true that the authority of the church is immediately enhanced if the church is represented as God's messenger, it turns out to be an entirely provisional and instrumental authority, won at the expense of the ultimate significance of the community in God's redeeming purposes. If the role of the community is simply to convey God's word to man, then the 'man' that is addressed by God's word is a humanity apart from community, an abstract individual for whose sake all the community's efforts are expended. And when, at the climax of history, this individual, multiplied an infinite number of times, is safely garnered into God's presence, the community's role will be over. If, on the other hand, the community does not merely speak *to* mankind but *is* the mankind that is spoken to, then the human response to God must display not only individual freedom but collective freedom. The community is then a true anticipation of the kingdom of God.

Angel-ecclesiology has had many forms, but within the sphere of Christian ethics the most striking has been the conception of an 'evangelical law'. The 'evangelical law' is the community-law which Christ is supposed to have given for the government of the church's life, and which it has been the task of the church to reapply in subsequent ecclesiastical legislation and administer by means of its discipline, both by excommunication and by the lesser disciplines attendant upon the confessional. The teaching and pastoral offices of the church mediate Christ's moral law to the individual and enable him to reach informed conscientious decisions. It is unjust to accuse this conception, as Protestants have sometimes done, of denying the individual the responsibility for his own decisions. It is also unjust to suppose that it claims a special grace of infallibility for the church offices which mediate moral instruction; for moral truths, as contemporary Roman Catholic moralists have been quick to assure us, cannot be the subject of infallible pronouncements. The point is simply that the individual's Christian judgment is formed *only* by this route; he has no other encounter with the moral authority of Christ than that which is provided for him by the tradition of church law and discipline. And such a conception, though without its moral formal legal aspect, still exercises a strong appeal among those who like to think of ethics as a function of sociology.

The visitor to the Sistine chapel in the Vatican who has gazed sufficiently upon the mighty ceiling and altar-piece of Michelangelo should not hurry away without studying the panels which cover the side-walls, where he will find a notable object-lesson in Moral Theology. These late fifteenth-century paintings, the work of various artists, comprise two parallel series of seven, one devoted to incidents from the life of Moses, the other to incidents from the life of Christ. The two series are contrasted and compared by the Latin titles, which describe Moses as the bearer of the law written on tablets of stone and Christ as the bearer of the new evangelical law, and, as in 2 Corinthians 3, they contrast the fading splendour of the one with the enduring splendour of the other. However, we may detect in the plan of these pictures a considerable departure from Saint Paul's emphasis. No longer is it a contrast between the written code that kills and the freedom of the Spirit which makes alive; it is a contrast between two kinds of *community-legislation*. Thus the crossing of the Red Sea bears the subscription, 'The gathering of the community to receive the written law from Moses', and is contrasted with the calling of Peter and Andrew, 'the gathering of the community to receive the evangelical law from Christ'. Moses on Mount Sinai is shown as 'the promulgation of the written law', and this is placed opposite the Sermon on the Mount, 'the promulgation of the evangelical law'. The punishment of the sons of Korah is 'the vindication of the authority of the written law', while the opposite panel shows Christ giving the keys to Peter, vindicating the authority of the evangelical law. Finally the two laws are 're-promulgated', the one at the entry to the promised land, the other at the last supper.

This conception can still be detected in the brief flowering of Anglican Moral Theology earlier in this century, and especially in the work of its most distinguished figure, Kenneth Kirk. Kirk's thought is often criticized today for being 'static' or 'metaphysical', or for the other vices which are supposed to adhere to those who admire Thomas Aquinas. Most of these criticisms are wide of the mark. Kirk was nothing if not aware of the need to loosen up the deductive rigidity of the Roman Catholic manualists. The real peril to which his thought was exposed was that of reducing morality to a function of community-legislation, with results that may be observed quite clearly in two short sections of *Conscience and its Problems* called 'the Relativity of Moral Law' and 'Custom and Re-interpretation' (pp. 71–86).

He begins from Thomas' division of the law into divine and human, the former subdivided into natural and revealed, the latter into civil and ecclesiastical. Only the 'first principles' of natural law, he reminds us, can be claimed to be beyond doubt. The same may be said of revealed law. 'Beyond doubt' means that we rest our conviction of these moral truths on an 'ultimate intuition' (p. 72). Some teachings of Jesus, some duties of religion taught by the church and certain moral positions established by the progress of Christian civilization share this apparent immunity to challenge (p. 73). From these first principles others are deduced, and sometimes they are believed to carry the same authority until 'sooner or later conscience begins to question' (p. 74). Many secondary principles once thought beyond challenge have thus proved 'unable to survive unchanged the storm and stress of time' (p. 76). But 'more disconcerting' is the discovery that even our supposed first principles are, after all, dissoluble by the same acid. 'That no reasonable Christian appears to question their validity is final evidence for their obligation today; but does it forbid the possibility of reasonable Christians legitimately questioning them tomorrow?' Such revision would be, of course, 'under the guidance of the Spirit', but there is no bar in principle to prevent anything whatever from being revised. Scripture is not such a bar, for 'every sentence . . . is capable of diverse interpretation' (p. 76). It is thus impossible to demarcate clearly between primary and secondary principles. But, then, neither can we distinguish sharply between secondary principles of divine law and human ecclesiastical law. Any expression of divine law is through human lips. This lays a great duty on the church of each generation to engage in a 'painstaking, conservative but brave revision of her moral code' (p. 79). This may happen by official action, but custom, too, if it is reasonable, established and acceptable to authority, can 'introduce, interpret or abrogate law' (p. 81). There are thus 'no limits to the action of custom and desuetude' (p. 82). There must, of course, be revolutionary moments at which new practice is striving to become custom, and the outcome is still unclear. This may mean that there is bad faith in the initiation of custom, but it need not do so; and even if there is, it may not affect the validity of the custom itself. 'We have to think, then, of the Church's code of obligations as . . . of any other living system of thought . . . Everywhere there is life, everywhere change, with a Church holding out her hands both to the past and to the future, and growing and developing with every moment of her existence' (p. 85).

It is clear that this 'softening of the sharp outlines of scholastic theology' (p. 80) is in fact a frontal attack on Thomas Aquinas' principles. Thomas believed that some immutable truths can be known with certainty. Kirk denies it. We accept, he thinks, some claimants to immutability 'more unhesitatingly' (!) – and in case anyone should miss the significance of the comparative form, he adds: 'Beyond that we cannot go' (p. 77). He has abolished immutable truths in two steps: first by assimilating revealed law to natural, so that even Christ's teaching is acknowledged (as in Kant!) on the basis of prior moral intuition; then in the second place by subjecting the moral intuition itself to a few routine sceptical feints which, in his view, are bound to overwhelm it. The principle which he claims to illustrate, that 'reason and revelation are different aspects of the same process' (p. 78), turns out in fact to be something quite different: that both reason and revelation are subject to the same ultimate criterion of being able to survive 'the storm and stress of time'.

But all this arises from a prior decision, which is to understand all morality in terms of community law, whether legislated or customary. Thomas Aquinas believed that there was a difference between ecclesiastical legislation and moral principle. Kirk curiously misunderstands Thomas' distinction, reinterpreting it in terms of certainty and doubtfulness. Thus he makes it impossible not only to criticize moral thought from the point of view of revelation, but to criticize community norms from the point of view of moral thought. For Kirk all moral thought is prescribed for us in the first instance by the community. 'The Church's code' includes both law and teaching indiscriminately. Conservative, because it has a long memory and expansive foresight, but not for that reason static or bound to any fixed point, this 'living system of thought', the church's tradition, is the norm by which all else is judged. The 'romantic vision' to which Kirk adheres is historicist through and through. And is that surprising? Hardly, for the very genius of institutional conservatism is its admiration for the adaptability of tradition, its delight in social institutions which can float gloriously down the stream of time, negotiating all its bends without accident.

The classic Protestant objection to this idea can be set out in three steps. First, by converting the moral teachings of Christ into legislation for organized society it imposes a consistently minimizing interpretation upon them. Is Jesus' uncompromising teaching about divorce completely accounted for by the church's firm but humane tradition on the conditions of nullity? Have we fully comprehended what it means to cut off the offending hand or foot when we have obeyed the church's ordered recommendations for a moderate ascetic discipline? Always the conditions of public justice, which bind the church as much as they bind any society, militate against recognizing the exceptional demand; but it is precisely that demand to which Jesus' moral teaching points. Secondly, by interpreting tradition in a mediating relation between the believer and the Scriptures, this approach is at least tempted to challenge the authority of the recorded words of Jesus. Ostensibly in the interests of protecting them against enthusiastic misinterpretation, it will always refer the believer back to tradition as the only reliable source of guidance, and so implicitly deny the direct claim of God's word. And so, in the third place, it has subjected the individual once again to the bondage of alienation. It has returned from Pentecost to Sinai, from the pouring out of the Spirit on manservants and maidservants to the mediation of the covenant through angels. But the spiritual liberty of the individual, claims the Protestant critic, rests upon the fact that he is immediately addressed by God, that God the Holy Spirit bears witness with his spirit, evoking assent to God's word in Jesus Christ.

Contemporary Roman Catholic thought has proved very sensitive to the complaint that the individual is liable to be improperly restricted by the authority of the community; and the fruit of this sensitivity may be seen in various remarks on the liberty of conscience which are found in the documents of the Second Vatican Council, especially in the fine Declaration on Religious Freedom, *Dignitatis Humanae Personae*. It is certainly to be regretted that 'conscience', with all its rationalist overtones, appeared to the Vatican fathers a suitable category for asserting individual freedom of religious decision. However, they did see the need to go beyond it. Freedom from religious coercion is defended at two levels. In the first place, it is said that the appropriate mode for seeking the truth is free enquiry, communication and dialogue (3); in the second place, the act of Christian faith itself is necessarily a free act (9). Thus the case for freedom is at heart a case for individual space, the space to think, argue, reach a conviction of the truth, and finally the space to commit onself in the existential decision of faith. This is important, and well said. But it falls short of an ecumenical convergence with Protestant concerns for what should be meant by evangelical liberty, which includes the epistemological freedom, given by the Holy Spirit, to attend to the teaching of the church critically, in the light of the apostolic witness of the Scriptures. All that the document can say in this connection is: 'In the formation of their consciences, the Christian faithful ought carefully to attend to the sacred and certain doctrine of the Church. The Church is, by the will of Christ, the teacher of the truth' (14).

But to these three objections, born of the Protestant insistence that all God's people are prophets, we must add a fourth, of a different character, which arises from what we have said above. This approach denies us the recognition that the church is itself a moral agent with its own freedom, that it has its own obedience to the word of God and its own public life to order in accordance with the gospel. This approach, therefore, renders the *discipline* of the church unintelligible. When in the early Middle Ages the church made the fateful exchange of public penance for private, it showed its forgetfulness of the fundamental rationale of community discipline. From that point on the system in its totality, even including excommunication, had to be justified in terms of its private service to the moral and spiritual formation of the penitent. But what if the penitent did not need or could not profit from such a service? This question was always implicit in Protestantism, and some parts of the Reformation came close to recognizing that another rationale altogether was required for the practice of excommunication; but with neither question nor answer made explicit, the recognition was not generally achieved before the Enlightenment swept away church discipline from all but sectarian Protestant communities. The point is that discipline does not exist first to serve the penitent; it exists to enable the church to live a public life of integrity. The community as a whole will decay, and lose its sense of its gospel calling, if its public life is not free to express the gospel. 'Expressing the gospel' means, of course, expressing the gospel of God's forgiveness of sin in Jesus Christ; so that any authentic church discipline must be centred on the reconciliation of the sinner rather than on his punishment. Nevertheless, even so its purpose is public. Public scandal is the community's corporate shame at its compromised standing; and it needs to find a proper resolution in communal confession and absolution of sin. Although the scandal may arise from private fault, though not inevitably, the function of discipline is to address the public problems that it poses for the church's common life. Until this is recognized, our churches will continue to be vexed by the all-too-familiar pattern of misunderstanding in which the people find themselves humiliated by some scandal and demand a firm line of their clergy or bishops, the bishops think the people harsh and unforgiving, the people think themselves betrayed, and everything is at cross-purposes. That is the necessary fruit of an attempt to render private and, in an individualistic sense, 'pastoral' what are in fact the church's rites of public justice, namely, the avowal of repentance and the assurance of forgiveness.

The freedom of the community to render corporate obedience to the gospel is the ground of its authority over the individual member. At the same time, his individual freedom to render obedience to the gospel in immediate responsibility to God defines the limits of the community's authority over him. It is obvious enough that these two freedoms are liable to conflict. The church is not free from the risk which all communities must face in the conditions of a fallen world, that limited possibilities for sustaining life and infinite aspirations of individual subjects may make the interest of the whole and the interest of an individual incompatible. However, the more important thing to say about the church is that these freedoms are finally convergent. The conflict between them, when it arises, is only provisional, springing from sin or from misunderstanding. For both these freedoms are authorized by the same eschatological reality, the kingdom of God, in which every individual vocation is fulfilled and brought to perfection in harmony with the whole. This means that within the church's life the eschatological reconciliation of individual and collective can begin to be realized. There can be a partial experience, at least, of living together in love. Both the church's freedom and the individual's freedom consist in their finding fulfilment in each other, and so displaying in outline the lineaments of the kingdom of God. But since the kingdom is founded on the victory of truth over falsehood in that decisive act of divine truth-telling which we call the Last Judgment, the freedom of church and individual consists also in their being given to *speak the truth*, to display the character of ultimate reality by which all deception will be condemned. We must be conscious of both these aspects of freedom as we look more closely at the church's authority over the individual.

A doctrine which had its origin in the patristic period, and was much developed in Western Catholicism, represented the meeting of these freedoms in terms of the contrast between *command* and *counsel*. There were moral prescriptions, it was said, which could be recommended to the individual but not required of him as a duty. Such were the renunciation of worldly possessions and of marriage. Those who embraced these counsels did so freely and uncoerced, to be rewarded the more greatly in the kingdom of heaven; but those who did not embrace them committed no sin and incurred no punishment. Relating the distinction to final reward and punishment was, of course, a great mistake. The Reformers took very justified offence at the doctrine because of its suggestion (in defiance of the parable of Lk. 17:7ff.) that God's demand was more limited than the total claim of the good. That was to drive a dangerous wedge between divine command on the one hand and the ultimate realities of good and evil on the other, so that theological ethics must become morally and metaphysically suspect. A metaphysic of ethics must be unitary. If an act is obligatory, it is so by virtue of its relation, whether direct or indirect, to the good; and by virtue of that same relation the performance of it is free. To divide actions up into those which are free on the one hand, and those which are obligatory on the other, destroys the very ideas both of freedom and of obligation.

However, there was in the distinction between command and counsel a valid perception that may be recovered from this criticism. The distinction properly concerns not the limits of God's demand but the limits of social demand. A double-standard moral theory is always a sign that ethics is being thought about in terms of social requirements, as politics or ecclesiology; but a social approach to ethics always ends with the recognition that there is an area of moral awareness which refuses to be accounted for in sociological terms. Once this recognition is reached, it may be interpreted in various ways. Secular liberal ethics, for example, is fond of demarcating an area where morality is deemed 'private', which consists of values which the individual chooses or opts into. The theological distinction between counsel and command is importantly different from this. The category 'counsel' does not admit that morality outside community norms is 'private' in the sense that nobody other than the agent has a right to an opinion; it is a sphere of public discussion and recommend-ation. Neither does it conceive of values in this area as 'chosen' – which tends to make them look more aesthetic than moral. They are a sphere of obligation which is rooted in the good and in divine command, as are all obligations. The point is simply that it is an area of direct address, in which the demand confronts the individual without the reinforcement of social constraint. Its content is that area of human fulfilment in which well-doing and wrongdoing are not susceptible to public observation: the inner life of thought, attitude and motive, and the response to individual vocation. To take the example of vocation: if Søren Kierkegaard had defied God by marrying Regine Olsen, only God and Kierke-gaard would have been the wiser; the Danish church could have known nothing of his disobedience. Thus the Danish church could bring no proper pressure on Kierkegaard not to marry Regine. However, it could certainly have known that such disobedience was a possibility in principle, and, as we sometimes detect Kierkegaard complaining, it could have done much more than it did to draw his attention to the vocation of singleness and exhort those who were called to it to be faithful to their calling.

The hiddenness which especially veils these areas of decision is present to a lesser extent in all the decisions of an individual, so that the church may counsel him, rather than command him, not only in the vocational sphere covered by the classical form of the doctrine but in all his moral decisions. Counsel, indeed, is the church's most characteristic form of address to the individual, because it respects his status as one whom God also addresses directly, and whose particular decisions are partly hidden from public gaze. It is not, however, that the church pretends to know nothing about the rights and wrongs of individual decision. When the church counsels, it points to the authority of God's revelation in Christ and to the moral teaching of Jesus, the prophets and the apostles; for it knows that right attitudes and decisions, however hidden and inscrutable in their detail, are those which come from a thoughtful obedience to that revelation. Thus the church counsels *with authority*. Its counselling is not fashioned on the non-directive model popularly favoured in a pluralist society, in which the coun-sellor's role is limited to helping the client discover and articulate his own convictions (which is not to deny the *instrumental* value of such an approach, especially in therapeutic situations); but then neither is it a veiled appeal to its own political authority as a society which, having made rules, expects obedience and loyalty. It is a didactic moral authority, appealing to the authority of a truth which stands above it and seeking to place the hearer in an equality of perspective with the teacher. The church commends its case by argument, persuasion and the exposition of Scripture, and regards itself as having in some measure failed if the matter is ultimately brought to the level of command. Its counsel, therefore, is authoritative without being coercive. It communicates the authority of revelation, by which its own words are authorized, and places itself alongside the hearer in obedience to that authority.

This double aspect of the church's counsel, at once exercising authority and standing under it, is perfectly expressed in the great climax to Saint Paul's defence of the apostolic ministry in 2 Corinthians 5:20 – 6:1, a passage which, it would seem, has been misunderstood in most English versions. I translate: 'We stand before you, therefore, as Christ's ambassadors; it is as though God were exhorting you through us. In Christ's name, then, we implore you: "Be reconciled to God! He has made the sinless one become sin for us, that we may become God's righteousness in him!" But we also speak to you as your fellow-workers, adding our exhortation that you should not let God's proffered grace go for nothing.' English translators, hypnotized by the parallel in 1 Corinthians 3:9 and ignoring that of 2 Corinthians 1:24, have supposed that the apostles are described as 'fellow-workers' (*synergountes*) to suggest their partnership with God. Chrysostom's interpretation, supplying 'with you' (*hymin*), is much preferable (*In ep. ii ad Cor. hom.* 12), making the two affirmations of 5:20 and 6:1 complementary, reflecting the carefully balanced view of apostolic authority which has emerged throughout this letter (*i.e.* Paul's last, probably fifth, letter to Corinth, consisting of 2 Cor. 1 – 7, excluding 6:14 – 7:1). Paul stresses throughout that he stands *with* the Corinthians *under* the authority of the gospel. At 1:20–21 all the promises of God find their 'Yes' in Christ, and the apostolic word adds, as it were, an 'Amen'; it is God who secures both apostle and disciple together in Christ. Three verses later (1:24) Paul says that he has cancelled his threatening visit, not to be authoritarian but precisely to avoid the authoritarian type of conflict: 'we are not lords over your faith, but collaborators (*synergoi*) of your joy. For it is by your faith that you stand' (*i.e.* not by ours!) The contrast of the apostolic ministry with that of Moses (3:4 – 4:6) stresses the difference between Christian communication which takes place in the open and without the veil of reserve which belongs to Mosaic authority. 'For what we preach is not ourselves, but Jesus Christ as Lord' (4:5). Yet there is a place, even in the same breath as this apostolic self-abnegation, for speaking of apostolic authority: ' . . . with ourselves as your servants for Jesus' sake.' The apostle shares with every man the expectation that he will stand before the tribunal of Christ (5:10), but with this difference, that for him the judgment will also touch on how he has discharged *this* service. Therefore he conducts his ministry in 'the fear of the Lord', open to the scrutiny of God and equally open to the scrutiny of those whom he serves (5:11). Together with reconciliation God has given the *ministry* of reconciliation and the *word* of reconciliation. Thus the apostle is not a medium of communication as Moses was a medium or as the angels on Sinai were a medium, whose authority consisted in their representation of God and concealment of his face. He is a part of what God has effected, and thus subject to what God has done, one with those to whom he speaks, open to their inspection and assessment, not to mention their love (7:2–3). His aim is to make his hearers independent of himself, to direct them to the gospel of Christ; yet he will always have a place in the communication of the gospel, pressing home its authoritative claim, 'Now is the "acceptable time"; *now* is the "day of salvation"!' (6:2).

It would be a mistake to think of the church's preference for counsel as some kind of self-denying ordinance, as though the community curtailed its own collective freedom in the interest of fostering individual freedom. For its own freedom could not anyway be expressed by the arbitrary demand for obedience to its rules, but only in being a community of agreement in the truth. Yet the church does have rules to which it may arbitrarily demand obedience. Its form in the world is that of an organized society, and as such it has a structure of political authority: it has institutions of government, rules for administration, sanctions against the breach of rules and so on. However, outside the Congregationalist tradition, Christian theology has always refused to understand this form as being the essence of the church, and has understood church-authority as something more than this purely immanent church-political authority. We have two adjectives which embody the distinction, 'ecclesial' and 'ecclesiastical'. The church's authority is genuinely *ecclesial* only when it manifests the church's identity as a witness to the kingdom of God. The arbitrary *ecclesiastical* order does not necessarily give expression to the authority which the church holds from God; it does so only if it is shaped to contribute positively to the church's witness to the kingdom. This arbitrary authority, to which we point when we speak of the church's transition from counsel to command, is alien to the true nature of the kingdom of God, though it can serve it. It thus imposes a constraint upon the life of the church as a community as well as upon the freedom of the individual. The reason that this constraint is necessary is that the church does not yet live in the full daylight of the kingdom of God, but shares with the world a life under the shadow of divine judgment. Just as the political structures of worldly society depend upon the representation of divine judgment in the form of coercive rule, so the structures of the church depend also upon a sign of divine judgment. What differentiates the church's sign, however, is that it points, entirely symbolically, to the last judgment, the judgment which will put an end to all judgment.

Confronted with the appearance of resolute disobedience to God, the church of the New Testament responded with a public act, a demonstration of the final separation of truth from falsehood on which the harmony of the kingdom of God is founded. Excommunication pointed to the gulf which must exist eschatologically between one who refused God's word and the redeemed community which lives by it. Equally important, public reconciliation of the sinner pointed to the removal of this gulf in repentance and faith. The authority with which the church invoked these acted signs of divine judgment was neither purely didactic nor purely political, but of a mixed form in which elements of both were present. Already in the church's didactic and political authority we have seen a tendency of these typically distinct forms to converge. Pure didactic authority, on the one hand, is not concerned with obedience, but only with understanding; but the character of the church's teaching is affected by the fact that the truth to which it witnesses is revealed and not merely discovered, and so carries with it the demand for obedience and faith. Pure political authority, on the other hand, is not concerned with understanding but only with obedience; but the church's political authority is also directed towards making the gospel perspicuous in its public life. In the practice of discipline the church acts politically, but in a way that is entirely concerned with declaring the word of God. In the New Testament practice of excommunication and reconciliation we come as close as possible within the conditions of this world to overcoming the gap between public action and the truth, for public action is here transformed into a simple acted word of witness, no longer oriented to the usual goals of community self-management and self-preservation.

That is why it is important to stress that this sign of divine judgment could properly be invoked only in response to the refusal of God's word, and not to the refusal of the church-political order. Suppose, to take some modern examples, the church had to deal with a layman who celebrated Communion, or with a bishop who, before the church had authorized it, ordained a woman. Such breaches of order, though grave, are merely breaches of order; they defy the church's regulations but not the word of God. The use of excommunication in such cases as these would debase it into an act of political authority, in which the self-defence of the ecclesiastical order was the first consideration. Such abuses in the past contributed more than anything else to the widespread collapse of the practice in the major Christian denominations. Imagine, on the other hand, that a church member publicly advocates and practises violent intimidation for monetary gain. This is a challenge not to the regulations of the church but to the authority of Christ's moral teaching to which the church is bound to bear witness. (I recall an occasion on which a class of liberal North American Protestant students were suddenly awakened to what church discipline was about when they saw televised pictures of lavish Catholic funerals provided for Mafia bosses in Sicily!)

In between these two poles lie more ambiguous cases. Presumably the authority of Christ's teaching cannot be limited to the actual words of the text, but must extend to the whole pattern of thought which they imply. Presumably, therefore, the church may command, with the sanction of discipline, in matters where a theological argument alone seems to require a certain conclusion. It can maintain, for example, that the practice of euthanasia is unconditionally inconsistent with biblical ethics, even though not explicitly condemned in the biblical text. In doing so, it will be bound to keep the argument open to public examination and discussion, to prevent the prohibition from being a mere ecclesiastical decree; but so long as the argument commands general agreement among those who accept the authority of Christ's teaching, a disciplinary sanction may be appropriate. But suppose a case where the argument was not simply theological, but involved also certain critical judgments of fact: for example, if the point in question were the church's support for economic justice, and some of its members were heard to argue that in a Western bourgeois democracy (let us say, Canada) only violent revolution could save the underprivileged from annihilation. The church should clearly not attempt to cast people out of Christ's fellowship simply on the basis of what would be, by any normal reckoning, pretty poor political judgment. (One could well imagine, however, forms of support for revolution which were more overtly ideological and therefore constituted a more direct challenge to the truth of the gospel.) We have no reason, on the other hand, to deny the church the right to give counsel in such areas. It may certainly advance arguments in which not all the premises are theological; the point is simply that it should itself understand, and encourage others to understand, the shape of those arguments, and to distinguish those disagreements which can, from those which cannot, be matters of direct obedience and disobedience to the word of God.

It might be thought that there was an inherent contradiction in the church's move from counsel to command. The point of counsel was precisely that the moment of eschatological disclosure has *not yet* arrived, so that the realities of individual decision are still concealed from public observation; but in sanctioned command, it is argued, the church pretends to identify disobedience to the word of God and to invoke divine judgment upon it. Would not the insights which recommend counsel rather than command lead us, if we were consistent, to recommend it exclusively? Would they not imply approval for the general disuse into which excommunication has fallen in the principal Protestant denominations? That conclusion need not follow if we recall that the point of church discipline (and this applies to reconciliation, no less than to excommunication) is to defend the public integrity of the church. Inevitably it belongs to the realm of appearances, and provides a sign rather than the substance of divine judgment. How, then, are we to assess this realm of public appearances in which the church necessarily functions? Evidently it does not amount to a full disclosure of the truth which will become visible at the end of time, when all that is concealed will be revealed. The church's public life is vulnerable to concealment in many forms. It may, without bad faith, condemn an individual whose integrity, in the best Kierkegaardian manner, is universally incomprehensible, who cannot become revealed. It may, much more commonly, accept as a member in good standing an individual in whom the outward show of obedience conceals an inner rebellion and refusal. Moreover its judgments are vulnerable to the hiddenness of the future: in that nobody knows what an individual will become, nobody can speak a final word of judgment upon him. In setting up the sign of judgment, then, the church can act only provisionally. The sign, too, belongs to the realm of appearances and will be judged by God; nothing, not even excommunication, can separate from the church one who is living in accord with the truth of the gospel. But that does not mean that the realm of appearances is a realm of absolute illusion. A provisional disclosure of reality is given to us. The importance of this sign is that it takes the church's public life seriously as a sphere of action in which eschatological reality can be seen. And although we may say that it is only a *witness* to that reality, operating under the constraints and ambiguities of public life, nevertheless it is a witness which the Holy Spirit has *authorized*, and through which God's word has been made known, constraints and ambiguities notwithstanding. A community of loving agreement in the truth can have existence, though fleeting and imperfect, in our midst, and can show us something of the life of heaven.

'Christ our passover is sacrificed for us. Therefore let us keep the feast, not with old leaven, neither with the leaven of malice and wickedness; but with the unleavened bread of sincerity and truth' (1 Cor. 5:7–8, AV). The question is simply: is the church as a community really free to celebrate this paschal feast with this unleavened bread? And the answer is: Yes, because it can define the shape of its public life by excluding from it scandalous, that is, known and unrepented sin. It can 'purge out the old leaven' and be 'a new lump' (7). That is the meaning of what Christ did for his apostles, according to Saint John, after the resurrection, when he breathed on them and said: 'Receive the Holy Spirit. If you forgive the sins of any, they are forgiven; if you retain the sins of any, they are retained' (20:22–23). This does not imply, of course, that the apostles have the right to forgive and retain sins *arbitrarily*, but in accord with the preaching of the gospel, which invites all to repentance and forgiveness.

Nor does it imply that the apostles can speak God's *final* word, that they may bind beyond hope of divine loosing or loose beyond fear of divine binding. That is not even implied in the Matthaean version of the promise (16:19; 18:18), where Jesus speaks explicitly of a binding and loosing *in heaven*. What is meant is that the exercise of such disciplinary powers in the church, in accord with the preaching of the gospel, is not a merely ecclesiastical measure, adopted by the church to protect itself as a social institution. It is a *sign* of the final judgment which the gospel proclaims and which is already present in the death and resurrection of Christ. We may compare it with the instruction given to missionaries to shake the dust off their feet when they leave an impenitent community. Such a sign enables the church to express itself unmistakably when it announces the gospel, to overcome the ambiguities which must cling inescapably to its message if it cannot repudiate unbelief and impenitence when it meets them.

But of course the gospel is not the gospel unless it speaks of pardon, and most particularly when it pronounces judgment. Pardon and judgment are not opposed poles, between which the church must vacillate, but are complementary aspects of the way truth impinges upon falsehood. Thus it is that in the rules recorded for us in Matthew's Gospel (18:15–20), the very way in which the exercise of discipline is approached declares the desire to speak this word of pardon clearly. (In the same spirit the patristic church devised a ceremony of reconciliation by the laying-on of hands for the reception of those who had previously been the object of excommunication.) This does not imply any hesitation, or bad conscience, about pronouncing judgment. Repentance, after all, is the *acceptance* of God's judgment upon us, as we see both it and its object in the cross of Christ. What is implied in the Matthaean provisions is simply the avoidance of premature publicity, a desire to hold back the final manifestation of the kingdom which will allow no more time for second thoughts. Yet even in this private dealing, the church, in the persons of its two or three, is still acting *as* the church, bringing the authority of the ascended Christ to bear upon the falsehood and sin which it confronts – that is the plain implication of 18:19–20. To make judgment present in reconciliation is the church's proper activity; but when it is opposed by stubborn impenitence it may defend its public life by maintaining the same authority in a different way: it may invoke public judgment.

From the story of Ananias and Sapphira (Acts 5:1–11) we may learn what Saint Luke thought was implied by this measure. We must remember that this is the Evangelist who has consistently sought to clarify the true character of eschatological expectation against enthusiastic attempts to invoke final judgment prematurely. We must recall Jesus' rebuke to James and John, recorded only by Saint Luke (9:52–56), when they wished to call down fire upon the Samaritan village. Yet in his portrait of the early Jerusalem church Luke includes this startling and formidable exercise of apostolic judgment. Like every incident in the early chapters of Acts it is intended to be seen, not as typical of the church's powers but as archetypical of them, displaying in the sharpest profile the lineaments of the Pentecostal authority which must undergird, though less explicitly, the life of the church throughout. The authority of the church, thus understood, consists in its power to maintain the truth against what obscures it, to penetrate behind deception and render a judgment by the prophetic word which makes hidden things plain. This judgment derives its terrifying decisiveness from its relation to the final judgment of God, which seems to cast its shadow back acrosss the penultimate judgments of men and make itself known in the midst of history. Of course, such a moment of prophecy is not something which will occur every time anyone exercises church discipline; nor does it imply anything about God's final word on any individual. The church can, and should wish to, do no more than to hand such a one 'to Satan for the destruction of the flesh', in the hope that God's last word upon his spirit may be quite different (1 Cor. 5:5). Yet in the mention of Satan the ultimate decision is taking shape within the penultimate. Even in its penultimate judgment the New Testament church understands itself to be making final judgment visible. In this way its public life is protected against erosion by the ambiguities in the midst of which it lives, and continues to be shaped by the gospel which is God's last word about man's ambiguous relation to the created good.

Part Three

The form of the moral life

9

The moral field

The theme of this third section of our study is the form of the moral life, which, as we indicated in chapter 1, is designated as love. Our task is to give an account of love, that 'bond of perfectness' (Col. 3:14, AV), a task which will seem to some to be either superfluous or impossible. It may seem superfluous because, when we have announced the good news of God's redemptive work both objectively in Christ and subjectively in the Holy Spirit, there is no more to be said. Can any addition to this fail to raise the suspicion that there is, after all, in defiance of all that we professed in chapter 5, a 'something else' to ethics, a moment of intermission in the evangelical proclamation, a Pelagian pause for human action? It may, on the other hand, seem impossible because love is not susceptible to any accounting. Can we do more than point to it? Can we attempt to unfold what it implies without emptying it of all that makes it love, turning it into a mere code-word for some other conception of the moral life, probably a legalistic one? For these reasons many theologians would counsel us to venture no further down this road.

It is not a conclusive answer to these doubts, but may yet be a useful warning against them, that it is just such a restraint on the part of contemporary theology that has effectively handed over the study of ethics to formalistic philosophical schemata. For this is the area in which modern philosophical discussion has been most busy. Here dwell the great formal theories of ethics which we learnt as students: emotivism, intuitivism, utilitarianism, universal prescriptivism and so on. From the point of view of some moral philosophers the study of ethics really begins here; and even one who was sympathetically disposed to think theology germane to

181

the study of ethics might still be inclined to regard our first eight chapters as an extended preface to our last four. Obviously we reject such a view, or we should not have written in the way we have. Nevertheless, if any theologian is going to say that formal questions have no rightful place in theological ethics, let him at least understand the nature of the barrier that he will erect. It was once fashionable for Protestant theologians to introduce any remarks about ethics with a kind of war-whoop, declaring that the concerns of Christian ethics had 'nothing to do with moral philosophy'. The result of such bravado was not a genuine contest between philosophical and theological conceptions of the right and the good (which could only have been helpful), but a confirmation of the idea that in its own formal sphere philosophical ethics was autonomous. At best it meant a theological abandonment of the field, at worst a covert admission of untheological categories of thought into the very heart of theological discourse itself.

For if anyone really thinks that nothing intelligible can be said about the shape that love takes in the world, then he should follow his conviction to its logical end and keep silent. Moral argument for such a one must be forbidden territory; his way will lie solely along the hidden paths of spiritual and ascetic theology. He cannot first make sweeping apophatic avowals, and then garrulously interject his opinion into every current ethical deliberation. Such an opinion could only turn out to be borrowed, an untheological opinion which reproduced in church dress some popular philosophy, perhaps utilitarian or existentialist. If we are to form and justify opinions on specific questions in ethics, we must do so theologically; which means bringing the formal questions of ethics to theological interpretation and criticism. This by no means implies, of course, that we shall accept the current understanding of these questions unhesitatingly from the lips of philosophers, for theology has something to say also about how the questions are formulated as well as about how they are answered. We do not have to abandon evangelical proclamation when we ask about the form of the human response to the gospel. We are asking, in Saint Paul's expression (Gal. 5:22), about 'the fruit of the Spirit'.

On two occasions in the writings of Saint Luke we are told that a crowd which heard the preaching of the gospel asked, 'What shall we do?' The answer was different in either case. John the Baptist (Lk. 3:10ff.) responded with some specific moral counsel: 'He who has two coats, let him share with him who has none; and he who has food, let him do likewise.' Saint Peter, on the other hand (Acts 2:37–38), replied, 'Repent, and be baptized every one of you in the name of Jesus Christ for the forgiveness of your sins; and you shall receive the gift of the Holy Spirit.' It would be mistaken to interpret this difference in terms of a contrast between law and gospel, between preaching before and preaching after the coming of Christ. John the Baptist was quite capable of giving the reply that Saint Peter gave (apart from the name of Jesus and the promise of the Spirit), while Saint Peter could easily have replied as John did. The point is, rather, that the question about the form of the moral life may invite two different approaches to an answer.

One approach has to do with the kinds of action which the gospel evokes. It begins to describe the content of the moral law; and because the moral law reflects all the variegated pluriformity of the created order itself, this answer has to choose a specific starting-point somewhere in the middle of things, addressing itself – as it happens in this case – to those who have two coats first of all, who by no means constitute the whole of mankind, and then proceeding to address other kinds of situation in turn, such as those in which tax-collectors, soldiers or other classes of the population may find themselves. The other approach has to do with the disposition of the moral agent. It is universal and simple, applying with equal immediacy to all. We may be tempted to think that the difference between these two is simply a difference of *specificity*; that Peter's words achieved their universal simplicity by being highly general, as though he had said 'Love your fellow-men' and so covered, with one broad sweep of the brush, all the detail of moral responsibility which John the Baptist had been at pains to etch out distinctly. But that would be to overlook the specificity of repentance, which is a distinct disposition among other dispositions, and of baptism, a distinct act among other acts. The counsels of prophet and apostle, then, differ by addressing polar and complementary aspects of the moral life, aspects which arise precisely from the complementary objective and subjective aspects of God's work of redemption, from his renewal of the world-order in Christ and his renewal of the moral agent by the Spirit. If the gospel tells of agents rendered free before the reality of a redeemed universe, then the form which their agency assumes will correspond *both* to the intelligible order which they confront *and* to the freedom in which they act. The form of the moral life will be that of an *ordered moral field* of action on the one hand, and of an *ordered moral subject* of action on the other. To use more traditional terms, it will be a form relating to *human acts* and also to *moral character*.

An ordered moral field: from plurality to pluriformity

We may begin from one feature of the category 'human acts': it is in the plural. One human agent in his time performs many acts, and not one only. To see the moral life as 'human acts' is to see it broken down into a series of discrete and distinct events of human agency, a plurality of responses to the world rather than a single response. It is important to notice that this analysis of our agency is already a moral analysis, and not one that could be reached by an ideal scientific observer. Imagine such an observer watching someone write a letter over a period of a couple of hours: in the course of this time the person under observation will get up several times from his desk, walk around the room for thought, idly pull a book from the shelf and put it back, make a cup of coffee, and then sign the letter and seal it; finally, having done something quite different for half an hour, he may reopen the letter and add a postscript. The observer who follows this behaviour may perfectly well chart episodes of movement and repose in the subject's limbs, but such episodes do not constitute acts. What he cannot do is identify, or even enumerate, the human acts involved. To do that he will need to be something more than an observer; he will need to be himself a moral agent, to whom the different acts will already have a moral intelligibility because he can recognize their ends. (Even so, of course, two moral agents may disagree about how many acts there were; but that will be a moral disagreement about what one or another phase of this behaviour was for, about whether it had an independent point.) But all this is to say that the difference between one human act and another arises not out of some disjunction intrinsic to the agent's behaviour, but out of the changing field of action, which, in the course of a few hours, sets a sequence of possible ends-of-action before an agent and elicits his response to some of them.

With this realization there arises a disturbing question. If the temporal distinction of our acts, and so the development of our agency, is not imposed by us upon the world but by the changing world upon us, then we must ask how we are to recognize and respond to *new* ends-of-action. The problem of novelty is the central problem of historical existence. 'Historical' existence is distinguished from merely 'temporal', as that form of existence which is conscious of its own temporal character and can ask about the meaning of temporal succession, *i.e.* about historical teleology. It therefore involves an awareness of novelty, a sense that each episode is 'new' in relation to what preceded it. But this awareness, as much modern philosophy has discovered, is alarming, for it implies that the field of action comes to us uninterpreted, and so possibly unintelligible.

Our anxiety may assume a more or less radical form. In its less radical form we may conceive that the succession of new events makes the good difficult to recognize; so that we conceive our human agency as a recurrent series of deliberative or reflective crises, in which we are at a loss to know what to do, or in which some past decision stands out from our memory to trouble us. We become aware of our agency primarily by way of these moments of crisis, focused around difficult decisions. The traditional 'casuistic' form of ethics has been shaped largely in response to this conception of what human agency is: it is a science of 'moral problems' or 'quandaries'. Although it is currently fashionable to decry 'quandary ethics' (and rightly, in so far as ethics is thought to be *confined* to crises), it would be a mistake to overlook what it tells us about the way in which we encounter the field of action. The task of acting is rendered perilous by the historical dimension of our path through the world; we are threatened at each turn by a universe which we do not know and cannot recognize, in which memory will not serve us or may even mislead us; life is a series of challenges, none of which conforms to the same rules as any other.

But our anxiety may take a yet more frightening turn. If what comes next is really unrecognizable in terms of what has gone before, there are implications for our continuity as acting subjects. To the extent that we do come to recognize and respond to a new good, we must *ipso facto* loose our grip upon the old, for the old and the new do not inhabit the same moral field. Thus in recognizing the unrecognizable we are changed, and become unrecognizable ourselves, our past no longer intelligible to our present as our present, when it was still future, was unintelligible to our past. Our identity is given to us in relation to the world in which we participate; correspondingly, a metamorphosis of the world must involve a transformation of our identity. The division of the moral field into a sequence of disjoined novelties must dissolve the acting subject in an acid of radically changing predicates. Instead of being one subject performing a multitude of acts, the agent becomes a plurality, a sequence of dissociated roles and responses evoked by the shifting self-transforming meanings of the world, or (perhaps we may even say) the sequence of different worlds into which he has to act.

The nature of this anxiety may appear more clearly if we glance at how two modern approaches to moral thought orient themselves to the problem of novelty. The first proposes to call upon *the experience of the past*, and to make use of memory, not only our own individual memories but those of our institutions and communities, as the best torch to light our path. We are to act into the unknown future in the same way that our predecessors acted into theirs; and although we know that our future and theirs are not the same, we hope, nevertheless, that, by our conscious resolution to imitate their mode of conducting themselves as closely as our new circumstances allow, we will establish sufficient continuity to tame the apocalyptic strength of novelty to the point where it can be managed by a comfortable process of adaptation. Such a policy for binding the unknown is what is properly called 'conservatism' – and that name should be reserved for such a policy which self-consciously addresses the questions of historical existence. But its cords are as inadequate to their task as the new ropes with which Delilah bound Samson. Quite apart from the question of whether memory can actually survive radical change, we are left with the problem that knowledge of the past *cannot* simply be transformed into knowledge of the present. It cannot tell us what it is that we confront now, and therefore it cannot tell us what precedents from the past are relevant, nor how they should be adapted. The only way to tame the unknown is to come to know it. Conservatism, because it offers no satisfactory route of knowledge, can present only the illusion of taming the unknown – an illusion which may have a considerable social value, no doubt (and that is why conservatism has more validity as a political attitude than as a philosophical one), but which still leaves us without the understanding which is existentially necessary for us to live our lives by.

The point of greatest value in the debate which raged two decades ago over Joseph Fletcher's 'situationist' account of moral rules was that it brought into the clearest possible light the difficulties inherent in the conservative policy for overcoming novelty by remembering the past. Fletcher, of course, was no typical conservative: his insistence on the uniqueness of every situation and the impossibility of measuring its requirements 'in advance' ran counter to the evolutionary conservative understanding of history as the barely perceptible emergence of new out of old. Yet once we make old and new the sole terms of understanding, and rule out, as historicism is bound to do, all transhistorical mediation, what difference does it make whether the transition from one to the other is gradual or sudden? Fletcher's discontinualism brought to light the true structure of all historicism, conservative historicism included. The evident impotence of the conservative proposal, as he used it, merely highlighted its inadequacy for any use. The form which the proposal takes in his thought is that of the 'summary rule', which appeals to him as a way of making a modest concession to normative rules which still falls far short of allowing the claims that have traditionally been made for them. Thus he writes that 'the most which can be hoped for any normative rule, such as the one against lying, is that it will be a "summary" wisely adumbrated and based on a wide, long and mature experience'. Of such normative rules it is said that they 'may illuminate a given situation in which we are trying to bring *agapē* and *kairos* together' ('What's in a Rule?', p. 331). But that is certainly too much to hope for. What illumination could a summary rule, drawn from however much experience of the past, shed upon a present in which 'there are *no* actions that should be predetermined in practice by *any* moral rule whatsoever'? To say (p. 332) that 'general principles in normative ethics may sometimes, even often, be relevant and obliging because they happen to be consistent in concrete situation with the transnormative criterion' (*i.e. agapē*) is to concede nothing at all of substance. For it is clear that such a coincidence of normative principle and *agapē* could be recognized only *post factum*, *i.e.* once the decision had first been taken without the aid of the principle. Which is to say that, when the future has ceased to be future and has become past, we may then observe rational continuities between it and the earlier past that preceded it – then, and not before! But was not Fletcher perfectly correct to claim that an ethics which thus 'makes room for both decisional freedom and generally valid principles' occupies a 'conservative position' (p. 327)?

The second approach proposes to overcome the perils of novelty by *anticipation*. Although the future is unknown to us, there are certain regularities in events which may allow us to form reasonable expectations and assume a limited measure of responsibility for what will happen. Each human act has a kind of reach into the future by way of its consequences. To a major tradition of thought in the English-speaking world this act-consequence nexus has offered the hope of getting a grip upon the threat of novelty and of bringing it within the scope of human discretion. What we call 'consequentialism' (or, less accurately, 'utilitarianism', which is, strictly speaking, a species within the genus) is, at its heart, a programme for robbing historical existence of its terrors by conceiving of history as a kind of human artefact. For although the consequences of any one act are so inconsiderable that they must be absorbed into insignificance quite early in the infinite chain of succeeding events, the accumulated consequences of many acts, all performed with a certain general policy, are not negligible. And even though the future can never be made up exclusively of the positively planned consequences of present acts, even surprises and unexpected contingencies can, nevertheless, be at least allowed for in general terms, so that they are brought within the scope of that for which we presently assume responsibility. Thus our present acts can be, as it were, a managerial choice in favour of a total future for the universe. When we encounter that future, it will no longer be quite new to us, for it will be the state of things which we ourselves, with greater or lesser discernment, have chosen.

Discussions which interpret modern consequentialism simply as a version of classical teleological ethics (comparable to the 'eudaemonism' of the ancient world), and which understand the issue between it and rule-based morality in terms of the contrast between teleological and deontic ethics, have simply overlooked its most striking feature, which is the reinterpretation of classical categories of the final good in terms of *historical consequences*. The value ordering 'for the sake of' (*tou heneka*) has been replaced by a quite different 'for the sake of', which means 'productive of'. All classical ethics, Christian and pagan, teleological and deontic, is challenged at its heart by the proposal to evaluate acts solely in terms of the consequences they tend to produce. Such a proposal can be understood only as a refusal to evaluate *acts* altogether. Indeed, we may go further and say that it is a proposal to abandon the *category* of acting altogether, for in reconstruing history as an artefact we abolish the only context in which acting can have any meaning. Acting implies risk – the risk of performing a completed deed and setting it loose in the world, laden with its perilous cargo of possible consequences, to encounter whatever fate may befall it from other people's actions, from chance, from accident or from decay, and committing it only to the care of inscrutable providence. To speak of acting implies a history *into which* we act. Once history is safely parcelled up into the act, so that we conceive every act as the choice of a total future, then there is no possibility left to us of acting at all. Everything we do becomes one vast process of manufacture.

There is, of course, a marked convergence between these two modern attempts to overcome the anxiety of history. For the consequentialist is bound to reflect that our present acts are not the first in the world's history. They are themselves a part of the universe which previous generations have chosen, part of the 'future' for which agents in the past were responsible. They were, of course, a multitude of agents, acting at different times and with different purposes and very variable success; but as they were each, in principle, choosing a total future for the universe, we can allow the various contradictory elements in past decisions to cancel themselves out and imagine the present world as the product of a single great collective decision, a decision which embraces our own acts, however we may act, and all possible futures arising from them. Thus our own present decisions now appear simply as *interpretative* decisions, in which we give substance to a world which has already been determined in outline by the choices of the past, choices accompanied, no doubt, by their share of miscalculation but which provide a framework of meaning for what we ourselves now do. Thus the conviction that we ourselves create an intelligibility for the decisions which our successors will face reinforces the belief that the deeds of our predecessors provide the meaning for the decisions which we now have to face. Thus our consequentialist may well end up agreeing with some words of Alisdair MacIntyre, approaching the matter from the conservative side: 'An adequate sense of tradition manifests itself in a grasp of those future possibilities which the past has made available to the present' (*After Virtue*, p. 207).

But nothing will bind the future unless the future, for all its unpredictability, is already bound, by being the future of God's world, the history of his created order. It is true that many have grown wise through the study of the past. But that happens only as the past has been used as a mirror in which the transhistorical order of things has been reflected and studied. For the understanding which enables us to live with confidence rather than terror in the face of history must provide a measure by which novelty can be comprehended, understood and integrated into our experience; but such a measure cannot merely be conjured out of our experience unless it is actually derived from the objective world-order with which our experience has put us in touch. Only if we are endowed with a vision of what it is in the world which measures change and so stands beyond it, can we dare to encounter change.

Such a vision is what the ancients meant by the term 'wisdom'. Wisdom is the perception that every novelty, in its own way, manifests the permanence and stability of the created order, so that, however astonishing and undreamt of it may be, it is not utterly incommensurable with what has gone before. This does not imply a pretence that the unlikeness of the new to the old is unreal. Even unlike things can be seen as part of the same universe if there is an order which embraces them in a relation to one another. The *plurality* of situations and events which characterizes the experience of history, the fact that every event is 'new' and different from every other, can be seen as a *pluriformity* in the world-order, which is a capacity for different things to transpire and succeed one another within a total framework of intelligibility which allows for their generic relationships to be understood. Without a generic order new things would indeed be incomprehensible, for they would be absolutely particular, which is beyond the power of human thought to grasp. The utterly 'unique situation', if we were ever to encounter it, would destroy us and the universe. Wisdom liberates us from the persistent fear of that unutterable and unknowable uniqueness by enabling us to interpret each particular thing, in all its newness to us, generically, and so measure its difference from other things and respond to it appropriately according to its kind. Thus wisdom greets new things with recognition, and new moral decisions can be made. And with this possibility comes also the possibility that the moral agent himself can be consistent in his moral attitudes, even though he is a historical being in constant encounter with the new.

It has often been said, quite falsely, that Israel did not have the same sense of stability and eternity, set in opposition to change and history, that marked Greek thinking. In support of this claim can be alleged the tendency to interpret wisdom, as spoken of in the tradition of proverb-making common to Israel and her neighbours, as *torah*, thus replacing, it is said, the eternal stability of things with the arbitrary and historically determinate command of God. Although this contention is based on an unbalanced reading of the Old Testament (how many times is it stated that God's command 'endures for ever and ever'!) there is something here to be explained. The re-presentation of wisdom as law declares, in fact, the central point of Israel's faith, which is the meeting of life-in-the-world with life-before-God. The point can be approached from two sides. On the one hand, the understanding of the world-order, so necessary for life in the world, was known to be the personal and gracious gift of the God who had chosen Israel for himself. On the other, the burning fire of election, that transcendent storm which swept through history as the Lord revealed himself, intended nothing other than the blessing of life upon the earth. Wisdom, with its cool observational detachment and its inherent restriction to the educated, was made immediately available to all in the form of law, and was co-ordinated in the covenant with the summons to worship and rejoice. The joy of life-in-the-world was a gift given together with the joy of life-before-God. At the same time the arbitrary command of the transcendent Lord of history had assumed responsibility for ordered life. The God of Exodus and Conquest had shown himself as God of creation too. In *torah* the moral authority of created order and the transcendent authority of the electing God were made one. That was the source of Israel's security, the watch-tower from which her prophets could comprehend the events of the ancient Near East, always threatening dissolution and meaninglessness, and make of them a song of praise and thanksgiving.

The tone of delight with which the worshippers of the Old Testament spoke of the *torah* can be understood only if we appreciate the existential problem which God's gift of law had met. The law evoked the most moving expressions of gratitude for rescue from the threat of 'death'. Who could meditate for long upon Psalm 119, for example, without being struck by the constant association of law (and all its synonyms) with life, health, delight and well-being? For it is nothing else than death to have to confront the future as entirely unknown, knowing only that one is oneself subject to the same insecurity as everything else in the world about one and that one may dissolve with any new constellation of circumstances that may emerge. But 'your word, O Lord, is eternal; it stands firm in the heavens' (Ps. 119:89, NIV). As the worshipper aligns himself and the world under the scrutiny of that word and that law, he has a stable point of reference and is secure. Can this admiration of the moral law lead to the legalism of which Christianity is properly afraid? Of course it can. It can become a cover for complacency, or it can become a new source of dread, as soon as the soteriological context of the law ceases to be vitally experienced. But in this lyrical outpouring it is precisely the meaning of law as salvation that predominates over every other thought.

Casuistry and moral learning

The moral agent approaches every new situation, then, equipped with the 'moral law' (which is how we shall refer to that wisdom which contains insight into the created order when it is formulated explicitly to direct decisions, *i.e.* deontologically). As he holds the moral law together in thought with the particular situation, it illuminates and interprets it, enabling him to reach a moral judgment about it. But at the same time this illumination reflects back upon its source, so that he comes to understand not only the particular situation but the generic moral law itself with greater clarity. It does not matter whether the situation is one in which he, or someone else, has immediately to act, or one in which he, or someone else, has already acted, nor even indeed whether it is a purely hypothetical situation put up merely to be thought about. Whether in deliberation, in reflection or in abstract moral exploration, the consideration of particular cases involves learning about the moral law, which is to say, about the created order itself. 'Casuistry', as it is called, is not just a matter of solving problems, but of growing in wisdom.

At this point it may be useful to clarify some of the terms which we shall use in this discussion. The *created order*, as must by now be apparent, is the structure of the world in its objectivity, which includes, as we have argued in chapter 6, its authority to evoke our action. The *moral field* is the world as it presents itself to us at any particular moment as the context and occasion of our next action. *Wisdom* is the knowledge of the created order; and the *moral law* is such knowledge conceived and organized explicitly in terms of the authority to evoke action, *i.e.* as an ordered and total demand. *Casuistry* is the application of the moral law to action in particular cases. A *moral code* is a didactic formulation through which we attempt to teach, learn or remember the moral law; it is an artefact of public culture, with all the strengths and limitations of such an artefact, which, in the acquisition of wisdom, we have both to make use of and to transcend.

It might appear to be otherwise. It might be thought that the whole task of moral reason in relation to particular situations was simply to classify them, 'subsuming' the particular case under the generic rule. Moral thought might therefore be understood as involving two distant and successive operations: in the terminology of mediaeval scholasticism, *synderesis*, which was the comprehension of the principles of moral law, and *conscientia*, their application to particular cases. *Synderesis*, we might think, must be presupposed by the exercise of *conscientia*. The morally educated person must know that adultery is wrong and charity right *before* he has to decide about any particular case. The casuistic question then takes the form, 'Is *this* act an act of adultery?' 'Does *this* behaviour embody charity?' And the answer to that question tells him nothing that he did not already know about the rightness and wrongness of adultery or charity, but only about the character of the particular case which he has been considering. A prominent ecclesiastical dignitary who visited South Africa some years ago remarked tartly to the press on his return, 'I didn't have to go to South Africa to learn that apartheid was wrong!' Presumably he had visited that country to learn whether *in fact* apartheid was practised on the scale and in the manner that he had been told. The exercise of *conscientia*, but not that of *synderesis*, would have been helped by his seeing with his own eyes.

A difficulty will arise, however, in that *conscientia*, as defined in this conception, must be purely an intuitive operation. Confronted with a particular, moral reason can do nothing with it if it has not first recognized it, placing it in a generic category. We cannot reason discursively about bare particularity; we cannot analyse a particular case before we have some generic purchase on it. But what if this task of intuitive recognition proves difficult? What if it is not immediately obvious whether what we are seeing is, or is not, the commanded charity or the forbidden apartheid? It would be possible to deny, perhaps, that such a difficulty ever arises in good faith, or to attribute it, if it does, to a purely spiritual malaise such as an over-scrupulous conscience – a course which has sometimes appealed to Protestant thinkers. The scholastic tradition, however, did not hesitate to admit that recognition could in itself be difficult. Indeed, in the eyes of a host of critics (of whom Pascal, in his *Lettres Provinciales*, was among the most effective) the scholastic tradition seemed to go out of its way to create difficulties where they did not exist and to confuse moral intuition by raising subtle doubts about what should have been straightforward judgments. In doing so, whether justifiably or unjustifiably, it counted confidently on being able to do something which seemed to be ruled out by the simple opposition of generic *synderesis* and particular *conscientia*. That is, it undertook to carry out a purely *formal* analysis of the human act as such, in order to facilitate the intuitive task of recognition.

Let us consider an example of such a formal analysis at its most helpful. Imagine that Mr Jones has driven his motor car into Mr Smith, and killed him. We have to decide whether or not this was murder. We are supposed already to have understood (by *synderesis*) the moral principle which forbids murder, and the only question before us is that of *conscientia*, whether *this* act is properly subsumed under that principle. If direct intuition fails us, or if we are led to doubt the reliability of its verdict, what kind of help is forthcoming? Scholastic moral theology offers us the assistance of the so-called Principle of Double Effect (better described as the distinction between directly and indirectly voluntary acts – or more simply, between intention and foresight). This Principle advises us: (a) that there is a difference between directly intending an evil effect of one's action and merely foreseeing that it will follow; (b) that one may foresee an evil effect of one's action without desiring it; and (c) that one may licitly act in such a way as will foreseeably produce an evil effect (which one neither intends nor desires as such) in order to secure some proportionate good or avoid some proportionate evil. This is very enlightening, as it helps us to frame some useful exploratory questions about the Jones-Smith case: (i) Did Jones *intend* to kill Smith, either as an end in itself, or as a means to some further end? (ii) If he did not intend to kill him, did he, nevertheless, *foresee* that Smith's death must follow from the way he was driving his motor car? (iii) If he did foresee it, did it occur to him as a *desirable* result? (iv) If it did not occur to him as desirable, was there any proportionate reason (*e.g.* avoiding a crowd of schoolchildren) which could reasonably make him prefer the course of action which killed Smith to any other that was open to him? If the answers to (i) or (iii) are positive, we may regard Jones as a murderer; if the answer to (ii) is negative, or to (iv) positive, we may count him blameless; if the answer to (iv) is negative, we may think him guilty of some lesser species of manslaughter.

But then we wonder where the Principle came from, and why, apart from its intuitively satisfactory results, we should entrust ourselves to its guidance. It presents itself as a formal analysis of the human act as such, which describes the structure and identifies the value-bearing elements (intention, proportion, goodwill, *etc.*) of *any* act, whatever its kind and whether good or bad. But what kind of reason could carry out such an analysis? Clearly it must be a work of moral reason, if, as we have seen, even the human act as such can be distinguished only by moral thought and not by any other kind of observation. But on the face of it such an analysis does not belong either to *synderesis* or to *conscientia*: *conscientia*, because it has to do with the particular, could never produce a general theory, while *synderesis*, concerned as it is with the normative principles of moral law, could never produce a formal theory. Scholastic casuistry may seem, then, to have generated a third operation of moral reason, *a priori* and analytic, which lays down formal rules governing the subsumption of particular cases under generic moral principles.

We would be wise to fight shy of such a conception. The enlightenment afforded us by the Principle of Double Effect can be accounted for by a different and more satisfying hypothesis, which is that it conveys not a formal truth about the shape of the human act as such, but a quite specific moral truth about murder. Indeed the Principle of Double Effect arose in the first place largely out of attempts to understand the morally significant differences between murder and other kinds of killing, and it often gives very unsatisfactory results when applied to other areas of moral concern. When used, for example, by an older generation of Roman Catholic moralists to recommend that certain life-saving abortions should be performed by hysterectomy in order to preserve the 'indirect' character of the attack on the fetus, it merely provoked scepticism. The moral order, we perceive, does not authorize such a distinction between an attack on the pregnant womb and an attack on the unborn child that we may call the one 'act' and the other 'effect'. Only reality itself can authorize or disallow different applications of the distinction between foresight and intention. When we have discovered that this distinction is relevant to the characterization of murder, we have discovered something specifically about murder, and not about any other thing. The Principle was wrongly understood as an analytic *a priori*, a formal rule governing the subsumption of particular cases under generic moral rules.

Thus Paul Ramsey concludes his defence of the distinction between direct and indirect voluntariety by complaining that, as Catholic moralists before the Second Vatican Council improperly extended it to cases to which it did not apply, so more recent Catholic moralists have improperly generalized in its place the principle of proportionate reason. 'A vice of Catholic moral analysis is the other side of its great virtue, namely, to seek always for a universal understanding of the moral life . . . . Our moral lives are more various than either generalisation' ('Incommensurability and Indeterminacy in Moral Choice', pp. 136f.).

We have every reason to doubt that there can be any such formal rules which apply with equal validity to acts of all kinds and which offer genuine help to someone who is at a loss to know how to view a particular case. It is open to anyone, of course, to suggest a possible candidate. We will suggest, and dismiss, one ourselves. Take: 'It is not only the act which counts, but the thought behind the act.' Is there any area of moral obligation to which this rule does not apply? Yet without it we would never be able to distinguish in practice deliberate sins from mere carelessness. But then we shall have to ask whether carelessness, too, is ever a sin. If it is, its sinfulness consists precisely in its not being deliberate; it would make no sense to excuse a careless person with the plea that it didn't occur to him that he was being careless! The rule about the thought behind the act, then, seems not to apply to at least one moral principle, the prohibition of carelessness. Although some strands of New Testament moral teaching, and especially of Jesus' teaching, lay great stress on the moral significance of thought, it by no means follows that this arises out of a general theory of the human act as such, rather than out of a sensitivity to certain specific areas of moral concern. For example, it is the nature of sexual motivation, rather than the structure of the human act in the abstract, which makes Jesus' concern with 'adultery in the heart' (Mt. 5:28) especially appropriate.

However, this is not a point of cardinal importance, for even if there is some analysis of the human act which applies equally to every area of moral concern, we shall still wish to say that the help which it affords is *moral* insight, derived from an understanding of the moral law. How do we discover that it is not only the act but the thought behind the act which counts? How did Thomas Aquinas ascertain, in his elaborate account of 'good and evil in human acts in general' (*Summa Theologiae* II–I.18), that the value-bearing elements of the human act are four: act-as-such, object, circumstance and finality? Only by discovering through moral insight that the created order demands of us right thought as well

194

as right action, good final intention as well as a good object. It is moral knowledge. But it is gained, nevertheless, as we deliberate or reflect upon particular acts which are, for one reason or another, ambiguous. And this provides the most conclusive argument for preferring our alternative account: it makes intelligible what is surely a datum of common experience, that we learn more about the moral law as we think about difficult cases. The particular discloses to us aspects of the generic to which we have not previously been sensitive. What was wrong with the simple account of casuistry from which we began was simply the assumption that *synderesis* is already complete before we approach the task of *conscientia*. In fact the work of comprehending the moral law goes on in parallel with the work of interpreting cases in its light, the difficulties of the latter providing new material for the former. We did not, after all, comprehend the prohibition of murder when we first addressed the case of Jones and Smith. Our casuistry had to discover not only whether Jones was a murderer, but also what murder really is. The engagement with the case showed up a measure of haziness and ill-definition in our understanding of the moral principle; the particular acted as a kind of magnifying glass through which the generic appeared with more clarity. We recall here what has already been said (chapter 4) about the character of moral learning, which is not a matter of accumulating new information about the moral order, but of discovering in closer detail that which we already know in broad outline. We penetrate behind the straightforwardness of the moral code through which we first learnt the moral law, to discover that that law is as complex and pluriform as the created order itself which it reflects.

And if we fail to learn in this way? If we cling to the simplicity of the code as we first knew it? In that case the pressure of new experience which historical contingency forces upon us will soon bring us to the breaking-point. We shall recognize suddenly that the categories of our moral understanding are no longer sufficient to interpret our situation, and we shall rebel wildly and disorderedly against them. The form which this rebellion takes in moral theory is the positing of random and meaningless 'exceptions' to moral rules. The exception is the case which our understanding cannot encompass, the absurd contradiction of the rule for which we cannot account. Once we concede the invasion of the absurd into our moral thought (not merely in the form of a problem, demanding resolution, but as a permanent resident which is there by right), we have, in effect, abandoned our responsibilities to reality. Unofficially the whole standing of morality has been shifted on to a voluntarist basis. Henceforth it will be something that we shall impose upon ourselves when and as we feel we can. The moral life will no longer be the consistent regard and delight elicited from us by the order of the real world which God has made.

195

'If the breadth and flexibility of good moral reason is lost from view, then all that once passed for rationality is bound to seem a cruel master.' So wrote Paul Ramsey in a wide-ranging article, 'The Case of the Curious Exception', which spoke the last word on the formal questions which had been agitated in the debate about situationism (p. 92). Ramsey noted two broad senses in which we speak of 'exceptions' to moral rules, a theologians' sense in which the exception falls *outside* the rule (and of this he noted three sub-classes which need not concern us), and a philosophers' sense, in which the exception belongs *within* the rule as a feature-dependent qualification. The strategy of the article was to use the philosophers' conception to overwhelm the theologians. A 'justifiable exception', he argued, is a contradiction in terms, since to be justified it must be feature-dependent, which makes it generic and so places it *within* the rule, no longer an 'exception' in the sense that the theologians demand. (Philosophers could presumably speak of a justifiable exception in their sense of the word, but Ramsey would perhaps prefer them to use a less ambiguous term.) What appear as justifiable exceptions are usually to be attributed to incomplete moral reasoning: 'someone stopped giving his feature-dependent reasons for the actions he puts forth' (p. 77). If there really were particular, non-feature-dependent exceptions to any moral principle, then it would not be a moral principle at all. Discussing the proposal (of situationist provenance) that the principle forbidding adultery should be observed 'except when it would do more good on the whole (not) to do so', Ramsey observes: 'This turns the principle into a maxim or guideline or summary of its past observances; a principle whose observance or whose violation has equally to be validated afresh in each case by appeal to one's ultimate norm . . . The attachment of an exception-making criterion to the marriage-principle has already destroyed that principle and set it aside, whether the decision in the present instance is to abide by it or actually to depart from it for the sake of doing good' (pp. 84f.).

This provides a context for understanding Ramsey's distinction between moral knowledge 'arising from' experience and 'arising with' it, a distinction which could be mistaken for a denial of what we have asserted about learning through attention to particular cases. Christian moralists, Ramsey maintains, should reject the idea that 'the terrain supplies the conditions for discriminating right from wrong'. 'There are meanings or stipulations or explications or qualifications *implicit* within the moral law.' These 'may be brought to light by experience'; they 'arise with' experience, but do not 'arise from' experience. They arise from 'the implied meaning of principles' (pp. 90f., italics added). These words do not deny learning through experience (though we should not overlook Ramsey's concern to include *thought* within the fabric of moral experience). They insist, rather, as we have done, that *what* is learnt through experience is nothing other than the shape of the moral life itself. We are not to imagine that there is an independent source of moral wisdom in the particular situation, which in some way qualifies the generic truths of the moral law. Rather, the particular situation acts as a catalyst for fresh discoveries about the moral law.

According to Ramsey the only aspect of moral judgment which can be attributed simply to 'the terrain' is the particular judgment, '*This* is a case which falls under such-and-such a rule.' The subsumption of cases is irreducibly particular, not to be thought of as the last stage in the narrowing specification of a moral principle, nor as the conclusion of any deductive process. Thus Ramsey can be seen to contend for the sharpest of distinctions between *synderesis* and *conscientia*. Curiously, he goes so far as to say that subsumption is not part of moral reason at all, but of 'actual practice', though he also consistently describes it as the work of 'prudence or practical wisdom' (pp. 104f.). It is clear what the point of forcing this distinction is: it is to protect against the suggestion that there is to be found in the particular case any *other* kind of moral wisdom than knowledge of the moral law itself. Prompted by the same concern Ramsey declares against the idea of a 'subsumption-ruling rule', which he understands differently from ourselves, not as a formal rule but as the last term in a casuistry which pretends to deduce the particular, thus improperly suggesting that moral wisdom was all the time an assemblage of particular judgments. The awkwardness of saying that a particular judgment is 'actual practice' illuminates a problem that remains unresolved in Ramsey's thought: how can we defend the generic character of moral wisdom, while still allowing that a particular judgment can be an exercise of rational thought?

The defence of generic judgments in this article is mounted largely (and unusually for its author) on the thought of Anglo-American moral philosophers who were maintaining one or another version of the thesis of 'universalizability'. Nothing suggests that Ramsey regards this as more than a falling-in along the way. In a final section he argues that Christianity provides its own distinctive 'normative meta-ethics', so he has clearly dismissed the claim that this philosophy propounds a neutral and universal meta-ethic, a 'logic of moral judgments' which may serve as a court of final appeal. It remains for Ramsey to show how the generic character of moral wisdom is necessitated by an authentically theological meta-ethic, which is, of course, exactly the opposite of what the serious theologians among his opponents, Karl Barth for example, were inclined to maintain. But to fill this lacuna adequately is at the same time to answer the unsettled question of the particular judgment. If, in keeping with a Christian account of creation, we root the generic character of morality in the order of the *world*, rather than in the structures of the *mind*, then we can see how it may be a rational judgment to subsume a particular under a generic principle. For it is not a *bare* particular which we encounter, until we randomly throw the cloak of generic order around it. It is already ordered generically and teleologically by virtue of its relations to other things, and it discloses to us its generic and teleological relations in disclosing itself. Subsumption, then, is a matter of truthful recognition. This has been one of our own persistent contentions, especially in chapter 2 above. What we have written there may be read as a modest footnote to Ramsey's article, supplying these omissions in its presentation.

An ordered moral field: from pluriformity to universality

Not every occasion for particular judgment is also an opportunity for moral learning. To take a simple example, from positive rather than moral law: in Ontario it is forbidden to pick the trillium, a wild flower of some charm which grows in woodlands in spring.

I may understand this prohibition very well, and appreciate the good reasons for it, without actually being able to recognize a trillium when I see one. If someone then points one out to me, saying 'That is the flower that you are not allowed to pick!', I have learnt something, certainly, but not something about the *law*. The particular judgments, on the other hand, which do afford opportunities for moral learning are those in which the situation is capable of more than one description and therefore demands of us not simple recognition (as of something quite obvious once we learn to see it) but an interpretative decision as to how we may call it by its proper name. That is to say, the judgments from which we learn are the dilemmas, or 'quandaries', which create a deliberative or reflective crisis for us because we can understand our situation in more than one way. If someone is wondering whether to sin or not, then, however anxious he may become, he is not engaged in moral deliberation, but is simply wrestling with temptation. His irresolution is raised to a moral level only when he can see a plausible reason why he should do something which might also, from another point of view, be looked at as a sin. This does not make it any less a temptation, perhaps, but its character as temptation is obscured, at least, in the form of a moral dilemma. Whether or not it is true, as classical Christian moral theory maintained, that all temptation implicitly takes this form, and that all human sin is performed *sub specie boni*, it is certainly the case that in a *genuine* moral dilemma each of the alternatives is viewed *sub specie boni*. But it is precisely this which forces us to come to a closer understanding of the good. Which provides a further reason for restraining ourselves from the inclination to dismiss 'quandary ethics' too quickly.

To take a typical dilemma such as moralists discuss: suppose I become aware that a friend is spending a great deal of money upon a mistress with whom he has suddenly been infatuated, and that his wife is in ignorance of the fact. In weighing the various courses of action and inaction open to me, I shall have to reach some generic view of the relational goods which are implied in my ties with both of them: does a man's loyalty to the friend of a lifetime count for more than the more recent and less intimate bond which he has with his wife? Or does the institution of marriage imply that he is related to the *couple*, even when they appear to be at odds with each other? Or does the nature of the information (with its hint of grave financial injury to wife and children) present a claim on justice that overrides all private bonds? And I shall have to reach some generic view of the relative importance of the different services I can render to each: to the husband, critical judgment, which he may need, or continued unjudging support, which he may also need; to the wife, the truth, with the opportunity to take defensive measures to protect her own and her children's financial position, or the peace of mind which belongs to ignorance of what may yet, in the end, be a short-lived lapse; to the couple taken together, a possibly healthy stimulus to mutual reckoning, or the mysterious good of privacy without which a marriage cannot thrive. The difficulty of reaching a particular judgment is posed precisely by the fact that *any* course of action may be justified in terms of *some* ordering of these goods. The value of doing so is that we must think more about the goods whose proper ordering we have to discern.

The dilemma arises because the moral field is pluriform. It does not arise out of the adequacy or inadequacy of the moral code which the agent may happen to have been taught, or to have formulated for himself. One code is not formally more likely to throw up moral dilemmas than another (though codes may differ in their tendency to encourage scrupulousness, and so make their adherents more or less disposed to notice dilemmas and be exercised by them). We may think of any two moral principles, true or false, and it will not require much ingenuity to imagine a situation in which they would make conflicting demands. Only a moral code which systematically reduced its principles to one could eliminate dilemmas. But such a code would be useless. For whatever the single principle might be, it could not satisfactorily interpret the agent's situation to him. It would be too crude an instrument to yield any understanding of the field of action. For pluriformity is not an accident or defect of codes. They are pluriform (consisting of ten commands in the Decalogue, six hundred and thirteen commands in the Pentateuch, or whatever) because the moral field itself is specifically differentiated. The order of reality holds together a multitude of different kinds of moral relation, and orders them without abolishing their differences. Moral codes must teach a moral law which corresponds to the order of reality in its differentiation and complexity.

But order also confers unity upon differentiation and complexity. It holds different kinds of moral relation together within a universe, giving them a common total meaning by which they coexist. That is why dilemmas do not merely arise, but are susceptible of rational resolution: the different descriptions which may be applied to an ambiguous situation do not belong to different universes of description, but to one and the same, which means that they can be weighed against each other. What happens when we think through a dilemma is that we gain some view of the universal order within which different species of moral claim are related. We described this as 'penetrating behind the straightforwardness of the moral code', a description which requires some explanation. A code presents the moral law 'straightforwardly' in so far as it presents it as a *catalogue* of moral claims, be there ten of them or six hundred and thirteen, without conveying any principle of order by which the relations among them may be understood as a moral whole. It does this, obviously enough, for didactic purposes. It would be pretentious to deplore it or to make it a ground for proposing to dispense with codes as a means of moral learning. We have to formulate our basic commitments somehow; but equally we cannot be content merely to repeat them, or even to add to them, as though we could, by mere accumulation of moral demands, express the whole content of the moral law. The items in a code stand to the moral law as bricks to a building. Wisdom must involve some comprehension of how the bricks are meant to be put together.

This has an immediate bearing on how we read the Bible. Not only is it insufficient to quote and requote the great commands of the Decalogue and the Sermon on the Mount (and there are still many who need persuading of this, in practice if not in theory); but it would be insufficient even if we added to them, if we could compile a complete list of things commanded or prohibited; it would be insufficient even if we included in such a list, with a shrewd awareness of the relativity of semantic forms, principles derived from other modes of moral teaching in the Bible, such as stories, parables or laments. We will read the Bible seriously only when we use it to guide our thought towards a *comprehensive* moral viewpoint, and not merely to articulate disconnected moral claims. We must look within it not only for moral bricks, but for indications of the order in which the bricks belong together. There may be some resistance to this, not only from those who suspect that it will lead to evasions of the 'plain' sense of the Bible's teaching, but from those who have forebodings of a totalitarian theological construction which will legislate over questions where it would be better to respect the Bible's silence. But in truth there is no alternative policy if we intend that our moral thinking should be shaped in any significant way by the Scriptures. For it requires only very limited talents at scepticism to raise doubts about the application of any biblical teaching, however plain, to any situation whatever; and if, when such doubts have once been raised, we are denied any biblical recourse in quieting them, then we are doomed to think the Scriptures inconclusive for any question that is worth stopping to doubt about in the first place. The result will be that all important moral questions will be settled explicitly on non-biblical lines. It hardly needs to be added that it is constantly stressed in the New Testament itself that to understand the moral law of the Old Testament we must attend to the principles of order which are to be found within it.

We take note here of a theme which is dear to Saint Matthew, who finds in a text from Hosea (6:6), 'I desire mercy, and not sacrifice', a principle of order which differentiates Jesus' understanding of the *torah* from that of his Pharisaic opponents. 'Go and learn what this means, "I desire mercy, and not sacrifice," ' says Jesus to the Pharisees who were offended at his dining-companions (Mt. 9:13). The quotation appears again, and with special weight, in the story of how the disciples plucked ears of corn on the sabbath (Mt. 12:1–8). The Evangelist's emphasis is laid on how the Pharisees were guilty of misinterpreting the law: 'If you had known what this means, "I desire mercy, and not sacrifice," you would not have condemned the guiltless.' He omits the saying in Mark 2:27 that 'the sabbath was made for man', and supplies an additional consideration from the law to strengthen the interpretative case. He also mentions, to draw out the parallel with David's soldiers, that the disciples were hungry. The whole argument thus goes as follows: (a) David's appropriation of the shewbread provides a precedent for regarding hunger as a factor which can override certain types of restriction. (b) There are examples in the Mosaic order of sacred tasks which have to be performed on the sabbath (*e.g.* the changing of the shewbread, Lv. 24:8, and the doubling of the burnt offering, Nu. 28:9–10). But the presence of the Messianic community gathered around Jesus invests this occasion with a greater sacredness than those. (c) These two considerations bring the incident under the scope of Hosea 6:6, which should have enabled the Pharisees to understand that the disciples were not bound to a strict observance of the sabbath regulation given their need and their status. 'For the Son of man is lord of the sabbath', a statement of priorities which is entirely in keeping with the law's intent. Hosea 6:6 also lies in the background of Matthew 23:23, one of the 'woes' against the Pharisees, in which they are accused of neglecting, among other things, 'mercy', which is among 'the weightier matters of the law' (contrast the parallel at Lk. 11:42).

Supreme among the principles of order which unify the obligations of the moral law is the so-called 'summary' of the law, by which Jesus taught us to find, in one text from Deuteronomy (6:5) and another from Leviticus (19:18), the two commands on which 'depend all the law and the prophets' (Mt. 22:37–40). What kind of precedence is it that is claimed for these commands, 'You shall love the Lord your God with all your heart, and with all your soul, and with all your might' and 'You shall love your neighbour as yourself'? Two contrasting ways of understanding it can be discerned within the New Testament references to the love-command. On the one hand it is thought to have precedence by virtue of its *inclusiveness*: all other commands are present within it. It 'sums them up', or they 'depend upon it'. On the other, it is suggested that the love-command takes *priority* over other commands, such that it should be preferred (as mercy is preferred to sacrifice) in a conflict of claims. It is 'the first' or 'the great' command. Clearly these two ways of understanding its precedence imply different conceptions of its definiteness. If it is to overrule other commands, it must have a high degree of definiteness and specificity; we must be able to say, with some clarity and objectivity, '*This* is the loving course of action, even though *that* is the just (or prudent, or courageous) course.' If, on the other hand, love includes the other moral demands within its scope, it must be correspondingly indefinite, permitting the requirements of justice, prudence, courage and so on to determine the specific forms which love will take in practice.

Jesus' account of the law in terms of Deuteronomy 6:5 and Leviticus 19:18 occurs at Mark 12:28–34, with a parallel at Matthew 22:35–40. Saint Luke (10:25–28) puts it in the mouth of a 'lawyer', not thereby denying that Jesus taught it, but suggesting that it had a certain currency. Saint Paul twice uses Leviticus 19:18 alone (Rom. 13:8–9; Gal. 5:14), and Saint James quotes it alone at 2:8. Mark's questioner asks for the command which is 'the first of all'. In Matthew this is rephrased: 'which is the great commandment in the law?', suggesting to commentators a Rabbinic distinction between great and little commands, distinguished by sanctions, means of atonement and in other ways. This could imply that the love-command *took priority* in cases of conflict, as mercy takes priority in Hosea 6:6 – and indeed there is an echo of that text in the scribe's reply at Mark 12:33, that to love God and neighbour is 'much more than all whole burnt offerings and sacrifices'. However, there are also suggestions that the love-command has a *universal inclusiveness*. Matthew's conclusion, 'On these two commandments depend all the law and the prophets', reminds commentators of Rabbi Simlai's complaint that halakoth (Rabbinic legal traditions) on the sabbath are like a mountain suspended on a hair, which is to say that they have too slender a derivation from the written law. Saint Paul, who says that the love-command 'summarizes' or 'sums up' every other command (Rom. 13:9), also says that the whole law 'is fulfilled' in this one text (Gal. 5:14) and, even more strikingly, that anyone who loves 'has fulfilled the rest of the law' (Rom. 13:8). There are a number of Rabbinic precedents for the attempt to identify key principles in which the whole law is implicitly present; of which the most famous is the story of Rabbi Hillel's reply to the man who wanted to be taught the law while he stood on one foot. (See Strack-Billerbeck on Mt. 22:35ff.)

Advocates of the situationist programme have liked to pose a dilemma about the definiteness of the love-command: either we must regard love as an empty concept, they argue, to be filled with substantial content from the rest of the law, or, in allowing that it has a content of its own which may overrule the rest of the law, we must make it the sole criterion by which we resolve every decision. We need not develop any further our objections to the idea that one single command with a definite content could be applicable to every kind of moral decision, an idea which ignores the differentiated pluriformity of the moral field. The dilemma is a false one, too, for another reason: definiteness and indefiniteness are not absolute but relative terms. We are not compelled to choose between a completely indefinite and formal love-command, which contributes nothing to the interpretation of the many commands, and a completely definite one which must either endorse or contradict them. In posing the choice in this way the situationist appears to share with the legalism he rejects an ill-founded conception that pluriform codes are by themselves sufficient to guide our moral thought without interpretation. But no moral code with more than one principle in it could be applied without some interpretation. That is what the single ordering-principle provides; and though it is less specific than the many commands which it orders, it is still definite enough to give a distinctive character to the way in which they are understood and obeyed.

But we may go further. If, as we have said, a code of moral rules is no more than a cultural form through which we communicate knowledge of the created order which is itself a whole, then it is clear that our ordering-principles will be something rather more significant than mere procedural rules-for-applying-rules. They will provide insight into what the rules are really about. When we learn, for example, that God requires 'mercy and not sacrifice' in relation to the sabbath, we are not merely learning when to apply the sabbath-rule and when not to. We are also learning something of what the sabbath, as a divinely-given institution, really is. For in the moral law the sabbath-command, together with its associated restrictions, has its meaning *in relation to* all other aspects of human response to God's grace. That meaning is illumined for us precisely by the way in which the restrictions are *not* applied beyond certain limits and outside certain contexts. It is this discovery of how every area of moral responsibility is illumined and interpreted by every other that makes the real difference between morality and legalism.

10

The moral subject

In the last chapter we took as our starting-point the dilemma of historical existence: constant encounter with the new, which comes to us in the first instance fragmented and uninterpreted, and threatens to dissolve the moral agent into a sequence of unrelated roles, without integrity as a subject. We then argued that the moral law, reflecting as it does the order of created reality within which all change occurs, brings the field of action to order by tracing the generic relations between each new situation and other situations. This order within the field of action, like the created order in the universe to which it corresponds, is both differentiated and unified. It reflects the multiplicity of created nature, while at the same time giving the whole a coherence, so that we can speak of 'an' order and 'a' moral law. Now we must return to the implications of this for the moral subject in his dilemma. The unity of the moral law ensures the unity and integrity of the moral agent who respects it. That is why, as we observed, the very existence of the *torah* was, for the Old Testament believer, a salvific reality. One thing is demanded of him – one thing which is highly differentiated in its forms, to be sure, but one thing all the same. One thing is demanded of him all his days from youth to age, whatever the differing tasks of those phases of life may be. In consequence, he is able to be one person, not merely the bearer of a multitude of successive and inconsistent roles. He can have that 'purity of heart' which Kierkegaard insisted 'is to will one thing'. 'Thou hast said, "Seek ye my face." My heart says to thee, "Thy face, Lord, do I seek" ' (Ps. 27:8).

So moral thought turns its attention back from the field of moral action to the moral subject. It asks not only about this or that act (whether of deed or thought) which he has performed or may perform, whether it is a good or a bad act and in virtue of what features it is so; but it asks also about himself, the agent who has performed or may perform these acts, whether he is a good or a bad person, and in virtue of what features he is so. It concerns itself with 'moral character' as well as with 'human acts'. Christian moral thought, indeed, has a special warrant for this concern, in that Jesus took issue with the casuistry of his own day precisely over its fussy concentration upon the circumstances of acts and its failure to think seriously about what he called 'the heart'. 'From within, out of the heart of man, come evil thoughts, fornication, theft, murder, adultery, coveting, wickedness, deceit, licentiousness, envy, slander, pride, foolishness. All these evil things come from within, and they defile a man' (Mk. 7:21–22).

How are we to understand this 'heart', this 'within' to which these corruptions are attributed? It is possible, perhaps, to interpret it as referring to acts of a special kind which is hidden from public examination, that is to say acts of thought. In that case Jesus will be understood to say (treating the first item in the list as a rhetorical excrescence) that all of these corruptions of outward behaviour originate in corrupt thoughts. On another occasion, in the famous teaching about 'adultery in the heart' (Mt. 5:28), Jesus certainly did use the term 'heart' to mean the seat of thoughts. But that interpretation does not make good sense of this text, nor of his other teaching in this vein. Could Jesus have meant that every act of foolishness was preceded by a foolish thought? that every word of slander was preceded by a slanderous thought? and that every act of pride was preceded by a proud thought? Did he perhaps mean that none of these acts would be a matter of serious moral concern if they were spontaneous and undeliberated? His words obviously demand a different understanding. These evils arise from the *personal agency* of the one whose acts express them. They 'defile a man', unlike the food he eats, because they really belong to him. He cannot dissociate himself from them. He the moral agent is himself the evil thinker, the fornicator, the thief; he is not merely one who happens to perform fornication, theft or slander, as it were incidentally. The individual is the subject of his own corrupt acts, he is the consummate moral reality which his acts declare. When we are told that God looks upon the heart of a man, this means, not only that God sees certain acts which, by their private character, are hidden from the scrutiny of human observers, but also that he sees and comprehends the subject himself in his totality as a moral being.

But it is equally clear from this text that Jesus did not propose to *substitute* agent-evaluation for act-evaluation and leave it at that. Thought about the subject and thought about his actions are correlates, not alternatives. How this correlation is to be understood is the most difficult question that faces an 'ethics of character'. What follows cannot pretend to be an exhaustive answer. We shall be content to make two stipulations which, it seems, any satisfactory answer will have to observe, and which will provide a point from which a provisional criticism of unsatisfactory answers can be developed. These two stipulations complement each other: (a) the subject's character must not be reduced to a function of his acts; (b) the subject's acts must be allowed to disclose his character, which will make itself known only through them.

These two stipulations attempt to give a formal expression to Jesus' teaching, directed against the 'hypocrisy' of the Pharisees, that 'the tree is known by its fruit'. The force of this image, and of the images which are associated with it in Saint Matthew's and Saint Luke's Gospels, is to deny that pretence can be ultimately successful. The pretence in question is the performance of acts which do *not* faithfully reflect the agent's character. False prophets come 'dressed up as sheep while underneath they are savage wolves' (Mt. 7:15, NEB). But their true character must eventually make itself known, just as the identity of a tree makes itself known when the fruiting season comes; and then the pretence is shown up as the absurdity it is. The inner reality is betrayed especially by speech, 'for the words that the mouth utters come from the overflowing of the heart' (Mt. 12:34, NEB). Human morality is a series of disclosures in which reality (the heart) forces itself into the realm of appearances (deeds and words) and declares itself, tearing apart the veil of pretence which has hidden it. Character is hidden from public view, while acts are open to it; but the shrewd observer will be able to read the character from the tell-tale act. For acts cannot be made entirely plausible on their own, without a character to support them.

In the Sermon on the Mount at Matthew 7:15–20 the context of the saying about the tree and its fruit is the warning against false prophets, the wolves in sheep's dress. Luke's parallel in the Sermon on the Plain (6:43–45) also refers the saying to the question of hypocrisy, prefacing it immediately by the parable of the mote and the beam. Luke then continues with a word that addresses specifically the issue of speech: 'the good man out of the good treasure of his heart produces good, and the evil man out of his evil treasure produces evil; for out of the abundance of the heart his mouth speaks.' Speech is the paradigm case for the general principle about acts. It may pretend to be good, but its pretence cannot succeed. It can be good only if its source is good. Both Matthew and Luke then follow with the criticism of those who say, 'Lord! Lord!'

Speech is again the concern of the section Matthew 12:33–37. Immediately beforehand comes the incident in which Jesus is accused of alliance with Beelzebub. He replies first with the saying about the blasphemy against the Holy Spirit, and then with the saying about the tree and its fruit. Then follows the rebuke: 'You brood of vipers! how can you speak good, when you are evil?' Clearly we are not supposed to think that the Pharisees' words actually are good, only that they pretend to be good. Their blasphemy against the Spirit is the tell-tale word that betrays what is in them. To reinforce the point there then follows the saying about speech which Luke included in the Sermon on the Plain. The paragraph concludes with a warning that the external evidence of speech will be taken with ultimate seriousness: 'By your words you will be justified, and by your words you will be condemned.'

To these texts we must add one of the 'woes' against the Pharisees (Mt. 23:25–26; Lk. 11:39–41): 'You clean the outside of cup and dish, which you have filled inside by robbery and self-indulgence!' (NEB). More than one of these denunciations concentrates on the contrast between appearance and reality, but this one is striking because of what follows: 'Clean the inside of the cup first; then the outside will be clean also' (so Mt.; Lk. is more obscure, but to the same effect).

The irreducibility of character

Our age has become familiar enough with a radical form of the act-analytical reduction of character against which the first of our two stipulations is directed. The 'behaviourist' tendencies of analytical philosophy have done much to encourage, as a habit of modern thought, the atomistic interpretation of character as a kind of shorthand for describing and predicting sequences of acts. Dispositional terms, it has been said, do not describe facts. The sentence 'John is talking' points to a particular event which is an item of reality; but there is no comparable item of reality corresponding to the sentence 'John is talkative'. It merely 'licenses' us to proceed inferentially from one event in which John talks to another event of the same kind. It draws attention to the regularity in sequence with which these events take place. It is clear that such a philosophy cannot employ the concept of an *agent's* disposition without irony; whatever status may be assigned to the regularities which dispositional statements report or predict, they are clearly not supposed to be anything properly pertaining to John himself, since if they were they would constitute a new fact about him. As well as defying our first stipulation, then, this philosophy can offer only *pro forma* acknowledgment to the second. For it is an empty thing to say that acts 'disclose' character or disposition when there is nothing in reality other than the acts themselves to be disclosed.

It may seem odd to associate with this radical reductionism the Aristotelian account of the virtues that is maintained by Saint Thomas Aquinas; for at the level of psychological metaphysics this offers a substantialist account of dispositions (or 'habits') which is entirely opposed to reduction. A habit is a fact about the person who has formed it. John's talkativeness is no mere shorthand for indicating a sequence of events in which John talks; it is a disposition of John's soul, fashioned by the repeated acts of talking and liable to give rise to further acts of talking. Yet at the level of evaluation Saint Thomas is much more inclined to an act-analytical approach. He will insist that dispositions are real; but it is not clear to him that they can be the objects of evaluation primitively and in their own right. John's talkativeness is a habit that can now be thought of independently of all those acts that formed it and continue to express it. But when we evaluate it and call it a vice, we do so because the speech-*acts* are uncontrolled. And when we praise Jane for her prudence, we do so because her disposition gives rise to well-judged deeds and words. It is the deeds, words and thoughts, the 'human acts', which are of primary moral significance, and we evaluate the dispositions which produce them only as 'principles' of human acts.

Saint Thomas Aquinas introduces the main section of his great treatment of morality in the *Summa Theologiae* as follows: 'Since it is by our acts that we must attain beatitude, our next task must be to consider human acts, distinguishing those that further us on our way to beatitude from those that hinder us. But operations and acts have to do with concrete situations (*circa singularia*); so that the science of practical affairs, taken as a whole, achieves its point only with the study of particulars. The study of morality, therefore, which is the study of human acts, proceeds from general questions in the first place to the particular after that. The general questions about human acts must be organized first into questions about human acts themselves and secondly into questions about their principles (*principia*) (II-I.6). These *principia* are then in turn divided into *intrinseca* and *extrinseca*. Extrinsic principles of human acts will turn out to be law and grace. Intrinsic principles are potency and habit.

Our presentation of the more radical position will, of course, be easily recognized as a reference to the views famously propounded by Gilbert Ryle in *The Concept of Mind*, and may (as the author says, 'harmlessly') be characterized as 'behaviourist', although Ryle professes to champion the cause of dispositions against more totally reductionist programmes. But his championship runs only to defending the usefulness of disposition-*statements*, and proceeds from the admission that they do not refer to anything 'actual'. 'The world does not contain, over and above what exists and happens, some other things which are mere would-be things and could-be happenings' (p. 115). Therefore there is a valid objection to any account of disposition-statements which 'construe such statements as asserting extra matters of fact'. A disposition-statement is, like a law, 'an inference-ticket . . . which licenses its possessors to move from asserting factual statements to asserting other factual statements' (p. 117). These statements of disposition 'apply to, or are satisfied by, the actions, reactions and states of the object: they are inference-tickets, which license us to predict, retrodict, explain and modify [?] these actions, reactions and states' (p. 119). 'Naturally the addicts of the superstition that all true indicative sentences either describe existents or report occurrences will demand that sentences such as "this wire conducts electricity" or "John Doe knows French" shall be construed as conveying factual information . . . .' But 'they narrate no incidents' (p. 120). We need not enquire to what an extent Ryle goes beyond denying that disposition statements *either* describe existents *or* report occurrences, to denying the very possibility that there might be descriptions of existences which did *not* report occurrences. It is enough for him that we should deny all in a heap the various claims that a disposition is a 'matter of fact', an 'existent', 'actual', that it is 'contained in the world' and that it is an 'incident'. Thus the disposition-statement can do no more than note a regularity between one fact, existent, actuality, thing-in-the-world or incident, and another. Or – remembering that a 'regularity' is no more a thing-in-the-world than a 'disposition' is – we must say more strictly that a disposition-statement is a regularity-statement, which licenses us to proceed inferentially from A to B. What kind of authority could be supposed to issue such licences for inference, we should not, of course, enquire!

It seems clear, though some defenders of the reductionist approach deny it, that act-analysis, whether of the more extreme or of the more moderate description, has an interest in accounting for dispositions in terms of *repetitive* sequences of acts of the same kind. Thus talkativeness is a repetitive sequence of acts of talking, wisdom a repetitive sequence of wise acts, and so on. For if there is a disposition, let us suggest 'adaptability', which consists of a sequence of acts of *different* kinds, then one can no longer say that the facticity of the disposition (or its value) resides exclusively in the component acts themselves. If disposition X consists of acts of kind a in the repetitive sequence a^1 a^2 a^3 a^4, etc., then the act-analyst has no difficulty in saying that X is valuable because acts of kind a are valuable (or, if he is a tough-minded empiricist, that a statement about X is no more than a licence to proceed inferentially from a^1 to a^2). When he encounters disposition Y, on the other hand, which consists of a series of acts of different kinds, a, b, c, d, then it appears that the value of Y does not consist in the value of either a or b or c or d, but in the value of a fifth kind of thing, which is the sequence a b c d as a whole. Whereupon he must either abandon his view that the value of a disposition consists entirely in the value of its constituent acts, or else he must elevate the sequence a b c d to the status of a complex mega-act, e; at which, of course, he is back with a repetitive sequence, since disposition Y is now accounted for in terms of the sequence e^1 e^2 e^3 e^4.

We find, therefore, a tendency of act-analysis for each disposition to look for the corresponding act that is repeated. So in the case of a virtue like 'adaptability' it will want to remind us that, since the generic order of a moral act is determined also by its circumstances, a series of acts which are otherwise of different kinds may, nevertheless, all qualify to be called 'adaptable' by virtue of their circumstantial relations. (It is not, after all, very different with 'wise' acts, which, apart from the common factor that they display wisdom, can be of an infinite variety.) What, then, of virtues and vices which are not focused in any single type of act, even one specified by circumstances? To what kind of act does the virtue of 'maturity' correspond? What has someone repeatedly done when we comment on his 'even-temperedness'? Or when we stigmatize his 'lack of initiative'? The defender of act-analysis is not to be refuted by this kind of objection, as though he cannot carry his programme through consistently. He will no doubt reply that restraint and inaction, on occasions which might invite action, are themselves a form of acting. These virtues and vices point to a series of repeated occasions on which someone might well have been silly but wasn't, might have lost his temper and didn't, might have been expected to set his hand to something useful but couldn't. Our objection is not that this reductionist approach cannot be pursued with rigour: it is simply that its consistent application distorts certain elements of the moral reality it pretends to interpret.

This seems to me to be the great *formal* importance (I do not deny that there are also points of great *substantive* importance) in the debate on contraception within and around the Roman Catholic Church. The point at issue, for those who believe, as the majority of Christians still seem to, that openness to procreation is a significant aspect of the virtue of chastity in marriage, is whether that disposition of openness is constituted only by a repeated sequence of 'open' sexual acts, each of them open to procreation in its own right, or whether it is comprehensible as a virtue of the married life in its totality, regardless of whether contraceptive measures are taken during some phases of it. Such a question cannot be settled by formal stipulation, but only by moral discernment of the nature of sexual and procreative life within marriage. What upset so many in the teaching of Paul VI's encyclical *Humanae Vitae* was that it seemed not to perceive the difference of structure between sexual relations in marriage and simple fornication. Chastity in marriage was analysed into a series of particular acts of sexual union, a proceeding which carried with it an unwitting but unmistakable hint of the pornographic. A married couple do not know each other in isolated moments or one-night stands. Their moments of sexual union are points of focus for a physical relationship which must properly be predicated of the whole extent of their life together. Thus the virtue of chastity as openness to procreation cannot be accounted for in terms of a repeated sequence of chaste acts each of which is open to procreation. The chastity of a couple is more than the chastity of their acts, though it is not irrespective of it either. This is not, of course, to recommend an alternative formal principle, a 'principle of totality' or whatever, to substitute universally for the formal principle of act-analysis. It is to say that the question of how any virtue is disclosed in its acts is not to be resolved by a *formal* principle at all, but depends on the substantive moral reality to which that virtue refers, in this case the proper shape of conjugal love.

The epistemological priority of act

This objection to the reduction of character may expect to gain the sympathy of those recent contributors to Christian moral discussion who, partly influenced by the reviving interest in Aristotle's ethics, have stressed the importance of the virtues in an account of the moral life. Our second stipulation, however, may provoke a measure of resistance from them. We have insisted upon an epistemological priority of act over character: the character is known only through the acts. It is impossible to speak of someone's 'courage' unless we have seen some evidence of courageous deeds. This is the truth which occasioned the errors of a reductionist act-analysis. For although it was wrong to say that the quality of courage resides only in the acts and not in the person, it was true, nevertheless, that it takes the acts to show us, as we say, 'what kind of stuff he is made of'. In biblical categories the quality of courage resides in the 'heart'; but the heart is hidden from man's eyes until deeds and words declare it. In the writings of the neo-Aristotelians, by contrast, we often find what appears to be a contradictory assertion to this, the epistemological priority of character over act. Impressed by the way in which two apparently similar deeds may assume quite different significances when viewed in the context of their agents' differing life-histories, they have argued that the meaning of any act depends on its being interpreted in the light of the personal whole of which it forms but a moment.

There is clearly a truth here, and we must enquire how it relates to our own contention. Who (to take an example that has figured largely in some discussions from this school) could pass judgment upon the moral quality of an abortion, without knowing what kind of person the agent was, what history of experiences had formed her, and what values she pursued in making her decision? Only a knowledge of the agent and her story can tell us precisely *what has happened* in this abortion from a moral point of view. But then let us notice from *what* moral point of view we need this knowledge. We need it in order to 'judge' the moral quality of the abortion; we need it to discriminate the abortion which this woman has had, or proposes to have, from other abortions, hypothetical or actual, which other women, with different characters and stories, have had or may propose to have. Information about the agent's character is necessary for an *evaluative* process of moral thought in which the thinker stands at an observer's distance from the agent and her acts and assesses them. (This raises the question posed by the Sermon on the Mount (Mt. 7:1), whether third-person evaluation of other people's acts is ever a proper or necessary activity. We shall take it, for the sake of argument, that it can be proper. We return to Jesus' words below, page 224.)

Suppose, however, that it is not evaluation but deliberation about an abortion that is needed. Suppose that I myself am the pregnant woman, that the decision is my own, and that the life-story in which the decision is set is my life-story. Some of the information about me, which the observer needs to know in order to judge my act correctly, would be inappropriate or even inaccessible to my own deliberations. Inaccessible, because I am the last person to form an accurate assessment of my own character; inappropriate, because even if some adviser gives me an accurate picture of myself, that picture ought not to contribute to my decision except in so far as it may clarify my view of the *moral field*. We must note carefully what this denial does not mean. It does not mean that I should ignore all personal factors which determine my field of choice and resolve to treat my decision as though it were exactly the same as every other woman's abortion-decision. I may properly consider the needs of my existing children, the extent of my financial resources, and so on. Nor does it mean even that I should ignore factors about my own disposition and personality in so far as they too contribute to an objective picture of the moral field. If I know, with some objectivity, that I am likely to break down under strain, that my emotional stability and mental health are delicately balanced, these too would be proper factors in my decision. (And so traditional casuistry has always maintained. It is true, of course, that in the matter of abortion it has not regarded them as probably *decisive* factors; but that is a substantive judgment about the overwhelming claim of the unborn child's life, not a formal judgment about what may be considered in principle.) What I cannot admit as relevant to my decision, however, are factors about my moral character which would short-circuit the process of deliberation and distort the proper consideration of the moral field.

The third-person judge may think that I have been 'conscientious'. He will have formed this view, not from looking at this one decision alone, but from the evidence of my life as a whole, which will give him a context for understanding this decision and reaching a favourable verdict on it. But suppose that this knowledge of my own conscientiousness is offered to me, perhaps by a well-meaning counsellor, as I wonder doubtfully whether to have the abortion or not. What difference will it make? It may perhaps incline me to be less anxious, believing that I have it within me to make a conscientious decision, and so, at the best, to take the decision more in my stride, or, at the worst, to become complacent and belie the character that I have so far earned. Or it may challenge me to be no less conscientious on this occasion, as I realize that nothing less than my character is at stake. In no case does it contribute to the substance of the decision; it can only relax or brace me as I confront the decision, and if it helps or harms the decision it will do so by relaxing or bracing me in the right way or in the wrong way.

But then we have chosen a rather under-specified example. Let us now consider a judgment of character which might well affect the substance of the decision. Let us say that the judge finds me to have been conscientious and practical in the care of my children, and praises my decision to have an abortion as one more example of my sense of parental responsibility. Could *that* knowledge of myself, if it were available to me, help me decide one way rather than the other? Clearly it could. I could say to myself: 'I have always been careful where my children's material welfare is concerned, and I don't intend to change now!' But that would be to narrow the field of moral claims prematurely. It would make for an unconscientious decision, because it would refuse to confront the possibility that where the life of an unborn child was at stake, even the material welfare of one's existing children might be a secondary consideration. In that case a strong self-consciousness about my own characteristic excellences, far from illuminating the meaning of the act which I have to deliberate, will have obscured it. It will have stood between me and the moral field to which I must respond.

In this discussion we have in mind some remarks made by Stanley Hauerwas, to whom theological moralists owe a debt of gratitude for reawakening their interest in questions of character as well as for raising other new questions to which we cannot attend here. In an article co-authored with David Burrell, Hauerwas makes a point of the formal inhibitions imposed on the discussion of abortion by what he calls 'the standard account of moral rationality' (which is actually rather difficult to attribute to anyone in particular): 'So in considering the question of abortion, questions like "Why did the pregnancy occur?", "What kind of community do you live in?", "What do you believe about the place of children?" may be psychologically interesting but cannot be allowed to enter into the justification of the decision. For such matters are bound to vary from one agent to another' (*Truthfulness and Tragedy*, p. 18. In his more recent writings Hauerwas has inclined to qualify such strong claims for the independence of the agent's perspective with a stress on the perspective of the community). A similar reproach against traditional modes of moral argument is made in James Gustafson's contribution to the symposium on abortion which was edited by John T. Noonan: 'Arguments pertaining to "saving the life of the mother" do not admit as important evidence such factors as whether she is the mother of six other children depending on her, or no other children. In some other ways of discussing abortion such information might make a difference in the argument. I am suggesting that the time and space limits one uses to isolate what is "the case" have a considerable effect on the way one argues' (pp. 104ff.). To both we may reply that two points are being confused: the substantive point that traditional Christian casuistry on this subject has not regarded certain factors as decisive, in face of the overriding claim of the unborn child's life; and the formal point that some considerations are inappropriate to the agent's own deliberations and can be taken into consideration only from the observer's perspective. Such is the case with the question of what the agent 'believes'. It must not matter to her what she *believes* about the place of children; it must only matter to her what the place of children *is*. That is to say, she must be open to correcting a false belief if she finds she has one.

This response is somewhat paradoxical, since Hauerwas, in common with others of the school, makes a point of stressing (in contrast to the 'standard account') the importance of 'agent-perspective'. He objects to the assumption that 'the observer is the ideal judge whose description of an action defeats all accounts' (*Vision and Virtue*, p. 79); and yet we have suggested that he introduces factors from the observer's exclusive viewpoint inappropriately into his account of moral deliberation. And we may be permitted to adduce in support of our charge a small but revealing piece of evidence: all the questions about abortion which he and Burrell think should be asked are framed in the second-person form, 'What do *you* believe about . . .?', as though asked by a counsellor, not in the first-person, as asked by an agent. (Similarly, Gustafson's essay sees the question in terms of 'the Christian moralist' who must 'respond to this woman' in 'a responsible relationship' (pp. 107f.). We might ask: do Christian moralists never have unwanted pregnancies themselves?) It is not that Christian ethics has nothing to say about the counsellor and his limitations; but one might expect it to say it *after* it has examined the simple case from a first-person point of view, and it is quite extraordinary that the counsellor's stance should be described as occupying 'the agent's perspective'!

But of course it is precisely the third-person judge who has to remember to *include* the agent's perspective in his purview, as part of what he is trying to assess. The agent does not have to include it, because he actually holds it, simply by virtue of being the agent. The judge must strive to remember the agent's viewpoint because he is *not* the agent; the agent must struggle to transcend it because he *is* the agent. The counsellor is in the dangerous position of both holding the third-person point of view on the one hand, and of contributing to the deliberative process on the other. That is why he must be self-disciplined, for he can easily become a tempter if he introduces his own compassion or admiration for the agent into the agent's deliberations. Gustafson's essay concludes, with reference to a case he has discussed at length: 'My own decision is (a) if I were in the woman's human predicament I believe I could morally justify an abortion, and thus: (b) I would affirm its moral propriety in this instance' (p. 117). The organization of this conclusion cannot be faulted: the moralist moves from an imaginative first-person judgment about what he would do in the woman's situation, to converting that judgment, and only that judgment, into advice. But then he immediately adds: 'It is a discernment of compassion for the woman'; which suggests that the third-party perspectives had *not* been excluded after all. Is this counsellor advising this agent to act in this way because he feels sorry for her? Is he, therefore, by implication encouraging her to act on the basis of self-pity? When 'agent-perspective' comes to mean this, it is simply a corruption of the counselling relationship!

Knowledge of the agent's character, then, cannot contribute to *deliberative* moral thought. It contributes to *evaluative* moral thought only because that kind of moral reflection supposes a closed narrative of actions from which the character has already emerged clearly into view, so that each element in the narrative can be interpreted in the light of the whole. Even in evaluative thought, then, we do not have an exception to the rule that the character is known through the acts. In deliberation, on the other hand, the narrative is not closed but open; the next act is undetermined. And when that is the case, our knowledge even of another person's character, let alone of our own, is rendered merely provisional, subject to the proof of further disclosures. The relevant character-knowledge is unavailable, because it depends on the decision which has yet to be made. The inappropriateness of character-knowledge to the tasks of deliberation is the clearest demonstration of the epistemological priority of acts in disclosing character.

To this argument, however, we may anticipate a further response. It will be said that we have not given sufficient weight to the role of the agent's *intentions* in determining the meaning of his acts. This introduces a new theme, focal to the neo-Aristotelian approach, which is the connection between character and intention. Acts are not self-explanatory, at least in one important respect: we can never be sure precisely what was done until we know what the agent meant to do. But that information is immediately known only to himself; it is part of his self-knowledge, which, therefore, is not only accessible to him in his deliberations, but constitutes one of the most important contributory elements to his decision. But in what sense can the agent's intention already be 'knowledge' while he is still deliberating? Is it not the end-result of deliberation to *form* an intention, and must not that intention, therefore, be still unformed while the deliberation goes on? Here our respondent replies that in an important sense the intention is already preformed, because it arises from his character. In deliberating, the agent draws on his self-knowledge to determine what *kind* of intentionality he brings to this choice from his past, to inform him, as it were, what range of possible concrete intentions with respect to this particular decision would be true to his own self. Thus every moral decision becomes a kind of self-interpretation, a way of conducting the self, which has been built up by past intentions and choices, in a manner that will give meaningful development to its career. The force of this response, therefore, is to challenge our claim that such character-knowledge is inappropriate to the agent's perspective on his own decisions. For if all decisions are understood in this way as a form of conscious self-development, then clearly this form of self-knowledge is the most appropriate asset that the agent can possess. And to our objection that this pre-empts an open consideration of the moral field, it will be replied that an *indeterminate* openness to the moral field is not what is required at all. Only such responsiveness to the moral field as will comport with the virtues and character that the agent brings to it can reasonably be demanded. To expect the agent to exclude himself, or to include himself only as object, as part of the moral field, is to demand that moral decision should be something that there is no reason for it to be.

Thus the epistemological priority of character is defended in a new form, which assimilates the notion of character to that of intention, *i.e.* essentially to that of will. It is the kind of argument that G. K. Chesterton called an 'argument of impenitence'. That is a useful title, in that it draws attention to the positive reason why Christian thought has tended to insist that every moral decision should be approached *de novo*, with complete openness to the moral field; namely, that it affords also an occasion of repenting. To demand that the new decision shall conform to that which we have brought with us, in our expectations and life-projects, is to close ourselves to the possible grace of God in judgment and conversion. (And the fact that from a third-person point of view absolute openness may appear never to be achieved, does not make openness any less the appropriate moral task for the agent. Here we may readily agree that the observer's account must not be allowed to defeat all other accounts!) When we deliberate on something we are about to do, or reflect on something we have done, we have, in the final analysis, a single point to resolve: is it, or was it, the *right* thing to do? We may, of course, ask more specifically about virtues and vices which the act may or may not express: is it a compassionate thing to do? Is it just? Is it cowardly? But these are only preliminary explorations to help us locate the challenge posed by the situation. It is as though we were asking: is this a situation which demands more compassion than I am inclined to show? Is it a situation which requires more scrupulous fairness? Is it a situation in which cowardice is a serious temptation? We cannot resolve in advance that, whatever the situation, we will do the compassionate thing, the just thing, the courageous thing; for that would be to conclude our moral enquiry before we had ascertained whether compassion, justice or courage was what this particular situation was most importantly about. It would be to close ourselves against the *corrective* influence of this situation upon our pre-formed moral inclinations. It may happen, of course, that someone who, at a formative stage of his life, finds himself constantly in situations where one virtue in particular, let us say courage, is required of him, will tend thereafter to interpret all the decisions he faces in terms of the need for courage. But this is not a virtue, it is a vice. It means that he cannot discern the reality of what he faces because of the presuppositions he brings with him. It is the problem of the soldier-turned-politician: we may praise him for a while for his firm resolution, but the more he persists in misinterpreting situations in terms that are alien to them, the more we come to feel the force of the argument in Plato's *Laches* that a man who fails to display understanding cannot be courageous, but only rash.

We may observe that the neo-Aristotelian position has here imposed upon Aristotle's concept of character a somewhat un-Aristotelian interpretation. Aristotle did, of course, envisage second-order deliberation about how we may train ourselves and our citizens to have good habits; but habit is not primarily a category of deliberation, but of description. In particular decisions it is the moral field, the field of pleasures and pains adjudicated by 'right reason', which is determinative (*Nicomachean Ethics* 1103 a 14 – 1105 a 16). Hence: 'habits are formed from their correlative activities' (1103 b 21). The conception of moral decision as conscious projection of one's character really arises from the modern voluntarist conception of the self as historical project, the very conception to which many representatives of this school boast that they have found an alternative.

Hauerwas's early article 'Towards an Ethic of Character' (*Vision and Virtue*, pp. 48–67) brings out this ancestry rather clearly, since it begins from those conceptions of 'freedom and responsibility' which 'focus on man as self-creator', and which lead both to a moral vacuum, in which 'we are simply forced to fall back on ourselves in order to make decisions that have no relationship to objective right and wrong', and to a concentration of ethical discourse on ' "problems", i.e. situations in which it is difficult to know what one should do'. It is clear that Hauerwas intends to offer us an alternative, but that alternative turns out to be not so much a repudiation of man's self-creation as a refinement of it. 'Unless the positive significance of character is appreciated, freedom and responsibility cannot be understood in their proper context; for we are more than just the sum total of our responses to particular situations.' Self-creating, in other words, has also to take account of linear continuities. 'By our actions we not only shape a particular situation, we also form ourselves to meet future situations in a particular way' (pp. 48f.). We need not stress, however, the strong claims made in this essay for the self-determination of character, claims which may not be, as Outka observes in his critique of the author's thought, entirely characteristic of Hauerwas' total view. Our interest focuses on the few pages in which the essay moves from this starting-point to assert the inscrutability of actions apart from the agent's self-declared character. Hauerwas maintains unproblematically that 'action can only ultimately be described and understood by reference to the intention of the agent' (p. 57). Intention is described in a broad way, to include the choice of perspective in which we interpret situations and not merely the choice of naked ends or goals: agency depends on man's 'ability to envision and fix his attention on certain descriptions and to form his actions (and thus himself) in accordance with them. A man's character is largely the result of such sustained attention' (p. 58). 'Result', of course, represents the orthodox Aristotelian view that character is formed by its exercise in the corresponding acts (*Nicomachean Ethics* 1103 a 31ff.). But a moment later a new conception of character emerges: 'Man's agency . . . is only effective when it is determined in one direction rather than another, i.e. when a man *chooses to live his life by certain beliefs and intentions* ... and embodies this *fundamental choice* in concrete choices' (italics added). What was the *result* of a series of concrete choices has now become itself a kind of mega-choice, a 'fundamental choice' or life-project, which is then to be embodied in concrete choices thereafter. The way is now free for Hauerwas to attribute to character all the interpretative force which has just been established for intention. But obviously this leads him immediately into a quarrel with Aristotle's doctrine mentioned above: 'Aristotle was fond of saying that "virtues develop from corresponding activities", which implies that it is possible to establish a rather direct relationship between the virtue and a certain set of actions that have a publicly agreed-on description. But Aristotle's understanding of this relationship is far too simple.' Hauerwas has identified the nature of his quarrel perfectly: it is about the public scrutability of acts and the hiddenness of character. Aristotle thought that acts, in so far as they were open to public interpretation, brought character out into the open too. Hauerwas thinks that the hiddenness of character drags acts back into the half-light of ambiguity. That is why, he argues, there are conflicting descriptions of acts. He thinks this because he has already shown that a certain ambiguity attaches to acts by virtue of the hiddenness of their agent's *intentions*, and he has now construed character as a kind of total intentionality for the life-project. Consequently he can write, as though the words 'intention' and 'character' were synonymous: 'Our *character* is always secret to some extent; no matter what our public *actions* may look like to the observer, only our own avowal can finally be taken as the description of *what we were doing*' (p. 59, italics added).

The plurality and unity of the virtues

Two features tend to go together in a moral theory, voluntarism and pluralism. And so it is with this modernized Aristotelian doctrine which understands character as life-shaping intention. Having once determined that the agent legitimately imposes his own interpretative matrix upon the situation into which he must act, it must go on to maintain the possibility of many different interpretative matrixes corresponding to many agents' different life-intentions, all equally valid. This may be qualified by allowing that some life-intentions are more capable of sustaining themselves than others. There may be more and less adequate interpretative matrices; some may be too crude to handle the reality that confronts them, and so may provoke a crisis which will result in some kind of conversion. Nevertheless, the criteria for forming one's life-intention must, it seems, be functional criteria; there is no immediate dictation to this decision by the demands of reality itself. There are many different life-intentions that could be sustained by a reasonably thoughtful agent, and which would sustain him on a consistent course throughout his life. Three different applications of this pluralist principle may be noted, though we shall address only the last of them. For some of its advocates moral pluralism is directly related to religious pluralism. For many of them it is the key to the understanding of tragedy, which is seen as the clash of incompatible moral visions. For most it presents a serious challenge to Plato's doctrine of the unity of the virtues.

Plato argued that the theoretical plurality of the virtues resolved itself concretely into a simple necessity that anyone who exemplified one virtue should exemplify all of them. Someone who was not wise could not be courageous, someone who was not courageous could not be prudent, someone who was not prudent could not be just (*Protagoras* 349–350). On the face of it this argument seems to ignore the fact that the virtues are differently represented in different people. If we praise someone as 'just' and someone else as 'compassionate', we are pointing to differences of moral character between them. This contrast may carry the implication that in certain situations they will act in opposite ways: when there is a decision which presents a *prima facie* tension between compassion and justice, the one will act justly rather than compassionately, the other compassionately rather than justly. But it need not imply this; and it certainly need not suggest that the just person is incapable of feeling the claims of compassion and *vice versa*. What it does imply is that the two lives display different salient features, and that both sets of features can properly and without dissimulation be called good. It suggests, moreover, that both sets of features could not easily be conceived of as characterizing one and the same life to the same extent. Here is a courageous woman who has lived out her life in the slums working for the socially disabled. Here is another of great family-loyalty, who has brought up her children with devotion and been a rock of support to her kin and community. And here is a third, who has given her energies to an intellectual quest which she has pursued with integrity and self-discipline. They may admire each other; they may even imitate each other's virtues to an extent. But in so far as each woman's life has been *shaped* by one virtue rather than others, it does not have room to accommodate the specialized excellences which the other women's lives display. There might, of course, be a fourth woman who combines elements of all these three careers and who has pursued each less single-mindedly; and this width of accomplishment might itself be viewed as a species of excellence. But the point is that this fourth woman would not necessarily be better than the other three. We cannot conceive their lives as mere defections from the ideal which she represents. (Plato's position, of course, is susceptible of a less stringent interpretation, and could allow for the virtues to be present in different people in different proportions. But even on this account he insists on a certain homogeneousness of virtue which it is the purpose of moral pluralism to challenge.)

These pluralist objections to Plato need cause no embarrassment to us. The ethic of character which we would wish to defend, confined as it is to an evaluative (third-person) stance, is free to acknowledge a plurality of moral excellences without being drawn into the relativism which a deliberative (first-person) pluralism is bound to involve. 'Relativism', as the word is commonly used, is simply an aspect of voluntarism. It is a posture of scepticism adopted in deliberative moral thought, in which we declare that there is, in principle, no rational resolution available to our deliberations: the choice between the alternatives must be nothing more than a bare choice, a raw exercise of the will. But we can be pluralist in our evaluations without ascribing diversity merely to the diverse choices of the agents' wills and without allowing deliberation to be caught in the relativist *impasse*. What made the three women of whom we spoke achieve such different forms of excellence? Their careers were shaped by their different habits; these habits arose as they confronted different occasions of choice; the different occasions were afforded them as a result of their different educations; and their educations were dictated by their different natural endowments. (That is the simplest form of the story, which does not venture into such other determinants as social or political circumstance.) The differentiation of their virtues, in other words, does not depend on their intentions. Of course, there will have been different intentions too, some of them of moral significance, some of them not so. But we can account for their differences of character without supposing that any of them approached a major decision with anything other than an open intention to discern and do what was right in the circumstances. We do not require prejudice of intention to produce moral diversity; variation in the moral field is sufficient to produce it. In theological discussion it is understood within the concept of 'vocation', or, in New Testament terminology, of 'gifts'. 'Having gifts that differ according to the grace given to us' (Rom. 12:6), we respond to the objectivity of that gift and live the life that God has summoned us to live in all its distinctiveness.

To his contemporary interpreters it seems that Aristotle provides a model for combining a pluralist account of the virtues with a unified teleological concept of 'the good for man' which defends against relativism and allows some way out of the deliberative *impasse* of modern voluntarism. In the opening paragraph of the *Nicomachean Ethics* (1094 a 1 – b 7) Aristotle starts from the observation that all human activity strives for some good; but there are 'many practices, arts and sciences' and so 'many ends-of-action'. But that does not mean that there can be no unified science of Ethics. For some goods and activities are hierarchically subordinated to others as means to ends; and we may therefore conceive of a single end-of-all-action to which all other goods and activities are subordinated and towards which they all strive. This 'good for man' (*tānthrōpinon agathon*)

Aristotle identifies as 'happiness' (*eudaimonia*). His modern exponents are quite justified in stressing that this account of the good allows much more to pluralism than Plato's account. Aristotle explicitly rejects a univocal sense of 'good' that is common to different activities (1096 b 25). And they are equally justified in stressing that the unity conferred upon Aristotle's ethics by the ultimate good, to which all other goods are as means to end, is of great importance for the possibility of rational deliberation.

But we may observe how difficult it is for the modern exponent (who will here be represented by Alisdair MacIntyre) to appropriate the train of thought in these paragraphs, given that he bases the plurality of practices and virtues not, as Aristotle was inclined to, on social determinants, but on will. MacIntyre proposes to identify a 'core concept of the virtues', derived from Aristotle but with two reservations. These reservations are: first, that Aristotle's natural teleology must be replaced with an alternative teleology; secondly that there must be a sufficiently marked pluralism to account adequately for tragedy, 'the conflict of good with good', which even Aristotle, tempted by Plato's doctrine of the unity of the virtues, was inclined to gloze over (*After Virtue*, pp. 152f., 183). He will reconstruct this 'core concept' in three stages. The first is to relate virtues to practices. This follows Aristotle's assertion of 'many practices, arts and sciences' with their many ends; it ensures the plurality of the virtues and, most importantly, suggests the alternative teleology which MacIntyre requires. It affords a teleology of 'goods internal to practices', that is, of implicit intentionality embodied in the variety of human enterprises. MacIntyre then asks himself what is inadequate about this account taken on its own, and replies quite correctly that it is indistinguishable from the modern relativist voluntarism which it set out to oppose (pp. 187f.). To overcome relativism he has to follow Aristotle further, from the 'many ends of action' to the single 'good for man'. But how can this be done without also adopting Aristotle's natural teleology? His second step undertakes this task, by extending the scope of implicit intentionality from discrete practices to 'each human life as a unity'. This certainly moves away from a pluralist fragmentation of the moral subject; but it hardly provides what is necessary to a unified good for man *qua* man. For there will be as many different valid answers to the question 'What is the good for me?' as there are persons to ask it. At this point MacIntyre attempts an astonishing manoeuvre: 'To ask "What is the good for man?" ', he says, 'is to ask what all answers to the former question must have in common' (p. 203). The good for man *qua* man, in other words, is reached by abstracting the common element from all the life-projects of individual men. But how do we know that these individual life-projects will have anything of significance in common? Only by assuming that they were in the first place valid interpretations of a common human calling! So far from the good-for-man being an abstraction from the multitude of goods-for-men, they are rather abstractions from it. But that makes it impossible to account for the normativity of the common human good in terms of the intentionality of the various life-projects. The intentions in these projects are to be judged as reasonable or unreasonable in the light of that good, which must, therefore, be known independently of them.

MacIntyre's third stage then attempts another way of reaching the unified good-for-man, by extending the implicit intentionality yet further to include the cultural tradition within which each individual life is lived. Again, this will not overcome relativism. It will merely leave us with its most common form, the cultural relativism which cannot choose between alternative traditions. In the end, then, MacIntyre cannot break with the modernity which he repudiates; and that is because he believes the moderns rather than Aristotle on the question of natural teleology.

But Christianity has never been prepared to leave the matter there, at the level of vocation or gift, which would amount to no more than an ethic of differentiated self-fulfilment. Individual gifts and vocations do play a significant part in the New Testament, especially in its understanding of the church as a community of God-given differences. Yet over against the 'varieties of gifts, varieties of ministries, varieties of expressions', there is the unity of God, Father, Son and Spirit, whose work underlies all these differences, and there is the unity of the confession 'Jesus is Lord' which marks the authentic presence of the Holy Spirit (1 Cor. 12:3–6*). This unity, too, must be discerned behind the plurality of individual moral characters; there must be a unifying factor in virtue which is the expression of the church's one faith. And so Saint Paul continues, 'I may speak in tongues of men or of angels, but if I am without love, I am a sounding gong or a clanging cymbal. I may have the gift of prophecy, and know every hidden truth; I may have faith strong enough to move mountains; but if I have no love, I am nothing' (13:1–2, NEB). In reading these familiar words we must be alert to the context of discussion in which they are situated: the great achievements which Paul thinks meaningless without love are gifts of the Spirit, vocations, particular callings to which one is summoned individually, which will distinguish this man's service from his neighbour's and will mark his history out as a unique and personal history. It is not that Paul deprecates the individual and personally distinctive; it is not that he suspects all striking manifestations of it of a secret hypocrisy. His point is simply that a life considered solely as the fulfilling of a personal destiny, the working-out of an individual charisma, is a vacant abstraction. The particularity of vocation must serve as a window through which the universal character of all Christian life may appear. Just as the variety of voices within the church are unified in a common confession, 'Jesus is Lord', so the variety of forms of life are unified within a common form of life according to God's order, the life of love.

The shape that Western Christianity gave to its doctrine of the unity of the virtues owes more to this passage of Saint Paul than it does to Plato. Plato's famous list of four 'cardinal' virtues is based on his tripartite analysis of the human soul (*Republic* 435a – 441e): temperance is the virtue of the appetite, fortitude of the spirit and prudence of the intellect, while justice is the virtue of the whole in which each part is properly subordinated to the next above it in a hierarchy where the intellect is sovereign. Contrast this with what we find in Saint Augustine (*De moribus ecclesiae* 15.25). True virtue is love for God, and the four cardinal virtues are manifestations of this love in certain typical relations into which human existence leads us. Temperance is the loving subject preserving himself unspoilt for God; fortitude is his glad endurance of all for God's sake; justice is his stance of subordination before God and command over the non-human creation; and prudence is his discrimination between that which helps and that which hinders his pilgrimage towards God. The most striking difference is that Augustine has described both virtue as such and its differentiation into the cardinal virtues in terms of the relation of an undifferentiated soul to a differentiated external reality that it encounters in its history, to God, to adversity, to the lower creation. Plato's account, on the other hand, is given in terms of the self-contained organization and operation of a differentiated soul; and in so far as this account presupposes his doctrine of the transcendent good, the soul is ordered to an undifferentiated reality, encountered unhistorically by the mind alone. Like Plato, Augustine thinks the unity of the virtues is important because it reflects the soul's orientation to its transcendent good. Unlike him, he thinks the differentiations of virtue important because the soul's pursuit of its good must take place in the context of a relation to other realities which form the circumstances and conditions of its life in history. Augustine's doctrine was taken over with only minor adaptations by Saint Thomas Aquinas, who referred to love as 'the form of the virtues' (*Summa Theologiae* II–II. 23.7,8).

Returning to the well-known passage from 1 Corinthians we now find a change of focus: 'Love is patient; love is kind and envies no one. Love is never boastful, nor conceited, nor rude; never selfish, not quick to take offence. Love keeps no score of wrongs; does not gloat over other men's sins, but delights in the truth. There is nothing love cannot face; there is no limit to its faith, its hope, and its endurance' (13:4–7, NEB). Here we are no longer dealing with vocations and gifts, but with the moral law. Martyrdom may be the calling of a select few, but freedom from envy is a demand made upon all. The significance of this step in Paul's thought is clear enough. The unity which can be seen behind the many forms of individual goodness is nothing other than the fulfilment of the moral law. That is what makes these differentiations of character good: they are true interpretations, each within a unique vocational matrix, of the one moral life, the life which is given to all men to live. Just as love is the one demand which is differentiated generically in the variety of commands in the moral law, so it is the one life-task which is differentiated particularly in the uniqueness of individual vocations. Love is the unitary orientation that lies behind all the uniquely varied responses to the generic variety of the created order.

The function of an ethic of character

There remains one question to be addressed, which arises out of our contention that an ethic of character is developed from an evaluative (third-person) stance, and cannot play a role in a deliberative train of thought. What, then, is its function in moral thought? And with this question we may usefully associate another, to which we have earlier alluded: is an ethic of character itself morally legitimate? Can it escape the condemnation implied in Jesus' warning, 'Judge not, that you be not judged' (Mt. 7:1)?

Assessments of character remind us, in the first place, what moral deliberation is about. They place it in its soteriological context, as a matter not merely of 'doing the right thing' but of 'saving one's soul'. The names of the virtues and the vices represent to us different aspects of the salvation and damnation of the soul. Courage, wisdom and loyalty are forms of well-being in the moral agent, while cowardice, ignorance and selfishness are forms of corruption. In observing such well-being and corruption we see what 'doing the right thing' and 'doing the wrong thing' actually do to us. They therefore become an object of practical consideration, not in particular moral deliberations but in a commitment to more conscientious moral deliberation in general. And inasmuch as they are differentiated, they may alert us to special temptations or challenges which we will be more prepared to recognize in future deliberations. An ethic of character, therefore, raises the soteriological question in relation to morality; that is why the Catholic tradition of moral theology has been right to retain it. But it does not answer that question sufficiently; that is why the Protestant tradition has been right to suspect its possible pretensions. We shall not learn how to save our souls by talking about the formation of virtuous characters. Nevertheless, such talk may teach us better than anything else what it is for a soul to be lost or saved, and so teach us to care about it for ourselves and others.

From this it follows, in the second place, that thought about moral character plays a central role in repentance. Evaluative assessments are made not only of other people but of ourselves. The observer's distance, which removes us from the deliberative situation, can, nevertheless, give us a perspective from which to review our own past lives. We can form judgments (partial, no doubt, but not valueless) on what kind of character our history has disclosed, and these, rather than judgments on particular acts, are what will make us feel most acutely the need of salvation. The prophet cried out, 'I am a man of unclean lips, and I dwell in the midst of a people of unclean lips' (Is. 6:5), not accusing himself or his people of any particular act of false speech, but summing up in that phrase his moral insufficiency to sustain the holy worship of the Lord of hosts. Of an ethic of character, then, we can say with particular point what Lutheran theology used to say about the moral law in all its forms, that by condemning us it drives us to seek the grace of God.

But, in the third place, such self-assessment is based on comparison of self and others. We stand under the law of God, which accuses our selfish ambition or indolence; but we learn to see those traits in ourselves when we recognize the similarities between our own character and others'. A provisional judgment of other people, too, is implied in a judgment of ourselves, because the moral law speaks generically. Happily, this judgment may very often be favourable. We observe the virtues as well as the vices of other people, and fortunate we are that this is so, since it is such observation that teaches us to love. Nevertheless, our observations, whether favourable or unfavourable, must be provisional, and in that sense we 'judge not'. Just as our favourable judgments on ourselves must be provisional, knowing that whatever has been given us by God's grace may be lost through complacency and carelessness, so our favourable judgments on others are tempered by the knowledge that they, too, are open to temptation. More importantly, just as our critical judgments on ourselves must be provisional, lest we despair of repentance and transformation, so our critical judgments on others must be expectantly open to God's grace. And when we look at others we have to think not only of repentance and transformation that may yet take place, but of that which may possibly have already taken place, though without being disclosed to our view. Thus Solon's warning, to call no man happy until he is dead, is less cautious than Jesus' warning. Even of the dead we do not know what hidden work of God may yet be shown us on the last day.

11

The double aspect of the moral life

We have said that love is the principle which confers unifying order both upon the moral field and upon the character of the moral subject. It is the fulfilment of the moral law on the one hand, and the form of the virtues on the other. Yet Jesus' command of love, as the Synoptic Gospels report it, is a twofold command, combining the rulee of worship from Deuteronomy 6:5, that 'you shall love the Lord your God with all your heart, and with all your soul, and with all your might', with the rule of social life from Leviticus 19:18, that 'you shall love your neighbour as yourself'. Ever since Saint Augustine gave to the Synoptic text its commanding position in Western moral thought, the church in the West has been fascinated, and perhaps a little alarmed, by the implications of this duality. 'Hardly could a more frightful thing be conceived', observed Kierkegaard, 'than that there might be a collision between love for God and love for the persons for whom love has been planted by Him in our hearts' (*Either-Or* II, p. 205). This 'frightful' conception has, in different guises, haunted the church. In the Middle Ages it appeared in classical dress in terms of Aristotle's distinction between the practical and contemplative lives. In the modern period it has presented itself as a conflict between the claims of worship and the claims of service, and again as a conflict between the claims of evangelism and the claims of works of mercy. These are, of course, distinct problems. Yet there is a root issue which is common to them: the 'frightful' conception is the thought that the universe might be at war with itself, and that man might be claimed by both sides as an ally. It would indeed be a terrifying collision between love for God and love for the persons for whom love had been planted by him in our hearts if, in the end, we had

226

to say of those two loves what the apostle says about love for the world: 'If any one loves the world, love for the Father is not in him' (1 Jn. 2:15).

If this is the correct interpretation of the church's recurrent anxiety about conflicts of obligation, we must meet it boldly with a dogmatic assertion: this collision does not and cannot occur in a universe where there is one God who is Creator of all things. Lying behind the anxiety is a covert Manichaeism, a belief in two first principles endlessly at war, the source of incompatible claims and counter-claims between which we are caught. But when we are warned of 'the world', we are not meant to think that there is a *real* alternative to God that we might love in his place. 'The world' in this sense is not the real and good world that God has made, nor any other real world, but a fantasy-world of the sinful imagination, a nothingness which will destroy us if we love it simply because it is nothingness and offers nothing on which we may nourish ourselves. Neither is the twofold command to be thought of as an attempt to build a bridge between love for God and some other love. Propounded, as Saint Matthew has it (22:36), in answer to an enquiry after the 'great' commandment, it presents a demand which, though it is twofold, arises within the unified demand of the one God. One God demands of us one love – for himself and for our neighbour. The unity of the demand is underwritten by God's own unity and singleness of purpose. Only as we seek to understand the demand as a unified demand does it reveal to us that our response must have two sides to it, like a stream bifurcating into two channels.

Yet perhaps even that simile might prove misleading. What, we might ask, is the primary stream, antecedent to its bifurcation into love of God and neighbour? Is it simply 'love' without a definite object? Is it love of reality, of all that is? But there is no such thing as love without an object; and as for love of reality, it must be an idolatrous love if it proposes for itself any object larger than the source of all reality. Love for God and neighbour cannot unfold out of love for an undifferentiated All, simply because God and neighbour have themselves not unfolded out of an undifferentiated All. Reality does not primordially embrace God and something else. Reality is God, who, in his ability to confer reality upon things other than himself, brings duality to existence alongside his unity. Creation is not the self-differentiation of a whole, but the making of a world *ex nihilo*. Thus the love with which we love reality must be twofold in the same way that the reality which we love is twofold: the secondary object is given by, and depends upon, the primary object. Just as God, in a certain sense, continues to be the sole reality, even though he has created a new reality apart from himself, so love for God continues to be, in exactly the same sense, the sole thing that is demanded of us: 'with all your heart, and

227

with all your soul, and with all your mind, and with all your strength' (Mk. 12:30), which leaves us, as Augustine commented, no room for any other love.

We may illustrate the point from Jonathan Edwards' treatise, *The Nature of True Virtue*, which begins with a definition of virtue as 'benevolence to being in general', expressed as 'union and consent with the great whole', and contrasted with 'benevolence to a private circle or system of beings, which are but a small part of the whole' (pp. 3f.). From there Edwards advances as follows: 'If being, simply considered, be the first object of a truly virtuous benevolence, then that object who has most of being, or has the greatest share of existence, other things being equal, so far as such a being is exhibited to our faculties, will have the greatest share of the propensity and benevolent affections of the heart' (p. 9). And this, he intends, will justify his concluding (but not until chapter 2!) 'that true virtue must chiefly consist in love to God; the Being of beings, infinitely the greatest and best . . . So that all other being, even the whole universe, is as nothing in comparison of the divine Being . . . And all true virtue must radically and essentially, and as it were summarily consist in this. Because God is not only infinitely greater and more excellent than all other being, but he is the head of the universal system of existence . . .' (pp. 14f.). We need not question the seriousness with which Edwards takes these theological assertions of chapter 2, but there must be a sense of discomfort about the relationship of this Edwards to the metaphysical Edwards of chapter 1. If one starts by treating 'being in general' and announces that one will regard God as a special case of such being, any subsequent assertions that the universe is 'as nothing' beside the divine being will inevitably tend to be discounted. One has already *derived* the love of God from a prior love of the universe. The finest Christian theological assertions about the relation of God to his creation will lose their force and significance if they are used merely as the *minor* premiss of an argument which takes as its major premiss the identity of virtue with love of the universe.

We may explore the duality-in-unity of the love-command by way of two complementary affirmations, the one starting from its unity, the other from its duality. In the first place, we are to love the neighbour *because the neighbour is ordered to the love of God*.

Self and neighbour are equal partners within a universe which has its origin and end in God. Neither is origin or end to the other. He (or she) is my ontological equal; he (or she) is given being on the same terms as I have been given being. But such parity cannot simply be self-subsisting. To recognize the neighbour as my equal is to recognize the generic ordering, prior to both of us, which relates us to one another as members of a common kind, as man alongside man. But generic order implies teleological order; real kinds are defined in terms of real ends. If human equality lays claim on me with the authority of reality, and is not merely an abstraction of thought, it is because one human being shares with another a common end. It gains its compelling power only as I see the neighbour as a secondary reality like myself, ordered alongside myself in common dependence upon the primary reality for being and significance.

Many times in the history of thought respect for fellow-men, divorced from its theological context of love for the highest good, has collapsed into one of two corruptions: the attempt to tyrannize over the fellow-man by taking the responsibility for his welfare out of his hands, and the enslavement of the self to the fellow-man who becomes an object of desire and need. The first corruption, however benignly inspired, can lead only to the sort of totalitarian mastery of man by man such as is constantly threatened by modern projects of managerial philanthropy. The second, which is the characteristic relation of a society to its heroes, provides the opportunity for tyranny by absolutizing the erotic subordination of the weak and impressionable to the natural authority of the beautiful and the strong. Take away love for God, and the ontological parity which makes true neighbour-love possible is upset; one human being takes the place of God and confers value and significance upon the other. Anders Nygren's famous opposition of Agape and Eros presumed to tell us, in effect, that no other form of love was possible: in love we must master or be mastered.

True neighbourliness requires the recognition of the supreme good simply in order that we may see the neighbour for what he is. But that means that our pursuit of the neighbour's welfare has to take seriously the thought that he, like ourselves, is a being whose end is in God. To 'love' him without respecting this fundamental truth about him would be an exercise in fantasy. Saint Augustine used to say that our first duty to the neighbour was to 'seize him for God'. This does not mean, as some critics would pretend to warn us, that every gesture or act of love towards the neighbour will have a religious goal as an 'ulterior motive'. It means simply that there is, in our love for the neighbour, a recognition of his high calling and destiny to fellowship with God and a desire to further that destiny in the context of concern for his welfare. It is possible, of course, that the evangelistic zeal which Saint Augustine recommends could become a cloak for some kind of religious self-aggrandizement; it is possible that it could go hand in hand with insensitivity to other aspects of the neighbour's welfare. There are enterprises in the past and more recent history of Christian mission which could lend plausibility to both charges. But can we without prejudice say that this has usually been the case? The surface of the globe is covered with Christian institutions of education and healing which belie the suggestion. We must ask instead whether the somewhat truculent repudiation of evangelism which has been fashionable in some ecclesiastical circles does not reveal a simple refusal to take the neighbour's vocation seriously, or, at best, a timidity which shrinks from putting the Christian understanding of man to the test.

In the second place, however, because creation is God's gift of genuine otherness to his creatures, we must insist also upon the duality of the love-command. Although love-of-neighbour originates in, and has its end in, the love of God, it is still *the love of something that is not God*, and therefore it is quite different from the love of God.

God's creative deed has involved the making, not merely of *one* other than himself, not of a single created subjectivity to which he can be the sole Thou, but of many. He has made a multitude of kinds; within the one kind he has made a race of men; he has called them to live together as a city; he has brought into being those who will have fellowship, not only teleologically with himself, but generically with each other. It is important to stress that plurality is not a state of fallenness, from which mankind must return into an undivided unity. The plurality of mankind, like the pluriformity of created order as a whole, is God's first and last word. He did not make Adam alone at the beginning, and he will not leave him to be alone at the end. Community of equals is that to which man is called and, indeed, that upon which his very capacity for self-conscious individuality depends. The Neo-Platonic mystical quest, in which the soul seeks to be 'alone with the alone', can never be Christian obedience, in that it refuses the communitarian character of redemption. This is not to deny the appropriateness, indeed the necessity, of solitude in Christian piety. But even in solitude, in the private chamber where one is seen and heard by God alone, freed from the oppression that community may impose upon the soul, even there one is a man with and for other men. The early solitaries defended their vocation of withdrawal on the grounds that they were praying for the church – an appropriate defence, for intercessory prayer is perhaps the most central way in which the Christian church functions as a community of individuals. In praying for one another the individual members of the church at once bear their personal responsibilities in seeking the face of God, quite probably in the solitude which that requires, and yet they come before God as a community, bearing each other's needs as well as their own individual needs before him.

The requirement of solitude cannot be glossed over, especially in the light of Matthew 6:5–6, where privacy in prayer is associated with secrecy in almsgiving and fasting. The theme which links them is stated at 6:1: 'Beware of practising your piety before men in order to be seen by them; for then you will have no reward from your Father who is in heaven.' The danger of public deeds of righteousness is that they lose their eschatological reference; their horizon is entirely occupied by the demands and satisfactions of the religious community in the present ('they have received their reward', 6:2,5,16). Secret alms, private prayer and concealed fasting, on the other hand, are open-ended. Their value is not spent upon the community of the present, so that they can expect acknowledgment in the eschatological community of God's kingdom. The contrast is only provisionally between community and solitariness; ultimately it is between the two communities, that of the present age and that of the eschaton. The believer whose heart is set on *that* community seeks a measure of distance from *this* one lest its demands and rewards absorb him. The glossator who, in verse 6 as in verse 4, added the words *en tō phanerō*, 'openly', to the promise of divine recompense did not misunderstand the text. For there is an openness implicit in the promise of eschatological reward, the openness which belongs to the community in which the secrets of all hearts are revealed. He who now attends to private prayer prepares himself for that publicity; for the link which binds his secrecy now with his openness then is the presence of the Father 'who sees in secret'. His public security then is assured by his private access now to the one whom he is taught to address as his 'Father in the secret place' (*tō patri sou tō en tō kryptō*, 6). Like the penitent of Isaiah 26:20, he goes into his chamber to survive the wrath. Like Elisha (2 Ki. 4:33) he exercises there a prophetic access to the powers of the kingdom.

But if the solitarist approach fails to express what is meant by redemption in community, so does another, paradoxically close to it, which proposes to rise above the sense of individual distinctiveness which we have as individual subjects before God, and cultivate a kind of universal self-consciousness. We are to love the neighbour 'as ourself' by losing all sense of the distinction between him and ourself, expanding our self-consciousness to include him in radical empathy. This is, in fact, simply the reverse side of the solitarist coin, for to be alone with the alone is to include the universe in oneself and thus cease to be oneself in distinction from the rest of the universe. But it is not what God calls us to when he calls us to live in community. The communal subject is not constituted by the suppression or abolition of the individual subjects who participate in it. It comes into being as individuals, who are attuned to one another and responsive to one another's actions, co-operate in common enterprises, so that they act as one while still being many. God's creative deed is not about the absorption of individuality into a unique transcendent self-consciousness; it is about the full realization of individuality in a commonness of sharing and reciprocation.

The many references within the New Testament to the 'unity' which should characterize the church are all concerned with the relationships between individuals which enable the formation of a community with common convictions and priorities. Thus Saint Paul, at Philippians 2:2–4, explains *to auto phronēte*, 'thinking the same', which might possibly be misleading, as *tēn autēn agapēn echontes*, 'having the same love'; then *sympsychoi*, 'together in soul', and *to hen phronountes*, 'thinking one thought', are developed as follows: 'Do nothing from selfishness or conceit, but in humility count others better than yourselves.' It might be possible again to understand the next words, *mē ta heautōn hekastos skopountes*, 'let not each consider what is his own', as implying some loss of the sense of difference between I and Thou, but that the conclusion restores it, *alla kai ta heterōn hekastoi*, 'but also what belongs to others'. The famous picture of the earliest Jerusalem church which Saint Luke paints at the beginning of Acts (4:32ff.) confirms this impression. Those who believed were 'of one heart and soul, and no one said that any of the things which he possessed was his own, but they had everything in common'. What sense is to be given to this 'unity' and this 'common' possession of goods? Apparently that which Saint Luke gives in the next verses: that richer Christians made their goods freely available for the needs of the poorer brethren, an act of sharing in which the dynamic polarity of giving and receiving is not abolished in the community of goods, the individual agency of rich and poor not lost in the collective agency of a morally united church. We may mention also the great prayer of Christ for unity in John 17:22, 'that they may be one even as we are one'. But the unity of the Father and the Son in the eternal life of the Godhead cannot either eradicate or overcome the 'I' and 'Thou' of their fellowship: 'I in thee and thou in me'. This was the chief point at issue in the controversy between the church and its Sabellian heretics.

Because God has made us a plurality of others, it is inevitable that our relationships must take on a double aspect: with God on the one hand, and with those who are not God on the other. There must be the distinction between the 'religious' and the 'secular' realms of practice. There must be prayer and praise directed to God in the first instance; there must be fellowship with the neighbour and service of his welfare which is not directed to God in the first instance. Yet these two distinct spheres of active love do not represent two loves; there is no competition which will threaten the purity of heart which is to will one thing. How, then, can we think them together as a unity? How, to use a classical expression, can we understand *caritas ordinata* – love differentiated and set in order? We will comment on two inadequate proposals for an answer before we point to a satisfactory way of conceiving things.

The ordering of love

An approach to the ordering of the two loves which has had much currency in popular piety understands it in terms of the priority of choice in case of conflict. 'Put God first, others next and yourself last,' we were taught when we were children. We are to imagine an occasion on which Kierkegaard's 'frightful conception' is realized, and resolve that in such an event we will treat God's claim as superior to the neighbour's. As with many other human apportionments, the claim of seniority wins the day. God is to have what he asks for; what is left will be offered to others, and then, when the carcass has been picked nearly bare, we will permit ourselves to take what is left.

This, of course, is to arbitrate between God and neighbour in the same way that we arbitrate between conflicting claims made upon us by our fellow human-beings The characteristic virtue of such arbitrations is the virtue of justice, which is to decide between claimants on the basis of the true relative worth of their claims. And there is, of course, a level at which such arbitration of claims has to be done, even with respect to our duties to God. Every one of us has to arbitrate between the claims upon his time of the sacred and secular realms of practice, between time for prayer, time for participation in the world, and time for sleep. Every one of us has to apportion his money between the claims of church institutions, of social and philanthropic works and his own need to stay alive. But there is an obvious inappropriateness in using this model for the ordering of our duties *as a whole* towards God and neighbour. A first objection is that although the presence of God to mankind creates a realm of sacred practice and obligation distinct from the secular, God's claim is not confined to the sacred realm but is total. There will never be a situation, then, in which his claim does not exclude all other claims that are made against it. Jesus taught his disciples to say 'We are unprofitable servants' when they had done everything required of them, because they had done no more than they had been commanded (Lk. 17:10). This stands as a warning against every attempt to mark off God's demand (as the realm of the sacred can be marked off) in such a way that it could be exhaustively met, leaving us free to go on to meet other demands or to take our rest. God's demand is not one among others. We may speak of the claims that different people or realms make upon us, claims that may conflict and have to be ordered in terms of their priority (and we may include even the sacred realm among such claimants); but God's claim is not among these. God's claim embraces the whole of our duty, ordering the other claims before us as they ought to be ordered. God does not stand in line waiting his turn at the wicket, not even at the head of the line. Rather, he brings this or that neighbour to the head of the line, and demands our best attention for him. And at another moment, perhaps, he closes the wicket, sends the whole line away, and demands to inspect our books.

A second objection to this model is that, by presenting the question in terms of a conflict in need of resolution, it obscures the fact that the neighbour's good can be realized only when God is the object of his love, and fully realized only when God is the object of all men's love. The inadequacies of 'quandary ethics' are never more apparent than here, for this is the kind of question which cannot be analysed properly in terms of a conflict of claims. By posing the question as an either-or between God and neighbour, the arbitration-model ensures a false perspective from the start. For loving someone is not the same as preferring his claim to other claims in a conflict – a conception which has been responsible for many of the difficulties which have plagued Western thought over the relation of love and justice. The twofold love-command is not intended to answer the question, 'Whose claim should I prefer?' – a question which is anyway not susceptible of a universal answer. We can love a neighbour even when we have to decide against him in a conflict of interest; we love him by taking him seriously as one whose claim must be heard and weighed, and as one whose ultimate good must be pursued even when his proximate interest must be denied. The inadequacies with the arbitration-model become even more marked when self is brought in alongside God and neighbour as a third object of love, as it regularly is in the ontological tradition of Western Christian ethics derived from Saint Augustine. To a conception of love as the preferring of a claim the very mention of self-love must be offensive, introducing as a rival to God and neighbour the very one who, as arbitrator of the conflict, ought to keep his own claims well out of things. But, of course, it is the conception which is at fault, not the mention of self-love (though the term is admittedly paradoxical). We should not be talking of conflicts of interest, nor of arbitrating rival claims. In understanding how the two loves, of God and neighbour, relate, we may not forget that the true good both of loving subject and of loved object is to be realized in their loving God.

A second interpretation of the ordering of love has at least the merit of taking this last point seriously. It conceives the relation of the two loves as the ordering of a means to an end. I am to love my neighbour as the necessary condition for achieving the supernatural end that is set before me in the love of God. I am, in Augustine's terminology, to love the neighbour 'for God's sake', or to 'use' him. This is one of those rare opinions in the history of thought which have had a more conspicuous influence through being rejected than through being held. Especially through Kant's insistence that we treat every 'rational nature . . . as an end withal and not as a means only', the denial of it has come to be regarded as a necessary condition for serious moral thought.

The first book of Augustine's *De doctrina Christiana* gave a wide currency in mediaeval thought to the association of the twofold command with the pair of terms 'use' and 'enjoyment' (*usus, fruitio*). 'To enjoy any thing', Augustine tells us (4.4), 'is to cleave to it in love for its own sake (*propter se ipsum*). To use something is to refer the object of our use to the obtaining of what we love – assuming that it is a proper object of love.' The universe of 'things' (*res*) is divided up into the proper objects of use (*utenda*) and the proper objects of enjoyment (*fruenda*). Or, more strictly, the *one* proper object of enjoyment, since only the divine Trinity is worthy to be enjoyed, and all other loves must be subordinated to that love. But then we ask about ourselves (22.20): 'It is a great question whether men ought to enjoy one another, or use one another, or both. For we have a command to love one another: but that leaves us with the question whether man is to be loved by man for his own sake, or for the sake of something else. If it is for himself, we "enjoy" him; if for the sake of something else, we "use" him. It seems to me that he is to be loved for the sake of something else.' Various attempts have been made to put a construction on Augustine's words which will escape the obvious censure. My own view (for which see my '*Usus* and *Fruitio* in Augustine, *De doctrina Christiana* I') is that Augustine's face cannot be saved. But *De doctrina Christiana* I is not representative of Augustine's mature thought, and it appears that in his subsequent practice he quietly reversed the answer that he gave there: the neighbour is understood as an object of 'enjoyment in (or, for) God'.

The opposition of 'means' and 'ends' is unsuited to express the ordering of love, equally unsuited whether we stand with Kant for the denial, or with the younger Augustine for the affirmation of this conception. 'Means' belong to planning; we determine them, they do not determine us, and are not determined for us. What is a means to what is entirely variable from agent to agent and from project to project. 'Ends' are more complicated, for it is certainly possible to speak, as we have done extensively, of ends which are given to us in the created order of things; but when the term 'end' is used in conjunction with the term 'means' it inserts itself into the same context of discussion and becomes an expression for the subjectively determined goal of some human project. The means-end pair belongs, then, to what we called, after Saint Basil (page 37, above), 'deliberative' rather than 'natural order'. Kant's protest could more aptly have been expressed by saying that relations between one human being and another cannot be reduced to a deliberative project. Love involves the grateful recognition of the neighbour's given reality, which is by no means the creation of the subject's will and does not derive its importance from his ambitions. We cannot love a neighbour 'as a means', and neither can we love him 'as an end and not as a means', for means and ends are things we determine for ourselves in practical deliberation, while love is determined for us by its object.

The offence which is given by speaking of another human being as a 'means' arises from the arbitrariness with which he is put to the service of some end. So long as we speak in terms appropriate only to human projects it must appear that the welfare of the brother, whom we pretend to love, is being wilfully subordinated to some purpose of our own. This 'love' is thus exposed as no more than manipulation. What we should wish to say, however, is that the neighbour's subordination to God, so far from being imposed by the arbitrary ambitions of the subject, is ontologically given. The teleology arises not from the subject's purposes, but from the neighbour's own being. He is in fact a creature, and his destiny is in fact to glorify God. 'Ordered love' does not approach the neighbour to impose this categorization upon him from outside; it comes recognizing that it belongs to him intrinsically. The neighbour's being imposes the order upon love, not love upon it. We are to love him as a creature destined for his Creator's fellowship, because that is what his nature demands of us. Any other conception of the neighbour's value – including one that treats him 'as an end and not as a means', *i.e.* as the final term of *our* project – is fantasistic and manipulative. Only that love which loves him at once 'for himself', and therefore at the same time 'for God', is truly humble before the reality of the neighbour.

This has already brought us to the third way in which the ordering of love may be conceived. It is the free conformity of our agency to the order of things which is given in reality. We have already remarked (page 110, above) how the mature Augustine based his presentation of reason and will upon the doctrine of the Trinity and especially upon the Nicene assertions of the consubstantiality and coeternity of the Son and Holy Spirit. The Love of the Father and the Son (*i.e.* the Spirit) is always will informed by reason, never will in isolation and independence. True human love, conformed to the image of God's love, must always involve an integration of will and reason in a rational and comprehending affection which accords with the truth of its object. Love cannot be love in a vacuum of intelligibility; the human soul loves only on the basis of an understanding of its object. The question, then, is whether the understanding on the basis of which it loves God and neighbour is a true understanding of them in their real relationship to each other. To follow Augustine further: we must love 'God as God' and 'neighbour as neighbour', that is 'as equal', that is 'as self' (*Sermo de disciplina Christiana* 3.3). Titania's love for Bottom was a monstrous love, not because he was a monster and she loved him as such, but because he, being a monster, appeared to her to be an object of beauty. The delusion lay in her eyes; her love was a love without truth. In the ordering of love it is truthfulness that is at stake: whether our love recognizes what the neighbour is, what God is, and what the true ordering of creature to Creator must be. The same principle governs the love of non-human created things. Love of the material world is good if it is built upon a recognition of what material goods are and what they are for. It is therefore dependent upon the love of the neighbour in the same way that the love of the neighbour is dependent upon the love of God.

The double aspect of the moral life

The love-command and respect for persons

We return, then, to the point from which we began, that the two loves, of God and neighbour, are one love, held together and differentiated by an order, just as the universe of God and world is held together and differentiated by the ordering of creature to Creator. We return, having learnt that the ordering of love is not a matter of one love cancelling the other out, nor of one being subjected to the other in a project of the loving subject; but it derives from the ordered and intelligible relations of its two objects, and presupposes that love is interpenetrated and shaped by the order of reality disclosed to the understanding. But this is not to say that the love of God and neighbour is simply the same as attention to the order of reality. It presupposes such attention, and, since we cannot obey the command to love otherwise, we must say that it requires it of us. But the command to love God and neighbour is more specific than a demand that we should attend to the order of reality. In the first place 'God and neighbour' define the object of our attention more closely. Not all created reality is included in those two terms. Nothing is said, for example, of the obligations which we may have to ourselves or to the non-human creation. In the second place, 'love' defines more closely the mode of attention appropriate to these objects. Not all reality is a possible object of love, though all may demand some form of respect.

This brings us back to the question at which we glanced above (pp. 201ff.): what kind of precedence do the two commands of love for God and neighbour have over other rules of moral obligation? It is possible to answer that when the law and the prophets are said to 'depend' upon them, what is meant is that they comprise the most general statement of obligation that can be framed. All other commands are logically implied in them. From this answer it will follow that no claims arise outside the most general state- ment. No demands are made upon us by any being other than God and neighbour: we owe ourselves nothing, and, more perilously, owe nothing to the world of inanimate and animal natures. If, in following this narrow reading of our obligation, we continue to take seriously the correlation of morality with reality, then we will project back upon reality itself an equally narrow metaphysic, in which only God and neighbour have absolute reality. Something of the kind is implied in Kant's famous 'metaphysical formulation' of the categorical imperative in terms of 'persons' as 'ends in themselves'. Through Kant's idealist successors it has been deeply influential in shaping the technological humanism of the West with its exclusive regard for 'personality' or 'rational nature'. For the love-command can be understood more easily as a *universal* summary of obligation when these generic categories are put in place of the concrete and relational terms 'God and neighbour'.

Classical Christian thought, too, conceived of the human being as a 'person', and a comparison between what it meant and what is meant by the modern use will show more clearly than anything else what is at stake in the disagreement between them. Christian thinkers of the patristic period, in the course of their debates about the Trinity and the person of Christ, brought the term 'person' into theological, and eventually into philosophical, currency in order to escape from an impasse created by classical patterns of thought about human individuality. They had inherited from the ancient world the conception that individuality resided in 'reason' (*nous*) or 'soul' (*psychē*). But when these generic categories were applied to the individuality of Christ, they led to a range of unthinkable options: either Christ, by virtue of being both God and man, was two individuals; or, being one individual, he did not have all the attributes of humanity and divinity; or (closest to the classical world) the highest attributes in man were anyway divine. Their solution to the impasse was to draw the sharp distinction between the concepts of 'person' and 'nature' famously maintained in the Chalcedonian definition. In speaking of Christ as 'one person in two natures' the Council of Chalcedon used the term 'person' (*hypostasis*) to represent the non-generic principle of individual existence, and 'nature' to represent the complex of attributes, divine or human, which constitute the generic distinctness of divinity and humanity. Through the influence of Boethius' Fifth Tractate upon philosophers this conception became generalized from the unique person of Christ to all persons. Thus the human individual was conceived not merely as a concretization of his human attributes, but as a bearer of them: he is not merely a chip off the block of total humanity, but *someone who is* human. This perception has its roots in the biblical understanding of individual vocation. Prior to those events which bring our humanity to being, we are called by God: 'Before I formed you in the womb I knew you' (Je. 1:5).

In modern idealism the term 'person' has lost the very element which once made it important for Christian thought, and is reduced once again to expressing an individuality which is rooted in generic attributes, either in 'rational nature' (Kant) or in 'personality' (Hegel). (The abstract form of the noun 'personality', replacing the concrete 'person', confirms this shift of understanding.) What the particular features of these attributes are varies from thinker to thinker; but usually they have to do with the exercise of reason, will and self-consciousness. It is, in fact, a return within the parameters of the pre-Christian conception of individual humanity as *nous*. What is meant by 'respect for persons' is a regard for the highest form of being as it achieves concrete existence in individual humans. Kant's famous formulation of the categorical imperative in its second form, bidding us to treat 'rational nature' as an end in itself 'whether in your own person or in that of another' (*Groundwork* 429), presents an exact formal contrast with the formula 'one person in two natures'. For the modern, as for the pre-Christian, world, individuality is the form in which rational nature exists. For the classical Christian world, on the other hand, rational nature is the mode in which the individual exists. It is not surprising, then, that for all the apparent seriousness with which the modern world has taken the human person, it has been constantly seduced by enterprises of totalitarian utility which subordinate the individual to the quantitative and qualitative betterment of a homogenized realm of personality. (I have developed this argument in connection with one such modern enterprise in my *Begotten or Made?*, pp. 49–66.)

We may contrast this answer with a classical alternative. Saint Augustine thought that the reason we were commanded to love only God and neighbour was that, if we would learn to attend properly to these two objects of love, all others would fall into place of themselves. The appropriateness of other loves, when ordered in obedience to the order of reality, was not to be denied. Love of self, for example, was apparently presupposed by the demand that one should love the neighbour 'as yourself'; but it would be quite mistaken from a pedagogical point of view to insist on self-love, in which men were never lacking; for once one had heard the command to love God with heart and soul and mind and strength, all the guidance one might need in directing self-love to its end had been given. This answer understands the precedence of the twofold love-command as a matter of pedagogical priority rather than inclusive generality. The priority is *only* pedagogical, because there is no ultimate conflict of claims between God and any other being; the immediate conflict of claims arises from the ascetic measures necessary to correct man's biased starting-point. Every human agent starts out as a moral solipsist, understanding the world as existing to satisfy his own needs and desires. God and the human being next to him are the paradigm of independent and other reality, reality which is capable of challenging and shattering his egocentric ordering of the universe around himself. The twofold command serves, in Kierkegaard's expressive phrase (*Works of Love*, p. 34), as 'a pick which wrenches open the lock of self-love'.

We can do no more than hint at how these alternative answers unfold into sharply contrasting patterns of moral thought. If we regard the love-command as the most general statement of moral obligation, we expect it to describe a decisive boundary about those areas of experience where moral obligation is presumed to arise. Subsequent moral exploration, then, is bent on discerning what is and is not included within that boundary. 'And who is my neighbour?' (Lk. 10:29). The lawyer's question is not only not out of place, but is the only question worth asking, the form of all possible moral questions, once we have understood the love-command in this way. The modern equivalent is to ask, 'Who is to count as a person?' But, as moral theologians have never tired of pointing out, the parable of the Good Samaritan does not answer the question 'Who is my neighbour?' on the terms in which it is put. The lawyer is not given the criteria of discrimination which he asks for. True, his question does receive an answer, inasmuch as it raises by implication the question of racially restrictive criteria and Jesus, also by implication, dismisses the idea. However, by the way in which he dismisses it, he defeats the presuppositions of the question as well as the supposed answer. Turning the concept of neighbour around and applying it to the agent rather than to the object of the loving act ('Which of these three, do you think, proved a neighbour to the man who fell among the robbers?') Jesus draws attention to the fact that neighbourhood is a *reciprocal* relation. 'Nobody can be a neighbour except to a neighbour,' commented Augustine. And by casting the story in the form of an adventure, with its 'as it happened', he emphasizes the *contingency* of the circumstances which can place us in an unlooked-for neighbourly relation with others. The Samaritan was discovered to be the Jew's neighbour, not by any judgment or evaluation on the Jew's part, but because he 'turned out to be' a neighbour in the event. Rather than decide from a distance who his neighbours were, the Jewish lawyer had to stumble upon them, or they stumble upon him, by chancing to be next to them in the contingencies of life.

The contingency of the neighbour-relation, the element of 'as it happened', is, of course, one form of *nearness*. The generalizing interpretation of the love-command is embarrassed by the element of proximity in the term 'neighbour' (in Latin, *proximus*); and some interpreters of Christ's teaching carry their embarrassment further, taking offence at other relations of nearness which assume importance in the ethics of the New Testament. Biblical commentators of our generation have been prone to find in the Household Codes of the epistles, or even in the Johannine form of the love-command (in which the disciples are instructed to love 'one another', *e.g.* Jn. 13:34), a declension from the lofty ethic of undifferentiated love to all which Jesus was supposed to have taught. This is rather thoughtless. An ethic of undifferentiated love which allowed of no application to proximate relations could have little relevance for embodied human beings who can be in only one place at a time and must needs be closer to some people than to others. Certainly, the parable of the Samaritan should not be used to support such an abstract moral schematization. When we render the love-command in terms of 'respect for persons' or 'equal regard', we strain out precisely the element of contingent proximity on which the parable most strongly insists. It counters the limiting structures of racial and communal proximities precisely by challenging them with a proximity of a different sort, the contingent nearness into which we constantly find ourselves thrown with all sorts of people.

The pedagogical and ascetic priority of the two pre-eminent commands becomes even clearer when, following the lead of Saint John, we bring the two together into a single command, that we should love Jesus. In Jesus God has reached out to us from heaven in love, and we love him in return by believing the one whom he has sent. But in Jesus, too, this love has taken on the form of neighbour-love, a service rendered us by one who has dwelt near us upon the broken terrain of our humanity and who asks of us our neighbourly loyalty and support in his testimony against evil.

'If you love me, you will keep my commandments. And I will pray the Father, and he will give you another Counsellor' (Jn. 14:15–16). 'He who has my commandments and keeps them, he it is who loves me; and he who loves me will be loved by my Father'(21). 'If a man loves me, he will keep my word, and my Father will love him' (23). What is startling in the repetitions of this passage is the self-conscious absence of any reference to the disciple's love for God the Father. The Father will love those who love his Son: that is what is implied by the unity of the two, 'I am in the Father and the Father in me' (10–11). There is no distinct way in which the Father is loved. 'Lord, show us the Father,' Philip has said, 'and we shall be satisfied' (8) – very much as a theologian might ask, 'Lord, define for us the love of God *as such*!' But the only answer he receives is, 'Have I been with you so long, and yet you do not know me?' (9).

A *theologoumenon* of the Alexandrian fathers, in expounding the parable of the Good Samaritan, used to say that the neighbour whom we are bound to love is Christ; for the neighbour turned out to be the Samaritan, and Christ is the one who, like the Samaritan, has bound up our wounds and poured on oil and wine. It is the kind of tradition which is too easily dismissed with a smile as part and parcel of their undoubtedly baroque taste for the allegorical. Obviously enough, it would not do to say *only* this, thereby deflecting into pietistic devoutness the very openness to the unexpected neighbour which is central to the thrust of the parable. But this is a point on which the fathers do not need us to instruct them. Clement of Alexandria, for example, proceeds from this identification (by way of Jn. 14:15 and Mt. 7:21, stressing that love of Christ means keeping his commandments and doing the will of his Father) to conclude with the parable of the sheep and the goats from Matthew 25:31–46. 'For whatever service a man does for a disciple, the Lord accepts for himself' (*Quis dives salvetur* 28ff.). Even more clearly Origen begins from the universal – 'charity counts all men neighbours' – and observes, again from the parable, that neighbourly love is due also to one who is sunken in wickedness. Neighbourliness is rooted in the *natural* relations of one man to another; yet in another sense we may 'become neighbours' by showing mercy. 'Wherefore also our Saviour became a neighbour to us, and did not pass us by' (*in Canticum*, prooem.). Augustine's use of the identification in his allegorical exposition of the parable is well known (*Quaestiones Evangeliorum* II.19, e.g.); but he, too, quite naturally associates it with the assertion of universal neighbourhood: 'Thus we should understand that he is our neighbour to whom the office of mercy should be shown if he needs it . . . (and) that he is our neighbour who in turn shows this office to us' (*De doctrina Christiana* I.31.30).

Once we have established good faith with the primary meaning of the text in this manner, we may say definitely that this *theologoumenon* is a helpful one. For Christ identifies himself as the object of our neighbourly concern in two complementary ways: by accepting works of mercy done to others in his name (Mt. 10:40–42; 18:5; 25:31–46; Jn. 13:20) and by arrogating to himself the loving attention which was due to the needy poor (Mt. 26:6–13).

It is possible to love Christ only where the gospel has been preached and received. Apart from Jesus of Nazareth, crucified under Pontius Pilate and raised the third day, the phrase 'love of Christ' is empty and without reference. It cannot possibly be conceived as a universal form of obligation, simply because it cannot have been an obligation to more than a fraction of humanity. If we attempted to conceive it so, we would set the name 'Christ' loose from the historically concrete figure of Jesus of Nazareth and so step outside the limits of Chalcedonian Christology. This would have one of two results. Either we would settle for a static Nestorian theism, in which the object of our love was, in truth, simply the divine principle, though accompanied, perhaps, by a sentimental fondness for the figure of Jesus of Nazareth; or, more characteristically of the modern period, we would embrace a monophysite humanism, in which what really secured our devotion was the emerging idea of a divinized humanity. If these two paths are closed to us, as they must be, then the love of Christ cannot be conceived in such a universalizing way, but must be viewed eschatologically, as the form which our moral obligations have taken in these last days, at the climax of God's redemptive work.

The same must be said of the love which most closely follows from it, the love of Christ's people for each other which assumes such importance in the Johannine writings. Jesus calls it 'a new commandment' (Jn. 13:34) – not that there could never have been communities held together by mutual love before his community, but that his community and its love depended upon something new. The new commandment was to love 'as I have loved you', in a love responsive and obedient to the divine and neighbourly love of Christ for mankind. Yet at the same time, paradoxically, it is 'an old commandment' (1 Jn. 2:7). The new reality confirms, clarifies and vindicates the reality which was always there, presupposed even in its denial by sin, the reality of human brotherhood. Far from denying universal love of man for man, the love of the believer for Christ and for his fellow-believer is the form in which it is restored and re-enters the world. For the church anticipates restored humanity, and all humanity lies implicitly within the church. To love the church, therefore, is to venture out beyond its present borders, to claim those who lie outside them for their place in the City of God.

'Beloved, I am writing you no new commandment, but an old commandment which you had from the beginning.' So writes the author of 1 John in a consciously paradoxical dialectic with the dominical saying of John 13:34, 'A new commandment I give to you, that you love one another.' He goes on: 'The old commandment is the word which you have heard.' Does the apostle mean simply that now, in the second generation

242

of the church, the command is no longer new because it was preached, together with the message of Christ itself, 'from the beginning'? He clearly does mean this, but there is more. His 'from the beginning' has a double reference: to the original apostolic preaching from which the church derived (1:1), and beyond that to the primordial originality of 'him who is from the beginning' (2:13–14), the God of whom the apostolic preaching spoke. This more far-reaching reference emerges here. 'Again, it is a new commandment that I write to you – a message that has its reality in him (*i.e.* Christ) and in you – because the darkness is passing away and the true light is already shining.' (2:8*). The newness of the command is the eschatological newness of Christ's appearing; its oldness, correspondingly, the aboriginal oldness of created order which is vindicated as the dawning light floods the world. Here, then, is the command: 'He who says he is in the light and hates his brother is in the darkness still' (2:9; *cf.* 2 Jn. 5).

Who is this 'brother'? Are we to think of the closed 'one another' of the faithful community, or of universal humanity? The apostle refuses to resolve the expression decisively in either direction. He will speak of loving 'one another' and 'the brethren', and will say that 'every one who loves the parent loves the child' (5:1), *i.e.* the believer. At the same time he will speak of each one loving '*his* brother', *i.e.* the person who happens in *his* case to be in this relation to him, and suggests that this may be someone in need who evokes compassion (3:17), or even someone whom he would like to kill (3:12)! And this ambiguity is entirely appropriate given that the church is simply that portion of mankind which dwells in the dawning light which is to flood the world. The term 'brother' mediates between the fellowship of a limited community and the universal brotherhood of restored humanity. If the light is the light of the world, how could we ever suppose that any given person was *not* our brother?

Love of Christ has priority over all other obligation because it is the love of Jesus *as* the Christ, the acceptance of him as the one whom the Father has sent. From it there follows that we are given to love the whole of reality in its due order: God, the neighbour, self and the world. And from it there follows obedience to the authoritative teaching and life which interpret what is given us in reality; 'If you love me, you will keep my commandments' (Jn. 14:15). It is a love which springs from faith, and which therefore loves the universal in the particular, finding in Jesus the head in whom every neighbour is summoned to appear before God and in whom the non-human creation awaits its redemption. This brings us back to where we began, to the divine act by which God has designated Jesus as the Christ and has vindicated creation in him, his resurrection from the dead. In this act all Christian love, from the universal to the familiar, finds its spring.

We may give the last word on this subject to the Tudor poet Edmund Spenser:

> Most glorious Lord of life! that, on this day,
> didst make thy triumph over death and sin:

and having harrowed hell, didst bring away
captivity thence captive us to win:
This joyous day, dear Lord, with joy begin,
    and grant that we, for whom thou diddest die,
    being with thy dear blood clean washed from sin,
    may live for ever in felicity!
And that thy love we weighing worthily,
    may likewise love thee for the same again:
    and for thy sake that all like dear didst buy,
    with love may one another entertain.
So let us love, dear love, like as we ought;
    love is the lesson which the Lord us taught.

                  (*Amoretti*. Sonnet 68)

12

The end of the moral life

Saint Paul's great hymn of love concludes with the assertion, 'Faith, hope, love abide, these three' (1 Cor. 13:13). Love, like faith and hope, has an eschatological reference which belongs to it essentially. It is not like the 'gifts' of prophecy, knowledge or ecstatic tongues, which have sufficient justification simply within the terms of the church's historical existence, quite apart from the end to which its existence is directed. To think of these gifts is to think of things which the church does, or which are done within the church, out of which the church's history is built up as a story of human activity, in itself both satisfying and self-justifying. The church proclaims the gospel, praises God, discerns the meaning of the times, serves mankind, thinks, theologizes and, no doubt, develops doctrine. All of which, as any well-wishing person could agree, are excellent ways for it to spend the time. If the church were to go on doing these things for ever, and the Son of man were never to come in glory with the sound of the trumpet, then nothing, at least, of the *intrinsic* value of these eminently worthwhile activities would be lost.

When we think of the church's faith and hope, on the other hand, we think of dispositions which are quite without point if they are viewed in isolation from the end. Faith and hope have no validity apart from what is believed and hoped in. The church believes and hopes throughout its historical pilgrimage, and yet no possible extension or development of that pilgrimage can make faith and hope sensible historical projects. If the Son of man were not to come in great glory, the very words 'faith' and 'hope', which already presuppose a positive answer to the question about what is believed and hoped in, would be inappropriate to describe the church's pointless expectancy: 'If Christ has not been raised, then our preaching is in vain and your faith is in vain' (1 Cor. 15:14). Only as the pilgrimage reaches the end which God has destined for it can the faith and hope of the church be validated and justified.

If we have understood why love, the form of the moral life, is grouped, not with the spiritual gifts, which have their own intelligibility, but with faith and hope which depend for intelligibility upon the end of history, then we have grasped how morality is related to salvation, how it is that Christian ethics is evangelical. The moral life of mankind is a moment in God's dealing with the created order which he has restored in Christ. Only as that restored order is fully disclosed can the meaning of human morality be comprehended. Various aspects of the church's activity can be abstracted from the totality of the church's life and discussed in terms of their immanent value: Christian thought and education, Christian missionary enterprise, Christian art, Christian politics, Christian family life can all be appreciated, criticized, and perhaps improved upon from this point of view. But if we add to this list something called 'the Christian ethic', then we are not merely abstracting, we are misrepresenting. The true moral life of the Christian community is its love, and its love is unintelligible except as a participation in the life of the one who reveals himself to us as Love, except, that is, as the entry of mankind and of the restored creation upon its supernatural end.

It has, of course, proved possible to understand Paul's assertion that love 'abides' in exactly the opposite sense, as though Paul meant that no eschatological transformation could render obsolete the indubitable achievement of love within the world as it stands. The immediate implication of this reading is that the association of love with faith and hope becomes incomprehensible. How can faith and hope be said to 'abide' in *that* sense, since they are clearly to be superseded? The coming of the eschaton must transform them into sight and possession. Faith is 'the evidence of things *not* seen' (Heb. 11.1, AV); and 'Who hopes for what he sees?' (Rom. 8:24). So we helpfully correct Saint Paul with Bishop Christopher Wordsworth:

> Faith will vanish into sight;
> Hope be emptied in delight;
> Love in heav'n will shine more bright;
>   Therefore give us love.

Perhaps we should not question the possible truth of these words. Perhaps we can and should claim for love (understood, with Wordsworth's hymn, as the Spirit's gift at Pentecost) a perdurance which cannot be attributed to faith and hope. Even so, love would not be quite unique, for some such continuity is implied, too, in Paul's words about knowledge: 'now I know in part; but then shall I know even as also I am known' (1 Cor. 13:12, AV), a verse which did not find its way into Wordsworth's hymn. And do we not also have to attribute a measure of discontinuity even to love? An older tradition spoke of the transformation of love from *desiderium* to *delectatio* (though 'delight', we notice, is now promiscuously associated with hope!). Be that as it may, whatever truth we allow to such words in themselves, their substitution for Saint Paul's words betrays a false conception: that in the perdurance of love we have to do with the reassuring permanence of something familiar to us and with which we are already at home. What (to return to the theme of the last chapter) did Jesus mean when he taught it as a *new* command 'that you love one another' (Jn. 13:34)? The point is that whenever we take love seriously, even within the perfectly 'natural' perspective of the twofold command of love to God and neighbour, we stand under the shadow of the last things. The order of love, the created moral order, does not have eternity in itself, but looks forward to a new creation to fulfil it and make it wholly intelligible.

The point which is made here in terms of the eschatological dimension of love is, of course, made in other terms too. When we speak of Christian morality in relation to the *kingdom of God*, for example, we assert the same dependence of the present upon the future. The conviction of a final triumph of God's will, in which every other created will is conformed to it, makes sense of our present relative and imperfect commitment to doing God's will. Again, when we speak of the Christian life as life *in Christ*, we indicate that our life, like his, is 'hidden' (Col. 3:3) and 'waiting' (Heb. 10:13) until his appearing, when his enemies shall be put beneath his feet. We do not even pretend to describe what the life of perfect participation in the restored order of creation will be like; for the only model for such a description was concealed from our sight by a cloud at the point of his glorification, so that the apostle must say that although we are now children of God, it has not yet been shown us what we shall be (1 Jn. 3:2). Again, when we speak of the Christian moral life as lived *in the Spirit*, we declare that this life is itself part of the divine self-disclosure, and as such points us forward to the goal of that self-disclosure. The Holy Spirit, outside of whose field of operation the Christian moral life is unthinkable, is a signpost to the future, 'the earnest of our inheritance pointing to the redemption of God's possession' (Eph. 1:14*).

Between faith and hope, however, there is a distinction to be made, although both relate us to the future transformation. In hope that future is present to our minds by anticipation; it encourages us and sustains us by promising to our present experience, with all its ambiguity, a completion which will render it intelligible. In faith our minds conceive that future as something apart from our present, wholly independent of it and standing in judgment upon it. These two complementary relations to the eschatological future qualify Christian love in distinct ways.

Love and its reward

We consider first what it means for love to be hopeful, which is to say, to carry with it a sensed incompleteness and to depend upon the anticipated future to render it intelligible. In the language of the Gospels, we have to consider love's *reward*. This is an idea which still requires some clarifying in response to certain familiar types of criticism which were made with especial force two or three generations ago in the heyday of philosophical idealism. We may classify the criticisms into two groups. First there are those which object to the thought that there can be another good, the reward, which is higher than this good of love in which we participate and which can lend it a completion which it lacks. Secondly there are those which find difficulty with the idea that such a higher good, on the assumption that it exists, can be a motive of moral action without compromising the agent's commitment to love.

Evidently the first group presents the more direct challenge to the theological authenticity of Christian love, in that it reveals quite clearly the pantheistic possibilities of idealism. To assert that there can be no higher good than that in which man presently participates is to abolish the difference between created and uncreated good, and so to divinize the exercise of human love. When Christians speak of the supernatural end of man as a participation in the divine life, they do, of course, run the calculated risk that they will be misunderstood in this way, as though they were saying that divinity were no more than a transferable quality of existence to which mankind too can aspire. The life of love which we are given to live with God is a life that is from first to last oriented towards him as the original Love, from whom this love is given to us. Man's life of love can never pretend to curl up on itself like a furry animal and keep itself warm with the insulation of its own divinity.

However, the objection is not bound to take an overtly pantheistic form. It is possible to confess that the divine life quite surpasses the life of human love, while still shying away from all talk of love as finding its eschatological reward in sharing the divine life. And we must concede at once that there is a valuable warning expressed in this shyness. The church can never boast with perfect confidence that it has altogether put behind it the sub-moral religious mythology that makes the moral life a mere means to an end, a troublesome burden to be carried for the moment which will be lifted from our shoulders at the last that we may enter an existence 'in glory', a glory that has, presumably, nothing to do with the glory of God's love. If the life of love to God and neighbour is a true participation in the restored order of creation, a responsive love to the divine love in which the divine mode of life becomes our own, what higher good can possibly be spoken of? Only a good that is essentially one with this good, a renewal and perfection of this good which we now have. The idea of reward must therefore always be clarified by some such expression as Augustine's famous *ipse praemium*: 'he himself is the reward!' What more can God give us than what he has already given us, his own being to be the light of our being?

When this warning has been duly taken, however, we are still bound to speak of an opposition between love now and love hereafter, between labour and reward, between *desiderium* and *delectatio*. This is necessary, in the first place, because participation in the restored creation is by conformity to the death and resurrection of Christ. If the life of love is not in itself a burden, it does, nevertheless, involve us in burdens. No account of the Christian moral life can be adequate unless it is allowed to point forward to the resurrection. The articulation of love into labour and reward in Jesus' teaching corresponds to the apostolic teaching that we must die with Christ so that at the last we may rise with him. It is necessary to speak in this way, in the second place, because the present hiddenness of God's new creation demands its fulfilment in public manifestation, the *parousia* or 'presence' of the Son of man to the cosmos in which God is to be all in all. The suggestion that the believer already enjoys so complete a communion with God and his new creation, that no further manifestation is necessary or possible, conceals, as did the teaching of Hymenaeus and Philetus of old, a gnostic pretension to private redemption apart from, and dispensing with, the public redemption of the cosmos.

But to what extent may the church or believer actually hope for or desire the final reign of God? Here we confront the second group of objections, which find that the idea of reward, however necessary it may be theologically, constitutes a temptation from the moral point of view. Desire, it is argued, introduces an element of self-interest which compromises the true loss-of-self-in-other which is the essence of love. In desiring, the subject loves himself. The good of God's final reign implies *his* welfare as a future glad participant, so that his desire for God's reign is implicitly a desire for his own welfare. Love is thus corrupted into self-seeking. Therefore our knowledge of future glory must be held, as it were, in an attitude of detachment and busy indifference, lest our longing for it should result in the displacement of God from his throne.

Clearly there is something suspicious in the paradoxical dissociation of morality from reality which this argument urges upon us. Indeed, precisely in this dissociation we may discover the clue to its real character, and recognize in it a reflection of that suspicion of teleological ethics which we have already discerned to be voluntarist in inspiration. We are not going to quarrel with the premiss that love must not be introverted into self-love. But how does this danger arise in *any* recognition of *any* object as good?

For that is what it amounts to. Simply to notice a good and to pass it by is not to recognize it as a good at all; the only true recognition of good is love, and love implies a desire for the good (in so far as it is merely in the realm of possibility) to be actualized. Certainly, if an object is good, I, the subject, am involved with that object; it is good also *for me*, by virtue of the fact that I am a part of the world in which and for which it exists as a good. But that 'for me' is a mere implication of its goodness. Why should I be so troubled by the 'for me' that I would rather turn away from the good altogether and hide my face from it, lest in gazing at it I find that I am gazing into a reflecting mirror? Presumably because I think that anything in the universe which is good for me *is* a reflecting mirror! I have not understood the *objectivity* of my good, given to me in the order of the universe as a reality which I can only acknowledge and welcome. At the heart of my anxiety is the voluntarist supposition that my good is something which I create or evoke for myself. To love the kingdom of God as my good, then, is to manipulate it to my own design, to impose my purposes upon it, and from this I rightly shrink back in holy fear. But where does the real idolatry lie? In the recognition of the kingdom of God as my good, or in the supposition that I have myself made it my own good? The paradoxical character of this objection arises from its attempt to challenge the self-involvement of the subject from within, using solipsistic categories to attack solipsism. It never breaks out of the circle of self-reference into a clear conception of the objective reality of good and the extroversion of love, but can only confront introversion with a negative reflection of itself, the empty phantom of 'self-forgetfulness'.

The Augustinian *ipse praemium* had no trouble with the *praemium*, the 'for me', because it laid its stress upon the *ipse*. Everything depended upon the object. The criticism of self-interestedness was expressed as a criticism of an inadequate object of love, a 'private', *i.e.* a diminished and restricted, good. When the object of love is God himself, the author of all love and of all subjects who love, there need be no more anxious enquiry about right and wrong love, selfish and unselfish love, noble and ignoble love. These questions have all been resolved when the question about the object of love has been resolved. In giving himself, the subject of love, to be the object of our love, he has given us also the love with which it is appropriate to love him. It is a love that need not be ashamed of itself in the manner of its hope nor fear for itself in the security of its possession.

Kenneth Kirk may be taken as representative of that tradition of moral theology which, under the influence of Kant, found a 'difficult and perplexing problem' in the references to heavenly reward in the teaching of Jesus (*The Vision of God*, pp. 140–146). 'It is not without plausibility',

Kirk thought, 'that Christianity has so constantly been condemned as "self-seeking" . . . (for) nothing would be left of Jesus's teaching if the references to reward and punishment were struck out as inauthentic.' And yet: 'the slightest condonation of self-centredness is no less than treason to the ideal of self-forgetfulness; and it is hard to believe that the Lord — whatever he may have done on matters of less significance — could for a moment have compromised on a matter so vital as this.' Following von Hügel's exposition of Jesus' teaching as a series of critical revisions to popular expectations of reward, Kirk concludes: 'Jesus promised reward only to those who were prepared to follow and obey him from some other motive . . . It is only those who did good in complete unconsciousness, not merely that it would be rewarded, but even that they were doing good at all, who were set on the right hand, and entered into the joy of the Lord.' But why, then, did Jesus confuse matters by speaking about rewards, and not preach an ethic of pure duty? Kirk replies: 'The true Christian is self-forgetful; but no one can become a true Christian by the *pursuit* of self-forgetfulness . . . The calculated practice of self-sacrifice is as self-centred as any other occupation.' An answer which hardly meets the point, since a teaching which mentions reward only to forbid the thought of it would seem more likely to evoke *calculated* self-forgetfulness than one which never introduced the idea of reward in the first place!

We say that the influence was that of Kant. But Kant was the inheritor of a tradition, associated especially with mystical theology and pietism, which assessed the affections not in terms of their object but in terms of their formal inner disposition. Kirk's antecedents also include Fénelon from the seventeenth century (of whose controversy with Bossuet he gives a memorable account) and from the Middle Ages Saint Bernard. The mediaeval source of this tradition is of great importance. Pierre Rousselot's fine monograph *Pour l'histoire du problème de l'amour au Moyen Age* traced with great insight the distinction between what he called the 'ecstatic' school, which interpreted love subjectively, and the ontological tradition which runs from Augustine to Thomas Aquinas. Clearly Kirk is a modern descendant of the ecstatics; and so in his way is Kant, since we must acknowledge a strong Protestant version of this tradition which can be detected among the pietists and puritans. It is, perhaps, something of a hallmark of the school in its classical mystical form that it was enthusi-astic about Saint Paul's prayer of Romans 9:3, 'I could wish that I myself were accursed and cut off from Christ for the sake of my brethren . . . .' Here, it felt, was a truly selfless love, a love for which we must all strive, in which Paul's service and love for God was unconnected with any hope for his eternal reward. 'If it is God alone that we establish as the cause of our love, then indeed, because he only does what is best, whatever he were to do to us or to others would make no difference to our love because the cause of our love would be unaffected' (Abelard, *Commentary on Romans* III, on 7:13). Obviously, this hypothetical 'whatever . . .' is only a hypothesis. The tradition does not doubt that God is in fact gracious according to his promises. But it finds it necessary, as an ascetic discipline for the soul, to conjure up a moment of forgetfulness, in which the soul overlooks the graciousness of God and sees only the pure divinity behind it, lest God's kindness prove to be an allurement to self-love. Such a moment in which all self-love is stripped away forms the climax of the ascetic programme.

Thus it concludes, rather surprisingly, that the only safe object for a Christian's affections is an abstraction. The actual self-revealed God of grace and forgiveness in Jesus Christ is a dangerous temptation. (Can we, then, be terribly astonished at a modern follower of the tradition, James Gustafson, when he resolves the tension between motive and reality by declaring that this God was, after all, only a fiction of man's self-centred imagination? See his *Theology and Ethics*.) When Kirk contrasts self-centredness and self-forgetfulness as two 'wholly conflicting modes of thought', and then substitutes 'God-centredness' for 'self-forgetfulness', as though they were synonymous, we may suspect, without being unduly mistrustful, that God-centredness is always to be understood in terms of self-forgetfulness; and that even Kirk's efforts to guard against 'calculated' self-forgetfulness are really directed not to fixing the soul's gaze upon its proper object but to preventing the project of oblivion from falling on its face under the weight of self-consciousness.

Is it possible, we may wonder, to carry through the ecstatic programme of purging the affections of covert self-reference without thus driving a wedge between God's promises and the disciple's motivation? We may at least give sympathetic consideration to a sensitive attempt from the eighteenth century. Jonathan Edwards set himself to differentiate between those religious affections that were 'truly gracious' and those that were not, a project with significant affinities, at least, to that of the mystics, though its ultimate intent was more ecclesiological than ascetic. He, too, wished to maintain that 'the first objective ground of gracious affections, is the transcendently excellent and amiable nature of divine things, as they are in themselves; and not any conceived relation they bear to self, or self-interest' (*Treatise concerning the Religious Affections*, pp. 240–253). He goes on to warn that an affection towards God that arises from self-love cannot be truly gracious, that 'gratitude is one of the natural affections . . . and there may be a kind of gratitude without any true and proper love'. This false gratitude, moreover, may arise not only from the thought of God's kindness to myself as an individual, but even from the history of man's redemption itself. The only true ground for love of God 'is that whereby he is in himself lovely'. Edwards has no place for the climactic moment at which the soul can bless God in the face of its own damnation. But he does have an analogue to it, which, in keeping with his puritan interest in conversion, comes at the beginning of the believer's spiritual career. 'The exercises of true and holy love in the saints arise in another way. They don't first see that God loves them, and then see that he is lovely; but they first see that he is lovely . . . and then, consequentially, they see God's love; and great favour to them.' We may still be perplexed about how one could insist, whether in conversion or in mystical crisis, on a merely *partial* vision of God as the best test for authenticity. But Edwards will now make a concession, which may possibly set our perplexities at rest. 'There is doubtless such a thing as gracious gratitude . . . In a gracious gratitude men are affected with the attribute of God's goodness and free grace, not only as they are concerned in it, or as it affects their interest, but as a part of the glory and beauty of God's nature. That wonderful and unparalleled grace of God, which is manifested in the work of redemption . . . is infinitely glorious in itself . . . 'tis a great part of the moral perfection and beauty of God's nature.' We do not, then, actually have to forget the work of salvation or ignore it. We do not have to go behind God's gracious self-manifestation to an abstract God-as-such. We simply have to conceive saving-history precisely as God's *self*-manifestation, as a revelation of *his* excellencies, and this provides the correct context for all thought of our own salvation. At this point the element of truth which underlay the ecstatic tradition has found adequate expression. May we not whisper that it has found it precisely by returning to the concerns of the ontological tradition, by reasserting the *ipse* of the *ipse praemium*?

Love and justification

Faith and hope each express our dependence upon the future: the present, in which we have to act, needs the future of God's kingdom to give it intelligibility, and so to give our acts a frame of meaning. 'Through the Spirit, by faith, we wait for the hope of righteousness' (Gal. 5:5). But the direction in which thought moves between the present nd the future is different in either case. When we hope, we begin from the problematic character of the present, from its ambiguity and unsatisfying incompleteness, and turn gratefully to the future judgment of God which perfects the imperfections of the present and promises completion. In faith we move in the opposite direction. Beginning from the final judgment with its affirmation of man's created life and love, we turn gratefully back to the present, our appointed scene of action, to claim and enjoy that affirmation not simply as an object of hope but as an immediate reality. Thus faith takes two decisive steps beyond hope. It corrects the orientation of hope about the incomplete present, and attends first to the objective completeness of the divine judgment in man's favour. And it moves *to* the present rather than *away from* it, giving practical 'substance' to what is hoped for (Heb. 11:1). It is thus at once more contemplative and more active.

'We wait for the hope of righteousness.' Paul's choice of the word 'righteousness' to express the final act of God brings us to the centre of the nexus which binds ethics and eschatology together, a centre that is safeguarded in Protestant thought (by no means satisfactorily, but still indispensably) by the concept of 'justification'. This concept subordinates morality to the divine promise in such a way that the moral life may never set itself free of its dependence upon God's prior kindness to become autonomously self-sufficient. To conceive God's final judgment of grace upon man's life as the hope of *righteousness* is to insist that any rightness which may belong to human act or character derives from this final judgment. It is not a question of man's doing what he can to please God, and of God's saying 'Yes' or 'No' in response to it; it is a question of man's being able to please God only because God will most definitely say 'Yes'. From that 'Yes' are derived both the possibility and the conditions of human morality. It is aboriginal as well as final, a creative 'Yes' by which God sets the seal of his good-pleasure upon human life and its relationships of love, now redeemed by the deed of his right hand, as on the final day of creation when he saw all that he had made and it was very good. What we accomplish, therefore, in human act or character today, depends for its form, meaning and value upon the justifying 'Yes' of God. Every achievement of eternal worth presupposes it; it is 'apart from works' (Rom. 3:28), in that it is the foundation of all possible works of love and presupposes none of them.

The Protestant term 'justification' corresponds to no distinct term used in the Greek of Saint Paul, upon whom the doctrine largely depends. Indeed, the very origin of the Protestant conception lies in the discovery that Paul uses one and the same noun (*dikaiosynē*) both for the moral status of 'righteousness' and as the active noun corresponding to the verb *dikaioō*, 'to put someone in the right'. (To state the lexicographical point a little more accurately: twice in the Epistle to the Romans Paul experiments with a noun formed from the active verb-stem, *dikaiōsis* (4:25; 5:18), and once uses a noun formed from the passive verb-stem, *dikaiōma* (5:16), which also means a 'deed of justice' and may here, in parallel with *katakrima*, 'condemnation', mean a 'verdict of acquittal'. But the bulk of Pauline references upon which the doctrine has been built use *dikaiosynē*, as for example the great programmatic statement of Rom. 1:17.) The original value of invoking the term *iustificatio* (derived from the Vulgate rendering of both *dikaiōsis* and *dikaiōma*) was to clarify the connection in Paul's thought between moral righteousness and the favourable verdict of God which puts man in the right. But of course the use of two terms to translate *dikaiosynē* can have exactly the opposite effect and may serve to *obscure* the connection, leading Protestantism back into the very uneschatological moralism from which it sought to deliver us. The correlate of a 'justification' which has nothing to do with 'righteousness' is a righteousness which has nothing to do with justification, and this soon presented itself to Protestant thought under the heading of 'sanctification'. The improper divorce of sanctification from justification bequeathed Protestant churches their characteristic tension between a gospel with no concern for life in the world and a concern for life in the world which has lost touch with the gospel.

If we are to grasp the point that is safeguarded by the doctrine of justification, it is not enough to speak in general terms of a dependence of human achievement upon divine favour. It proved easy for some streams of Protestant thought to understand this dependence as a mere biographical succession, so that the ground for works of love seemed to be sufficiently given in a believer's experience of conversion, a moment in his past when God has intervened in grace and justified him freely. Nor were matters much better when to this was added a reminder of the believer's continuing dependence on grace for perseverance. For dependence on divine aid can quickly become a secret self-legitimation for all the activity which we value most. We may cheerfully attribute our doings to divine aid so long as it remains our prerogative to resolve on them, and God's to invest them with importance! Both conversion and co-operating grace, of course, must be spoken of with proper respect in their place. The point here is simply that to speak about them is not to say all that needs to be said about our dependence upon God's favour, for neither of them have to do with God's last and decisive word. When Christian thinkers prefer to speak only of these penultimate words and avoid that last word, they are guilty of pre-empting God's final judgment 'apart from works' and of attempting to replace it with a judgment based on the strange warmings of their hearts and the success of their most passionate and sustained endeavours.

Such a pre-emption, perhaps, is unavoidable unless we look for that final judgment to the place where God has revealed it, which is to say, to Jesus and to the justification of mankind which God has effected by raising him from the dead (Rom. 4:25). Apart from that event our talk of a final word of God must either be an ideological attempt at self-justification or must relapse into agnostic silence. Only as we talk of what has been done in Christ can we give content to a judgment 'apart from works', for there we have set before us the future judgment already manifest, God's final decision on mankind, in a form which allows of no supplement (as though it were provisional or incomplete) but which is decisively creative for all ages before and after, so that works of love spring into life where God has once and for all declared his approval. The core of the doctrine of justification is not expressed in the tag 'by faith' (important as that may be) but in the *solus Christus*, 'that *in him* we might become the righteousness of God' (2 Cor. 5:21).

In speaking of judgment, we keep in mind the correlation of justification with condemnation, the 'No' which accompanies and gives form to the 'Yes'. Where God has said 'Yes' to mankind in Christ, he has said 'No' to all refusal of him, to the rebellious authorities which, as the Psalmist has it, the Lord 'laughs to scorn' (Ps. 2:4, New English Bible). This 'No' does not in any way qualify the 'Yes' that he has spoken to his creation; it does not make it into an ambiguous and vacillating 'Yes and No'. 'For the Son of God . . . was not Yes and No; but in him it is always Yes' (2 Cor. 1:19). And that is because the Creator is not dependent to the least degree upon his individual creatures – not even to provide him with the material for judgment, since that is present in Christ. It is enough that he has spoken his word upon creation in the person of its head, in whom all and everything are represented. In accepting him, God has accepted mankind totally, and the created universe with mankind. In rejecting all that rejects him, God has rejected nothing of mankind and nothing of the created universe, but only that which denies and detracts from them. No act that is performed, no life that is lived in refusal of what God has done, has any claim upon him – not even the claim that if he will not capitulate to it on its own terms, something will be lacking from his restored creation.

Our faith, then, when it has contemplated the final 'Yes' of God to man, can return from the future to the present with all that it needs, knowing that its works of love are justified. We do not have to assure ourselves of anything else. In particular, we need no reassurance about our *past* lives and actions and about the achieved formations of our character. These may, or they may not, fall under the condemning 'No'. But in so far as we, the agents, stand under the 'Yes' which God has spoken to Christ, then our pasts, too, are brought within the favourable meaning which that 'Yes' confers upon our lives as a whole. There is no need for us to save the faces of our past selves, for they are saved through what God is doing for our present selves. All that we need fear in relation to our pasts is that by trying to defend them against the divine 'No' we may cease here and now to live in the light of the divine 'Yes'. Faith, therefore, is always open to repentance, able to relax the compulsive grip of self-justification upon the past. Love which is qualified by faith is free from 'self-love' in that sense of the word – which is to say, it does not have to adjust its perceptions of reality in order to sustain a consistency and continuity of present deeds and attitudes with past. It is renewed and sustained, not out of the agent's established character but by continual conversion. Yet this is not to deny that love does imply a coherence and intelligibility in the agent's life as a whole. How this may be so is the first of two aspects of the qualification of love by faith which we must examine a little more closely.

Conversion and the meaning of a life

The prophet Ezekiel speaks of the wicked man who gives up his sinful ways and keeps God's laws, who will 'live'; and conversely of the righteous man who turns back from his righteous ways and will 'die' (Ezk. 18:21ff.). What, we may ask, of the virtues and vices of these two men, the settled dispositions which they formed over the years? Presumably the wicked man will carry some of his vices with him to wrestle with in his righteous period? And the righteous man will display many virtues in his pursuit of wickedness? And what of the objective historical records of what each man did, especially if the first period in each case was long, and the second period short? Clearly these things can still be discussed. But in terms of the final assessment of these two men, the assessment that God will make, they are secondary. The turn that each has taken, to or away from the law of God, has marked his life and imposed a shape upon it which is decisive for the whole. There has been a formative moment, a moment of conversion, from which the rest of the man's career has taken its meaning for good or ill. In saying this Ezekiel draws upon the wisdom that was common to the scribal schools of Israel, that the end of a career settles the value of the whole.

Jesus, too, drew upon this wisdom, and gave it an extraordinary resonance in his words to the penitent thief upon the cross. But in the conversion of the thief there is also a new element. For him it is not merely a question of a deathbed repentance, a turning of the will which, even at the last moment, could transform the story of his life; it is a moment of recognition and acknowledgment, in which something confronted him and exacted his worship. That moment shaped his life, not simply because it was, in biographical terms, his last act of will, but because in it he encountered the decisive reality which must shape his life one way or the other whenever he met it. Jesus told a parable about two debtors, one with a large and one with a small sum owing, who were forgiven their debts outright. 'Which of them', he asked, 'will love [the moneylender] more?' (Lk. 7:42). The encounter with God's pardoning grace is a formative moment in a life because it evokes love. The presence of that love determines the meaning of the whole. Once again we must say that though settled dispositions and character, though the record of good things done or not done, are important features in human morality, they take second place to this formative moment, the meeting with the divine presence in Jesus which stamps the life with the mark of love.

Such a moment, of course, is elusive of observation. In the case of Ezekiel's two men, though one could not have foreseen the moment of conversion in each life in advance, the phenomenon would have been evident enough once it has occurred. With this moment of encounter, on the other hand, the possibility of outward ambiguity remains. Love as the shaping force of a life may not declare itself immediately in observable ways. The most outward and public gestures of reformation and change may be the most illusory. Without recanting what we said in chapter 10 about the revelation of character through acts, we have to recognize that the shaping moment of conversion complicates this revelation, since it introduces an inner contradiction, a conflict of 'flesh' and 'Spirit', as Saint Paul calls it (Gal. 5:17), into the hidden reality of the character itself. And that is why Christians are warned not to 'judge' people. We are not able to draw quick conclusions from appearances as to whether someone is a good or a bad person, a saved or a damned soul. The invasive reality which touches and shapes human lives is nothing other than the eschatological judgment of God in Christ; and only when that judgment is finally manifest can we expect to see clearly with what design it has cut through the fabric of human conduct. The words 'Judge not, that you be not judged' (Mt. 7:1) are not intended, as a liberal indifferentism can so easily construe them, to forbid moral judgment. There is a tolerance which comes from not taking moral questions seriously, from regarding the difference between right and wrong sceptically because of the ambiguities with which human behaviour confronts us. There is another tolerance, quite different in spirit from this, which comes from taking moral questions so seriously that we recognize the point at which they exceed our competence to resolve them. We can speak and think about the right and wrong of acts, the value of virtues and traits of character; but when it comes to pronouncing a verdict on a human being's life in its totality, we know that too much is hidden from us to permit any anticipation of God's final word.

But the ambiguity which surrounds other people's acts and experiences, revealing, yet at the same time hiding, that which gives their lives their final shape, also attaches to our own. We are, of course, in a very much better position to understand ourselves. We have a more ample memory of our own doings, and (what is of the greatest importance) a memory of our intentions and internal experiences. We do not have to be simply agnostic about ourselves, but can make provisional judgments as to the direction of our lives, finding in our memories material both for repentance and for thanksgiving. Yet even so our judgments are provisional. We can misremember our internal experiences under the stress of present emotion, and we can find our own past actions entirely puzzling, as when we have to search our motives in a painful struggle for self-understanding. The subjective access which we have to our own histories, then, does not provide a platform from which we may leap to certainty about ourselves. We cannot claim that the final meaning of our lives is luminous to us by introspection. There is a place for certainty, for the 'assurance' upon which Calvinist Christians have insisted so rightly, but it is founded not on introspection but on faith in the objective word of God. In examining the apparent meaning of our own past lives, we have to confess its ambiguity, its failure to give clear expression to the reality which must shape it. Therefore we continually turn back from these appearances of ourselves to the reality itself. In this sense it is true to say that conversion happens not once but many times. Yet it is always the one eschatological reality, and the transformation it effects in any life is, in the light of the end, the one decisive transformation; so that we may say, and more profoundly, that conversion happens only once, and that each successive turning back claims and reclaims the one decisive encounter.

In contrast to the hiddenness of the formative moment we are given a public sign that keeps it before our minds and prevents our ignoring it, as we can so easily ignore what is hidden about other people. The sign is baptism. It is a ritual, and therefore liable to the loss of significance which can befall any ritual when it is taken outside its proper context of understanding. It is a sign, and therefore distinct from the reality to which it points. Nevertheless, a ritual sign is the only appropriate way for the hidden moment of conversion to take public form; for without such a form the reality, given from outside man's sphere of activity, lying beyond the scope even of his religious capabilities, will be in danger of confusion with the merely human acts of repentance and belief which it produces. Neither an individual's belief, nor his love for God, nor his appearance of repentance and moral seriousness, however impressive they may be, can assure us of the redemptive presence of Christ. Only the sign itself, because it is given by Christ, can give a public assurance that God's redemptive grace is active in the world and that this person too will encounter it, so entitling us to read the indications in the candidate's subjective and active life hopefully, as evidence of the Spirit's activity. Baptism does not point to the high moments of devotion or to the sustained achievements of moral fibre of which the human spirit is capable, but to the formative moment in which the whole of a person's life, past and future, is taken up and pronounced upon by God in the 'Yes' that he has spoken and will speak in Christ. It represents the redemption of the whole passage of life from birth to death, including all within it that in itself falls under the 'No'. It stands over the individual's life as Christ stands over world-history, marking the point at which eternity has established its hold upon the temporal.

Simplicity of decision

It is by this moment of encounter, the gospel tells us, that the shape of a human life is decisively established. This is not to dismiss or ignore all the other elements which characterize a human life from the moral point of view; it is not to pretend that criminality is no different from honest citizenship or asceticism from self-indulgence; it is not to deny that some of the possibilities of human life are precious and others worthless. It is simply to say that about all these elements, about the varied constellations and patterns that they may form, about the worth and worthlessness which they may embody, there is yet one final question to be asked: what do they constitute for eternity? And it is there, in that question, that final judgment is rendered, rendered by criteria that are not immanent to the created order itself but which come from beyond it, from its supernatural end. The final question is whether this life, this act, this character, belong to the renewed and transformed world which God is bringing into being, and that question can be answered only in terms of the relation to Christ in whom the transformed world is already present to us.

In the light of that question, the issues of morality which are as complex and diverse as the created order which gives rise to them are reduced to a stark and awesome simplicity. We can speak of the simple choice for or against God's new creation, the simple alternative of a broad way and a narrow way, the straightforward either-or opposition of sin and virtue. We can speak of the life of the believer as one in which there is love and no sin, and of the life of the unbeliever as one in which there is sin and no love. This is the second way in which love qualified by faith takes on a distinctively eschatological form. Such absolute oppositions cannot be avoided in Christian thought, for without it morality loses its eschatological relation to the new creation and becomes no more than a reflection of the ambiguities and complications of this world. At the same time it is clearly possible to misapply the language of eschatological simplicity and allow it to obscure the manifoldness of created good and the ambiguities to which it gives rise.

The most famous passage of 'perfectionist' language in the New Testament, 1 John 3:1–12, luminously illustrates the eschatological and revelatory context within which the either-or can properly be posed. The chapter begins with the Father's 'gift of love', which is the adoption of mankind to become God's children, the eschatological transformation declared in its most simple form. This status is not merely a name, but a present eschatological reality: 'that we should be called children of God; and so we are.' But this act of transformation involves a division between 'us' and 'the world' which 'did not know him'. Did not, we observe; because the eschatological gift was given once for all in Christ, and final judgment is already past history in the division that he brought about. This present eschatological status still awaits full disclosure: 'it does not yet appear what we shall be'. But the future disclosure, though its content is hidden, is assuredly a disclosure of life *in Christ*. So the apostle is to discuss a mode of existence which is already ours, yet not fully clear to us, and which is, before it can be our mode of existence, Christ's mode of existence. The Christian life, then, lived in hope of that disclosure, is one of self-purification, 'as he is pure', that is a disciplined and serious laying-hold of that mode of existence which is his already.

This is the preface for the opposition which the apostle will now develop between the sinful man and Christ. The one breaks the law (thus pointing up the theological, God-defying heart of sin), the other was manifest to do away with sin. In him there is no sin; therefore, 'every one who abides in him sins not' (6*). The assertion is, of course, absurd, unless we hold in mind what the apostle has just told us, that our existence in Christ is not fully manifest. The eschatological dimension of that 'sins not' is given in the verb 'abide'. To 'abide' in Christ is not simply to pass time with him, but to conclude history with him, to endure with him to the end, in which the sinlessness of Christ's life is manifest clearly also in us. Similarly, just as the end discloses the sinless character of the life in Christ, so it discloses the character of the alternative: a sinful life is a life without

Christ. 'Children, let no one deceive you!' The deception is not to imagine that there are ambiguities in the moral experiences of history, that there are believers who commit sin and need an advocate with the Father, or that there are unbelievers who perform worthy and worth-while good deeds. The deception is to think that these ambiguities represent the *ultimate* state of affairs, to foist upon God's judgment a kind of decent, understanding, man-of-the-world set of assumptions, when the nature of his judgment has already been made clear in Christ. When we speak in terms of ambiguities, we speak only of history which has come and will go; when we speak of the source and end of history, we speak of opposition: 'The devil has sinned from the beginning. The reason the Son of God appeared was to destroy the works of the devil.'

There is, then, in our status as God's children – John recapitulates this in the phrase 'born of God' (9) – a certain impossibility: he cannot sin. This impossibility is not a historical impossibility rooted in capacities and inclinations, not even in the converted capacities and inclinations of the believer; it is an eschatological impossibility rooted in the 'seed' which now dwells in the believer ('abides', again with an eschatological reference.) The manifestation of the status of sons (for which, of course, we still wait, though not without anticipations of it in the church) is precisely this, the manifestation of 'him that does no right' over against 'him that does right', the child of the devil over against the child of God. But that rather formal phrase must be expressed in terms of its content: love of the brother over against hatred. For John, as for later Christian thinkers, Cain and Abel represent the moral sources from which the ambiguities of history are mixed. What he is most anxious that we should understand is simply this: in the last analysis these sources are quite distinct and will be seen to be so. Our task, therefore, is to refuse to accept ambiguities in our own behaviour or to hide behind a supposedly necessary unclarity or compromise, and instead to purify ourselves as he is pure.

But it is not only Christian moral thought that displays this reduction of complexity to simplicity. The more directive moral thinking attempts to be, the more it needs to establish categories of disjunction, which differentiate the possibilities for action into two opposed classes. The language of morality is built around such pairs of opposed terms: good and bad, right and wrong, noble and base. It was not Jesus who first propounded the idea that moral decision was a choice between two ways of life; it was an old and recurrent theme of Western ethics. To this extent, then, the announcement of God's final judgment simply told mankind what it already knew implicitly: that beneath the ambiguity of concrete decisions, beneath every hesitation between alternative goods in alternative courses of action, there lay a simple and final choice between good and evil, a choice on which the fate of the soul depended.

The difficulty is that when moral thought has not made or has lost contact with the eschatological ground, the emphasis on simplicity of choice will be immanentized, and so will obscure the complexities and ambiguities which concrete moral decisions actually present. Legalism, proverbially the hallmark of Pharisaic morality but often reproduced in Christian ethics since, provides a clear example of this. It attempts to ensure the simplicity of the concrete decision by making the codified law entirely comprehensive. If every eventuality can be foreseen and provided for in an elaboration of the moral code, then, when the moment of decision arrives, it is confronted in its simplest form as a choice for or against obeying God's law. The ambiguities have been cleared out of the way by the experts, so that the moral agent, provided that he will take expert advice, need not be troubled by the tasks of discernment but has only to take the simple decision of will seriously. Something comparable can be seen in a tradition which runs, with variations, from the Stoics to Kant, and has much influenced modern romanticism. There are conceived to be two levels at which moral thought proceeds: a fundamental level of intention – the will, in Kant – which makes a simple moral decision in favour of duty and the universal moral law, and a secondary level of empirical discernment which, as it were, merely administers that decision concretely. The moral element of choice is narrowed down to the formal relation of the will to duty, while the discernment of complexities is allowed no real moral significance.

Legalism and moralism of these kinds intend to do justice to the ultimate simplicity of moral choice by locating it exclusively in a certain element of actual decision, an element which supposedly can be separated out from the task of discerning complexities, and which can therefore be identified as the 'purely moral' element, owing nothing to skill, insight or successful performance. The result is that every moral decision has to be taken with a great deal of seriousness because on it, in a sense, depends the fate of the soul. Each time the agent confronts a decision, he confronts the possibility of absolute apostasy from the good. Even though his responsibility is narrowed down to a formal disposition of the will, so that there is no danger of his damning himself by mistake, the burden is not lessened. Indeed, the more sharply the responsibility is focused on the will, the more awful does the prospect of a simple defection of will appear. When these voluntarist traditions are embodied in Christian devotion, they make for great scrupulousness and lack of evangelical freedom. This must surely be the inevitable result when man attributes to his own decisions the capacity to invoke the apocalypse of final judgment which properly belongs to God's decision.

In reaction to this are a variety of antinomian stances which tend so to separate the eschatological decision from all historical decisions that it is no longer clear how the one affects the others at all. Luther's famous paradox, *Pecca fortiter*, however much it may merit judicious exegesis, at least illustrates the tendency. Sin will not be sin, except in an ironic sense, if the final decision of justification has been so absolutely rendered 'apart from works' that what we ourselves decide can bear no relation to it. Thus arises the second of the two forms of 'perfectionism' that have haunted the history of Christianity. The legalist form immanentizes the simple final decision, so that it is constantly encountered as an immediate possibility; the antinomian form absolutizes it, so that it can be presumed upon as an impotent abstraction, unrelated to the dynamics of human decision.

We can, then, only admire the discovery of Kierkegaard, with his horror of antinomianism, that an ethic of simple decision could emerge clearly only with Christianity, and was dependent upon the incarnation. For it is only when mankind is confronted by the God-man that all decisions are reduced to the one decision, the decision between 'faith' and 'offence'. The opposition of sin and faith, peculiar to Christianity, 'transforms the definition of all ethical concepts. At the bottom of this opposition lies the decisive Christian concept, "before God" ' (*The Sickness unto Death*, p. 214). Sin presupposes revelation (p. 226). The Socratic understanding of sin as ignorance did not achieve an understanding of sin at all, for it lacked the notion of 'defiant will' (p. 220). Sin, therefore, is 'not a negation but a position' (p. 227). The cardinal sin, the 'sickness unto death', is despair of the forgiveness of sins; for this is to be 'offended' at the God-man who forgives our sins.

We must admire it, however one-sided we must concede it to be; for it has grasped the extent to which Christian eschatology has brought the simplicity of moral decision into focus, and to which an ethic such as Kant's, which deals heavily in simplicity, is trading in unconfessed theological contraband. We may add, however, that Kierkegaard's interest in Socrates and the problem of ignorance did not allow him to see how pre-Christian classical ethics really did attempt to articulate simplicity and defiance of will (as, for example, in the Stoic concept of virtue); nor how Christian eschatology itself qualifies the immediacy of the simple decision 'before God' on which Kierkegaard is eager to insist. We live in the time of divine forbearance, in which the Lord, not wishing that any should perish, holds back the day when he will come like a thief, that all should reach repentance (2 Pet. 3:9). In faith we begin to discern the ultimate and simple decision taking shape through the complexities of our immediate and provisional decisions. When we are ready, we shall see it, and make it, clearly. We may well pray to be spared too hasty a revelation of the dizzying choice between heaven and hell, between perfect love and the sin against the Holy Ghost, lest it invoke prematurely the impenetrable despair of final destruction and the condemnation of God.

The author of the Apocalypse, with his characteristically vivid way of expressing paradox, tells us that at the great judgment the 'books were opened. Also another book was opened, which is the book of life. And the dead were judged by what was written in the books, by what they had done . . . And if any one's name was not found written in the book of life, he was thrown into the lake of fire' (Rev. 20:12ff.). The final judgment of God is, on the one hand, a judgment rendered on human deeds; on the other, it is a creative new word rendered from a source that is independent of human deeds. These two aspects of divine judgment are complementary. Human deeds become what they are not in themselves, the story of God's gracious purposes, when their books are interpreted out of that 'other book'. The works that men have done become the basis of God's favourable or unfavourable judgment when they are read in the light of God's work of sovereign grace. The ultimate and simple decision is not found in the books of human deeds, but in the book of life, where it is a question of Yes or No: either a name is there, or it is not. But the book of life does not supplant the books of men's deeds; rather, those books, when read in the light of that book, take on the character of a correspondingly simple and final decision, a Yes or No to God's grace. However much our moral decisions strive for clarity, they are never unambiguous or translucent, even to ourselves. But – and is this not the gospel at the heart of evangelical ethics? – it is given to them by God's grace in Christ to add up to a final and unambiguous Yes, a work of love which will abide for eternity.

Bibliography

Only works mentioned in the text are included in the Bibliography. In order to assist the non-professional reader, biographical dates are provided where the publication dates cited do not fall within the author's lifetime. With a few exceptions non-English works are given in an accessible English translation where a suitable one is widely available.

The following standard abbreviations are used for series:–

ANCF: *The Ante-Nicene Christian Fathers.* Grand Rapids: Eerdmans, 1975.

CCCM: *Corpus Christianorum Continuatio Mediaevalis.* Turnholt, 1971– .

NPNF: *The Nicene & Post-Nicene Fathers.* Grand Rapids: Eerdmans, 1974–76.

PG: *Patrologia Graeca*, ed. J.–P. Migne. Paris, 1857– .

PL: *Patrologia Latina*, ed. J.-P. Migne. Paris, 1844– .

Abelard, Peter (1079–1142). *Commentaria in epistulam Pauli ad Romanos. CCCM* xi.

Aquinas, Thomas (*c.* 1225–1274). *Summa Theologiae.* Ed. T. Gilby, with translations. London: Eyre & Spottiswoode, 1963– .

Arendt, Hannah. *Between Past and Future.* New York: Viking Press, 1961.

Aristotle (384–322 BC). *Nicomachean Ethics.* Tr. W. D. Ross. *The Works of Aristotle*, ed. W. D. Ross, ix. Oxford University Press, 1925.

Arndt, W. F. and Gingrich, F. W. *A Greek-English Lexicon of the New Testament*, 4th ed. University of Chicago Press, 1952.

Athanasius of Alexandria (*ob.* 373). *Against the Arians* (*Contra Arianos*). NPNF (2nd ser) iv.

Augustine of Hippo (354–430). *Against Faustus* (*Contra Faustum*). NPNF (1st ser) iv.

—*The City of God* (*De civitate Dei*). Tr. H. Bettenson. Harmondsworth: Penguin Books, 1972.

—*On Christian Doctrine* (*De doctrina Christiana*). NPNF (1st ser) ii.

—*On the Holy Trinity* (*De trinitate*). NPNF (1st ser) iii.

—*On the Morals of the Catholic Church* (*De moribus ecclesiae catholicae*). NPNF (1st ser) iv.

—*On Nature and Grace* (*De natura et gratia*). NPNF (1st ser) v.

—*Quaestiones Evangeliorum*. PL xxxv.

—*Sermo de disciplina Christiana*. PL xl.

—*Speculum* 'Quis ignorat'. PL xxxiv.

Barth, Karl. *Church Dogmatics*. Tr. G. W. Bromiley and T. F. Torrance. Edinburgh: T. & T. Clark, 1956– .

—*The German Church Conflict*. Tr. T. H. L. Parker. *Ecumenical Studies in History* i. London, 1965.

—'Gospel and Law'. In *God, Grace and Gospel*. Tr. J. S. McNab. Edinburgh: Oliver & Boyd, 1959.

Basil of Caesarea (*ob.* 379). *Adversus Eunomium*. PG xxix.

—*On the Holy Spirit* (*De Spiritu Sancto*). NPNF (2nd ser) viii.

Boethius (*c.* 480–524). *Tractates*. Tr. H. F. Steward *et al.* (Loeb Classical Library). London: Heinemann, 1918.

Bonaventure (*c.* 1217–74). *Commentaria in iv Libros Sententiarum* (Commentary on the Sentences). In *S. Bonaventurae Opera Theologica Selecta*, i–iv. Florence, 1934–49.

Brunner, Emil. *Justice and the Social Order*. Tr. M. Hottinger. London: Lutterworth Press, 1945.

—'Nature and Grace'. In *Natural Theology: comprising 'Nature & Grace' by E. Brunner & the reply 'No!' by K. Barth*. Tr. P. Fränkel. London: Bles, 1946.

Butler, Joseph (1692–1752). *Sermons*. Ed. W. E. Gladstone. Oxford: Clarendon Press, 1896.

Calvin, John (1509–64). *Institutes of the Christian Religion*. Tr. F. L. Battles (Library of Christian Classics). London: SCM, 1961.

Chrysostom, John (*c.* 347–407). *Homilies on the Statues* (*De statuis*). NPNF (1st ser) ix.

—*In epistulam ii ad Corinthios homiliae*. PG lxi.

Church of England (Mortimer Commission). *Putting Asunder: Divorce Law for Contemporary Society*. London: SPCK, 1966.

Clement of Alexandria (*fl. c.* 200). *The Rich Man's Salvation* (*Quis dives salvetur*). Tr. G. W. Butterworth (Loeb Classical Library). London: Heinemann, 1919.

Cranmer, Thomas (1489–1556). 42 Articles. In Charles Hardwick, *A History of the Articles of Religion*. Cambridge, 1851.

D'Arcy, Eric. *Conscience and its Right to Freedom*. London: Sheed & Ward, 1961.

Dooyeweerd, Herman. *The Christian Idea of the State*. Tr. J. Kraay. Nutley, NJ: Craig Press, 1968.

—*A New Critique of Theoretical Thought*. Tr. D. Freeman and W. Young. Presbyterian & Reformed Publishing Company, 1969.

—*Roots of Western Culture*. Tr. J. Kraay. Toronto: Wedge, 1979.

Edwards, Jonathan (1703–58). *The Nature of the True Virtue*. Ed. W. K. Frankena. Ann Arbor: University of Michigan Press, 1960.

—*Treatise Concerning the Religious Affections*. Ed. J. E. Smith. New Haven: Yale University Press, 1959.

Finnis, John. *Natural Law and Natural Rights*. Oxford University Press, 1980.

Fletcher, Joseph. 'What's in a Rule?'. In *Norm and Context in Christian Ethics*, ed. P. Ramsey and G. Outka. London: SCM, 1969.

Grant, George. *Time as History*. Toronto: Canadian Broadcasting Corporation, 1969.

Grotius, Hugo (1583–1645). *On the Right of War and Peace (De iure belli et pacis)*. Tr. F. W. Kelsey *et al.* (Classics of International Law). Oxford, 1925.

Gustafson, James M. *Theology and Ethics*. Oxford: Blackwell, 1982.

—'A Protestant Ethical Approach'. In *The Moralty of Abortion*, ed. John T. Noonan. Cambridge, Mass.: Harvard University Press, 1971.

Hauerwas, Stanley. *Truthfulness and Tragedy*. University of Notre Dame Press, 1977.

—*Vision and Virtue*. Notre Dame: Fides, 1974.

Hegel, G. W. F. (1770–1831). *The Philosophy of Right*. Tr. T. M. Knox. Oxford University Press, 1952.

Hume, David (1711–76). *A Treatise of Human Nature*. Ed. L. A. Selby-Biggs. Oxford: Clarendon Press, 1888.

Irenaeus of Lyons (*ob. c.* 202). *Against Heresies (Adversus haereses)*. ANCF i.

Jonas, Hans. *Philosophical Essays*. University of Chicago Press, 1974.

Junghans, H. *Ockham in Lichte der Neueren Forschung*. Berlin, 1968.

Justin Martyr (*ob. c.* 165). *Dialogue with Trypho.* ANCF i.

Kant, Immanuel (1724–1804). *Critique of Practical Reason.* Tr. Lewis White Beck. University of Chicago Press, 1949.
—*Fundamental Principles of the Metaphysic of Morals* (Groundwork). Tr. T. K. Abbott. London, 1925. (Page references to Prussian Academy edition)
Kierkegaard, Søren (1813–55). *Either-Or.* Tr. D. Swenson and W. Lowrie. Princeton University Press, 1944.
—*Fear and Trembling* and *The Sickness unto Death.* Tr. W. Lowrie. Princeton University Press, 1954.
—*Training in Christianity.* Tr. W. Lowrie. Princeton University Press, 1941.
—*Works of Love.* Tr. H. and E. Hong. New York: Harper & Row, 1962.
Kirk, Kenneth E. *Conscience and its Problems.* London: Longmans Green, 1927.
—*The Vision of God.* London: Longmans Green, 1931.

Lombard, Peter (*c.* 1095–1160). *Sententiae in iv Libros Distinctae* (Sentences). Rome, 1971–81.
Luther, Martin (1483–1546). *Lectures on Galatians.* (Luther's Works xxvi-xxvii). St. Louis: Concordia, 1963.
—*The Sermon on the Mount.* (Luther's Works xxi). St. Louis: Concordia, 1956.
(References to volume and page of the *Weimar Ausgabe* (*W A*).)

MacIntyre, Alisdair. *After Virtue.* University of Notre Dame Press, 1981.
MacNamara, J. V. *Faith and Ethics.* Dublin: Gill & Macmillan, 1985.
Mann, Thomas. *Doctor Faustus.* Tr. H. T. Lowe-Porter. New York: Vintage Books, 1971.
Maximus Confessor (*ob.* 662). *Disputatio cum Pyrrho.* PG xci.
Melanchthon, Philipp (1497–1560). *Loci Communes.* Tr. W. Pauck (Library of Christian Classics). London: SCM, 1969. (References to volume and page of *Corpus Reformatorum* (*C R*).)
Milton, John (1608–74). *Paradise Lost.* In *Poetical Works*, ed. D. Bush. Oxford University Press, 1966.
Moltmann, Jürgen. *Hope and Planning.* Tr. Margaret Clarkson. London: SCM, 1971.

Nygren, Anders. *Agape and Eros.* Tr. P. S. Watson. London: SPCK, 1932–39.

O'Donovan, Oliver. *Begotten or Made?* Oxford University Press,

1984.

—'*Usus* and *Fruitio* in Augustine, *De doctrina Christiana* I'. *Journal of Theological Studies* xxxiii (1982).

Ockham, William of (*c.* 1285–1347). *Quaestiones in ii Librum Sententiarum.* In *Guillelmi de Ockham Opera Philosophica et Theologica* v. St. Bonaventure, NY, 1981.

Origen (*ob. c.* 254). *Commentary on the Song of Songs* (*In Canticum*). Tr. R. P. Lawson (Ancient Christian Writers). New York: Newman Press, 1957.

Outka, Gene. 'Character, Vision and Narrative'. *Religious Studies Review* vi (1980).

Pannenberg, Wolfhart. *Theology and the Kingdom of God.* Ed. R. J. Neuhaus. Philadelphia: Westminster Press, 1969.

Pascal, Blaise (1623–62). *Provincial Letters.* Tr. A. J. Krailsheimer. Harmondsworth: Penguin Books, 1967.

Paul VI, Pope. *Humanae Vitae.* In *Humanae Vitae and the Bishops,* ed. J. Horgan. Shannon: Irish University Press, 1972.

Pierce, C. A. *Conscience in the New Testament.* London: SCM, 1955.

Plato (*c.* 427–348 BC). *Laches. Protagoras. Republic.* Tr. E. Hamilton *et al.* In *Collected Dialogues.* Princeton University Press, 1961.

Rahner, Karl. *Theological Investigations* xiii, xiv. Tr. D. Bourke. London: Darton, Longman & Todd, 1975–76.

Ramsey, Paul. *The Just War.* New York: Scribners, 1968.

—'The Case of the Curious Exception'. In *Norm and Context in Christian Ethics,* ed. P. Ramsey and G. Outka. London: SCM, 1969.

—'Incommensurability and Indeterminacy in Moral Choice'. In *Doing Evil to Achieve Good,* ed. P. Ramsey and R. McCormick. Chicago: Loyola University Press, 1978.

Rousselot, Pierre. *Pour l'histoire du problème de l'amour au Moyen Age.* Paris: Vrin, 1933.

Ryle, Gilbert. *The Concept of Mind.* Harmondsworth: Penguin Books, 1963.

Schleiermacher, Friedrich (1768–1834). *On Religion: Speeches to its Cultured Despisers.* Tr. J. Oman. New York: Harper & Row, 1958.

Scotus, John Duns (*c.* 1266–1308). *Ordinatio.* In *Ioannis Duns Scoti Opera Omnia* i–vii. Vatican City, 1950–73.

Spenser, Edmund (1552–99). *Poetical Works.* Ed. J. C. Smith and E. de Selincourt. Oxford University Press, 1912.

Strack, H. L. and Billerbeck, P. *Kommentar zum neuen Testament aus Talmud und Midrasch.* Munich, 1922–61.

Strauss, Leo. *Natural Right and History.* University of Chicago Press, 1953.

Thielicke, Helmut. *Theological Ethics* i. Tr. W. Lazareth. London: A. & C. Black, 1968.
Torrance, Thomas F. *Theological Science.* Oxford University Press, 1969.

Vatican Council. *Documents of Vatican II*, ed. W. Abbott. London: Chapman, 1967.

Index of biblical references

Index of authors

Index of subjects